LIVING ABROAD IN
MEXICO

JULIE DOHERTY MEADE

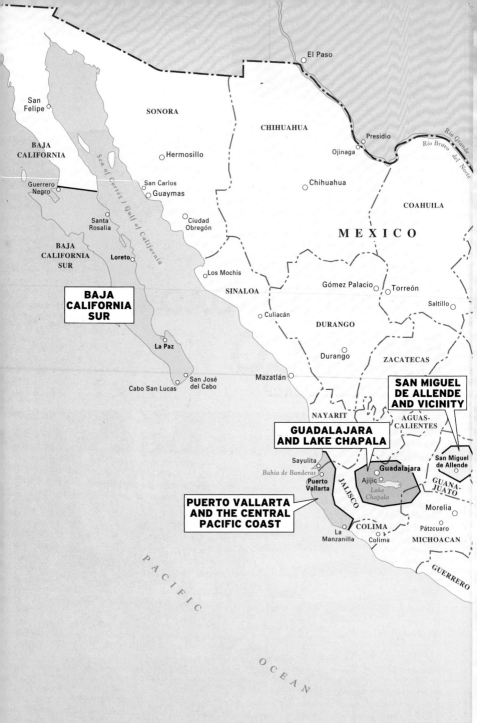

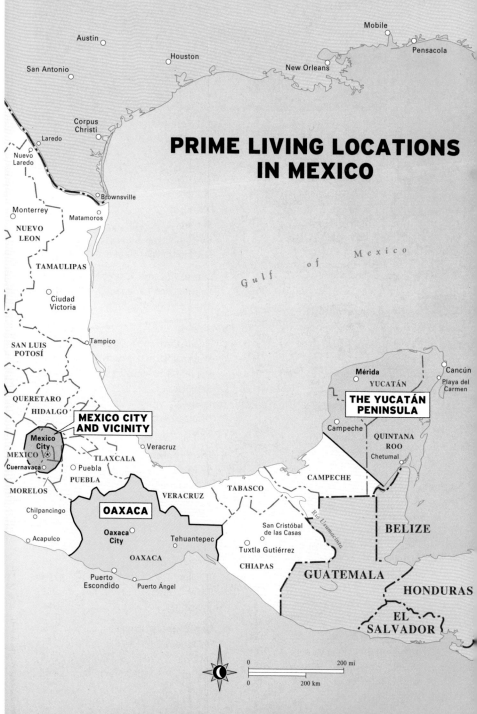

Contents

At Home in Mexico

Mexico is a hospitable place, in every sense of the word. The people are warm, the sky is perpetually blue, and the days, though technically comprised of the same number of hours, seem to stretch just a bit longer. It's easy to feel at home amid the cactus-studded plains of Old Mexico, where small pueblos still brim with old-fashioned friendliness and tradition. Along the coast, the lifestyle slows from laid-back to leisurely; sunsets and simple pleasures define daily existence, even as modern luxuries are accessible and abundant in Mexico's many famous beach towns. Even in the country's big cities, life moves at a different, less regimented pace, and there is always time in the day for a long lunch or a late night with friends.

The home of mariachi and the birthplace of chocolate, Mexico's vivid culture plays perfect accompaniment to life's easy rhythm. Mexico is astonishingly rich with tradition and history, from the diversity of its dried peppers and *mole* sauces to the colorful altars constructed during Day of the Dead, a uniquely Mexican holiday. Through the fusion of European and Native American cultures, Mexico developed unique traditions in the arts, music, and dance, as well as spectacular architectural achievements, exemplified by the country's many colonial-era cities. At the same time, life in Mexico is far from folkloric. In this changeable country, the economy continues to develop as the cultural landscape evolves beneath the ever-present influence of the United States. Since the inauguration of NAFTA (North American Free Trade Agreement), the manufacturing industry has surged across the country, and a new wave

of urban migration has burdened Mexican cities with contamination and traffic. Multitheater cinemas, imported clothing, and international chain restaurants are increasingly common, catering to the growing national appetite for cable television programs and caramel lattes.

While Mexico shares a border with the United States, it is surprisingly distinct from its neighbor to the north. As you will quickly learn, Mexico has its own way of doing things, and that way may not always seem to be the most efficient or logical. There are fewer rules and regulations governing daily life, despite the maddening penchant for paperwork and bureaucracy throughout the country's public systems. Moving to Mexico often means relearning how to perform everyday activities and errands, like paying the water bill or buying tomatoes at the market. Sometimes, simple tasks can seem remarkably difficult to accomplish, yet the key to life is learning to live more simply, too. In truth, the effort it takes to adjust to life in Mexico is minimal when compared to the many rewards south of the border.

If you are ready for a change, Mexico will change you. It will lower your blood pressure and improve your vitamin D levels – and it will likely change your outlook on life, as well. In this warm and welcoming culture, foreign residents fall into step with the country's sunny disposition, becoming a part of the diverse and colorful tapestry of modern Mexican society.

► WHAT I LOVE ABOUT MEXICO

- The jubilant strains of mariachi music filling an open plaza on a warm summer night.

- The fiery smell of poblano peppers roasting on a grill, and their savory taste when stuffed with cheese and deep fried in egg batter.

- Standing beneath a fluttering ceiling of colorful cut-paper flags and star-shaped piñatas, strung over the streets during the winter holidays.

- The Mexican custom of greeting other diners and wishing them a nice meal in restaurants.

- The refreshing chill in the air after a furious summer thunderstorm; the blooming cactus in the days that follow.

- Feeling like the essence of elegance in a hand-embroidered manta tunic, bought from a traditional artisan in the market.

- The proliferation of industrious small business owners and creative one-person enterprises, from the lone street-side ice cream scooper to the ubiquitous *tienda de la esquina* (corner shop).

- Sitting in a classic cantina while sipping aged tequila with *sangrita,* a delicious chaser made with tomato juice, spices, and hot sauce.

- Between cities, the vast expanses of rugged and undeveloped countryside, dotted with tiny pueblos and grazing burros.

- Watching the sun set in a pink blaze over the Pacific Ocean.

WELCOME TO MEXICO

INTRODUCTION

If you've been dreaming about a sunnier life in Mexico, you're not alone: Mexico is a decidedly magnetic place. Every year, millions of tourists visit the country's golden beaches and charming colonial towns, and writers and artists have sojourned down south since before Jack Kerouac wrote *Mexico City Blues* from the capital. Lured by practical considerations, like the lower cost of living, many foreigners decide to retire in Mexico, though many more choose the country simply because they love its unique culture and warm people. Today, Mexico is home to expatriates from across the globe, including the largest American community outside the United States. It is a popular place to take Spanish classes, to volunteer, or to teach English, and a number of cities have become well-known destinations for North American artists and retirees. You can find expatriates living in almost every part of the country, and many foreigners naturalize, marry into Mexican families, open businesses, or otherwise build a full and well-integrated life south of the border.

Despite its distinct national identity, Mexico is a country rather used to outsiders.

During the course of its tumultuous history, Mexico has been shaped by numerous cultures and foreign influences. The land was ruled by a succession of Mesoamerican empires before it was conquered by the Spanish. After independence from Spain, Mexico fell briefly into the hands of Napoleon III of France, followed by a quick but devastating occupation by the American forces. As political and social power changed hands, the country was continually reshaped and restructured, and, from its vast deserts to its famous coastline, regional cultures developed their own distinct flavor. In the 20th century, new immigrant groups, from Lebanese to Korean, left their subtle mark on local cultures, just as emigration and cultural hegemony from the United States has deeply influenced modern life. Here, assimilation and acceptance are the norm, and culture is strong but changeable.

Speaking of diversity, your experience as an expatriate will depend largely on where you choose to live. For some, life in Mexico is as simple as tying a hammock between two palm trees and watching waves crash on the shore. For others, it is a place to rush to work alongside the denizens of the western hemisphere's largest city. While some like the camaraderie of life in an established expatriate community, others seek out a tourist-free city or quiet beach town where they can live a more traditionally Mexican lifestyle.

With so many options, Mexico is a good fit for a wide range of people, but it isn't for everyone. Mexico marches to the beat of its own brassy and well-dressed mariachi band, and some foreigners can never fully adapt to the distinct social climate. Among other pervasive factors, there is less emphasis on speed and efficiency in Mexico; as an expatriate, you will likely get used to long lines at the bank, stifling bureaucracy in government offices, and the perpetual tardiness of your electrician. As a developing nation, Mexico's environmentalism, social programs, and safety regulations still fall short of contemporary standards. While some foreigners cannot bear the widespread poverty that blights the country, others are frustrated by the lack of stoplights at large intersections or the ubiquity of roadside litter.

Without a doubt, Mexico is a place governed by fewer rules and formalities, and you'll definitely feel the bumps in the road as you learn to navigate life without a safety net and with a greater sense of adventure. For many expatriates, daily life in Mexico can be a string of discoveries, triumphs, frustrations, and surprises: You never know when a municipal parade will come marching down a city street, delaying traffic, but also adding a touch more color and delight to your day. Mexico is best for those who choose color over consistency and looseness over law, though the friendliness of the people and the consistency of the sunshine invariably smooth the transition, even for the most rigid of Mexico's foreign residents.

The Lay of the Land

From the fertile valley around present-day Mexico City to the tip of the Yucatán Peninsula, Mexico has been continuously inhabited for thousands of years. A particularly vibrant and volatile piece of territory, it has been conquered, controlled, and influenced by myriad civilizations, and today, a plurality of people and cultures define the modern environment. The country expresses its mixed identity in many ways—even geographically. While Mexico is politically classified as North America, the Mexican states below the Isthmus of Tehuantepec are geographically grouped with Central America. Poised between two worlds, Mexico is heavily influenced by the United States yet retains a prominent position as the northernmost nation and second largest economy in Latin America. Even the land itself is a diverse mix of landscape and terrain, with ecosystems ranging from tropical wetland to high desert plain.

GEOGRAPHY AND TERRAIN

From its northern border with the United States, Mexico curves southeast toward Central America. The country's backbone, a massive plateau called the Mexican Altiplano, covers most of north and central Mexico. The plateau is bordered to the east by the Sierra Madre Oriental and to the west by the Sierra Madre Occidental, two long mountain ranges that form a part of the larger American cordillera. Below the mountain ranges, coastal plains stretch from the foothills to the sea on both the east and west coasts of the country.

Near Mexico City, the great plateau and the Sierra Madre merge with the east–west trajectory of the Mexican transvolcanic mountains, a particularly active seismic region. Part of this spectacular range, the twin peaks of Popocatepetl and Iztaccíhuatl flank Mexico City to the south, with the former sporadically spewing volcanic ash into the atmosphere. The mountains continue to rise into the eastern state of Veracruz, reaching their apex at the Pico de Orizaba—the country's highest mountain—before the landscape sinks into the balmy coastal plain.

Heading south from the capital, Mexico slims to just 125 miles from east coast to west coast at the Isthmus of Tehuantepec. This narrow strip of land was once considered a possible location for the transoceanic canal, today located in Panama; it remains the point of speculation for those looking to link the world's oceans. From the Isthmus of Tehuantepec to Mexico's southern border, the landscape is decidedly more tropical, with lush and humid jungle covering much of the low-lying plains in the states of Veracruz, Chiapas, and Tabasco. To the east, the Yucatán Peninsula juts like a thumb into the turquoise

RING OF FIRE

On September 19, 1985, Mexico City awoke to a 8.3 magnitude earthquake. The massive seismic tremor shook the city for more than three minutes. Built atop the water-rich sediment of a dry lakebed, Mexico City's centuries-old architecture trembled violently with the force of the quake. Hundreds of apartment buildings, schools, and hospitals came crashing to the ground, while drainage pipes burst beneath the city streets, contaminating the water supply. More than 10,000 died. Even today, the memory of this massive tragedy lingers in the popular consciousness.

Located at the inauspicious juncture between three major tectonic plates, Mexico is one of the most seismically active places in the world. In the north, the Baja California peninsula runs right along the edge of the large Pacific Plate, which meets the North American Plate along the southern extension of the San Andreas Fault. These two plates rub against each other, sending tremors through the north. Along the Pacific Coast in Southern Mexico, the Cocos Plate is sinking beneath the North American Plate.

It was this powerful juncture that rocked Mexico City in 1985; the epicenter of the quake was located more than 200 miles from the capital, off the coast of Michoacan.

The subduction of the Cocos Plate also creates volcanic activity throughout Southern Mexico. A beautiful threat, dramatic volcanic mountains, both active and inactive, dot Mexico. At almost 18,500 feet, the Pico de Orizaba is Mexico's highest peak and also an active volcano. Currently dormant, its 1,300-foot crater is covered in glaciers. Displaying a little more crackle and pop, Popocatepetl is an active volcano just 40 miles outside Mexico City. Today, plumes of smoke regularly escape from its snowcapped peak, occasionally throwing ash onto the capital. In December 2000, communities residing on the slopes of Popo were evacuated just before a major eruption. While volcanoes erupt less frequently than earthquakes rumble over the land, they have nonetheless caused some spectacular devastation in Mexico. In 1982, El Chichón in Chiapas unexpectedly erupted, killing thousands.

---

waters of the Caribbean Sea. A remarkably flat expanse of limestone rock, the peninsula is devoid of rivers or mountains but filled with deep sinkholes called cenotes.

On that note, water is abundant in Mexico but woefully distributed. More than 70 percent of the country's important watersheds flow through the southern states. In the north, reservoirs and other water supplies often run dangerously low in the dry season, and droughts are not uncommon. Water from the mighty Rio Grande, which forms a part of the border between the United States and Mexico, has been a serious point of contention between the two countries for decades.

A fact made famous by many glossy tourist brochures, Mexico has more than 5,500 miles of coastline, bordered by the Pacific Ocean to the west and the Gulf of Mexico and the Caribbean Sea to the east. In addition to its numerous resort towns, the Pacific Coast is the site of a highly active geologic fault, where the Pacific plate and the North American plate collide with explosive activity.

STATES AND REGIONS

Politically, Mexico is divided into 31 states, plus one *distrito federal* (federal district) in Mexico City. In everywhere but the capital, states are further divided into *municipios* (municipalities), political districts overseen by an elected local government. There are 2,440 municipalities in Mexico, plus 16 boroughs called *delegaciones* in Mexico City.

Mexico's northern border with the United States is the most trafficked international border in the world. It is delineated by a massive system of fencing, flowing rivers, and forbidding desert. Incredibly, the long run of the Rio Grande (known as the Rio Bravo in Mexico) forms 1,200 miles of the border's 2,000-mile trajectory, running all the way from Ciudad Juárez–El Paso to the Gulf of Mexico. Down at the opposite end of the country, the Usumacinta, Salinas, and Suchiate Rivers all make up segments of Mexico's 240-mile border with Guatemala; Belize also borders Mexico to the south, adjoining the Mexican state of Quintana Roo along the Caribbean Sea.

Aside from political divisions, the country can be loosely grouped into several large geopolitical regions, each quite distinct from the other.

Northern Mexico

The vast Sonoran Desert dominates the northwest swath of Mexico and is adjoined by the even larger Chihuahuan Desert to the east. With an arid climate unfit for agriculture, this forbidding yet beautiful region is largely dedicated to ranching. Up in *el norte,* culture is a modern-day version of the classic Mexican countryside: Cowboy

© GABRIELA PEÑA GARAVITO

Among other cultural markers, Northern Mexico is known for its vast cattle ranches and trio music.

MEXICO BY THE NUMBERS

- Total population: 112 million
- Median age: 27
- Population growth rate: 1.1 percent
- Percent of population living in cities: 78
- Average years of education: 8.6
- Percent of the population that identifies as part of an indigenous group: 10-14
- Percent who speak an indigenous language: 6
- Number of indigenous languages spoken: 89
- Total territory (in square miles): 1,217,420
- Miles of coastline: 5,600
- Percent of land that is arable: 12
- Number of cactus species: 700
- Number of endemic cactus: 518
- Acres dedicated to corn cultivation: 19,141,919
- Acres dedicated to chili pepper cultivation: 356,104

- Public markets: 2,300
- Open-air markets: 5,726
- Airports: 77
- Total households: 28,607,568
- Households with a computer: 8,279,619
- Miles of highway: 221,081
- Annual transit accidents (2009): 428,467
- Tons of sugarcane produced per year: 52,089,356
- Ounces of silver produced annually (2010): 128.6
- World rank for silver production: 2
- Percent of mine workers who are female: 10
- Percent of energy derived from oil: 88
- Number of offshore oil rigs operated by PEMEX (Petróleos Mexicanos, a Mexican state-owned petroleum company): 193

boots, cattle, saguaro cactus, fajitas, and trio music are ubiquitous signatures of the north.

Thanks to its proximity to the United States, Northern Mexico is highly influenced by its neighbor. Big cities, like Monterrey, take pride in their modernity, with many national and multinational corporations based in the city. Along the border, there has been steady urban growth and industrial development, especially since NAFTA (the North American Free Trade Agreement) went into effect. Today, Ciudad Juárez and Tijuana are among the country's biggest and most important cities, each blending into the larger metropolitan areas of El Paso and San Diego respectively.

Since the mid-2000s, the northern states have also been the unfortunate locus of violent clashes between rivaling drug cartels and the Mexican government. Cities that were once safe and livable have become increasingly unstable. Although cities throughout the region have suffered from a tremendous increase in crime, Ciudad Juárez is the most notorious, with some years seeing thousands of homicides.

Central Mexico

Between the great northern deserts and Mexico City, the population density slowly increases as the land become more hospitable. Descending from the western edge of the great plateau, the state of Jalisco is the birthplace of tequila and mariachi music; its capital, Guadalajara, is often cited as the most Mexican of Mexican cities. Farther south, the lake-filled state of Michoacan is one

© ARTURO MEADE

Cities of the Bajío region are known for their colonial-era Baroque architecture and cosmopolitan atmosphere.

of the country's cultural capitals, sharing a border with the state of Guanajuato to the southeast.

Guanajuato, along with the state of Querétaro, make up the majority of the Bajío region, a large plain on the southern Mexican Altiplano. Often considered the country's heartland, the Bajío does robust business in manufacturing, agriculture, and tourism. No longer a quiet or rural region, the Bajío boasts wineries in the countryside and a convivial atmosphere in its cosmopolitan cities and pueblos.

Valle de Mexico

Home to an estimated 22 million inhabitants, the Mexico City metropolitan area is the throbbing heart of the country. Spread across the Valle de Mexico (Valley of Mexico), urban sprawl has blanketed this once-fertile plain with smog, traffic, and industry. Even beyond the official metropolitan area, Mexico City seems to exert a gravitational pull on the ranches and pueblos that surround it, with thousands of automobiles entering and leaving the city every day. Cities throughout the surrounding state of Mexico—and even Morelos—exhibit a strong cultural link to the capital.

With the country's most robust economy, the capital area attracts urban migrants from across the country, as well as foreigners looking to live in one of Latin America's most vibrant cities. The result is a melting pot of Mexican and Latin culture, where you'll find authentic Argentinean steak houses next door to Yucatec *fondas* (casual restaurants). While home to a diverse population, the capital has its own particular character, including a substantial slang lexicon and a number of tasty dishes rarely served outside the capital.

Eastern Mexico and the Gulf Coast

From southern Tamaulipas to Veracruz, and westward into the Sierra Madre Oriental, the Huasteca is a distinctive region named for the indigenous Huastec people and famous for its lively *huapango* music. Throughout the region and along the Gulf Coast, the countryside is evergreen and tropical, covered with fern-filled rainforest and coffee plantations. In the city of Veracruz, there is a distinct Caribbean influence, where swaying palm trees, strong coffee, and marimba music flavor the balmy and tropical climate. The Gulf Coast also has a gritty side: Mexico's largest oil reserves are located in the states of Veracruz, Puebla, and Hidalgo, in a region known as the Chicontepec Field, while offshore drilling has converted some of the region's small towns to polluted industrial cities.

The Pacific Coast

Like the rest of Northern Mexico, the Pacific states of Baja California Sur and Baja California Norte are arid, sparsely populated, and largely influenced by the United States. On the mainland, some of the country's most famous beach towns are located along the Pacific corridor, including Puerto Vallarta, Ixtapa, and Acapulco. Small fishing towns and rustic hideaways dot the coast between major resorts, where roadside stands sell fresh coconuts and bunches of bananas. The coast becomes incrementally more tropical, humid, and remote the farther south you travel, with a distinctly bohemian vibe within Oaxaca's coastal communities.

The Yucatán Peninsula

A flat limestone peninsula dividing the Gulf of Mexico from the Caribbean Sea, the Yucatán Peninsula is a major destination for vacationers and cultural tourists, boasting gorgeous beaches, several important archaeological sites, and a large indigenous Maya population. Though they have many cultural similarities, three distinct states share the peninsula: Quintana Roo, Campeche, and Yucatán. The area is the home of the hammock, and there is often little way to beat the heat other than dozing in one through the warm afternoon.

The Yucatán Peninsula has been inhabited by Mayan people for centuries, and their unique traditions in food and culture continue to influence the region. Here, you can try distinctive dishes flavored with achiote (a rust-colored seed) and served with itty-bitty corn tortillas. The lightweight Mexican men's shirt, known as the *guyabera,* is also produced—and widely worn—throughout the Yucatán Peninsula.

Southern Mexico

Below the Isthmus of Tehuantepec, Mexico's culture is vibrant and traditional. Once the home of great Olmec, Mayan, and Zapotec cultures, the states of Tabasco, Chiapas, and Oaxaca are known for their tropical habitats, large indigenous communities, and vibrant regional culture. Both Chiapas and Oaxaca are major cultural destinations, with wonderful traditions in the arts and handcrafts, beautiful architecture, rich local markets, important archaeological sites, and lively regional festivals. They are also known for their ecological diversity, with some of the country's most precious wilderness located in eastern Chiapas and the sierras of Oaxaca.

WEATHER

The Tropic of Cancer slices through the tip of Baja California, hitting mainland Mexico in the state of Sinaloa. As a result, most of central and Southern Mexico is squarely situated in the tropics. Typical to all tropical zones, Mexico's climate is moist and balmy at sea level, with only slight gradations in temperature between the seasons. However, the country's varied terrain creates dramatic changes in elevation across the land, which likewise causes some significant differences in the climate across the country. Located on the southern tip of the central plateau, Mexico City is perched at over 7,000 feet. Sunshine is subdued by altitude, and the city maintains pleasantly temperate weather throughout the year, with average daytime temperatures in the mid-70s. By contrast, the coastal city of Puerto Vallarta has an average temperature of 86°F and humidity of 75 percent.

Throughout most of Mexico, the year is divided into the dry season, which runs from November to May, and the shorter wet season, from June to October. During the rainy season, heavy thunderstorms fall with a fury during the afternoon and evening but rarely last longer than a few hours. The amount of rain that falls varies greatly by region. In the north, including the Baja California peninsula, the climate is arid, with an average rainfall of 12–23 inches a year. Southeastern Tabasco receives close to 80 inches annually.

Speaking of rain, Mexico occasionally gets a lot of it. Both the Atlantic

© GABRIELA PEÑA GARAVITO

After the annual summer rains, colorful flowers bloom across south and central Mexico.

and Pacific coasts of Mexico are located at the heart of the world's hurricane belt, with major storms coming to shore from June to November. Both coasts take a frequent beating, through hurricanes in the Caribbean tend to be the strongest and most destructive. Hurricane Wilma, the largest tropical storm ever recorded, hit Mexico's Caribbean coast in October 2005. Even if you don't live on the coast, you may still feel the effects of these tropical storms in Mexico. A big hurricane can often produce days of wet weather throughout the country, including destructive flooding in the southern states.

FLORA

Mexico is one of the world's most biodiverse countries, with varied ecosystems supporting an enormous variety of plant and animal life. The unofficial symbol of the Mexican wilderness, the wonderful water-saving cactus proliferates throughout the country. Among the most famous genus of cactus, large multi-leaf agave grow in abundance throughout central Mexico. Harvested for centuries, juice from the agave's stalk is distilled to create mescal and tequila, two ubiquitous Mexican spirits. The tiny peyote button is another famed cactus, found in the vast deserts of San Luis Potosí. Peyote is sacred to the Huichol people, who consume its flesh to stimulate potent hallucinations.

Atop the Mexican Altiplano, grass and scrubland cover the central states, though much has been converted to farmland today. In the few remaining natural habitats, you'll see organ cactus, barrel cactus, and the ubiquitous prickly pear—the edible cactus depicted on the Mexican flag—shaded by the hearty mesquite and acacia trees. Tall trees are scarce in this low-water environment, though the majestic *ahuehuete* (cypress) often grow alongside rivers and streams in south and central Mexico. The oldest and largest *ahuehuete* trees are estimated to be more than 2,000 years old.

Altitude tempers the climate across the Mexican Altiplano, but the coastal plains are tropical in both weather and habitat. Around Puerto Vallarta, the hills are carpeted with fruit trees, orchids, and hanging vines, while mangrove estuaries and coconut palms line the shore in the Pacific's savanna grasslands. On the eastern coast of Mexico, remote cloud forests cover the coastal foothills of Tamaulipas,

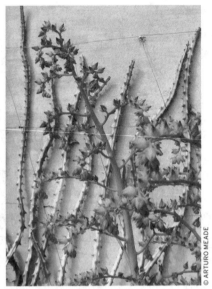

Cactus and succulents thrive in Mexico's semi-arid environment; here, a cactus climbs a wall in Oaxaca.

while the Sierra Madre Oriental harbors large swaths of pine-oak woodlands and fern-filled rainforest, where papaya, banana, and mamey trees grow naturally. The tropical coast of Veracruz is the original home of the world-famous vanilla bean.

In Southern Mexico, there are broadleaf evergreen jungles covering the low-lying regions of Chiapas, Tabasco, and Oaxaca—the most biodiverse states in a country celebrated for its biodiversity. Here, precious hardwoods like mahogany and cedar are mixed with towering rubber, tamarind, and ceiba trees, giving life to the many species that thrive beneath the rainforest's thick canopy. A famous native of the New World, the cacao plant grows wild in Mexico's southern jungles and was so prized by native Mesoamerican people that its seeds were used as money. To the east, the limestone sediment on the Yucatán Peninsula is covered in grassland and low evergreen jungle, brimming with hardwoods and fruit trees. Along the Caribbean coast, white-sand beaches and mangrove estuaries shelter marine life.

FAUNA

Almost 10 percent of the world's animal species live in Mexico, or, like so many North American vacationers, spend a season there during their annual migration. Mexico claims the largest abundance of known reptile species on earth, though its diversity of mammals also ranks within the top five worldwide. While Mexico's largest and most exotic creatures can often be difficult to spot in the wild, the multitude of wildlife makes it a popular destination for ecotourism, bird-watching, snorkeling, and scuba diving.

© ARTURO MEADE

The tropical climate in Mexico nurtures a range of flora and fauna, including many colorful insects.

On Land

Though the landscape appears inhospitable, Mexico's vast northern deserts are filled with creatures great and small. Desert tortoises, rattlesnakes, mice, coyotes, and prairie dogs are among the many adaptable animals that survive in the arid ecosystem. Though bighorn sheep and longhorn antelopes are rarely spotted today, they still make their home in remote corners of the desert wilderness.

Throughout the central plateau, coyotes, foxes, cottontails, jackrabbits, squirrels, mice, skunks, opossums, badgers, raccoons, and other furry creatures make a good living in the semiarid grasslands, while an abundance of hardy lizards and snakes warm their blood in the Mexican sunshine. From the scorpion to the deadly coral snake, venomous critters also find a comfortable habitat in much of Mexico, though, thankfully, most are reclusive.

Of Mexico's many reptiles, slow-moving green iguanas are among the most beloved and ubiquitous specimens; they often loiter around the backyards of vacation homes in Puerto Vallarta or in the archaeological ruins of the Yucatán Peninsula. Along with the iguana, a rich variety of animal life thrives in Mexico's tropical jungles, from the coatimundi, a raccoon relation, to the jaguarundi, a species of big cat. Down south, the jungles of Chiapas and Tabasco are home to ocelots, tapirs, armadillos, and the elusive jaguar. It may be hard to catch a glimpse of these larger creatures, but visitors to the jungles in Chiapas are often treated to a high-branch acrobatics show by playful spider monkeys.

At Sea

Mexico's long coastlines are rich with animal life. Between Baja California and the mainland, the Sea of Cortez shelters one of the most distinctive marine ecosystems on the planet. In addition to the multitude of fish, crustaceans, and sharks living in the warm coastal waters, an astonishing array of migratory animals spend a season off the Baja coast, including elephant seals, sea lions, and gray, blue, and sperm whales. Farther south, Pacific beaches are a major breeding ground for sea turtles. For sport fishermen, the Pacific Ocean boasts an abundance of marlin, halibut, tuna, swordfish, and other

Brown pelicans sun themselves in the harbor in Cabo San Lucas.

prized catch. A favorite sight on sunset cruises, dolphins leap over the waves just offshore, while crocodiles lurk in the quiet of coastal estuaries.

Off the east coast, marine mammals, eels, stingrays, sharks, jellyfish, and other sea creatures live within this giant semienclosed Gulf of Mexico. Bordering the Gulf to the south, Mexico's Yucatán Peninsula is fringed by the great Mesoamerican Barrier Reef, the second largest barrier reef in the world, home to dozens of coral species, as well as barracuda, lobsters, mollusks, sea turtles, manatees, manta rays, and tropical fish. The elusive whale shark gathers to mate along the northern stretches of the reef.

In the Air

The diverse ecosystems throughout Mexico create varied habitats for a wide range of birds. In temperate zones and grasslands, hawks, falcons, and owls keep watch over the semiarid plains of central Mexico, while hummingbirds, woodpeckers, and roadrunners roost in the cactus below. Beautiful small birds, like the vermillion flycatcher, are abundant year-round, and even water birds, like egrets, can be seen along the lakes and rivers of central Mexico.

The most impressive variety of birds lives along Mexico's tropical coastlines. Amazon parrots and hooded orioles are two of the colorful birds that live in the jungle near Puerto Vallarta, while pelicans and blue-footed boobies patrol the coastline. In the southern jungles of Chiapas and Tabasco, a pair of binoculars can help you pick out macaws and toucans among the leafy canopy of trees. Of the diverse shore birds of the Caribbean, the pink flamingo is the most flamboyant, gathering in large colonies along the west coast of the Yucatán Peninsula.

The Gulf Coast has the greatest diversity of birds in Mexico, with varied habitats supporting birds like fork-tailed flycatchers, parakeets, toucans, herons, wood storks, and ibis. Veracruz is also the site of the world's largest annual raptor migration; during September and October the skies are filled with falcons, hawks, vultures, and osprey.

While birds reign the sky, it is impossible to forget another, more delicate flying creature: the monarch butterfly. Every year, millions of monarchs spend weeks flying thousands of miles from the United States to the central Mexican state of Michoacan, where they winter in the Monarch Butterfly Biosphere Reserve.

ENVIRONMENTAL CONCERNS

In disappointing contrast to its ecological diversity, Mexico is plagued by numerous environmental problems. Throughout the country, there has been massive deforestation to accommodate farming, ranching, logging, and human settlements. According to some estimates, only 2 percent of the original old-growth forest remains standing in the Sierra Madre. In the Mexican Altiplano, the floodplains around the Río Lerma have suffered from severe erosion, which causes dramatic flooding during the rainy season.

Water is abundant in many parts of Mexico; however, many of the most populous regions suffer from depleted and contaminated water supplies. Industrial dumping, agricultural runoff, and human waste have contaminated many of the country's lakes and rivers, which are already woefully scarce in much of central and north Mexico. One of Mexico's most important watersheds, the Río Lerma is has been deeply affected by untreated waste dumped directly into the river.

Along the coasts, marine diversity has been compromised by dumping and topsoil runoff, as well as oil drilling in the Gulf of Mexico. Although oil did not reach Mexico's shores, the 2010 BP/*Deepwater Horizon* oil spill had an adverse effect on ocean creatures, with the full effects yet unknown. Many of Mexico's richest marine ecosystems have been badly damaged by overfishing and bycatch, as well as the damming of rivers that once flowed to the sea. The damming of the Colorado River is a notable example, as it has vastly reduced its output into the Sea of Cortez's estuaries and fisheries, significantly reducing their size.

Mexico's grassroots environmental movement has made some strides in the past decade, despite the monumental challenges it faces: In the Caribbean and the Pacific Coast, there are protected sea turtle hatcheries; in Mexico City, an aggressive program that limits automobile circulation has been very successful in reducing emissions and smog; there is a growing interest in organic agriculture throughout the country; and remote Oaxacan communities have developed community-based ecotourism programs to protect the region's natural beauty.

Social Climate

Mexico is the most populous Spanish-speaking country in the world, a major tourist destination, and one of the most important economic and industrial centers in Latin America. While Mexico doesn't have the diversity of, say, New York City, it supports a surprisingly pluralistic society. In addition to the mixed ethnic heritage of the Mexican people, the country sustains a large population of foreign residents from the United States, Canada, Europe, and Latin America, as well as a growing number of immigrants from more distant parts of the world, like Japan and Korea. While the conservative Catholic Church still holds sway over a large majority of the populace, Mexico is a surprisingly tolerant society, where different people and lifestyles coexist without excessive friction.

STANDARD OF LIVING

Despite Mexico's rapid economic growth and abundant natural resources, wealth is unevenly distributed throughout the country. Mexican society is highly stratified by class, and even basic services don't reach many marginalized communities in the remote countryside and urban slums. Social programs have made great strides over the past three decades, yet Mexico retains one of the largest impoverished populations in the world. Today, more than 40 percent of Mexicans live below the poverty line.

Though facts and figures reveal a grim reality, visitors expecting to find a country blighted by poverty are likely to experience very little of it on a day-to-day basis. In most Mexican cities, poor neighborhoods and shantytowns crop up outside the city center, while historic downtown districts are nicely restored and populated by an affluent population. Even in Mexico City, most of the central neighborhoods boast a higher standard of living than what you find in many of the outlying areas.

© ARTURO MEADE

Basic services and luxuries like eating at restaurants can be far more inexpensive in Mexico than in developed nations.

As an expatriate, you will likely live much more comfortably than the majority of the country. Mexico's middle class—which includes most foreign residents—is able to maintain a very high standard of living. Basic services are inexpensive, food is abundant and cheap, and basic health care is affordable. Even luxuries like hiring household help and eating at restaurants can be far more inexpensive than in developed nations.

However, it is important for foreigners to have realistic expectations with regards to cost. Though cheaper than most of North America, Mexico isn't a shoestring destination. Frugal residents find they can nicely subsist on their social security earnings, while others need a higher budget to maintain a comfortable lifestyle. Depending on where and how you choose to live, you might even find the cost of living can be comparable to some parts the United States and Canada.

Mexico is modernizing quickly, and there are few goods and services you can't find south of the border. Unless you live in a rural area, you can get phone and Internet service at home, as well as cable or satellite television broadcasting many of the same programs (in English!) as you'd find at home. Some imported items, such as brand-name clothing, electronics, and computers, may cost considerably more in Mexico than in the United States—in fact, affluent Mexicans often head to the United States to do their shopping, hauling back bursting suitcases of cheaper goods. At the same time, almost everything you might need, crave, or desire is accessible, though you might pay a bit more for it.

GRINGOS, GABACHOS, AND GÜEROS

You won't be in Mexico long before you hear the popular term *gringo* in use – especially if you are a gringo yourself. Who (or what) does it refer to? What are its origins? And – the most intriguing question for most foreigners – is it derogatory or simply descriptive?

Let's begin with the first question: Who (or what) is a gringo? In Mexico, *gringo* usually refers to something or someone from the United States. It can be used a noun, as in, "the gringo is taking photographs of a pelican," or as an adjective, as in "McDonald's is a gringo restaurant." Like all Spanish words, it has both a masculine and feminine form; the feminine form is *gringa*. (For taco eaters, a *gringa* also refers to a rubbed pork taco served with melted cheese in a flour tortilla.)

Though everyone has a pet theory about the origins of the word *gringo*, its etymology is unclear. The most popular explanation is that Yankee soldiers sang the song "Green Grow the Lilacs" during the Mexican-American War, prompting Mexican soldiers to shout "Green Go" in response. However, the term was in use before the 19th century, making this explanation unlikely. Other theories suggest that the word derives from *griego*, the Spanish word for Greek (and possibly a term applicable to any foreigner speaking a foreign tongue).

Finally, is the term derogatory? There is a persistent rumor that the term *gringo* is pejorative, and, in some cases, it is. When used in a sentence such as, "fast food is a gringo invention," the word can imply a certain low grade from the United States, which is generally disrespected in Mexico. However, in the great majority of cases, the word *gringo* is simply a descriptor, much easier on the tongue than the cumbersome official term *estadounidense* (U.S. citizen). As you'll quickly learn, many expatriates freely refer to themselves as gringos, and Mexicans use it without any implied offense. As an alternate to *gringo*, the word *gabacho* also refers to people or things from the United States. Though it is used less frequently, it is a synonymous with *gringo* and can be used interchangeably. For this word, we have a stronger sense of its origins, since the Spanish used *gabacho* to describe the French.

Finally, the popular moniker *güero* is a much more general term, though it's commonly used to describe foreigners. *Güero* refers to any person with fair hair and skin. There is no political connotation to the term *güero*, and Mexicans will even refer to fair-haired compatriots as *güeros*.

SAFETY AND STABILITY

Mexico has maintained a representative democracy since the end of the Mexican Revolution. The country's economy is rapidly developing, and the standard of living has improved across demographics. At the same time, Mexico has a history of revolution, unrest, and political instability deeply rooted in the collective psyche. As recently as 1994, an army of indigenous rebels took armed control of several cities in the southern state of Chiapas. Known as Zapatista Army of National Liberation, or EZLN, they brought indigenous politics to the forefront of international consciousness through a gutsy and well-planned military and political campaign.

On a much smaller scale, there are ongoing protests throughout the country, sometimes with major consequences. In 2008, the city of Oaxaca was brought to a near standstill during nine months of organized protests by the teachers' union. In 2002, residents of the small town of Atenco took control of the streets when the government proposed the construction of a new international airport on their land. There is a general sense of mistrust between the Mexican people and their governors and an ongoing air of political tension.

Since the government began a large-scale offensive against the drug cartels in Northern Mexico, there has been a major increase in violence throughout the north, especially in the regions bordering the United States. There has also been intermittent violence and drug-related activity in the central states, like Michoacan and Guerrero. Since the mid-2000s, the United States Department of State has issued ongoing travel warnings for those planning to visit the Mexican border region, including restrictions on American consulate workers in Ciudad Juárez.

In most Mexican communities, the clash between the government and the drug cartels has little to no effect on residents' daily life. Drug-related violence rarely occurs in the destinations discussed in this book, and most visitors and expatriates feel completely safe in Mexico. Understanding the importance of international tourism to the country's economy, the Mexican government has taken many steps to keep tourists out of the line of fire.

At the same time, ongoing violence has had a strong affect on the country's morale, even in places where *narcotraficantes* have not become an everyday problem. Ongoing reports of mass graves and brutal murders have created widespread disillusionment with the federal government. In 2011, the U.S. Ambassador to Mexico resigned under pressure from the Mexican government, whose handling of the drug wars he had criticized publicly.

MEXICO AND FOREIGNERS

The Mexican people are a melting pot of cultures and ethnicities, and foreigners are generally welcomed into this ever-changing society. It's not unusual to meet expatriates who have spent decades south of the border, married into Mexican families, naturalized as Mexican citizens, and speak Spanish with all the slang and flourishes of a native. In fact, there are so many North American and European expatriates living in Mexico that their presence rarely warrants a second glance.

Mexicans are generally accepting of newcomers, though attitudes toward foreigners differ by region. Tourism is a billion-dollar industry in Mexico, and the largest resort towns are used to a constant wave of international visitors—as well as plenty of part-time and full-time foreign residents. Those living at the beach will likely find their presence welcome and appreciated, if rather commonplace. In smaller communities without a large expatriate population, foreign residents may stand out a bit, and it may take more time to build relationships in the community. In bigger cities, foreigners fly under the radar, less visible among the diverse denizens.

Americans—known as gringos throughout Mexico—often worry that a bad international reputation precedes them. In reality, many Mexicans express ambivalence about the United States. Like most of Latin America, Mexico leans left on the political spectrum. The vast majority of Mexicans disagree with their northern neighbor's imperialist tendencies, and some bemoan the cultural hegemony that has brought McDonald's and Hollywood to a country that has plenty of culture of its own. At the same time, the United States is an integral part of most Mexicans' lives. Almost everyone in Mexico has a friend or family member who is living in the States, and it is a popular vacation destination with Mexicans of every class. Even if they disagree with American politics, Mexicans rarely take a personal issue with their gringo friends. As long as you don't mind a spirited political debate, you will rarely have a problem in Mexico.

On that note, spirited debates can be a lot more fun with a little bit of Spanish under your belt. You can certainly live in Mexico without learning how to

© ARTURO MEADE

Expatriates live in every corner of Mexico, from small towns to big cities.

speak Spanish (a large number of expatriates do!), but your experience will be much richer if you can interact with the people in your adopted home. Mexicans are welcoming to guests in their country, and it's well worth the effort it takes to speak the same language.

THE EXPATRIATE COMMUNITY

Mexico is a large and diverse country, which attracts foreign residents for a variety of reasons. Some foreigners relocate to Mexico to oversee their company's operations or to help develop new markets south of the border. Mexican law makes it fairly easy to work legally, so others take jobs in the tourist industry, at language schools, or in nonprofit organizations, among other industries. Those who don't have paperwork can often find jobs under the table, while others open a business with their own capital. Thanks to the magic of the Internet, many foreign residents take advantage of the dollar-to-peso exchange rate and telecommute to jobs in the States.

Obviously, not everyone comes to Mexico to work. For many North Americans, Mexico is a very attractive retirement destination—close to home, more inexpensive than the United States or Canada, and blissfully sunny year-round. Retirees often choose to settle down in one of the popular American and Canadian expatriate communities, like San Miguel de Allende, Ajijic, or Puerto Vallarta. Expatriate culture has a big sway in these cities, though they remain quintessentially Mexican places. Even if you eschew expatriate enclaves, you'll likely bump into another gringo or two; there are foreign residents scattered throughout the country, from big cities and tourist resorts to small towns and remote beaches.

HISTORY, GOVERNMENT, AND ECONOMY

Mexico has many stories to tell. Its history is long and extraordinary, often tragic, sometimes funny, and defined by conflicting ideas and charismatic personalities. Even as the country moves quickly into the 21st century, the past weighs heavily on the national consciousness. In Mexico, history is visible and close at hand, from the colonial-era architecture in the streets of San Miguel de Allende to the magnificent ruins of Teotihuacan. Most Mexicans know their country's history and are proud of it—just as they are conflicted about it. Understanding the country's past is a vital part of understanding its people.

War, strife, and hardship are not uncommon to Mexico or its people, and even today, there are great inequities within Mexican society. At the same time, Mexico has enjoyed a century of stable government and economic growth, creating a new society with more economic and social possibilities than at the turn of the 21st century. Mexicans are aware of their greater context as an ally in Latin America and a trading partner to the United States, and there is both hope and growing pains as the country negotiates a new and more important position in the world.

© ARTURO MEADE

History

EARLY CIVILIZATIONS

More than 30,000 years ago, the majority of the North American continent was covered in sheets of ice. Amid this forbidding landscape, the first human settlers migrated from Siberia to North America via a narrow land bridge across the Bering Straight. These first people were followed by another wave of migrants, likely of Asian descent. Arriving toward the end of the Stone Age, they eventually migrated all the way to the southern reaches of the Andes Mountains of South America.

Even with most of the continent blanketed in ice, conditions were agreeable in the southern plains of modern Mexico. Tribes of hunter-gatherers began to organize into communities; stone artifacts and evidence of living sites have been found throughout central and south Mexico, some of which date back more than 20,000 years. Many tribes were concentrated in a region known as Mesoamerica, a culturally linked swath of territory that covers Southern Mexico, Belize, Guatemala, Honduras, El Salvador, and Nicaragua. As the glaciers melted and the oceans rose, the American population was physically isolated from Eurasia, and independently developed farming techniques, with maize cultivation dating back 9,000 years.

THE OLMEC

A mysterious people called the Olmec are recognized as the first complex civilization in Mesoamerica, flourishing along the Gulf Coast between 1500 and 400 B.C. Though little is known about their daily life, Olmecs left behind the ruins of several great city-states, built around tall, stepped pyramids. A highly expressive culture with a deep belief in magic and shamanism, Olmecs produced art that is both technically impressive and aesthetically beautiful. Culturally, they are best known for their colossal stone heads, hand-carved from boulders of volcanic basalt, as well as their fantastical human or animal figures, carved into stone or jade.

The temple-pyramid would become emblematic of Mesoamerican cities, and anthropologists have found evidence that Olmecs were a major influence on succeeding cultures in other ways, too. For example, Olmecs had courts for the *juego de pelota,* or Mesoamerican ball game, a sport played by the Mayan, Zapotec, and Aztec cultures, among others. They also participated in ritual bloodletting, which would become a mark of Classic Mesoamerican cultures.

CLASSIC CIVILIZATIONS

Anthropologists generally divide Mexico's pre-Columbian past into several periods of time. About 250–300 B.C., the Classic Period in Mesoamerica began. The Classic Period was an era of great human advancement, as tribes began to gather in large city-states throughout Mexico and Mesoamerica.

During the early Classic Period, an unknown people founded the great city of Teotihuacan in the Valley of Mexico. Teotihuacan's largest structure, the 230-foot Pyramid of the Sun, was completed around A.D. 100, though the city reached

pyramid at the pre-Columbian city of Teotihuacan

its peak several hundred years later. With an estimated population peaking at 150,000 (and possibly more), Teotihuacan's influence reached throughout Mesoamerica. It was overtaken and destroyed around A.D. 800, though today it is one of Mexico's most famous cultural destinations.

Meanwhile, in the southern jungles, one of Mesoamerica's most celebrated civilizations was awakening. The Maya people rose in prominence between A.D. 250 and 900, building elaborate city-states throughout the Yucatán Peninsula, Southern Mexico, Guatemala, Belize, and Honduras. Accomplished astronomers and mathematicians, the Maya used a complex and highly accurate calendar system, which was later adopted by civilizations throughout the Americas. Their written language was a mix of syllabic signs and logograms, inscribed onto temple walls or into paper books. They were also accomplished artists and architects, with many elaborately wrought stone, ceramic, and jade pieces surviving to the present day, as well as beautifully painted frescoes. Though Mayan civilization experienced a steep and mysterious decline in the 8th or 9th century, they never totally disappeared from the land. Today, there are six million Maya people living in Mexico, Guatemala, and Belize.

Although their history dates back to the 6th century B.C., the Zapotec culture flourished in the Valley of Oaxaca during the Classic Period. The great city-state of Monte Alban was founded in 400 B.C. but reached preeminence during the Classic Period. Like their contemporaries, the Zapotecs were accomplished architects, artists, and scientists. They employed a writing system to record their people's history, which new evidence suggests may have been the first writing system in Mesoamerica.

POST-CLASSIC CIVILIZATIONS

Most large Mayan cities and the Zapotec cities began to decline after A.D. 1000, though a few continued to support smaller populations in the Post-Classic era. Even as populations declined, scientific and political advances continued throughout central Mexico and Mesoamerica as new tribes descended from the north. Among these, a strong and bellicose people known as the Toltec dominated central Mexico about A.D. 800–1000. They controlled trade routes from a massive city in Tula.

To the south, the Mixtec people had taken control of southern Puebla and Guerrero, and extended their influence south to overpower the Zapotec city of Monte Alban. The Zapotec fanned out to cover the Isthmus of Tehuantepec while maintaining an ongoing conflict with the Mixtec.

THE AZTEC EMPIRE

In the 15th century, Nauhatl-speaking people dominated Mesoamerica from the powerful tri-city alliance of Tenochtitlan, Texcoco, and Tlacopan, near modern-day Mexico City. The most powerful of the three cities was the great Tenochtitlan, home of the Mexica. The Mexica had arrived in central Mexico during the 12th century, founding their city when they saw a prophesied vision of a golden eagle eating a snake on a cactus (today, the symbol on the Mexican flag.) The Mexica, in conjunction with other Nahuatl-speaking people of the era, are commonly referred to as the Aztecs.

Known as brutal warriors and feared for their merciless treatment of prisoners, the Mexica and their allies were feared throughout Mesoamerica. At the same time, they were a highly developed and creative society, with advanced city planning and agricultural capabilities, as well as complex religious beliefs. Huizilopochtli, the god of war, and Tlaloc, the god of rain, were central figures in their pantheon. The Mexica gained Huizilopochtli's favor by performing massive human sacrifices in their temples, often searching for victims in neighboring city-states.

On the eve of the Spanish conquest, Tenochtitlan was one of the world's largest cities, ruling over an expansive territory that spans from the Gulf Coast to the Pacific Ocean. The island metropolis was filled with temple-pyramids, hydroponic gardens, and large public squares, connected by waterways that were navigated by canoe. Early Spanish accounts of the city marvel at its size, color, and orderliness.

THE SPANISH CONQUEST

When Christopher Columbus returned to Spain from his first Atlantic voyage, Iberian conquest of the New World swiftly began. The Caribbean islands fell easily to the Spanish crown, but mainland Mexico proved a greater challenge. In 1519, a young Spaniard named Hernán Cortés set sail from the Spanish colony in Cuba, landing in North America near modern-day Veracruz. Although the governor of Cuba had officially canceled Cortés's expedition, the young Spaniard forged ahead in his mission: to secure the land for Spain.

After an arduous journey into central Mexico, Cortés and his soldiers were welcomed to Tenochtitlan by emperor Moctezuma. Several weeks went by without event, but tensions brewed between the Mexica and their foreign guests. When the Spanish panicked and killed 200 Mexica nobles, the Spanish were forced to flee Tenochtitlan. Trying to escape under the cover of darkness, the Spanish lost hundreds of soldiers in a massacre remembered as the Noche Triste (Sad Night).

Planning their retaliation, the Spanish redoubled their forces. Playing on the widespread resentment of the Mexica throughout the region, the Spanish recruited help from many tribes near Tenochtitlan. The Spanish were further assisted by the smallpox virus, which they had unwittingly introduced to the Americas. In a matter of weeks, thousands of native people fell sick and died, including Moctezuma's successor, Cuitláhuac.

After months of preparation, the Spanish launched a waterborne attack on Tenochtitlan in January 1521. Months of conflict ensued, concluding with an 80-day siege of the city. Led by Moctezuma's son, Cuauhtémoc, the Mexica resisted the Spanish, even as the citizens of the besieged city ran low on food and water. Finally, Cortés and his military forced the Mexica to flee to the adjoining community of Tlatelolco, where they were overcome. The Spanish razed Tenochtitlan and built a new city on its ruins. They called the city Mexico and christened it capital of New Spain.

THE COLONIAL ERA

Not long after Cortés defeated the Mexica, Spanish missionaries and settlers began to arrive on the North American continent. The first viceroy of Mexico, Don Antonio de Mendoza, took his post in 1535. Conquest and colonization were brutal for the native people, both physically and culturally. Where they encountered resistance, the Spanish used ruthless tactics to subdue native tribes. Many indigenous people were enslaved, while others succumbed to foreign disease. As a result of these changes, the native population dropped significantly during the early years of New Spain.

Fifteenth-century Spain was a deeply Catholic place, entrenched in the Inquisition by the time Cortés conquered Tenochtitlan. Converting the native population to Catholicism was a top priority for the Spanish crown, and by the mid-1520s, Franciscan missionaries had founded settlements among native communities in Puebla, Oaxaca, and Mexico City. They continued to reach throughout the New World, building missions and outposts throughout Central and North America.

In addition to seeking converts, the Spanish came to the New World in search of wealth and fortune. To encourage settlement, the crown doled out land grants throughout the territories, and Spanish families established large haciendas, clearing the native land for agriculture and cattle grazing. Having admired the gold and silver jewelry worn by Mexica nobles, the Spanish aggressively sought precious metals within the craggy Sierra Madre. Fortuitously, a Spanish expedition discovered a large silver vein outside the modern-day city of Zacatecas in 1546. Several more bountiful mines were discovered shortly thereafter.

The discovery of silver immediately changed the power dynamic in the colonies, creating massive trading power for the New World with the Old World. New Spanish-controlled governments were established and registered, as wealthy new-world aristocrats invested heavily in new Spanish-style cities. Today, Mexico's colonial cities are filled with impressive sandstone architecture, Baroque churches, large public plazas, and opulent Spanish mansions. By the early 17th century, the Spanish had established control over the land, and development continued.

Colonial society was highly stratified. Throughout New Spain, Spaniards born in Spain were afforded the highest place in society and were consistently appointed to all of the most important political posts. Mexican-born people of Spanish heritage were referred to as criollos, and, despite their common heritage, had a lower social and political standing. Mestizo people of mixed ethnic heritage held a far lower place in society, only better than the abysmal position of poorly paid indigenous workers and slaves.

WAR OF INDEPENDENCE

After close to 250 years of Spanish rule in the New World, Bourbon king Charles III ascended the Spanish throne. A strong believer in "enlightened absolutism," he immediately made changes to the governance of New Spain.

Undermining the colony's economic autonomy, he established royal monopolies on seminal industries like tobacco, gunpowder, and mercury (an element needed for silver extraction in the mines). He also forbade church loans, which were a major source of credit within Mexican communities. Finally, he expelled the highly popular Jesuit order from Mexico. For many Americans—especially those who had already come to resent the colony's strict hierarchies and distant Spanish rulers—these changes stirred up immediate resentment within new-world communities.

In the Bajío region north of Mexico City, criollo landowners began

© ARTURO MEADE

A public mural by artist José Clemente Orozco in Guadalajara depicts the great Independence hero, Miguel Hidalgo.

to envision New Spain as an independent country, meeting secretly in Querétaro and San Miguel de Allende to conspire against the Bourbon monarchs. When Napoleon invaded Spain in 1807, the conspirators decided to exploit the Spanish weakness and stage a revolution. In September 1810, the conspirators' plan was uncovered prematurely; with little other option, the rebels decided to declare war on the Spanish without delay.

On September 16, 1810, Miguel Hidalgo made an impassioned call to war from the steps of the parish in Dolores Hidalgo, Guanajuato. His famous cry, "Viva Mexico!" is shouted to commemorate independence day every year. Despite his ragtag army and small cavalry, Hidalgo was able to easily take the cities of San Miguel de Allende and Celaya; however, he sustained major casualties in taking the city of Guanajuato. Thereafter, a major loss at Battle of the Bridge of Calderón threw the army into chaos, precipitating the upcoming 11 years of chaotic armed conflict.

After Hidalgo's capture and assassination, José María Morelos took charge of the army. He in turn was captured and executed. The battles continued for almost a decade until the government of Ferdinand VII was overthrown in Spain. As a result of the change in Spanish governance, Colonel Agustín de Iturbide, a fierce royalist, switched sides to join the Mexican army. With Iturbide at the helm, Mexico achieved independence with the Treaty of Córdoba in 1821.

POST-INDEPENDENCE

After signing the Treaty of Córdoba, Mexico took its shaky first steps toward establishing autonomy. Twenty-four states were named in the First Mexican Empire, with independence leader Agustín de Iturbide crowning himself emperor of Mexico. Hostilities stemmed from the clash between liberals and conservatives, who envisioned different roles for the independent states, the Catholic Church, and the monarchy.

Just eight months after Iturbide took control of the government, Vicente Guerrero and Antonio López de Santa Anna led a successful revolt against the government. They

Mexican flags for sale in San Miguel de Allende before the annual Independence Day festivities

© ARTURO MEADE

established the first Mexican republic, and another hero of the War of Independence, Guadalupe Victoria, became the country's first president. Guadalupe Victoria would be the only Mexican president to serve a full term for the next 50 years, which were characterized by instability and ongoing government overthrowal. Amid turmoil, Vicente Guerrero assumed the post of president when Guadalupe Victoria stepped down, though the conservative forces of General Anastasio Bustamante quickly ousted him from office.

MEXICAN-AMERICAN WAR

In 1831, Independence hero Santa Anna was elected to the presidency. During this time, the United States was aggressively expanding westward, and U.S. citizens began to settle in the Mexican territory of Texas. Though they arrived with permission from the government, new settlers were little interested in submitting to Mexico's laws. When Mexico's constitution centralized power and abolished slavery in 1835, Texas declared independence from Mexico. In response, Santa Anna sent troops to Texas. He sustained a major victory at The Alamo, but the brutality of the fighting galvanized Texans against the Mexican president. After numerous confrontations, the Texan army overpowered Santa Anna's forces, gaining independence.

On June 16, 1845, the United States annexed Texas, though the state's independence was never formally recognized by the Mexican government. Shortly thereafter, President James Polk began to prepare the United States for war. When a skirmish broke out between Mexican and U.S. military along the Texas border, Polk asked Congress to declare war.

Aggressively recruiting new soldiers to join the effort, the United States advanced into Northern Mexico under General Winfred Scott. Conquering the important central city of Puebla, Scott's army launched an offensive on the capital. After numerous battles, he won control of Mexico City. The capital of Mexico was temporarily relocated to Querétaro. In Querétaro, Santa Anna signed the infamous Treaty of Guadalupe, which ceded half of Mexico's territory to the United States, including California, New Mexico, Arizona, Texas, Colorado, and Nevada. A remaining segment of land was later sold to the United States.

REFORM AND FRENCH RULE

Benito Juárez became president of the republic in the middle of the 19th century, spearheading a series of liberal reforms over the course of his five terms in office. Among his most significant acts, Juárez abolished church property and amended the constitution to officially recognize freedom of religion. Juárez's presidency was repeatedly threatened by conservative and royalist forces, though he is remembered today as one of Mexico's most just and visionary presidents.

Failing to oust liberals from power, conservative leaders conspired with the government of France to overthrow Juárez's government. France invaded Mexico under Napoleon III, and, after a disastrous defeat in Puebla, came back to successfully overwhelm Juárez's forces. The French established the Second Mexican Empire, placing Emperor Maximilian I of Austria in charge of the state. In 1867, there was yet another successful uprising by the liberals, and Maximilian was executed in Querétaro. Benito Juarez returned to the presidency, and he remained in power until his death in 1872.

THE PORFIRIATO

Not long after Juárez's successor, Sebastián Lerdo de Tejada, had won his second election, army general Porfirio Díaz took office in a coup. A hero in the war against the French, Porfirio Díaz was originally a liberal. However, his politics changed in office. He became a powerful and conservative political leader with a strong military outlook. Commonly remembered as a dictator, Díaz held the presidency for 26 consecutive years.

Under Díaz, Mexico entered into an era of relative stability, though the regime's despotic and militaristic tendencies did not play out positively for the majority of Mexicans. While the country's wealth increased, social conditions for the poor worsened under Díaz's iron-fisted control. Díaz's presidency is known as the Porfiriato.

REVOLUTION OF 1910

After almost 30 years of the Porfiriato, wealthy politician Francisco I. Madero announced his presidential candidacy, in opposition to Díaz. Madero stirred up a great deal of popular support, and in response, President Díaz threw him in jail. In return, Madero declared a revolt against the Díaz government on November 20, 1910, now remembered as the Day of the Revolution.

The Mexican Revolution inspired some of Mexico's most colorful personalities. Leading the División del Norte (northern division), the wily and charismatic bandit Pancho Villa recruited thousands to the revolutionary cause. From the state of Morelos, Emiliano Zapata was a middle-class landowner who joined the revolution to promote land reform among peasants. Zapata rode to war dressed as a traditional Mexican *charro* (cowboy), with a wide-brim sombrero and thick moustache. He is still revered for his populist politics and his strong commitment to rural populations.

Within six months, the people's army defeated Díaz's military. Madero took the presidency, but to the disappointment of many, he made good on few of his promises. Observing Madero's political weakness, Victoriano Huerta ousted Madero in a coup and claimed the presidency for himself. In response, Venustiano Carranza, Álvaro Obregón, Pancho Villa, and Emiliano Zapata led yet another revolt against Huerta's government, with additional support from the U.S. army. They toppled Huerta's regime in August 1914.

Venustiano Carranza made a bid for the presidency, initially opposed by both Villa and Zapata. However, Carranza was able to win a broad base of support by promising constitutional reform. He oversaw the writing of the Constitution of 1917, which included land, law, and labor reforms. Carranza was eventually forced out of power and replaced by General Álvaro Obregón.

POST-REVOLUTIONARY MEXICO

The post-revolutionary period was a time of great progress, culture, and intellectual achievement in Mexico. During Obregón's presidency, José Vasconcelos served as the secretary of public education, overseeing the establishment of the National Symphonic Orchestra as well as the famed Mexican mural program, which brought celebrated artists such as Diego Rivera and David Alfaro Siqueiros to a larger audience. Economically, the outlook was brighter,

LÁZARO CÁRDENAS AND OIL EXPROPRIATION

At the beginning of the 20th century, Emiliano Zapata joined the popular uprising against longtime president and dictator Porfirio Díaz. The one true idealist of the Revolution of 1910, Zapata demanded "*tierra y libertad*" (land and liberty) for the Mexican people, envisioning the country's land redistributed and put into the hands of the people who work it. His populist notions drew citizen fighters to the revolutionary cause, and he is remembered as one of Mexico's great heroes. After the fighting ended, there was some limited land reform in Zapata's home state of Morelos, but the promises of the revolution were largely forgotten until the presidency of Lázaro Cárdenas in the 1930s.

Born in Jilquilpan, Michoacán, Cárdenas came of age during the Revolution of 1910. Though he never fought with Zapata, he fought in the Revolution alongside Francisco Madero and later joined up with Pancho Villa in the north. Cárdenas reached high ranks in the military, and, after the war had concluded, he was elected governor of Michoacán. Politically sharp, he traveled to remote parts of the state and occasionally asked local leaders to deliver his message in indigenous languages. He later served in the cabinet of President Pascual Ortiz Rubio and was elected president of the National Revolution Party (today's PRI), drawing great popular support. When President Plutarco Elías Calles's term ended, Cárdenas was his natural successor. Leading up to his election, Cárdenas traveled the country promising to enact widespread social and economic reform, as promised by the leaders of the Revolution of 1910.

Unlike many before him (and many after him), Cárdenas made good on his promises once elected president. He redistributed 45 million acres of land, converting them to *ejidos* (communally owned territory). He lobbied to create term limits for judges, favored unions over business, and began to implement a system of rural education. He became known for granting political asylum, and his administration accepted Republican refugees from the Spanish Civil War; in a famous move, he also accepted political exile and Bolshevik revolutionary Leon Trotsky, who lived the final years of his life in Mexico City.

As president, Cárdenas made his most famous move in 1938. After a long conflict between unionized workers and foreign-owned oil companies, the government intervened on behalf of the unions. On March 18, 1938, Cárdenas declared that a single, government-owned oil company would take control of all of Mexico's oil resources, amid great celebration of both petroleum workers and the people. Though its birth was shaky, Pétroleros Mexicanos, or PEMEX, overcame difficulties and became one of the country's top economic contributors.

While Cárdenas was popular with the people during his presidency and remains a charismatic and well-regarded figure in Mexico's more socialist past, not all of his endeavors were successful: The majority of his reforms were modified during his presidency or overturned by successive governments. The *ejido* system was officially terminated during the presidency of Carlos Salinas de Gotari.

too. After the 1920s, the Mexican economy began to grow annually. Politically, Mexico was on the road to a one-party system. President Plutarco Elías Calles, Obregón's successor, founded the National Revolutionary Party, which would eventually become the Institutional Revolutionary Party (PRI). The PRI ruled Mexico, virtually uncontested, until 2000.

In 1937, Lázaro Cárdenas was elected to the presidency. Cárdenas enacted land reform and redistribution as laid out in the Constitution of 1917. In a move that would serve as a model for other oil-rich nations, Cárdenas expropriated oil reserves from the private companies that had been running them. He established Petróleos Mexicanos (PEMEX), concurrently founding the National Polytechnic Institute to ensure a sufficient engineering force in the country.

Music and cinema flourished during the 1930s and 1940s, with Mexican movies outselling Hollywood films during World War II. During and after the Spanish Civil War, many European intellectuals took up residence in Mexico, adding to the thriving art and cultural community. In the 1950s, Luis Buñuel, the famous Spanish filmmaker, made some of his most influential pictures in Mexico, eventually naturalizing as a Mexican citizen.

THE 1960S AND THE TLATELOLCO MASSACRE

Having made substantial economic and social progress, Mexico was selected to host the Olympic Games in 1968. For Mexico's government, the Olympic Games were a major financial investment, as well as an important opportunity to boost the nation's economy and bring Mexico to the world stage. Inspired by the hippie movement, feminism, and world events, Mexican students saw the international publicity as an opportunity to draw attention to Mexico's oppressive government. There were widespread protests against the government in the months preceding the opening ceremony, many drawing tens of thousands of protestors.

Ten days before the Olympic Games were set to begin, thousands of students marched in protest to the Plaza de las Tres Culturas in Tlatelolco, a neighborhood in Mexico City. The gathering was meant to be peaceful, but military troops fired indiscriminately on the crowd as tanks rolled in behind them. While the government stated that only four students had been killed, eyewitnesses saw hundreds of bodies left in the wake. The official events were never fully uncovered, yet the event permanently tarnished the PRI's reputation with the people of Mexico and engendered deep suspicion of the government.

ECONOMIC CRISIS AND GROWTH

In the early 1980s, falling oil prices and high worldwide interest rates created a massive recession in Mexico. President Miguel de la Madrid was forced to drastically cut government spending, the economy stagnated, and unemployment soared. Recovery was incredibly slow, with the GDP growing just 0.1 percent per year until 1988. Finally, economic recovery began under the next president, Carlos Salinas de Gotari, who renegotiated the country's external debts and embarked on a policy of trade liberalization.

THE MODERN REVOLUTION

On January 1, 1994, the North American Free Trade Agreement (NAFTA) was officially inaugurated, opening up a new, more unrestricted economy between the United States, Canada, and Mexico. The same morning, the Zapatista Army of National Liberation (EZLN) burst from the remote southern jungles, taking armed control of several cities in southeastern Chiapas. Executing a very well-planned campaign, this small guerilla army, comprised almost entirely of indigenous soldiers, was able to maintain their stronghold on Chiapas for several days until they were, inevitably, overwhelmed by the Mexican military.

The EZLN issued a declaration of war against the Mexican government, calling attention to the great gap between rich and poor in modern Mexico. Indeed, as the government prepared to inaugurate NAFTA, the Mayan communities living in the deep jungles and remote highlands of the state of Chiapas were among Mexico's poorest and most disenfranchised citizens. The long and thorough marginalization of Mexico's indigenous communities had left these people forgotten by the greater society; most had insufficient access to basics like clean water, schools, or health care. In their revolution, the EZLN envisioned agrarian reform, as Emiliano Zapata had during the Revolution of 1910, and called for a new bottom-up (rather than top-down) political system. They demanded more indigenous control of the land, and women's rights were included on their agenda.

The EZLN sustained major casualties before armed conflict ended on January 12, with a ceasefire brokered by Bishop Samuel Ruíz, a popular figure with indigenous communities in San Cristóbal de las Casas. EZLN leadership took refuge in the jungle of Chiapas; the military was unable to locate them, though there were several instances of unwarranted brutality against rural villages suspected to sympathize with the EZLN. The group entered talks with the new administration overseen by Vicente Fox, but they were unable to reach agreement. Peace talks dissolved in 1996.

While they failed to make political inroads, the EZLN's forward-thinking political agenda, as well as their Internet-savvy and postmodern self-awareness, appealed to the international community and brought the struggles of Mexico's indigenous communities to the forefront of the world's consciousness. Since the initial conflict, the Zapatistas have been involved in only nonviolent organizing, publishing communiqués under the name the Other Campaign.

The economy improved under Salinas. However, shortly after PRI president Ernesto Zedillo was sworn into office, Mexico's currency collapsed and recession returned. The U.S. Treasury and the IMF (International Monetary Fund) put together a massive financial bailout, and recovery was much swifter. Mexico was economically stable enough to sign as a member of the North American Free Trade Agreement (NAFTA) in 1994. With the passage of NAFTA, Mexico's economy has continued to grow annually, and trade between NAFTA nations has more than tripled.

THE ZAPATISTA MOVEMENT

The same morning that NAFTA went into effect, a small but well-organized indigenous army called the Ejército Zapatista de Liberación Nacional (Zapatista Army of National Liberation), or EZLN, took armed control of several cities in the southernmost state of Chiapas, including the historic capital (and tourist magnet) of San Cristóbal de las Casas. Known as the Zapatistas, the army, in their first communiqué, declared war on the Mexican military and government, citing the years of poverty and oppression suffered by the country's native people. In response to the uprising, the Mexican government quickly dispatched thousands of troops to Chiapas, pursuing the EZLN as they retreated into the southern jungles.

This rebellion was small in scope but wide reaching in consequences, inspiring widespread support for indigenous people throughout Mexico—and throughout the world. The army's unofficial leader, Subcommandante Marcos, became a national spokesman for the indigenous cause and, along with a convoy of EZLN leadership, met repeatedly with Mexican government leaders. The EZLN has never been able to reach an agreement with the Mexican government regarding indigenous rights, but they remain a vocal and respected opposition presence in the country.

PRI OPPOSITION AND THE PAN

In 1988, leftist politician Cuauhtémoc Cárdenas (the son of Mexico's great post-revolutionary president, Lázaro Cárdenas) split from the ruling PRI party and announced his candidacy for president against Carlos Salinas de Gotari. Cárdenas was defeated in a highly suspect election, during which the voting systems failed to function for several hours. He lost another race against the PRI in 1994 but was elected mayor of Mexico City two years later, bolstering the notion that Mexico was ready for a change from the one-party system.

After the collapse of the peso, support for the PRI continued to erode. In the meantime, the conservative PAN party (Partido Acción Nacional, or

National Action Party) had made inroads into politics. As early as the 1980s, they had garnered several important government posts in the northern states. In the elections of 2000, popular support began to rally around the tall and mustachioed Vincente Fox Quesada, a native of Guanajuato state and a former Coca-Cola executive. Campaigning more on the ticket of change than on the conservative politics of the PAN, Fox won a tidy and much-celebrated victory over PRI candidate Francisco Labastida. The PAN did not control the congress, however, and Fox's presidency was largely marked by inefficiency.

Government

As laid out in the Constitution of 1917, Mexico is a democratic federal republic. Like its neighbor to the north, it is a federation of individually governed states, plus one *distrito federal* (federal district), known as Mexico D.F., overseen by a national government.

FEDERAL GOVERNMENT

Mexico is overseen by the federal government, which is divided into three branches: executive, legislative, and judicial. Head of government and chief of state, the president is elected to a single six-year term, with no option for reelection. The legislative branch is divided into two houses, the Senate and Chamber of Deputies, with 128 and 500 members respectively. Each state has two elected representatives in the Senate, plus a third representative, appointed by the leading minority party. There are an additional 32 senators, divided between major parties in proportion to their percentage of the vote. The Chamber of Deputies has one representative for every 200,000 citizens. Of these, 300 deputies are directly elected from member districts, while the remaining 200 are appointed by proportional representation. There is a single supreme court, with justices appointed by the president. The federal government operates in the *distrito federal* (federal district) in Mexico City, or Mexico D.F.

STATE AND LOCAL DIVISIONS

Mexico is divided into 31 states, plus one federal district in Mexico City. State government is elected periodically and located in the state's capital city. Like the federal government, state power is divided between the executive, legislative, and judicial branches, with an elected governor overseeing executive activities. States write their own laws, though technically none can contradict the country's federal constitution.

States are further divided into discreet units called *municipios* (municipalities). Municipalities generally encompass several cities and towns, and they are overseen by autonomous local governments known as *ayuntamientos,* usually located in the municipality's largest community. In more sparsely populated regions, municipalities can cover a large geographical region.

Mexico D.F., the country's federal district, operates its own local government. It is surrounded by the state of Mexico on three sides and the state of Morelos to the south, but it is not a part of any state. The *distrito federal* is divided into 16 *delegaciones* (boroughs).

ELECTIONS

As laid out in the constitution, Mexican elections are secret, free, and universal. They are overseen by the Instituto Federal Electoral (Federal Electoral Institute). IFE credentials, or voting cards, are the official form of identification across the country. State and regional elections may or may not be held concurrently with federal elections.

After years of PRI dominance, elections continue to be a hot issue in Mexico. Elections are often fraught with controversy, and the public's suspicion of the government quickly fuels fires when suspected fraud has taken place. At the same time, apathy and electoral absenteeism is a major problem.

POLITICAL PARTIES
PRI

Although the PRI no longer maintains unilateral power in Mexican politics, it remains one of the most important political parties in the country. After its losses in 2000, it regained majority of the legislature in 2003. The PRI also continues to dominate regional politics; 19 of the 32 state governorships are held by the PRI.

The PRI was traditionally considered a leftist party, espousing many of the socialist viewpoints common to Latin American governments. Over time, it has become more centrist, especially in its new role as an opposition party.

PAN

The PAN is a traditionally conservative party, established in the 1930s to protect the rights of the Catholic Church. Economically, the PAN generally supports a market economy and free trade, and socially, they also toe a traditionally conservative line, opposing both same-sex marriage and abortion. It grew strong with conservative voters in Northern Mexico, and PAN candidates won the national presidency in 2000 and 2006.

© ARTURO MEADE

political propaganda for the right-wing PAN and left-wing PRD parties, pasted to a wall in Mexico City

PRD

The PRD (Partido de la Revolución Democrática, or the Party of the Democratic Revolution) is the most leftist of the three major political parties in Mexico, and it is associated with the international organization Socialist International. The PRD grew out of the leftist opposition with the PRI, originally led by Cuauhtémoc Cárdenas. The party maintains an important presence throughout the country for its leadership in Mexico City's government during the 1990s and 2000s, where PRD mayors have instituted strong urban planning programs as well as progressive social programs. It was on the PRD's watch that abortion and gay marriage were legalized in the capital.

Other Parties

Aside from the three major parties, there are a number of smaller political parties in Mexico, including the Labor Party and the Green Party, which also have representation in the congress. In many cases, these smaller political organizations will work together with one of the three major parties to back a candidate. In 2005, the Labor Party officially backed PRD presidential candidates Andrés Manuel López Obrador. The Green Party joined the PAN in supporting Vincente Fox Quesada in 2000.

FOREIGN POLICY

Mexico's government traditionally focuses on domestic rather than international issues, though several strategic principles define its foreign policy. According to its constitution, Mexico supports policies of sovereignty and self-determination of all states, nonintervention, and the peaceful resolution of conflicts. In line with its policy of self-determination, Mexico was the first Latin American country to open diplomatic relations with communist Cuba in the 1960s.

Mexico has more free trade agreements than any other country in the world, which has helped to stimulate strong diplomatic relationships across the globe. Since NAFTA began negotiations in the early 1990s, former president Carlos Salinas made great efforts to convince Washington of his country's allegiance to capitalism and growth. After signing the tri-lateral agreement, the United States, Canada, and Mexico entered into a special trade relationship that increased Mexico's ties to Canada and deepened its relationship with the United States. Also of note, Mexico was the first country to reach a trade agreement with the European Union in 2000.

The United States has considerable influence over Mexico, though Mexican foreign policy has traditionally sought to maintain its independence from its neighbor. Mexico's support for the Cuban government in the midst of the Cold War is one important example of how the country has sought to distinguish itself. In addition to economic policy, Mexico and the United States share myriad issues, including border security, immigration, and the drug trade. As Mexico's relationship with the United States has improved, its relationships with Cuba and Venezuela have deteriorated.

Mexico is a founding member of the United Nations and the 10th-largest contributor to the U.N. budget. However, Mexico's foreign policy principles do not permit Mexico's involvement in U.N. peacekeeping missions. Mexico has a standing military, but military spending accounts for just 0.5 percent of all government expenditures. All Mexican citizens must complete 12 months of compulsory service in the military, though many have the obligation waived.

Economy

Mexico has a free-market economy, ranked within the 15 largest economies worldwide. Rich in natural resources, Mexico's biggest industries include energy, agriculture, ranching, fishing, and forestry, in addition to manufacturing. The country's economy has grown steadily since the beginning of the 20th century, and the economic outlook is positive, despite numerous lingering challenges. The country has little foreign debt, strong dollar reserves, and plans to continue reducing poverty. Free trade agreements have bolstered exports, and the country has been included in the G20 group of major advanced and emerging economies.

MAJOR INDUSTRY

Mexico built its first oil well in 1896, and today, it is the world's sixth-largest oil producer. All natural resources, including oil, are state property, and Petróleos

© CARLOS MEADE

Banks, hotels, corporations, and government buildings line the Paseo de la Reforma, a major avenue in Mexico City.

Mexicanos, or PEMEX, is the state-run company in charge of extracting, refining, and distributing oil. Although it has faltered over the years, PEMEX is the single largest source of income for the country. Mexico meets almost 90 percent of its own energy needs internally.

Manufacturing is also huge contributor to Mexico's economy. As of 2011, manufacturing accounted for up to 90 percent of the country's exports and 20 percent of the GDP. Although a large percentage of Mexico's population is involved in agricultural activities, farming has slowly become less important to the nation's overall economy.

TOURISM

Mexico is one of the world's most popular destinations, and tourism is vital to its economy. Although its contribution to the overall GDP falls well below oil or manufacturing, tourism is regionally important and can be the basis of a local economy in tourist-heavy regions like Cancún, Acapulco, Puerto Vallarta, or other well-known destinations. The Mexican government invests heavily in tourism, including massive international marketing campaigns designed to attract potential visitors to the country.

NAFTA AND INTERNATIONAL TRADE

Mexico has one of the most open trade policies in the world. In 1994, it became party to NAFTA, which created a new tri-lateral free trade zone between Canada, the United States, and Mexico. In the decades following NAFTA's acceptance, trade between Mexico and the United States tripled, accounting for a quarter of Mexico's total GDP. Trade ties between Mexico and Canada have also strengthened.

The passage of NAFTA also resulted in the passage of hundreds of American factories to new locations south of the border. *Maquiladoras,* Mexico's large manufacturing plants, were initially welcomed as a way to increase the manufacturing industry in Mexico. Many Mexicans headed to border cities like Juárez to take jobs in the factories. To date, *maquiladoras* have not realized their initial promise; low wages and poor conditions have made them a source of social instability.

Mexico has signed more than 11 free trade agreements that include more than 41 countries. Although the United States remains Mexico's largest trading partner, new trade agreements should help reduce the country's dependency on the United States.

THE UNITED STATES

Mexico's economy is closely linked to the economy of the United States. The United States is Mexico's biggest trading partner, accounting for 80 percent of all Mexican exports and 50 percent of its imports. In addition, 65 percent of Mexico's direct foreign investment comes from the United States, and U.S. financial institutions own a third of Mexico's bank assets.

In addition to their trade partnership, roughly 8–10 percent of the Mexican population lives and works in the United States. Remittances from Mexicans living in the United States add up to about $21 billion each year, the second-largest source of foreign currency after energy.

ECONOMIC CHALLENGES

Mexico's economy suffered several setbacks during the second half of the 20th century. In 1982, the economy was on the verge of collapse when the government was unable to pay back its debt obligations. After making a slow recovery, the peso was devalued in 1992. During the global financial crisis of 2008, Mexico's GDP dropped 6.5 percent. However, the economy's recession ended in 2009, with good economic growth and increasing foreign investment thereafter.

Today, Mexico faces numerous economic challenges. The country's heavy dependency on the United States remains a serious concern; a collapse of U.S. markets could be catastrophic for Mexico. Mexico has attempted to resolve this problem by establishing new free trade agreements. However, it faces significant competition from China, which has similar products in many of the same markets. The country is also highly dependent on oil revenue, which is also projected to dwindle within the next decade.

Despite macroeconomic stability, widespread poverty continues to plague Mexico as one of the country's greatest problems. In the countryside, lack of education and job opportunities have created a depressed rural economy, as well as encouraged a massive migration to cities. According to the World Bank and other sources, redistributing wealth is one of Mexico's greatest economic challenges.

PEOPLE AND CULTURE

A large and multiethnic country, modern Mexico is culturally rich and vibrant, with deep ties to both traditional Spanish and Mesoamerican cultures. The birth of the nation was difficult, initially rife with social strife and ethnic divisions (some of which persist into the present day); yet, over the centuries, Mexico slowly shaped a distinct identity, typified by its unique cultural traditions, like *charreada* and mariachi bands, and duly expressed in its celebrated cuisine. Through the centuries, family, tradition, and the Catholic Church have played an important role in shaping the daily life of most Mexican people, though a prevalence of leftist politics have always kept the country on a progressive and forward-thinking track.

Though Mexico expresses a cohesive national identity, it is largely defined by regional culture. Daily life can be surprisingly distinct from one end of the country to the other. A photographer from Tijuana likely has little in common with a truck driver in Michoacan, just as a journalist from Mexico City lives a very different life than does an ethnic Maya from the Caribbean Coast. In the

Huasteca, families come together for foot-stomping dance and fiddle music, while ranchers in Sinaloa gather for rodeos. It is hard to sum up a country so large and diverse, yet Mexicans do seem to share a certain warmth, charm, and love for life no matter where they come from.

Ethnicity and Class

Mexico's tumultuous history is reflected in its modern ethnic makeup. Today, the vast majority of Mexicans are mestizo, or mixed race. Genetic studies have confirmed that most people are predominantly a mix of Spanish and indigenous American heritage; however, *mestizo* implies a mixed ethnic background, and it may include other ethnicities. Though to a much smaller extent than in the United States or the Caribbean, some African slaves were brought to New Spain during the colonial era, and they also mixed with the Mexican population.

According to Mexico's 2010 census data, the country's population is about 10–12 percent indigenous. Indigenous people, or *indigenas,* are direct descendants of the pre-Columbian people of Mexico, and many still speak native languages. White Mexicans, who comprise about 10 percent or less of the population, are generally Spanish descendants, though there have also been other waves of European migrants to Mexico over the course of the country's history, including Irish, German, and French, among others. Mexico is also home to smaller populations of Turkish, Lebanese, Chinese, Japanese, and Korean people.

© GABRIELA PEÑA GARAVITO

Mexican society is deeply stratified by class. Since the colonial era, rich landowners took the lion's share of the country's resources and profits, while indigenous and mixed race people were afforded a lower social status and little political power.

The Mexicana Airlines corporate headquarters rises above a stack of traditional, handwoven baskets.

Today, social stratifications are not entirely inalienable, yet social mobility is highly limited. In Mexico, your economic class will determine a great deal about your possibilities in life. Those born into middle- and upper-class families are far more likely to finish their education, pursue professional careers, and maintain a strong influence in their local communities. Lack of opportunities and hard economic realities make it far more difficult for the rural or urban poor to improve their economic situation; many leave school early to continue in the same profession as their parents or migrate to the city in hopes of finding a steady job.

INDIGENOUS LANGUAGE AND CULTURE

An estimated 30 million people were living in Mesoamerica when the Spanish arrived in the 15th century. Immediately following the conquest, the native population was drastically reduced, both through violence and through diseases introduced by European settlers. Though many ethnic groups disappeared entirely, a significant indigenous population has survived to the present day, with the largest communities living in Oaxaca, Chiapas, Yucatán, Quintana Roo, Hidalgo, Puebla, Morelos, and Mexico City. About 6.7 million people in Mexico speak an indigenous language. With more than 1.5 million speakers, Nahuatl is the most widely spoken native tongue in Mexico. It is the language that was spoken by the Mexica and other inhabitants of the Valle de Mexico during the 15th century, collectively known as the Aztecs. Many indigenous communities in remote or rural areas have maintained native customs, craftwork, and dress. In the state of Chiapas, ethnic Maya from the highlands still wear the handmade and colorful costumes of their native pueblos. In the remote Sierra Madre Occidental, the Huichol people have continued to practice native shamanic traditions into the modern era. The ethnic Zapotec from the state of Oaxaca gather to buy and sell at the very same public markets they did before the conquest.

The Spanish language—along with English—has incorporated a large number of words from indigenous Mexican tongues. Among notable examples, the word *chocolate* comes from the Nahuatl word *chocolatl*. *Coyote* is a derivation of the term *coyotl,* also from the Nahuatl. In Mexico, many indigenous plants or animals, like the *guajolote* (wild turkey) and *mapache* (raccoon), are still more commonly referred to by their indigenous name. In addition, Mexico retained many indigenous place-names after the conquest. Oaxaca, Guanajuato, Tlaxcala, and Cancún are a few of the many cities that have Castellan versions of the indigenous place-name—not to mention, the term *México* itself, which took its name from the Mexica people of Tenochtitlan.

While Mexicans are fiercely proud of their pre-Hispanic past, native people have been highly marginalized since the beginning of the colonial era. Disrespected and often enslaved by the Spanish, indigenous communities were largely dispersed in New Spain. Today, predominantly indigenous communities suffer from a lack of basic resources, education, and infrastructure. They are at a further disadvantage from a deeply embedded racism that has been perpetuated since the colonial area. Today, 75 percent of indigenous people live below the poverty line. Not surprisingly, many of Mexico's indigenous populations have a complex and often fraught relationship with their country, feeling a much deeper allegiance to their native culture than to the society at large.

POVERTY

Mexico is a wealthy nation with abundant natural resources and one of the world's largest economies. Yet wealth is poorly distributed throughout the population, and vast extremes in standard of living define the economic climate. Mexico's most successful businessman, Carlos Slim, has been named the world's wealthiest person by *Forbes* magazine, yet 10 percent of Mexicans do not have access to sufficient food or medical care. According to government figures in 2010, more than 40 percent of Mexico's population lives below the poverty line.

Wealth is also unevenly distributed by region. Most of Mexico's money is concentrated in and around the capital, Mexico D.F., and along the U.S. border. Conversely, southern states tend to have far less capital. Chiapas is the poorest and most southerly state of Mexico, where almost 77 percent of the population lives in poverty and the annual per capita income was less than US$4,000 in 2007.

In the past few decades, falling birth rates and more wide-reaching social programs have helped ease the class divide. Through a program called PROGRESA (Programa de Educación, Salud, y Alimenación), the Mexican government has offered cash transfers to poor families to assist with childhood education and health services; the successful model was replicated in Brazil. International and nongovernmental organizations have also been active in helping to bring services and education to marginalized communities. Even so, there are still major challenges to eradicating poverty in Mexico.

EMIGRATION

Currently, somewhere between 8–10 percent of all Mexican citizens live and work in the United States. Mexican emigration to the United States has had a major influence on the country's economy and culture, especially in states where emigration is high. Remittances from Mexicans living overseas account for about $21 billion of annual income, the country's second largest source of foreign currency after oil. With the worldwide financial crisis of 2008, these remittances have begun to drop off. However, they remain an important source of income throughout the country.

In addition to the economic repercussions, emigration has affected Mexico's traditional communities in many ways. For example, in states where emigration is particularly high, many households are run by single mothers, who may also work outside the home.

Family, Sexuality, and Gender Roles

For the past 500 years, the Catholic Church has played a major role in shaping Mexican society, with a traditionally conservative stance on sexuality and family planning. As Mexico enters the 21st century, the church's influence has softened considerably. Social dynamics are rapidly changing, and formerly taboo subjects like divorce and homosexuality are becoming increasingly mundane in the modern world. Despite its large Catholic base and traditionally Latin culture, Mexico is a rather modern country when it comes to family, dating, gender roles, and sex.

Still, Mexico's culture remains traditional in many aspects. Family is still the cornerstone of Mexican society, with strong bonds between blood relations forming the base of social life and the economy. Although there are increasingly open-minded attitudes about women in the workforce, women are far from attaining income equality, and major feminist issues remain unresolved.

THE (EXTENDED) MEXICAN FAMILY

In beginning Spanish-language classes, students will often begin their studies by learning the names for different members of the family: *madre* (mom), *padre* (dad), *tía* (aunt), *primo* (cousin), *sobrino* (nephew), *abuela* (grandma), and so on. Learn these lessons well! In Mexico, family is fundamentally important, and you may be using the word *suegra* (mother-in-law) with more frequency than you'd expect.

Though society is generally arranged around the nuclear family, depending on economic and social factors, Mexican households may be large and multigenerational. It is not uncommon for grandparents to live alongside their children and grandchildren, just as children often live with their parents through adulthood. Married couples may even spend a few years with their parents

© ARTURO MEADE

A family leaves church after their daughter's first communion, an important milestone for children in many Mexican communities.

before establishing an independent household. Children maintain relationships with both the mother's and father's side of the family, and extended family members like aunts, uncles, cousins, and grandparents often play a very large role in home life. In addition to the extended family, the figures of *comadre* (godmother) and *compadre* (godfather) may also play an important role in the life of a child, as do the family's close friends. Children will often know and trust their parents' good friends, despite the difference in age.

Until recently, large families were the norm in Mexico, where the influential Catholic Church opposed family planning and discouraged the use of birth control. Since the government began widespread family planning campaigns in the 1970s, the birth rate has dropped dramatically. Today, the average Mexican couple has only two children, and the population grows by a modest 1 percent each year. Still, children remain highly present and beloved members of society.

MARRIAGE

As in most Catholic countries, marriage is considered an important rite of passage in Mexico. Yet, like many social institutions, customs with regards to both marriage and divorce are changing in the modern environment. It is still common to see young couples wed and have children before the age of 25, but today, the average marriage age for men and women in Mexico is 28 and 25, respectively. Today, only 25 percent of women marry before the age of 20. In accordance with Mexico's strict division between church and state, only civil marriage is recognized. Nonetheless, weddings are often celebrated with a Catholic mass.

Once a major taboo, divorce has become more common in Mexico, with around 14 percent of marriages ending in permanent separation. Although it is still a rather modest figure (in the United States, about 40 percent of marriages end in divorce), it is more than four times the divorce rate in the 1970s.

GAY AND LESBIAN COMMUNITY

Mexico is a generally laid-back and accepting society, and most people are unlikely to raise a fuss about someone else's business. At the same time, the Catholic Church has held a hard line against gay and lesbian relationships, making it less acceptable for homosexuals to come out within conservative Catholic households. Today, as in many aspects of society, Mexican attitudes toward homosexuality are becoming more liberal. In the capital, same-sex marriage was legalized in 2008, and same-sex couples may legally adopt children. Despite opposition from the conservative PAN (National Action Party), Mexico's supreme court upheld the new marriage law in September 2010. Popular support for same-sex marriage is split, with about half the country supporting it.

Generally speaking, the gay community is more visible and comfortably accepted in big cities than in small towns. Mexico City, Guadalajara, Tijuana, Puerto Vallarta, and Cancún all have large gay communities, and progressive cities like San Miguel de Allende have liberal outlooks on sexuality. Of particular note, within several of Mexico's native cultures, alternative gender roles are accepted and recognized. In the coastal areas of Oaxaca along the Isthmus of Tehuantepec, a *muxe,* or a man who dresses as a woman, is a traditional gender role in society. In these communities, there is often a greater acceptance of homosexuality as well.

While tolerance is growing throughout the country, discrimination is still an issue. Homophobia is not uncommon, especially in more conservative regions where macho attitudes are more prevalent. Hate crimes occur infrequently, but when they do, they are often unpunished. Since the 1970s, there have been large gay, lesbian, bisexual, and transgender movements in Mexico. Both Mexico City and Guadalajara host annual gay pride parades.

WOMEN

In Mexico, women and men share equality in the law, and since 1953, women in Mexico can vote in political elections. Second-wave feminism arrived in

Mexico in the 1960s, and there are numerous nongovernmental and nonprofit organizations working to improve conditions for women, both socially and politically. In 1994, the EZLN's (Zapatista Army of National Liberation) rebel army included both male and female soldiers and commanders, and listed women's rights within their greater agenda for social justice. At the same time, the feminist movement in Mexico has never received a wide base of support; its aims are unclear to many Mexicans, who mistakenly view feminism as an antimale movement.

During the first half of the 20th century, female children often left school while still young to help their mothers in the household. As a result, there has traditionally been a large gender gap in Mexico's workforce. In today's Mexico, economic realities, social changes, and increased education have changed women's relationship to the workforce. Mexican women work in the paid labor force across all sectors of society, from the small entrepreneur who cleans homes to the high-ranking political leader. Interestingly, many of the *maquiladoras* (factories) along the U.S.-Mexico border predominantly employ women. At the same time, women earn less than men, across the board, and continue to play a larger role in the household. In poor communities, women are still more likely to take on traditional gender roles.

Violence against women is a problem throughout Mexico. Programs to combat domestic violence have led to more reporting of intramarital crimes, but it remains widespread. Of particular note, Mexico has been regularly criticized for its poor handling of the ongoing disappearance and murder of women and girls in Ciudad Juárez, Chihuahua. Investigations into the decade-long crime wave against women have been limited and, at times, entirely wanting in professionalism. In some cases, local law enforcement waited days or weeks before beginning a murder investigation, and, on some occasions, cases were closed before the victim was identified. Local nongovernmental organizations have helped to bring more international media attention to the problems in Ciudad Juárez, but the representatives from these advocacy groups have themselves become targets of threats and violence.

Religion

CATHOLICISM

When Hernán Cortés and his forces vanquished the city of Tenochitlan, the Spanish razed the Mexica temples and built a massive Catholic church atop their remains. Today, that same church is the largest cathedral in the Americas, located just beside the national government buildings in Mexico City's central plaza. Its conspicuous position clearly indicates the enormous importance of the church to both the state and the people of Mexico.

After the fall of Tenochtitlan, the Spanish crown insisted on converting the native people of Mexico to Christianity. Missionaries were extremely active in New Spain, establishing an abundance of churches, Catholic schools, and hospitals, often with the financial assistance of wealthy Spanish nobles. There were massive conversions among the indigenous population to Catholicism, which spiked after the apparition of the Virgin of Guadalupe in Mexico City in 1531. Today, around 85 percent of Mexicans identify as Catholic, and it is the second-largest Catholic country in the world (surpassed only by Brazil). Pope John Paul II visited the country five times during his tenure, and he canonized the first Mexican saint, Juan Diego, in 2002.

Throughout Spanish rule of Mexico, the Catholic Church was one of the country's biggest landowners and a major player in politics. After independence,

© ARTURO MEADE

Revelers gather in San Miguel de Allende's central square to celebrate the town's Saint Day.

liberals wanted to free the country of its relationship with the church, while conservatives sought to establish an officially Catholic country. In the 1850s, liberal president Benito Juárez began to secularize the country's constitution and laws. Among other reforms, he limited church power, prohibited public religious schools, and appropriated church property for the state. After the Revolution of 1910, the Mexican constitution also limited the church's powers. Today, despite the Catholic Church's strong popular appeal, it has very little political power in Mexico.

Inside a church in Guanajuato, the statue of a popular saint has been decorated with colorful satin ribbons.

The Catholic Church continues to hold a very important place in Mexican society, even for those who aren't actively religious. Catholic schools are among the best and most popular options in private education, while Catholic mass is the traditional celebration for life's milestones: baptism, important birthdays, marriage, and death. Throughout the country, social values continue to be tied to Catholic values. In conservative families, premarital sex, homosexuality, and abortion are still taboo. Catholic ritual lends a set of colorful traditions to daily life. Catholic holidays are widely and exuberantly celebrated, with the entire country taking a vacation for Holy Week and the Easter holidays.

OTHER RELIGIONS

Mexicans who don't identify as Catholic are generally Protestants, though the country also has a small and historic Jewish community. One of the fastest growing Christian sects, the Church of Jesus Christ of Latter-day Saints has numerous Mexican branches and does active missionary work throughout the country. In addition, there is a growing interest in Eastern religions, especially Buddhism.

OUR LADY OF GUADALUPE

At any hour, on any day of the year, there is a crash of fireworks exploding over the Basilica de Nuestra Señora de Guadalupe in Northern Mexico City. Push through the crush of crowds at the gates to the shrine, and you'll see hundreds of pilgrims climbing the well-worn stairs, many on their knees, and Catholic groups from across the country carrying banners, flowers, and other sentimental offerings. They have come here to pray to, pay homage to, or snap a photo of Mexico's beloved "mother," the Virgin of Guadalupe.

According to 16th-century history, the Virgin de Guadalupe, dressed in robes of green, white, and red, and rimmed by angels and roses, first appeared to the Aztec nobleman Cuauhtaoctzin on December 9, 1521. Speaking in the native Nahuatl language, she instructed Cuauhtaoctzin – later to be baptized Juan Diego – to build a shrine in her honor. Church authorities initially ignored Juan Diego's entreaties, but the virgin appeared again on December 12, instructing Juan Diego to carry a cloak to the local church. When Juan Diego unfurled the shroud before the bishop, it was filled with roses and miraculously imprinted with the likeness of the virgin herself.

The story spread across Mexico, inspiring thousands of native people to convert to Catholicism. The virgin's dark skin, her Nahuatl tongue, and her appearance on the hill at Tepeyac (a place already sacred to the goddess Tonantzin in the native pantheon) helped this new figure appeal to the people. As instructed, her shrine was built at Tepeyac, and it was rebuilt several times over the following centuries. Today, there is an interesting assortment of old chapels along the hillside, most from the 1700s, while Juan Diego's original cloak hangs behind the altar in the modern basilica, which was designed by renowned Mexican architect Pedro Ramírez Vázquez in the 1970s.

The shroud itself – which can viewed up close from a moving walkway that runs behind the altar – has numerous peculiarities. For instance, a variety of the colors in the image were not available pigments at that time, and their origin is still unknown. On top of that, these colors have not been muted despite their age, as well as the continual flash photography from pilgrims. Skeptics, however, have many reasons to doubt the validity of the virgin's miraculous appearance, among them the existence of a very similar Virgin de Guadalupe from a remote corner of Spain where Hernán Cortés, among other Spanish conquistadors, once lived. Some historians even claim that there is no evidence Juan Diego himself existed.

No matter what the origins of the story, the power of this iconic image is hard to deny. During the War of Independence, father Miguel Hidalgo, a Catholic priest and the head of the Mexican army, used a banner depicting the virgin as the official flag for the Mexican army. Today, her image remains remarkably popular and distinctly Mexican, adorning thousands of T-shirts, key chains, posters, fabrics, and works of art. The Basilica de Nuestra Señora de Guadalupe is the second most-visited Catholic shrine in the world, eclipsed only by the Vatican itself. On her feast day, December 12, more than six million pilgrims arrive at the shrine to pay homage to her image.

Customs and Etiquette

Though you'll notice different attitudes and customs throughout the country, Mexicans are generally charming, courteous, and polite. Even in casual encounters, Mexicans generally address each other with formality and respect. While good manners are universally appreciated, Mexicans understand that foreigners may not understand the country's codes and customs. If you make an effort to be polite, show patience, and smile, you'll generally be appreciated in Mexico.

HOLIDAYS

In addition to the religious and national holidays listed below, every city (and indeed every neighborhood in every city) has their own fiestas and saint's days, often celebrated with much fanfare.

- **January 1: New Year's Day.** As in most countries, Mexicans usually spend New Year's Day recovering from New Year's Eve. It is a national holiday.

- **January 6: Los Santos Reyes (Three Kings Day).** On Three Kings Day, families gather to eat a *rosca de reyes*, a traditional fruitcake with small dolls of baby Jesus baked inside. Whoever finds the doll in their slice of cake is responsible for dressing and blessing the baby Jesus from the family's nativity.

- **January 17: Blessing of the Animals.** Many Mexicans take their beloved pets to church for a special blessing.

- **February 2: Día de la Candelaria (Candlemas).** On February 2, families dress up the baby Jesus from the nativity scene and take him to the church to be blessed. Whoever was charged with this duty on Three Kings Day must also invite the whole family to tamales and *atole*.

- **February 14: Día del Amor y la Amistad (Valentine's Day).** Greeting-card haters beware: You won't escape the sappy sentimentality of Valentine's Day in Mexico.

- **February 24: Dia de la Bandera (Flag Day).** No one gets the day off work, but there are often parades on Flag Day.

- **March 15: Natalicio de Benito Juárez (Benito Juárez's birthday).** The liberal president and champion of the people is celebrated with a national holiday.

- **March-April: Semana Santa (Holy Week).** The year's most important holidays take place during Holy Week, which starts on Palm Sunday and concludes the following week with Easter Sunday. There is massive ritual and celebration throughout the country, and almost everyone takes off school and work.

- **April 30: Día del Niño (Children's Day).** Ever wonder why there is a

TERMS OF ADDRESS

Mexicans are polite and formal when interacting with people they do not know well. When speaking to an elder or to someone with whom you will have a professional relationship, it is customary to use the formal pronoun *usted* instead of the informal *tú*. Most English speakers find themselves a bit daunted by the use of *usted,* uncertain of when it is appropriate and when it is overkill. When in doubt, you can always err on the side of caution by using *usted* with anyone other than children and close friends.

When addressing someone you don't know well, it is common practice to

---

mother's day and a father's day, but no kid's day? In Mexico, kids are commemorated on April 30.

- **May 1: International Workers Day.** Mexico joins numerous international countries in remembering the struggle of laborers on the anniversary of the Haymarket Massacre in Chicago. Mexicans take the day off work.

- **May 5: Cinco de Mayo.** Celebrations for this regional holiday are biggest in Puebla, where local troops achieved an important victory over the French on May 5, 1862.

- **May 10: Mother's Day.** Mother's Day isn't a national holiday, but it might as well be. Mother's Day is widely celebrated in every corner of the country.

- **June 20: Father's Day.** Sadly, dads aren't celebrated with the same fanfare as mothers.

- **September 16: Día de la Indepencia (Independence Day).** Every year, the president repeats Miguel Hidalgo's famous battle cry – Viva Mexico! – from the national palace on the night of September 15. Celebrations continue into the following day, a national holiday.

- **October 12: Día de la Raza (Columbus Day).** This holiday commemorates not just Christopher Columbus's voyage, but the birth of a new race.

- **November 20: Aniversario de la Revolución (Revolution Day).** The Mexican Revolution is remembered on the day war was declared against president Porfirio Díaz.

- **December 12: Nuestra Señora de Guadalupe (Our Lady of Guadalupe).** Millions of pilgrims visit the hill at Tepeyac on the anniversary of the day when Our Lady of Guadalupe appeared to Juan Diego. Although it is not an officially recognized holiday, celebrations abound, kicking off the Christmas season.

- **December 25: Navidad (Christmas).** Christmas is a family-oriented holiday in Mexico.

speak to that person using a polite title, such as *señor* for a man, *señora* for a married or older woman, and *señorita* for a young woman. When speaking with a professional, Mexicans may also use the person's professional title, such as *doctor* or *doctora* (doctor), *arquitecto* (architect), or *ingeniero* (engineer). The title *licenciado* or *licenciada* is often used to address a college graduate, as a term of respect. In addition, the term *maestro,* which means both master and teacher, can be used when addressing a skilled tradesman or a teacher.

GREETINGS

When greeting someone in Mexico, it is customary to make physical contact, rather than simply saying hello. A handshake is the most common form of greeting between strangers, though friends will usually greet each other with a single kiss on the cheek or a quick hug. The same physical gestures are repeated when you say good-bye. When greeting a group of people, it is necessary to greet and shake hands with each person individually, rather than address the group together. Yes, it's time consuming, but you'll need to individually say good-bye to everyone in the group, too.

Even in big cities, Mexicans will often treat each other with respect and courtesy. If you need to squeeze past someone on a bus or reach for a tomato over his shoulder at the market, it is customary to say *con permiso* (with your permission). If you accidentally bump into someone (or do anything else that warrants a mild apology), say *perdón* (sorry). It is common courtesy to make eye contact and greet the salesperson when you enter a store, as well as to greet other diners in a restaurant when you enter. Commonly, Mexicans will say *discuple* (forgive me) before asking a question of a stranger.

TABLE MANNERS AND TIPPING

When you are sharing a meal, it is customary to wish other diners *buen provecho* before you start eating. *Buen provecho* is similar to the well-known French expression *bon appetit,* and it generally means "enjoy your meal." If you need to leave a meal early, you should excuse yourself and again wish the other diners *buen provecho.* As in most countries, it is customary to wait for everyone to be served before starting to eat. Finger foods, like tacos or tortas, can be eaten with your hands, even in restaurants. If a meal is served with tortillas, you can help yourself to the basket in the center of the table. Same goes for salsa.

When dining out with friends or acquaintances, Mexicans very rarely split the bill. Usually, one of the parties will treat the others. If you were the one to invite a friend or business associate to a meal, you should also plan to treat.

In a restaurant, waitstaff receive a tip of 10–15 percent on the bill, though foreigners are generally expected to tip on the higher end of the scale. In bars, a 10 percent tip is standard. A customer may choose to leave a smaller or larger tip based on the quality of the service, but tipping is obligatory.

NEGOTIATIONS AND AGREEMENTS

Mexicans like to please, and, as a result, they are often reluctant to give a negative or unpleasant response. For example, if the mechanic doesn't think he can fix your transmission, he is unlikely to tell you so right away. You may not hear the full truth until the next day, when you come to pick up your car and learn it's time to buy a new transmission. As a result, foreigners occasionally perceive Mexicans as evasive, misleading, or even dishonest. However, the motive isn't deception, but the desire to avoid unpleasantness. Certainly, it can be frustrating to those who'd like to get a straight answer right away, but you'll only complicate matters further by becoming excessively angry when the truth becomes clear.

PUNCTUALITY

Mexico has a well-earned reputation for running on a slower clock. Certainly, there is less urgency in Mexico, and it is not considered excessively rude to arrive tardy to a social engagement. In fact, guests are usually expected to run about a half hour (or more) late for a party at a friend's home. However, when it comes to doctor's appointments, business meetings, bus schedules, or any other official event, punctuality is just as important in Mexico as it is anywhere else.

Food

Eating is one of the great pleasures of life in Mexico, and Mexicans are justifiably proud of their rich culinary traditions. One of the most popular cuisines worldwide, Mexican food boasts a diversity of ingredients, preparations, and flavors that you'll rarely find outside the country itself.

In Mexico, wonderful food is not reserved for the privileged class, and simple, common foods are often the most delicious. Even the simplest and most ubiquitous element in Mexican cuisine—the tortilla—can be a surprisingly complex combination of crisp crust, savory corn flavor, and warm, chewy interior. Taco carts are society's great equalizers, where a street sweeper and a wealthy executive stand cheek by jowl with their plates.

STAPLES OF THE MEXICAN DIET

Corn, beans, chili peppers, and squash have formed the base of the Mexican diet since the pre-Columbian era, together with other native foods, like turkey, avocado, papaya, cacao, and sweet potato. (Today, many popular dishes in Mexico, such as tamales, are based on popular pre-Columbian recipes.) When the Spanish began to settle the New World, they brought their seeds, domesticated animals, and culinary traditions with them. With the introduction of European beef, pork, chicken, dairy, olive oil, wine, almonds, rice, and herbs, Mexican cuisine began to evolve. Fusing indigenous traditions with Spanish heritage, a new and wholly original gastronomy developed.

Traditional Mexican food ranges from a simple warm tortilla wrapped around melted cheese (the ubiquitous quesadilla) to an elaborate *mole* sauce made with dozens of ground ingredients. Typical dishes include enchiladas (tortillas bathed in chili sauce), chiles rellenos (stuffed poblano peppers), and flautas (stuffed and deep fried tortillas), among many others. Mexican food is often heavily condimented with herbs and spices, like cinnamon, clove, cilantro, and epazote. There are hundreds of varieties of chili peppers cultivated in Mexico, which range from mild and smoky to bright and blisteringly hot. Spicy food is popular throughout the country, and almost everything in Mexico is served with salsa, a condiment made of ground chili peppers and spices.

In the southern highlands, both coffee and chocolate are cultivated, and

© JULIE DOHERTY MEADE

Sweet bread and *café con leche* (coffee with warm milk) are popular breakfast options throughout Mexico.

they are widely consumed through-out Mexico as a hot beverage. Distilled from the juice of agave cactus, tequila and mescal are popular Mexican spirits. Mexico also has a nascent wine industry, mostly centered in the north of the country and the Baja peninsula.

MEALTIMES

Most Mexicans begin the day with breakfast, or *desayuno.* Depending on your appetite, breakfast can be as simple as piece of bread and glass of milk, or as filling and hearty as a plate of carne asada (grilled meat) with beans and tortillas. A later breakfast or brunch is called *almuerzo,* which is usually eaten 10 A.M.– noon and is often more substantial than traditional breakfasts.

On Sundays in Mexico, families often visit market stalls to enjoy *menudo,* a beef-stomach soup in a clear or chili-based broth.

The largest meal of the day is the *comida,* which is eaten at about 2 P.M. If you are invited to share a midday *comida,* you should set aside a few hours. A complete *comida* usually consists of three or four courses: soup, a pasta or rice course, a main dish, and, sometimes, dessert. Families traditionally eat the *comida* together. In small towns, businesses often close for several hours to accommodate the *comida,* as well as a short nap. Although the nap is entirely optional (and less common today), this afternoon break is popularly referred to as the siesta.

Dinner is usually lighter than the *comida* and is eaten late in the evening, after 8 P.M. Popular dishes for dinner include *pan de dulce,* tamales, pozole (a hominy soup), or quesadillas.

© ARTURO MEADE

The Arts

Mexico has colorful and varied traditions in the visual arts, music, literature, and film, as well as robust traditions in popular art, textiles, craft, and clothing. Both traditional and contemporary forms are widely enjoyed, with fine-art museums, popular art museums, galleries, concerts, and festivals throughout the country.

POPULAR ART AND CRAFTS

Mexico has celebrated traditions in popular art and handcrafts, or *artesanía*. Most Mexican craftwork relies on centuries-old techniques that unite pre-Hispanic and Spanish aesthetics. Among other disciplines, Mexico is famous for textiles, embroidery, ceramics, blown glass, baskets and weavings, woodworking, toymaking, and tooled leather.

Like most aspects of Mexican culture, traditional handcrafts are highly specific to the region in which they are produced. In Puebla, for example, the Spanish introduced tin glazes and kiln firing to skilled indigenous potters. The resulting blend of traditions created a new-world version of Spain's decorative Talavera ceramics, but with more color and whimsy. In Tonalá, Jalisco, artisans create an entirely different line of burnished and painted pottery, much of which can be used for cooking.

Popular art is sold throughout the country in shops and public markets. Usually, you get the best price when shopping for a regional product, though

© ARTURO MEADE

Woven palm figurines are a craft tradition in the small town of Pátzcuaro, Michoacán.

beautiful handmade items are remarkably inexpensive everywhere. More recently, folk artists have begun to sign their work, and exhibitions of folk art have elevated the status of arts and crafts in Mexico.

MUSIC AND DANCE

Native Mesoamerican, African, and European musical traditions all contributed to the development of unique new-world music and dance. In Mexico, folk musical styles, or *sones,* developed in various regions, with diverse rhythms and instrumentation. The Gulf Coast was heavily influenced by Caribbean sounds, while music from the Huasteca incorporates violin and foot-stomping dance. These *sones* form the base of traditional Mexican music.

Mariachi, Mexico's most well-known musical ensemble, is a derivation of *son jarocho,* the musical genre from the state of Jalisco, characterized by its brassy sound and robust vocal style. Dressed in formal *charro* suits and large sombreros, mariachi bands usually feature an impressive lineup of violins, trumpets, guitars, bass guitars, and *guitarrón* (a fretless six-stringed acoustic bass). Mariachi musicians often wander the streets, seeking a commission, and mariachi music is a fixture at special events, like weddings or birthday parties, throughout Mexico.

During the 19th century, there was a rise in Mexican *corridos,* popular ballads originally based on the Spanish romance style. *Corridos* became a popular way to rally support during the Mexican Revolution. Today, they continue to tell stories, forming the mainstay of popular *norteño* music. A highly popular musical style throughout Mexico, *norteño* features the *bajo sexto* (a 12-string guitar) with the button accordion, an instrument that was introduced by German immigrants to Northern Mexico.

VISUAL ART AND ARCHITECTURE

Though most pre-Columbian cities were abandoned or destroyed by the 16th century, their ruins offer a glimpse into the accomplished architecture, city planning techniques, and artistic achievements of early Mesoamerica. The most distinctive features of Mesoamerican cities are the stepped temple-pyramids, which are generally surrounded by wide public plazas, palaces, and Mesoamerican ball game courts. Early civilizations, like the Olmec, were imaginative and impressive sculptors, carving detailed large-scale stone pieces. Their successors, the Maya, displayed an original and beautiful artistic aesthetic, from detailed frescoes on palace walls to laboriously carved stone urns and decorative pieces. Today, pre-Columbian art and artifacts can be viewed in the country's numerous and fascinating anthropology museums.

EVERY SEASON IS SOCCER SEASON

It is with delight, anticipation, and some undeniable anxiety that Mexicans crowd around their televisions to watch Mexico's national soccer team take the field in the World Cup. A win provokes a cacophony of car horns, celebration in the streets, and half days at the office. A loss is greeted with silence and dejection.

Sure, it's a sport. But soccer is more than just a pastime in Mexico. It is a point of national pride, and a celebratory experience shared by most of the country. During World Cup matches, televisions suddenly appear above stacks of fresh oranges in the local marketplace or behind the register at the corner store — sometimes with crowds gathering around them. If you happen to be flying in Mexico on the day of a match, the aircraft's pilot will likely announce the score from the control deck.

While universally beloved, Mexico's national team's rocky record on the world stage has made them a point of contention among the populace. The Selección Mexicana has made it to the quarter finals twice in World Cup history, in 1970 and 1986. While their overall record has improved in the past two decades, the team's inability to move past the second round is a source of endless speculation and debate. Players are deplored and berated for foolish errors, just as they are exalted and adored for achievement. Mexicans critique the politics behind the team's leadership, and the coaching staff changes so often it feels like the set of a telenovela.

World Cup brings the country to fever pitch, but in the four years between the big event, the Liga Mexicana (Mexican's club soccer league) keeps everyone entertained, if not a bit frustrated as well. Open any Mexican newspaper, and you'll find the sports section updated daily with almost nothing but soccer news. The papers closely follow the progress of Mexican players in prestigious European leagues (the career of youthful forward Javier Hernandez — or El Chicharito, as he is lovingly called — has been followed closely since his top World Cup performance won him a spot with English club Manchester United).

The regular soccer season — which seems to be on an endless repeating cycle — runs twice yearly, culminating in a two-game playoff. Regional alliances are not particularly important with soccer. People from across the country are fans of América from Mexico City and Las Chivas from Guadalajara. Major rivalries draw enormous crowds and raucous fandom. Attending a live game — especially in Mexico City's massive Estadio Azteca — can be a true cultural experience. No matter who is playing, you'll likely find rowdy youth and multigenerational families in equal measure.

As the Spanish began to colonize the Americas, they built new cities in the European style. Catholic missionaries and Jesuit educators were active throughout the country, and wealthy benefactors helped support their efforts by funding massive religious projects. Baroque art and design, which originated in Italy, was the dominant aesthetic during the colonial era. Inside chapels, religious oil paintings and elaborate *retablos* (altarpieces) show enormous creativity and skill on the part of Mexican artists. Among the most famous names of the era, indigenous artist Miguel Cabrera contributed hundreds of religious paintings to chapels in Mexico City, Guanajuato, and other colonial capitals.

The French occupation and the ensuing dictatorship of Porfirio Díaz also left a mark on the country's architecture, especially in the capital. Emperor Maximilian oversaw the construction of the Paseo de la Reforma in Mexico City, a large and central avenue that was designed to resemble a Parisian boulevard. During his decades of presidency, Porfirio Díaz followed in the emperor's footsteps, investing in buildings, monuments, and sculptures that would transform Mexico City into a European-style capital with public monuments and neoclassical buildings.

At the same time President Díaz was constructing marble monuments, a new and more national strain of art was emerging in Mexico. The wildly original printmaker José Guadalupe Posada produced political and social satire in lithography, woodcut, and linocut for local publications, often depicting Mexican aristocrats as *calaveras,* or skeletons. His wry wit and whimsical aesthetic would become synonymous with Mexico, and today, his pieces are often used as illustration during Day of the Dead.

After the Revolution of 1910, art, culture, and intellectual thought flourished in Mexico. Through progressive movements in government, the folk arts began to receive institutional support, while a new, government-sponsored public murals program brought artists Diego Rivera, José Clemente Orozco, and David Alfaro Siquieros to a greater public and international fame. American photographer Edward Weston spent extensive time living and working in Mexico, not long before Manuel Alvarez Bravo began photographing nationalistic scenes in Mexico, rising to international prominence. A fixture in Mexico City's political circles and wife of muralist and political painter Diego Rivera, Frida Kahlo was another expressive oil painter of the post-revolutionary era, who became internationally renowned for a series of powerful self-portraits.

Today, Mexico has a small but growing contemporary-art scene. The National Autonomous University of Mexico in Mexico City opened a large contemporary art museum, and Mexico City's annual art fair, MACO (México Arte Contemporáneo), has become increasingly diverse and prestigious. Mexico's most celebrated international artist, Gabriel Orozco, presented a massive retrospective at the New York Museum of Modern Art, not long after he opened the gallery Kurimanzutto in the capital with a team of partners. The wildly famous British artist Damien Hirst has spent months living on the Mexican coast (and shows new work at the Hilario Galguera gallery in Mexico City), while Belgian ingenue Francis Alÿs lives and works in Mexico City. Collectors have also been important in stimulating Mexico's art scene, particularly Eugenio López Alonso, the owner of the Colección Jumex, a vast and important collection of Latin American and contemporary art.

LITERATURE

Literary historians often cite Hernán Cortés's descriptive chronicles of the conquest as the birth of a distinctly Mexican literature. After the conquest, Mexican-born writers continued to make a distinguished contribution to literature in Spanish. Baroque dramatist Juan Ruiz de Alarcón and writer Carlos de Sigüenza y Góngora were two important literary figures during the colonial era, surpassed in reputation only by the beloved Baroque poet Sor Juana Inez de la Cruz. During the 19th century, Mexican writers contributed to the Spanish Romantic Movement and, later, to modernism.

During the 20th century, Mexico's national character was more strongly reflected in its literary traditions. Writers like Rosario Castellano and Juan Rulfo began to describe a distinctly Mexican environment, exploring the country's identity and consciousness. In the 1990s, Mexican poet and essayist Octavio Paz received the Nobel Prize in literature. His famous meditation on the Mexican people, *The Labyrinth of Solitude,* is his most famous work, though he is also remembered as an able poet.

FILM

Though Mexicans have been making films since the genre was invented, the 1930s and 1940s are known as the golden age of Mexican cinema. During this era, Mexican directors prolifically produced feature films, even surpassing Hollywood in exports during World War II. The glamorous and charismatic film stars of the golden age—Mario Moreno Cantinflas, Tin-Tan, Dolores del Rio, Pedro Infante, and Maria Felix, among others—are some of the country's most beloved personalities. In the 1940s and 1950s, Spanish filmmaker Luis Buñuel made many of his most celebrated films in Mexico, including *Los Olvidados.* Mexican film output began to decline by midcentury, though a few experimental young filmmakers contributed to the canon, including Arturo Ripstein and Alejandro Jodorowsky.

Since the turn of the 21st century, Mexican film and filmmakers have made a prominent resurgence. In 2000, Alejandro González Iñárritu's widely acclaimed *Amores Perros* was heralded as the beginning of a new era in Mexican filmmaking, focused on gritty modern themes. The following year, Alfonso Cuaron's film *Y Tu Mamá También* was nominated for several Golden Globes and Academy Awards. Cuaron and González Iñárritu, like many of Mexico's filmmakers and actors, work extensively in Hollywood; González won Best Director at Cannes for his 2006 release, *Babel*. Another lauded director from Mexico, horror film director Guillermo del Toro won major accolades for his 2008 release, *El Labarinto del Fauno* (*Pan's Labyrinth*).

PLANNING YOUR FACT-FINDING TRIP

Mexico is a wonderful place to travel. Its natural beauty, sunny skies, delicious food, relatively low prices, and warm people have made it one of the world's most popular tourist destinations. As many residents will tell you, daily life in Mexico retains many of the stellar qualities that make the country such a perpetually popular place for vacationers. At the same time, practical considerations become more important when you settle down in Mexico permanently. How do you imagine your life in Mexico, and how will you make friends, get a job, or a rent an apartment when you get there? What factors will help you feel at home, and how will you make a smooth transition? Do you want the excitement of a big city, or are you looking to get away from it all? You may love a remote beach town for a week at the shore, but is it a place where you could see yourself spending years of your life?

Fortunately, you can learn a lot about life in Mexico with a well-planned exploratory mission. Before you make the move, plan a fact-finding trip to Mexico, and use the time to create a larger game plan, get an idea of where

© JULIE DOHERTY MEADE

you'd like to live, and decide, once and for all, if expatriate life is for you. As beautiful and enticing as Mexico can be, some folks find day-to-day life is a difficult adjustment and end up returning home after a few disappointing seasons. Others feel immediately at home in Mexico's looser and less-formal environment, thriving on the idiosyncrasies of daily life and the warm Mexican culture. It's hard to know where you'll fit in until you make the move, but a research trip is a great way to get off the ground.

Preparing for Your Trip

Mexico is a large and diverse country, but it is generally an easy and comfortable place to travel. At the same time, you can make the most of your trip with a little research and preparation before you leave.

LEARN BASIC SPANISH

Your trip to Mexico will be much more successful if you can speak a little Spanish. If you have no background in Spanish, learn the basics of pronunciation, and try to memorize key terms, including greetings, please and thank-yous, numbers, common foods, and directions. Mexicans will appreciate your using *por favor* rather than *please,* and, in less touristy areas, you may find a little Spanish is necessary for basic functions, like buying bus tickets, paying for your hotel, or ordering a plate of fish tacos. There are plenty of ways to get a head start on the language, from books to DVDs to Spanish classes at a local community college.

RESEARCH

These days, few people pack for a vacation without spending some quality time on the Internet perusing pictures, selecting restaurants, and getting a feel for the place they're going. For those considering a move down south, the Internet is an amazing resource. Mexico's expatriates are a chatty bunch, and many of them write blogs, participate in online message boards, or maintain cultural websites about their new home. Not only can you read about other people's experiences, you can ask questions, get ideas about what to do, and contact real estate agents, tour guides, or future amigos. Finally, you can get a head start on looking at prices and real estate, which may help tailor your itinerary. (When it comes to looking for a job, you're likely to use the local newspapers as much as—if not more than—the Internet.)

Good old-fashioned books can also be a great way to learn about Mexico's

© ARTURO MEADE

Many of Mexico's colonial towns have been recognized by the United Nations for their unique aesthetic and beauty.

culture. History books and even novels about Mexico can be a great way to get inspired for your trip. For the places you'll be visiting, a good guidebook to the region can also be invaluable.

HEALTH

There are few health risks related to travel in Mexico. In some cases, visitors will experience mild stomach upset or traveler's diarrhea from the change in food or water. Visitors are always advised to drink purified water, and, until they get used to the food, to eat in restaurants, rather than street-side stands. As difficult as it can be, try to avoid the bonanza of eating, drinking, and general indulgence that accompanies a Mexican vacation. If you do get an upset stomach, the symptoms will usually clear up with a few days of hydration, rest, and an antidiarrhea medication. On some occasions, stomach upset can be serious enough to warrant a doctor's care.

Many of Mexico's most popular destinations, including Mexico City, San Miguel de Allende, Guadalajara, and more, are located on the Altiplano Mexicano, a massive plateau that covers the center of the country. As a result, these cities are located at more than a mile of elevation, though the natural environment belies their altitude (it can be hard to remember that you are in the mountains when all you see are great plains and cactus). Some visitors may suffer mild illness caused by altitude, including headache, stomach upset, and dizziness. Usually, your body will naturally acclimatize after a few days. If symptoms don't improve, seek medical attention.

Vaccines and Immunizations

There are no required vaccines for travel to Mexico. Some people take the hepatitis vaccine series before travel to Mexico; hepatitis can be transmitted through contaminated food sources. You do not need to take antimalarial medication unless you will be traveling in highly remote jungle, where there is still some instance of the disease. If you are considering any vaccinations, talk to your doctor.

WHAT TO BRING

When packing for Mexico, the most important factor is climate. Coastal towns are often hot and sticky, especially in the summer, while the highlands are warm and dry. In most parts of central Mexico, temperatures drop significantly in the evening, so be sure to bring layers, especially if you are visiting in the winter. As everywhere, people in cities tend to dress a bit more formally and conservatively than they do in small towns and coastal resorts. If you are going to a job interview or plan to make professional contacts, err on the formal side with regards to dress.

If there's one thing you can't leave home without, it's comfortable shoes for walking. Most Mexican cities were founded long before the introduction of paved roads, automobiles, and pedestrian sidewalks; no matter where you visit, you're likely to find yourself ambling along cobblestone lanes, strolling along a sandy boardwalk, or climbing two flights of stairs from the metro to the street. Go easy on your feet to avoid a sprained ankle. In addition, since a large part of the country enjoys year-round sunny weather, hats, sunscreen, and sunglasses are travel essentials.

It's easier to bring along your toiletries and travel supplies, but anything you may have forgotten, from toothpaste to sunscreen, is readily available in most Mexican cities. Pharmacies generally carry the same products as you'll find in the United States or Canada, though women should note that tampons can be hard to find in more remote locations.

Money

Mexico is still largely a cash-based economy. In larger resort towns, like Puerto Vallarta and Cabo San Lucas, more merchants are likely to accept credit cards. Anywhere else (including the capital and Guadalajara), you'll always want to have cash on hand. Most people use ATM cards to withdraw pesos via their bank account at home; ATMs (called *cajeros*) are available throughout the country. You will be charged a fee by most ATMs in Mexico (plus your bank's own fees), though they usually offer the best exchange rates. You can also use a credit card with a PIN (personal identification number) for cash advances via ATMs.

Bringing dollars can also be a smart move, especially if you will be traveling anywhere more remote (the coast of Oaxaca or the coast of Nayarit, for example). Many small towns have only one ATM (or none!), and sometimes they run out of cash. A few greenbacks will help tide you over.

Maps

If you plan to do any long-distance driving, it is worth investing in a road atlas for the trip. Guia Roji makes excellent state highway maps, as well as a comprehensive flip-book atlas that covers the entire country. If you will be exploring Mexico City in depth, it may also be worth investing in Guia Roji's comprehensive map of the capital. Though its dizzying size and detail make the map difficult to use for basic navigation, it can be a big help if you're lost or disoriented.

Those visiting Guadalajara should also consider buying Guia Roji's city map, as tourist maps rarely include details on the city's outlying neighborhoods. For any other destination, the maps provided by the tourist office or in travel guidebooks are usually a sufficient jumping-off point.

Electronics

Mexico uses the same electrical system as the United States, Canada, and most of the Americas: 110 volts. Unless you are coming from the eastern hemisphere, you do not need to bring a power adapter for your cell phone, computer, or other electronics. Outlets are usually made for standard two-prong plugs. To use computers or other electronics with a three-prong plug, you may need to purchase a simple three-to-two-prong converter. These are generally available in any hardware store in Mexico.

Medications

Almost all over-the-counter drugs are available in Mexico. Many travelers bring pain reliever, antidiarrhea medication, antacids, or antihistamines with them, but these drugs can be purchased at a pharmacy if you leave them at home. Unfortunately for scuba divers, Sudafed and any other pseudoephedrine-based decongestants are illegal in Mexico. Leave them at home.

If you take any prescription medication, bring along enough for your trip. Most medications are available in Mexico—and often can be purchased without a doctor's prescription. However, some medications, like birth control pills, may not be available in the same brand or dosage. Once you move, you can bring your prescription medication to a doctor or pharmacy in Mexico to determine the appropriate equivalent.

Take note that Mexico has very strict laws with regards to drugs and narcotics. If you are traveling with meds, only bring enough for your personal use. If you take any form of narcotic for pain, bring a note from your doctor; these substances are highly controlled in Mexico.

Phone

Travelers are increasingly likely to bring their cell phone on vacation, and most foreign cell phones function well on Mexico's Telcel network. At the same time, roaming charges or high cost-per-minute rates can really add up. If you want to bring your cell phone along, check with your carrier to determine the cost per minute for both local and international calls. If you have a smartphone, don't forget to check the cost of data usage.

Even if you don't bring your own phone with you, you may benefit from having a telephone while you're on the road, especially for researching rentals and real estate. Fortunately, buying and activating a cell phone in Mexico is inexpensive and easy. Any of the major cell phone companies will sell you a phone with a local telephone number; usually, you don't need to spend more than US$50 for a basic model (and there are often more inexpensive options, if you don't mind a simple piece of hardware). Thereafter, you buy credit for your cell phone, which is used up as you make calls and send text messages. You can buy additional credit at most convenience stores or pharmacies.

To make calls overseas from Mexico, many people use VoIP (voice over IP) or Internet-based technologies, though hotels usually offer international service at a flat rate per minute. While traveling, Internet cafés will often offer telephone service via VoIP technology. You can also call overseas from a Telmex pay phone; it will cost you about a dollar per minute.

Paperwork

You need a valid passport to enter Mexico, and that document can serve as your identification throughout the trip. Generally, it is a good idea to pack a photocopy of your passport, in case it is lost or stolen, and to leave another copy at home. Alternatively, you can often use a foreign driver's license as ID (as long as it has a photo) in most places, and you should definitely bring it along if you plan to do any driving (foreign driver's licenses are valid in Mexico).

WHEN TO GO

Almost any time of year is a good time to visit the cities of north and central Mexico. Almost year-round, the climate is warm and sunny during the day, cooling off considerably in the evenings. At the same time, altitude on the central plateau keeps the weather from getting too hot, even in the summer.

The rainy season runs from June to October. During that period, there are dramatic rainstorms in the afternoons and evenings, though these rarely last more than a few hours.

If you are visiting the coasts, you will enjoy a cooler and more comfortable climate during the winter. The best weather generally occurs during the tourist high season, from November through April annually. Along the Pacific Coast or on the low-lying Yucatán Peninsula, summer weather can be brutally balmy and hot (generally, July and August are the warmest months, though the summer season runs from June through September). In fact, many residents spend those months "north of the border" visiting friends and family. On the flip side, the low summer season is the best time to get deals on accommodations, especially at the beach. If you are pinching pesos, consider a summer trip.

Arriving in Mexico

ENTRY REQUIREMENTS

To enter Mexico, foreigners must present a valid passport. For citizens of most countries, a 180-day travel permit is granted automatically at entry. These travel permits, officially known as the Forma Migratoria Multiple (FMM), are issued to all travelers at the point of entry and ratified by immigration officials. Hold on to your stamped FMM; you will need to turn it in at the airport or to an immigration official when you leave the country. If you are driving to Mexico, you will need to stop at an immigration office (most are located close to the border crossing) and purchase a temporary import permit for your car. You must have the car's registration (in your name), a driver's license, and proof of citizenship (passport). You must pay a fee (about US$45) and a deposit. The car's permit will thereafter be linked to your FMM.

A note for families: When entering of leaving Mexico, children must be accompanied by both their parents, or they must present a notarized letter from the absent parent or parents, authorizing the trip. These laws are designed to prevent kidnap and human trafficking, and they are taken very seriously.

TRANSPORTATION

There are plenty of ways to get around in Mexico; the key is to plan a trip that fits your itinerary and budget. If you are traveling long distances or will be visiting a number of destinations, a mix of air and bus travel will probably be your best bet. Since most cities offer ample public transportation (as well as ample taxi service), those visiting just one or two destinations will rarely need to arrange for more than a flight down and back again. Alternatively, you can rent a car and travel the country by highway. Though not a necessity, having a car can be a great way to explore residential neighborhoods.

Air

For those covering a lot of ground, there are airports throughout the country (any sizable city has one). Even if you head farther off the beaten track, very few destinations in Mexico are more than a few hours' drive from an airport— though you may pay more to fly into a regional airport rather than a larger, international airport. Usually, you can book a shuttle, take a taxi, or rent a car at the airport to get to your final destination.

Bus

On the ground, the most popular and inexpensive way to travel between cities is by bus. There are comfortable first-class buses connecting most Mexican cities, including rural communities. First-class buses are a generally safe, comfortable, air-conditioned, and well priced, though it is generally best for those who will be traveling to cities on the mainland. If you are going to be traveling between central Mexico and Baja California or the Yucatán Peninsula, consider flying—or prepare for a long trip!

Car

For those considering more remote and off-the-beaten path locations where bus service is less reliable, taking your own car or renting a car is often the best option. Driving on Mexican highways is generally comfortable and safe; do invest in road maps.

Public Transit and Taxis

For intercity travel, most Mexican cities have a good public transportation system, as well as inexpensive and abundant taxis. In addition, since many cities are oriented around a central square, walking is often the best way to get to know a town, especially smaller towns or popular vacation resorts.

If you are visiting a larger city, you can take a taxi to various neighborhoods or rent a car and do the driving yourself. In Mexico City, use only registered taxi service, if you use a taxi.

Sample Itineraries

Good planning is the backbone of an easy move, so heading down south for a fact-finding mission can help you make a smooth transition. How you spend your time will depend on where you are in the planning process. You may still be toying with the idea of moving down south, and therefore want to cast a wide net. For those on the hunt for the perfect destination, the monthlong itinerary can serve as a jumping-off point for your exploratory mission. On the other hand, you may already know Mexico well and have decided where you want to relocate. If you are in the latter group, you can use the city-based or regional itineraries presented here to create a travel schedule that will prepare you to make the move.

Mexico's laid-back atmosphere doesn't lend itself to excessive planning. Even though you want to gather as much info as you can, let your intuition guide you as much as your itinerary. Take the opportunity to chat with locals, walk down a side street just to see where it leads, or follow your nose into a local restaurant. Don't hesitate to call a For Rent sign in a promising apartment window or answer an intriguing job ad, even if you won't be moving right away. Reach out to people whenever possible. Often, you'll find fellow foreigners are more outgoing in Mexico than they might be at home, and you may even make a few friends.

ONE WEEK IN A CITY

If you have already settled on a destination, one week will provide just enough time for a useful reconnaissance mission to Mexico. With seven well-planned days, you can explore residential neighborhoods, get a feel for local culture, talk to real estate agents, and possibly make some new friends among your fellow expatriates. You might need a few more days to adequately explore a larger city like Guadalajara, especially if you plan to go to Lake Chapala as well, but this itinerary, using San Miguel de Allende as an example, could be adapted to fit any small- to medium-size city in Mexico.

Day 1

Fly into the León-Bajío International Airport (BJX) and take a shuttle to San Miguel de Allende. After a long day of travel, enjoy your first night with an evening in the *centro histórico*. Sip something cold on a rooftop bar, then have a bite at one of the many jovial restaurants in town.

In most of Mexico, the Internet has yet to eclipse local papers as the best source of information. During your upcoming wanderings around town, look for a copy of San Miguel's weekly bilingual newspaper, *Atención San Miguel* (it comes out on Friday), and *El Trueque,* a local paper dedicated to real estate, car sales, jobs, and other classified advertisements. Both papers will be invaluable in your search for a home, especially if you plan to rent. Check fliers on bulletin boards and shop windows.

Day 2

Over breakfast, open a city map and plot an exploratory walking tour of the central neighborhoods. You might want to wander the main streets of the *centro* before heading south to the enchanting neighborhood surrounding Parque Juárez. Meander down to the Instituto Allende (an art school and shopping center), then cross into the San Antonio neighborhood. If your legs aren't protesting, do a lap around Guadiana, a popular enclave with the town's expatriates. Bargain hunters may also want to explore Cinco de Mayo, a popular neighborhood a bit farther south off the Salida a Celaya.

If you are moving to San Miguel with children, start planning visits to local schools. There are several bilingual private schools that are popular with expatriates (some are listed in *Resources*), and you can plan and budget better if you already have an idea of admission, tuition, the school calendar, and transportation options. Likewise, you might spend the afternoon visiting and collecting information on San Miguel's excellent language schools.

Day 3

Start the morning with breakfast at the Biblioteca de San Miguel, a wonderful lending library, nonprofit organization, café, and cultural center, as well as an expatriate nexus. Next, browse the Mercado Ignacio Ramirez (located on Colegio just north of Mesones), a traditional covered market and a great place to buy local fruits and vegetables. From there, you can take a taxi up to the Balcones neighborhood, an upscale and relatively new development with

© GABRIELA PEÑA GARAVITO

the sandstone contours of the *parroquía* (parish) in San Miguel de Allende

great views of the town below. Alternatively, walk down to Guadalupe and Aurora, two Mexican neighborhoods that have become more popular with expatriates. Take a turn through the Fabrica La Aurora, an art and design center housed in a converted textile factory—a great place to buy art, unique furnishings, and design accents for the home.

You'll note that many real estate agents post available properties and prices in their office windows or in binders on their coffee tables. If you see some listings, note what neighborhoods tend to fall within your price range and plan to visit them. It's also not uncommon to see For Rent (or For Sale) signs in the windows of residential houses; if you see something that interests you, call to get more information and possibly schedule a viewing (in San Miguel, most properties are represented by an English-speaking agent).

Days 4 and 5

Rent a car for days four and five, which will give you an opportunity to explore more outlying neighborhoods around town. If you don't want to get behind the wheel, you can hire a taxi or a driver; many tour guides and shuttle services will charge a daily rate for transportation. You might want to begin by taking a spin around the leafy Atascadero neighborhood east of the *centro,* then head south to explore the cobbled streets of Los Frailes, a beautiful suburban community just outside the city. For good prices on rentals and real estate, take a turn around the Independencia, a more outlying but increasingly popular neighborhood northwest of downtown.

You may also want to spend a day farther afield, especially if you are thinking about buying land. The small communities of Atotonilco and La Cieneguita are both popular places to buy (to a smaller extent, you may also find rentals in these neighborhoods). If your schedule allows, consider spending a few hours at one of the many natural hot springs near Atotonilco.

Don't miss the opportunity to get a taste of the expatriate lifestyle in San Miguel, whether its through a salsa class at the Arthur Murray dance studio, a performance at the Teatro Angela Peralta, or a yoga class in English. Look for fliers around town, or check out the numerous event listings in *Atención San Miguel*'s weekly insert, *Que Pasa.* Pick at least one event and go!

Day 6

By now, you've gotten a good introduction to the city and its layout, as well as a sense of its major neighborhoods. You've gotten your hands on the local papers, you've toured a traditional market, and you've been out at night with the expatriate crew. Hopefully you've located a few nice restaurants, seen some places where you'd do your grocery shopping, and noted some classes or activities you might pursue as a resident.

Today, drop in or make appointments with several real estate brokers to start discussing your options, either to rent or buy. Real estate agents may also be able to help you with other relocation particulars, like finding an immigration expert to assist you with paperwork or locating movers that will do an overseas transport. You can also research these particulars on your own; check the papers for advertisements. Ask for a *sección amarilla* (yellow pages) at your hotel (sometimes restaurants will also have them on hand) and look up *mudanzas* (movers), *colegios* (schools), and other essentials.

Day 7

If you aren't rushing to make your flight, use your last morning to resolve any unanswered questions you have before making the move. Do you have an idea of where you want to live, and how much it will cost to rent or buy? Do you know where you will shop, and if you need a car? Did you get enough information on prices for food and entertainment? Use the trip home to make note of everything you learned on your travels.

TEN DAYS ON THE COAST

Ten days will give you enough time to explore a larger region in Mexico. The following itinerary uses the Pacific Coast as an example, and the pace is a bit leisurely; after all, who wants to rush their way through a beach trip, even with an international move to plan? If you are considering Southern Baja, the Yucatán Peninsula, the state of Oaxaca, or any other region of comparable size and scope, a similar itinerary could be adapted to fit your destination.

Days 1–3

Once you've gotten off the plane and settled in your digs, spend the first few days getting to know downtown Puerto Vallarta. During the day, wander through Old Town and check out Playa de Muertos, Vallarta's most popular beach. Walk the *malecón* (promenade) to the Zona Hotelera (Hotel Zone). Try some of the restaurants and cafés popular with the expatriate crowd, poke into shops to review the price of food and furniture, and, of course, enjoy a bit of beach time. You may also want to take a taxi out to the residential neighborhoods east of Puerto Vallarta's central district, where you can find good deals on properties.

Puerto Vallarta has more information online than you'll find for some other destinations. Even so, you'll find a lot more printed material on the ground.

Pick up a copy of *Mano a Mano,* a classifieds newspaper that is good for rentals, as well as printed newspapers and brochures (even publicity aimed at tourists can provide some good information). If you find something that interests you in town—whether it's an art walk or a cocktail hour—drop by.

If you are considering buying into a condominium complex or gated community, you'll have a lot of options in Puerto Vallarta. After you've gotten the lay of the land, get in touch with real estate agents who can help you visit and decide between properties. If you plan to buy or rent privately, spend your time exploring other residential neighborhoods in the city before you meet with a broker.

Days 4 and 5

Once you've gotten a feel for the city, rent a car to explore the greater region (you can also take the bus to any of these locations). Start by driving north up the Nayarit coast, stopping first in modern Nuevo Vallarta. Continue along the coast to Bucerias, a mellow community right on the Bay of Banderas. Have lunch on the beach, then climb back into the car for the drive up the coast to Sayulita, where you can spend the night in a bed-and-breakfast in town. Alternatively, explore The Four Seasons resort at Punta Mita, where there are also high-end vacation properties for sale.

The next day, have a leisurely morning, then take the car farther north to San Francisco and La Peñita. You can return to Sayulita or spend the night

Sayulita's main square at night

© LUCIE ERICKSEN

in La Peñita; either way, make it an early night, because tomorrow you'll be on the road again.

Days 6-8

Now that you've explored the Nayarit coast, head south from Puerto Vallarta to experience the Costa Alegre, one of the least developed and most beautiful coastlines in Mexico. Exploring this region can take time, and you should definitely research the most interesting destinations before you hit the road. As an example, you might spend the first day in El Tuito, heading south to the Chamela Bay the following day. Get up early on the third day to reach La Manzanilla, on the southern stretches of the Costa Alegre. Spend the night there, enjoying a simple meal on the beach, then get up early to head back to Puerto Vallarta in the early morning.

Days 9 and 10

Return to Puerto Vallarta for your last full days. Now that you've seen smaller beach communities, you have a good idea of what the pros and cons are of choosing a bigger city. Now's a good time to check in with real estate and rental agents, if you haven't already. Pick up more newspapers and tourist brochures to take home with you. Scan prices in shops and grocery stores, noting what you find. Before you bid good-bye to the Pacific, have a nice brunch in a popular restaurant and review your findings.

TEN DAYS IN MEXICO CITY

If you are planning to move to Mexico City, you can prepare for the transition by getting to know the city's diverse residential neighborhoods, exploring its markets, and learning to navigate its transit and communications systems. Needless to say, you could spend years exploring this megametropolis, but save the street-by-street adventures for later. With 10 days, you'll have just enough time to get a solid introduction to life in the capital.

The following itinerary assumes that you have spent very little time in Mexico City, and that you would like to get a general idea of its neighborhoods and atmosphere while also getting a head start on practical details. It also assumes you don't want to do too much driving (and, unless you have great maps and a very strong sense of direction, it is probably better to let someone else take the wheel). If you are like most people, living in relatively close proximity to your job is a priority; if you already know where you will be working, you may be able to trim several days off this itinerary by focusing your efforts on places that will be most accessible from your workplace.

Days 1 and 2

There's no better place to start a Mexico City tour than in the heart of it all: the *centro histórico*. Explore the blocks between the *zócalo* and La Alameda, and be sure to wander down the lovely pedestrian street, Regina. From the there, head south toward Reforma, stopping into the Mercado San Juan on Ernesto Pugibet, a good local produce market with some exotic fruits, vegetables, and meat; it is one of the best (and only) options for food shopping in the *centro*.

Hop the metro or call a taxi to take you south toward the Zona Rosa, where you can explore the beautiful residential streets in the neighborhoods just east and west. Cross the Paseo de La Reforma and explore the Cuauhtemoc, a residential neighborhood behind the American Embassy with both accessibly priced apartments and early-20th-century homes. Head back to the *centro* and finish off your day with an evening at Bar La Opera, one of Mexico City's classic cantinas.

Days 3 and 4

One of the best ways to get a beat on the city is to start your day with a stack of local papers—*El Universal* has one of the most extensive classified listings in the city, so it's a good place to look for jobs. You can also find home rentals in the paper; however, for better or for worse, a large number of rentals are simply announced with a For Rent sign in the window. As you pound the pavement, don't be shy about calling promising apartment buildings and asking to see the place. While there, ask what the landlord requires for rentals, as rental agreements can be thorny for foreigners in Mexico City.

Armed with your stack of newsprint, head south to have breakfast in one of the chic cafés in the Condesa neighborhood. Stroll along beautiful Amsterdam Street and through the Condesa's twin parks, Parque México and Parque España. Cross Insurgentes to Alvaro Obregón, one of the main streets in the Roma, a slightly more inexpensive and highly popular neighborhood. Later, have dinner or a drink at Casa Lamm, or one of the other hip spots in these historic neighborhoods.

The following day, head a little farther south to explore the Colonía del Valle, a large residential neighborhood just south of the Roma. Take the MetroBus south and get off near the World Trade Center and Poliforum, then wander the streets, with their many apartment buildings, trees, and cute cafés. At the same latitude but east of Insurgentes, the Napoles is another extensive neighborhood with a good prices and a great old-fashioned Mexico City feel.

© GABRIELA PEÑA GARAVITO

On a particularly clear day, the twin volcanoes of Popocatepetl and Iztaccihuatl are visible above the Mexico City skyline.

Days 5 and 6

There are no metro stops in Coyoacán, which has helped this pretty neighborhood retain a small-town atmosphere. You can take a taxi all the way to the neighborhood's main plaza, or you can take the metro to Viveros and walk into the center of Coyoacán, noting corner shops and restaurants as you go. Do like the locals and have a mocha at Café El Jarocho and take a turn around the lovely central produce market, just behind the main plaza. In the evening, see an art film or old movie at the Cineteca Nacional de Mexico, or drink a beer in Coyoacán's old cantina.

Set aside the next day to explore San Ángel. You can get to San Ángel by taking the MetroBus south on Insurgentes. From there, explore the Plaza San Jacinto and wander the adjoining neighborhoods.

Days 7 and 8

The fresh air emanating from Mexico City's large urban park, Bosques de Chapultepec, is a good incentive to take a turn around Polanco and Anzures, lovely and upscale neighborhoods to the east of the *centro histórico*. You can take a *pesero* (city bus) along Reforma or the metro to the Polanco stop. In the evening, you can dine in one of the excellent restaurants in the area, or have a drink in the bookstore-café El Pendulo.

The next day, hire a driver to show you around Las Lomas, an upscale neighborhood near Chapultepec, or take the opportunity to breathe some fresh(er) air in Tlalpan, a large and pleasant neighborhood in the far south of the city. If you aren't absolutely wedded to living in the city, you might consider spending the day in Cuernavaca, a large neighboring city with an atmosphere similar to the capital.

Days 9 and 10

Use your last two days to get more specific information about the neighborhoods you are considering or to focus your explorations. If you liked certain parts of town, visit them again to gather a bit more information. Write down the name and contact information for real estate agents and rental brokers, note grocery stores and supermarkets, and figure out which bus lines and metro stops are most convenient. You might also want to cast a wider net. If you liked the Napoles and the Colonia del Valle, for example, you might consider spending a few hours exploring other southern neighborhoods like Mixcoac, La Florida, or San Jose Insurgentes.

ONE MONTH

If you are still deciding where to live in Mexico, you've got the perfect excuse for a road trip. Presumably, you'll want to get a feel for as many different destinations as possible, so this itinerary will take you to big cities, small towns, beach resorts, and coastal hideaways. If you are more interested in coastal towns than big cities, you might forgo your time in Mexico City and San Miguel de Allende and instead go to Los Cabos, catching a flight to Guadalajara to continue this itinerary from day 11. Alternatively, you could head straight to Oaxaca from Guadalajara (passing through Mexico City again on the way) and explore the Oaxacan coast, rather than Puerto Vallarta and vicinity.

Days 1-4

No matter where you ultimately decide to live, you will benefit from familiarity with the capital. Spend your first four days getting to know Mexico City, starting with the *centro histórico* and then heading to the most popular neighborhoods for expatriates: Cuahtemoc, Polanco, La Condesa, La Roma, and Coyoacán. Learn to use the extensive metro system, ride the Metrobús, and wander through urban markets. Be sure to pick up copies of the local papers.

Days 6-10

After the buzz of the capital, it's time to unwind in the beautiful expatriate enclave of San Miguel de Allende, just a four-hour bus ride from Mexico's northern bus terminal. If you've never been to San Miguel de Allende, four days will give you enough time for a little bit of everything: eating, going out, and a jaunt to the hot springs. Be sure to pick up the local newspaper, *Atención San Miguel,* and try to attend an event or two. There are gallery openings, music performances, yoga classes, and many other activities that will give you a taste of expatriate life.

Days 11-13

From San Miguel, catch a bus to Guadalajara. You'll arrive in the evening, just in time for *cena* (dinner) and a shot of tequila, Jalisco's favored drink. Though it is a big city, Guadalajara is much more manageable than the capital. Within a few days, you'll get a good sense of this friendly metropolis and its major neighborhoods. Be sure to spend a day in the *centro histórico* and in the residential neighborhoods of Minerva-Chapultepec and Chapalita. Take the double-decker tour bus or hop a cab to Tlaquepaque, one of the city's most charming districts and a great destination for shopping.

Days 14 and 15

From Guadalajara, it's only an hour's bus ride to the lovely little towns surrounding Lake Chapala. Get there early and plan to spend the night in Ajijic. With a couple of days, you can get a feel for the region, meet some other expatriates (the Lake Chapala Society is a great place to start), and meet with a few real estate agents.

Days 16-20

It will take six or more hours to get to Puerto Vallarta from Lake Chapala, but once you're there, you can treat yourself to a shrimp cocktail and a cold beer on the beach. Spend your time in Puerto Vallarta exploring the downtown area. If you are interested in a condominium or gated community, meet with real estate agents right away to take some tours of possible properties. If you are planning to buy a private home or a piece of property, explore the neighborhoods in and around the *centro*.

Days 21-22

Head just a half hour up the coast of the Bay of Banderas to Bucerias. Spend the afternoon sipping juice on the beach and wandering among the pretty, tropical streets of this laid-back town. The next day, head farther north to the beach community of Sayulita, where you can rub elbows with laid-back surfers from the west coast of the United States and check out some inexpensive properties.

Dine on fish tacos, then return to Puerto Vallarta for an early start the next morning.

Days 23-28

Puerto Vallarta to Oaxaca is the longest haul on your trip. You may want to cut down the transit time by flying between the coast and Oaxaca (transferring through Mexico City). If time is no issue, you can take a bus the whole way there (also transferring through the capital), though you may want to break up the trip into two days.

Once you arrive, spend a day getting to know downtown Oaxaca and its wonderful markets, restaurants,

Mexico is connected by a network of efficient and inexpensive first-class buses.

© JULIE DOHERTY MEADE

and architecture. Spend the next day in the northern neighborhoods of La Reforma and San Felipe del Agua, two of the nicest residential neighborhoods in town. Check bulletin boards at language schools for information and groups, seek out volunteer opportunities, and take a spin around the galleries.

Practicalities

ACCOMMODATIONS

There are accommodations to fit every budget in Mexico. Luxury travelers can easily find slick accommodations in all but the most rural destinations, while budget travelers will never lack for a simple hotel room. That said, hotels that offer the best deals will often get booked in advance, especially in small or medium-size cities like Oaxaca or San Miguel de Allende. Likewise, if you will be visiting a beach resort during the winter high season, book your hotel accommodations well in advance. Conversely, if you are visiting the beach in the low season, ask if the hotel offers discounts.

Mexico City and Vicinity

One of the most popular budget hotels in Mexico City is the **Hotel Isabel** (Isabel la Católica 63, tel. 55/5518-1213, www.hotel-isabel.com.mx,

US$42 d), located in an old colonial-style building in the *centro histórico*. Rooms are basic but clean, spacious, and comfortable, with creaky old furnishings, TVs, and telephones. Young travelers and backpackers favor this spot, though it isn't a party hotel; you'll get a good night's rest in this historic abode. Another inexpensive option in the *centro histórico*, **Hotel Catedral** (Donceles 95, tel. 55/5518-5232, www.hotelcatedral.com, US$45 d)—not to be confused with the similarly named Hostal Catedral—is a modern hotel with clean, quiet, carpeted rooms, each with private bath and television. Though not the most stylish accommodations, Hotel Catedral is very comfortable and convenient; it is located just behind the cathedral and around the corner from the *zócalo*.

A hip boutique hotel, **Condesa DF** (Avenida Veracruz 102, Colonia Condesa, tel. 55/5241-2600 or tel. 55/5241-2640, www.condesadf.com, US$200–300 d) is located in a redecorated colonial home overlooking the beautiful Parque España in the Condesa neighborhood. Interior decor is a stylish mix of aquamarine walls, dark wood furnishings, and glowing globe lamps; the downstairs restaurant is popular with the sushi-eating Condesa set, though beware that some rooms may be troubled by noise from the late-night crowds. Rooms are attractive and comfy, with flat-screen TVs, iPod docks, sitting areas, and rain showers.

There are a number of upscale hotels towering over the edge of Bosques de Chapultepec in Polanco, one of the most classic of which is the **Camino Real Mexico City** (Mariano Escobedo 700, tel. 55/5263-8888, www.caminoreal. com, US$100 d). The massive lobby and grounds are home to numerous restaurants and bars, and it's easy walking distance from the posh downtown district in Polanco. Rooms are spacious and comfortable, decorated with a 1970s color-block flair.

Guadalajara and Lake Chapala

A friendly and convenient place to stay, **Hotel La Rotunda** (Liceo 130, tel. 33/3614-1017 or tel. 33/3658-0224, tel. 800/964-8700, www.hoteleselectos. com, US$60 d) is as centrally located as they come. Set in a large colonial mansion just a block behind the cathedral, the hotel's guest rooms are airy and spacious, with high ceilings and ceiling fans, televisions, and private bathrooms. The desk staff is incredibly helpful, and the whole place is set up with Wi-Fi. In Tlaquepaque, **Quinta Don Jose** (Calle Reforma 139, Tlaquepaque, Jalisco, tel. 33/3635-7522, U.S. toll-free tel. 800/700-2223, www.quintadonjose.com, US$90–110 d) is a small hotel at a good price. Rooms are all different (and some are a bit nicer and more spacious than others), though they all

HOME EXCHANGE

Thanks to the Internet, it has become fairly easy to arrange a home exchange for a short- or long-term trip to Mexico. If you are planning a fact-finding trip down south, there are numerous benefits to arranging a home swap: It provides you with a free place to stay on your trip, someone will be watching your home while you are away, and you will have the opportunity to really *live* in Mexico for a short period of time. From your new home base, you can shop at markets, cook at home, use local transportation, and get a feel for residential neighborhoods. It's a great way to really get your feet on the ground.

If you are considering a home exchange, there are numerous online companies that help connect you with other people looking for a swap. Most of the major online companies charge a monthly membership fee to view listings and meet other swappers, though they do not guarantee or broker the arrangement. You may also be able to arrange a home exchange privately, either through friends or by posting a classified ad in a local newspaper. Craigslist (www.craigslist.

com) also offers a home swap section. No matter what route you take, there are home exchanges available at every level, from luxurious multibedroom homes to low-key one-bedroom apartments in residential neighborhoods.

A successful exchange is based on trust, so you'll need to spend some time getting to know the family on the other line, exchanging photos, and sharing personal references. If you know someone in Mexico, it may be helpful to send a friend to meet your home-swap partner. Clearly, it takes a little more legwork than booking a hotel, but there is plenty of payoff, especially if you plan to spend an extended time in Mexico.

If you are planning to swap your home for a place in Mexico, here are a few other items to keep in mind:

LOCATION

If you plan to swap your home for one in Mexico, pick a place where you'll really get a sense of day-to-day life. Ask about the home's location: suburban, countryside, or inner city? Are there transportation options and markets nearby?

have private bathrooms, air-conditioning (not that you need it in Guadalajara's perfect climate!), and televisions. There are beautiful gardens and sitting areas throughout the property, and it's a short walk from the bustling shops and restaurants in Tlaquepaque.

In Ajijic, try **La Nueva Posada** (Donato Guerra 9, Ajijic, tel. 376/766-1344, fax 376/766-1444, www.hotelnuevaposada.com, US$75–95 d), a well-priced boutique hotel set in a stately, aqua-colored colonial mansion. The pretty, pastel-colored rooms are equipped with cable television and Wi-Fi, and some have lake views. The hotel's proprietors can help you get a beat on the town, and there are weekly and monthly rates for those who plan to spend a little time lakeside.

What type of people live and rent in the area?

TRANSPORTATION

Make sure you'll have access to a car or public transportation while you are in Mexico so you can get to know the area. Many home exchanges will also include a car, and having a set of wheels can be a good way to get to know a city. If you decide to include your car in the exchange, be sure to add third-person liability insurance. Find out how you will be covered in Mexico.

PETS

Most home exchanges do not include pet sitting, though you may be able to find people who are willing to care for your animal (or who also have an animal that needs care). If you do include pet sitting in the exchange, get information on local veterinarians and pet supplies in Mexico, while providing the same information for your swappers. If not, consider the additional cost of boarding a pet.

INSURANCE

Double check that your home insurance covers anything that might happen while you are away, like fire or theft. Also ask your house-swap partner about their insurance situation; if they have home owner's insurance, how high is the premium? What does it cover?

PUT IT IN WRITING

Most home exchange companies help connect interested parties, but they cannot guarantee the swap will be problem free. Make sure you put all the most important agreements in writing (some exchange companies provide boilerplate contracts, which you can tailor to your situation). Include how utilities will be covered; if your home has air-conditioning, for example, you may want to include a clause requiring your swap partner to pay for the utilities.

PREPARING YOUR HOME

Before you leave, clean the house, prepay your utility bills, leave emergency contact numbers for your houseguests, and write out any instructions for plants, pets, or general maintenance. Hold or forward mail service and newspapers.

Puerto Vallarta and the Central Pacific Coast

In Puerto Vallarta, you'll find more inexpensive accommodations south of Rio Cuale and more full-service luxury resorts in the Zona Hotelera. Travel agents, as well as online sites like Expedia and Travelocity, can be great for getting deals on big hotels. If you prefer something simpler, there's an old-fashioned Puerto Vallarta atmosphere at **Casa Andrea** (Calle Francisca Rodriguez 174, tel. 322/222-1213, www.casa-andrea.com). Here, small studio apartments surround a pool and garden, each equipped with a kitchenette, wireless Internet, and air-conditioning. It is a good place to hunker down and call home while exploring the Puerto Vallarta area, and the hotel's proprietors can offer some tips on the Pacific lifestyle. Book in advance if you plan to visit during the high season. One of the more popular accommodations on the Playa de los Muertos is the hotel **Playa Los Arcos** (Olas Altas 380, tel. 322/222-0583 or tel. 322/222-7100, U.S. tel. 800/648-2403, Can. tel. 888/729-9590, fax 322/222-7104, www.playalosarcos.com, US$80–100 d). Rooms have a Mexican atmosphere and are simple, comfortable, and reasonably priced. For a bit more, you can get a room with ocean views and a kitchenette. The grounds include a large swimming pool, which opens right onto the beach, where the hotel manages a small bar and coffee shop, often with live music during the high season. The same company operates Suites Los Arcos, which has a small number of studio apartments for rent a few blocks from the shore. A small bed-and-breakfast in Old Town, the **Hacienda Alemana** (Basilio Badillo 378, Col. Emiliano Zapata, tel. 322/222-2071, www.haciendaalemana.com, US$135 d) isn't on the beach, but it's a friendly, charming, and comfortable place to stay. Rooms are tastefully decorated and equipped with air-conditioning, wireless Internet, small sitting areas, and balconies. Suites have kitchens, dining areas, and patios. The adjoining German restaurant is a popular place, even with nonguests, for Continental food and drinks.

San Miguel de Allende and Vicinity

The brightly colored guesthouses at **Casa Crayola** (Calzada de la Aurora 48, tel. 415/152-8900, U.S. tel. 202/391-0004, www.casacrayolasanmiguel. com, US$75 d) are the ideal home base for an exploratory mission around San Miguel. Surrounding a tree-filled courtyard and fishpond, each of these independent casitas is fully equipped with comfy beds, a sitting area, and a small kitchen. Surprisingly spacious, rooms can easily accommodate a family of four. Just north of the central square, the perennially popular **Casa Calderoni** (Callejón del Pueblito 4, tel. 415/154-6005, www.casacalderoni.com, US$110–140 d) is a warm and well-located bed-and-breakfast. Each room is individually decorated in honor of an artist, and some have private decks and sitting areas. The hotel's friendly proprietors know a lot about life in San Miguel, and breakfasts are delicious and included in the night's cost.

In the quiet and tree-filled Guadiana neighborhood, the **Guadiana Bed and Breakfast** (Mezquite 11, Colonia Guadiana, tel. 415/152-5171, US$48–52 d) is a relaxed and reasonably priced place to stay. Guest rooms aren't particularly fancy, but they are clean, large, and light filled. This low-key neighborhood is one of the quietest in town, and it's a relatively easy walk to Parque Juárez and the *centro histórico*. A San Miguel classic, **Casa Schuck** (Garita 3, tel. 415/142-6618, U.S. tel. 937/684-4092, www.casaschuck.com, US$200–275 d) is a gorgeous boutique hotel housed in a stately colonial mansion. The individually decorated guest rooms are decked out in jewel tones and traditional crafts. Each has a fireplace, and many have pretty French windows opening onto the tree-filled patio and small pool.

Oaxaca

Simple, tastefully decorated, Mexican-style rooms are scattered throughout the lush gardens at **Las Golondrinas** (Tinacos y Palacios 411, tel. 951/514-3298 or tel. 951/514-2126, www.hotellasgolondrinas.com.mx, US$55–60 d). This well-priced hotel is right in the center of Oaxaca, and it manages to offer a clean, clutter-free environment while still making good on all necessary services, like Wi-Fi and laundry. There are no televisions in the rooms (though there is a TV in the lobby), but simple pleasures are far more attractive here anyway. On the west side of the *centro*, **Las Bugambilias** (Reforma 402, tel. 951/516-1165, U.S. tel. 866/829-6778, www.lasbugambilias.com, US$70–115 d) is an incredibly friendly, comfortable, and impeccably decorated bed-and-breakfast, filled with unique art and crafts. Rooms are brightly colored and cool, with beautiful Mexican accessories; some have private decks. Though located on a busy street, the hotel is tranquil, set behind a restaurant and garden. A stylish boutique hotel, **Casa Oaxaca** (García Vigil 407, tel. 951/514-4173 or tel. 951/516-9923, www.casaoaxaca.com.mx, US$185–350 d) is a sophisticated and centrally located place to stay. Decor is elegant and modern but incorporates just a touch of Oaxaca-inspired color to the wood and white color schemes. The in-house restaurant is a top-notch option for creatively executed Oaxcan food and cocktails.

Baja California Sur

Los Cabos caters to high-end tourists, and there many options for luxury accommodations in both Cabo San Lucas and along the corridor to San Jose. If you want to stay in a full-service resort, you can often find specials in conjunction with your airline tickets. Otherwise, there are plenty of good options at smaller hotels, some quite reasonably priced. Downtown, the **Cabo Inn Hotel** (20 de Noviembre s/n, between L. Vicario and N. Mendoza, tel. 624/143-0819, U.S./Can. tel. 619/819-2727, www.caboinnhotel.com, US$55–60 d) is a friendly and inexpensive place to stay with cheerful, Mexican-inspired decor. The place attracts low-key travelers from around the world who are more interested in enjoying the area than lounging around a slick guest room. Though not a luxury accommodation, it has some key amenities like a shared library and kitchen, roof deck, and wireless Internet, and some rooms are pet friendly. Set on a hillside above Cabo, **The Bungalows Hotel** (Dorado and

Lienzo Charro, tel. 624/143-5035, U.S. tel. 888/424-2226, www.cabobun-galows.com, US$95–150 d) is a recommended bed-and-breakfast with cute, beachy rooms equipped with kitchenettes and television. The friendly hotel is a great place to get away from the noise and bustle of downtown Cabo, and there's a pool on the grounds for guests. Rates include breakfast.

Right in the middle of San Jose del Cabo's downtown district, the **Tropi-cana Inn** (Blvd. Mijares 30, Colonia Centro, San Jose del Cabo, tel. 624/142-0907, www.hoteltropicana.com/tropicana_los_cabo, US$80–125 d) has an old-fashioned Baja feeling. The hotel's comfortable and spacious rooms have flagstone floors, air-conditioning, private baths, and little patios, and they are set around a swimming pool with comfy chairs for guests.

The Yucatán Peninsula

A casual, cheap, and centrally located spot in Playa del Carmen, **Posada Freud** (Avenida 5 at Calle 8, Playa del Carmen, tel. 984/873-0601, www.posada-freud.com, US$65–85 d) is popular with a youthful crowd. Each of the basic but comfy rooms has a hammock swinging outside its doorway, and there's air-conditioning if you need it (though you pay extra to use it). It isn't a place for luxury, but a "fun in the sun" mentality. Another reasonably priced option in Playa is **Hotel Posada de las Flores** (Avenida 20 Norte at Calle 4, Playa del Carmen, tel. 984/873-2898, www.hotelcasadelasflores.com, US$80–100 d). Spacious guest rooms at this downtown establishment have a nice, simple, Mexican atmosphere and are equipped with ceiling fans, minifridges, and free Wi-Fi. At these hotels, like all Playa establishments, prices go up during the high season, especially at Christmas.

You can shack up in one of the many beach bungalows along Tulum's laid-back shoreline, some of which start at rock-bottom prices and rustic accom-modation, but **Posada Margherita** (Carretera Tulum-Boca Paila Km. 4.5, Tulum, tel. 984/801-8493, www.posadamargherita.com, US$200 d) man-ages to translate Tulum's casual atmosphere into a comfortable hotel. Rooms feel beachy and casual, with many opening up to the sand or a small private deck. Everything here is ecofriendly, with even the kitchen wind and solar powered.

In Mérida, **Casa Mexilio** (Calle 68, no. 495, Mérida, 999/928-2505, U.S./Can. tel. 888/819-0024, http://casamexilio.com, US$75–85 d) is a recom-mended bed-and-breakfast with artfully decorated rooms joined by walk-ways and patios. The Mexican-style furnishings include antiques, textiles, art, and iron bed frames. They all have windows opening onto the courtyard and gardens.

FOOD
Mexico City and Vicinity

For a comforting plate of enchiladas, stuffed chili peppers, or tortilla soup, there is no nicer atmosphere than **Café Tacuba** (Tacuba 28, tel. 55/5521-2048, 8 A.M.–11 P.M. Mon.–Sun.), an old-fashioned eatery and one of Mexico City's classic restaurants. There are no electrical appliances in the kitchen, so everything is ground, mixed, and seasoned by hand. The atmosphere is traditional Mexico City, with tiled walls and impossibly high ceilings, and there is a pleasant hum of diners from morning to night.

For a drink and a snack in a pleasantly historic atmosphere, **Bar La Ópera** (Cinco de Mayo 10, tel. 55/5512-8959, 1–11 P.M. Mon.–Sat., 1–5:30 Sun.) is one of the *centro histórico*'s oldest cantinas. With mirrors, dark wood furnishings, creaky booths, and high ceilings (rumored to be riddled with bullet holes shot by Pancho Villa and his gang), it is the perfect place to order a fine tequila, accompanied by *sangrita,* a spicy chaser of tomato juice and spices. The menu covers Mexican standards like *arrachera* (skirt steak) or enchiladas, plus appetizers like guacamole.

In the Condesa neighborhood, **Café La Gloria** (Vicente Suárez 41, Col. Condesa, tel. 55/5211-4185, 1 P.M.–midnight Mon.–Sun.) was one of the neighborhood's first cool bistros and remains one of the best places to eat in the area. Here, fresh and well-prepared salads, sandwiches, meats, and pasta dishes are served in a comfortable dining room, always bustling with a hip and youthful crowd.

© JULIE DOHERTY MEADE

For centuries, corn has been the base of the Mexican diet. Here, *chalupas* (thick corn tortillas) are served with red and green salsa, chicken, and onions.

TACOS DE NOPAL, POR FAVOR

Eating is one of the great pleasures of life in Mexico, and, despite what you might have heard, vegetarians won't miss out on the opportunity to enjoy the country's celebrated food. True, a variety of meat is enthusiastically consumed throughout the republic, but the country's diverse cuisine leaves plenty of room for vegetarians to enjoy delicious and unique Mexican cooking. Mexicans generally view vegetarianism positively, and there are a surprising number of vegetarian restaurants throughout the country, in addition to restaurants with a range of nonmeat options. Though you may occasionally be obliged to explain that fish and chicken are not a part of a meat-free diet, most restaurants will accommodate your menu substitutions if you want something prepared *sin carne* (without meat).

For those who eat eggs and dairy products, there are a range of options, and popular dishes can often be prepared with cheese instead of meat (enchiladas, for example, can almost always be made with a cheese filling, rather than meat). Traditional breakfasts are a bastion of great vegetarian eating – though, less so for vegans, unfortunately. Even those who don't eat eggs or cheese will find some interesting eats within Mexico's bountiful produce and creative dishes, from wonderful prickly-pear salads to the ubiquitous fruit and juice stands throughout the country. The following is a basic primer on great vegetarian food in Mexico.

IN THE MARKET

Markets are the best place for fresh produce, as well as a variety of prepared foods, from green beans to handmade tortillas. Here are a few more exotic items to look out for.

- chayote: A green gourd native to Mesoamerica.
- chile poblano: A large, mild, green chili pepper.
- *flor de calabaza:* Squash flower.
- *huitlacoche:* Corn fungus.
- *maracuya:* Passion fruit.
- nopal: Prickly pear cactus.
- tuna: Fruit of the prickly pear.

IN A RESTAURANT

When eating out at a traditional Mexican restaurant, you will generally find several vegetarian options on the menu. Vegans may be able to adjust a meal to fit their diet, ordering something without the traditional cream or cheese.

- *chilaquiles:* Fried strips of tortilla bathed in salsa and sprinkled with onion, cheese, and sour cream. Often accompanied with a fried egg.
- chiles rellenos: Large peppers (usually poblano) stuffed with cheese or another filling, then fried in egg batter and bathed in salsa.

In Coyoacan, **Corazón de Maguey** (Plaza Jardin Centenario 9-A, Col. Villa Coyoacan, tel. 55/5659-3165 or tel. 55/5659-2912, www.losdanzantes.com/web/restaurantes/mayahuel, 1:30 P.M.–midnight Mon.–Thurs., 1:30 P.M.–2 A.M. Fri.–Sat.) is a newer restaurant, best known for its menu of top-shelf mescal (a distilled spirit made from agave and a cousin to tequila), which you can order

- enchiladas: A stuffed or folded tortilla smothered in chili sauce.
- *enfrijoladas:* A stuffed or folded tortilla smothered in bean sauce.
- guacamole: Mashed avocado and chili pepper dip.
- *molletes:* A *bolillo* (white roll) cut in half and spread with beans and cheese, and served with *pico de gallo.*
- *papadzules:* A traditional Yucatec dish of hard-boiled eggs wrapped inside a tortilla and topped with a pumpkin-seed sauce and more crumbled egg.
- *pico de gallo:* A fresh salsa of chopped tomato, onion, and ci-lantro, usually served with corn tortilla chips.
- *rajas:* Strips of roasted chili pep-per (usually chile poblano, a mild green chili), often served with corn or cream.
- *sopes:* Thick hand-rolled corn flatbreads, often topped with beans, cheese, lettuce, cream, and salsa.
- *queso fundido:* Cheese melted in a casserole and served with torti-llas and salsa.

ON THE STREET
Though tacos are the most popular street-side meal, there are plenty of vegetarian options in the country's ubiquitous outdoor stands. Here are some good snacks to try.

- *aguas frescas:* Fresh fruit drinks.
- *elotes:* Steamed or grilled corn on a stick, topped with lime, cheese, mayonnaise, and chili powder.
- *esquites:* Corn kernels served in a cup and topped with lime, cheese, mayonnaise, and chili powder.
- flautas: Stuffed and deep-fried tortillas, often filled with *papa* (potato) or *queso* (cheese).
- quesadilla: A warm tortilla wrapped around melted cheese.
- *tacos de guisado:* Tacos prepared with a variety of different fillings; you'll almost always find a veg-etarian option.
- *tlayuda:* A large and toasted corn tortilla filled with beans, cheese, and salsa, from Oaxaca (vegetar-ians should ask to have theirs pre-pared *sin asiento*, or without lard).

Strict vegetarians and vegans should take note that a lot of food in Mexico will be seasoned with or cooked in animal fat. Lard, called *manteca* or, in some places, *asiento,* is often incorporated into common dishes like refried beans or tamales. In fact, you should assume a tamale contains animal fat unless specifi-cally told otherwise (vegetarian tamales can be made with olive or other vegetable oils and often cost more than regular tamales). In addi-tion, chicken broth (*caldo de pollo*) is frequently used in soups and rice dishes.

by the glass or in a tasting flight. However, the food is just as attractive as the bar. The interesting menu includes Oaxacan-inspired dishes like *chapulines* (seasoned grasshoppers) quesadillas with *huitlacoche* (corn fungus), and *mole negro,* among other interesting dishes. The warm, convivial dining room is often crowded, especially on the weekends.

Located in downtown Guadalajara, Birriería Las Siete Esquinas is an atmospheric and tasty restaurant that serves traditional slow-roasted goat and lamb.

Guadalajara and Lake Chapala

The romantic atmosphere in **Fonda San Miguel Arcangel** (Donato Guerra 25, Centro Histórico, tel. 33/3613-0809, 8:30 A.M.–9 P.M. Sun. and Mon., 8:30 A.M.–midnight Tues.–Sat.), located in a former convent, is the perfect backdrop for the restaurant's homey, traditional Mexican dishes. You can sit aside the bubbling fountain and order a *sopa azteca* or enchiladas, then wash it all down with a *limonada* (limeade) or top-shelf tequila. Food is spicy and well prepared, and the service is formal and attentive.

With several locations around town, the inexpensive food and drinks at **Chai** (Av. Juarez 200, Col. Centro, tel. 33/3613-0001, and Av. Vallarta 1509, Col. Americana, 33/3615-9426, www.chai.com.mx, 8 A.M.–midnight daily) have garnered a loyal following with locals. Breakfasts here are particularly tasty, many incorporating traditional ingredients like nopal (prickly pear cactus) or chipotle into omelets or egg dishes. There are also salads, sandwiches, and pastas, in addition to a wide range of coffee drinks, tea, beer, wine, smoothies, and, of course, chai.

Slow-roasted goat, or *birria,* is a specialty of the Guadalajara region, and you can try a delicious version of this classic dish at the charming **Birriería Las Siete Esquinas** (Colón 384, tel. 33/3613-6260, www.las9esquinas.com, 9 A.M.–10 P.M. Mon.–Sat., 9 A.M.–7:30 P.M. Sun.). This wonderful restaurant serves flavorful *birria* in a savory, lime-tinged *caldo* (broth), *barbacoa* (slow-roasted lamb), and soups, all brought fresh to the table with a basket of hand-made tortillas and spicy homemade salsas.

When lakeside, join the locals at **Ajijic Tango** (Morelos 5, tel. 376/766-2458, 12:30–10 P.M. Mon. and Wed.–Sat., 12:30–6:30 P.M. Sun.), an Argentinean restaurant in a pretty courtyard setting, serving steaks, chicken, salads, and pasta. It's a good place to get a beat on the local expatriate crowd.

Puerto Vallarta and the Central Pacific Coast

Puerto Vallarta is a dining destination, and there are dozens of great places to eat, from humble street-side taco stands to fine-dining restaurants. Fresh fish is definitely a highlight of the local cuisine, brought fresh from the neighboring seas, though you'll find a wide range of options here. A popular Mexican restaurant, **Cafe de Olla** (Basilio Badillo 168, Col. E. Zapata, tel. 322/223-1626, www.cafedeollavallarta.com, 10 A.M.–11 P.M. Wed.–Mon.) serves traditional dishes like enchiladas, fajitas, and chiles rellenos. Attended by a super friendly staff, the casual dining room is comfortable, though there is also outdoor seating for mild nights. During the high season, there can be a wait for a table at this inexpensive eatery.

Another traditional Mexican joint with a low-key atmosphere, **El Arrayan** (Allende 344, tel. 322/222-7195, http://elarrayan.com.mx, 5:30–11 P.M. Wed.–Mon.) serves more experimental Mexican fare like plantain empanadas and duck tostadas, as well as traditional but more uncommon dishes like grasshopper tacos (a Oaxacan specialty) and *cohcinita pibil* (seasoned pulled pork from the Yucatán Peninsula).

If you'll be in Sayulita, you'd likely find **Choco Banana** (Calle Revolución s/n, Sayulita, tel. 329/291-3051, 6 A.M.–6 P.M. daily) without a guidebook to aid you, as it's right on the town square and packed all morning with contented breakfasters. In addition to its egg dishes and signature chocolate-banana muffins, they make burgers, sandwiches, and bagels.

San Miguel de Allende and Vicinity

For breakfast, locals favor **Café de la Parroquía** (Jesus 11, tel. 415/152-3161, 8 A.M.–4 P.M. Tues.–Sat., 8 A.M.–2 P.M. Sun.), a tasty and inexpensive half-day joint set in a colonial courtyard surrounding a gurgling fountain. It is one of the most relaxing places to brunch alfresco while flipping through the latest edition of *Atención San Miguel*. The menu includes traditional Mexican dishes like fried eggs in *mole negro,* huevos rancheros (fried eggs in tomato salsa), and chicken and cheese tamales in black bean sauce, as well as French toast, fruit, or oatmeal.

For a hearty dinner, **Tio Lucas Restaurant and Bar** (Mesones 103, tel. 415/152-4996, noon–midnight Mon.–Sun.) is a lively steak house best known for its

Mexican cuts of beef, like *arrachera, puntas de filete,* or *norteña.* The atmosphere is always upbeat, with a nightly jazz band, constant crowds, and Mexican pottery and stamped metal decorations adorning the walls of the open-air dining room.

The dining room at **La Posadita** (Cuna de Allende 13, tel. 415/154-8862, noon–11 P.M. Thurs.–Tues.) has a beautiful view of the city, nestled on an open rooftop beneath the Parroquía and overlooking the valley beyond San Miguel. The menu sticks to classic Mexican dishes like enchiladas *mineras,* pozole, and guacamole, as well as a tequila-heavy cocktail menu. It's a great place for a relaxing lunch or to watch the sunset.

Oaxaca

Oaxacan food gets a modern twist at **La Biznaga** (Garcia Vigil 512, tel. 951/516-1800, 1–10 P.M. Mon.–Thurs., 1–11 P.M. Fri.–Sun.). The restaurant's large chalkboard menus list an exciting array of options, with unusual but well-executed plates like blackberry *mole,* fish tacos rubbed with *adobado,* and cheese-stuffed hibiscus flower. This is delicious, rich food, which goes well with a fiery mescal, served here in a pretty ceramic tumblers. Tables are arranged around an open-air courtyard, allowing fresh air and a starry sky to complement the dining experience.

A Oaxacan specialty, the *tlayuda* is a giant corn tortilla filled with beans and Oaxacan cheese, then grilled till crisp on a bed of charcoal. Several restaurants make a version of the *tlayuda,* served with a knife and fork and plenty of napkins, but the best place to eat them is at a street-side stand, still hot from the grill. Though many places vie for the title of best *tlayuda* in town, the most popular is the delicious **Tlayudas Libres** (Libres 212, 9 P.M.–4:30 A.M. daily), a late-night dinner spot perpetually thronged with Oaxacans seeking a massive and inexpensive meal with fiery salsa. There are seats inside the restaurant, but you can also huddle around the grill outside, set up right in the middle of the street.

In the Reforma neighborhood, the uniquely fresh and delicious food at **Itanoni** (Belisario Domínguez 513, Col. Reforma, tel. 951/513-9223, www. itanoni.com.mx, 7 A.M.–4 P.M. Mon.–Sat., 8 A.M.–2 P.M. Sun.) is among the best in Oaxaca. The simple menu revolves around fresh cornmeal tortillas and flatbreads. Though it appears simple, an avocado taco or a bean-and-cheese tostada can take on surprising dimension when prepared fresh in Itanoni's open kitchen. Service is friendly, and the atmosphere is definitively casual, with most guests seated at plastic tables or picnic benches in an open-air dining room.

Baja California Sur

Start your day with a serious meal at the perennially popular **Mama's Royal Café** (Hidalgo s/n, at Zapata, tel. 624/143-4290, www.mamascabosanlucas. com, 7:30 A.M.–1 P.M. and 4–10 P.M. daily), where the menu ranges from sweet French toast to huevos rancheros, and the portion sizes are enough to keep you satiated well past lunch. While breakfasts are the restaurant's claim to fame, it converts into a traditional Mexican restaurant in the evening, where you can get famous mainland dishes like pozole and enchiladas, as well as fresh fish and shrimp dishes. The outdoor dining room is always packed, and there is often a wait for breakfast.

The best taqueria around, **Taqueria El Ahorcado** (Pescadores and Marinos St., San Jose del Cabo, tel. 624/172-2093, 6:30 P.M.–midnight) serves northern-style tacos with meat or cactus, bean stews, and *queso fundido* (melted cheese). This casual, open-air eatery is incredibly popular with locals, and it fills up in the evening as revelers make their way home from a night out in San Jose.

Along the corridor between Cabo San Lucas and San Jose del Cabo, **7 Seas Restaurant** (Acapulquito Beach, Km. 28, San Jose del Cabo, B.C.S., tel. 624/142-2666 or tel. 624/142-2676, U.S. tel. 858/964-5117, mercedes@7seasrestaurant.com, http://7seasrestaurant.com) at the Cabo Surf Hotel is a romantic place to eat some fresh and creatively prepared seafood. Try the delicious shrimp or fish tacos, a specialty of the Baja region, or order a plate of coconut shrimp, fresh tuna steak, or grilled sea bass. The atmosphere is beachfront dreamy, with a *palapa*-roofed dining room overlooking a beach where surfers are continually catching gentle waves.

The Yucatán Peninsula

There are an abundance of places to eat along the Quinta Avenida (5th Avenue) in Playa del Carmen, many of which are quite tasty and atmospheric. One place to try is **Yaxche** (5th Ave. at 22nd St., tel. 984/873-3011, www. mayacuisine.com, noon–11 P.M. daily), which serves cuisine based on traditional Yucatec recipes. Here, you can get a true taste of the regional cuisine with dishes like *panuchos* (stuffed corn cakes) and Maya-style tamales. The garden seating is decked out with Maya-inspired decor.

For a taste of fresh seafood or perfectly prepared ceviche, check out **El Tabano** (Carretera a Boca Paila Km. 6, tel. 984/134-8725, 8 A.M.–10 P.M. daily) in Tulum. In addition to seafood, the restaurant serves a range of traditional Mexican dishes, like seasoned pork and chicken in *pipian,* a pumpkin-seed sauce. The atmosphere has a rustic, romantic, beach vibe, with a thatched

Papatzules (egg-stuffed tortillas bathed in a pumpkin-seed sauce) is a traditional dish from the Yucatán Peninsula.

palm roof, chalkboard menus, sandy floors, and wooden tables. In the evenings, flickering candles complete the scene.

In Mérida, **La Casa de Frida** (Calle 61 at Calle 66, tel. 999/928-2311, www.lacasadefrida.com.mx, 6–11 P.M. Mon.–Sat.) is a well-loved place for traditional Mexican plates, like enchiladas with *mole,* guacamole, quesadillas, and *sopa azteca.* There are also some creative takes on Mexican standards, like an eggplant flan. The brightly painted dining room is decorated with traditional crafts and creates the perfect accompaniment to the menu.

DAILY LIFE

MAKING THE MOVE

Moving to a foreign country inevitably involves some planning and paperwork, but Mexico makes it easy for outsiders to legalize their status. The country's immigration policies are fairly liberal, and foreigners have historically been welcomed into society. Of particular interest, the country has long been generous in granting political asylum, accepting many exiled liberals during the Spanish Civil War, as well as famous revolutionaries like Leon Trotsky, who died in his home in Mexico City.

For regular folks, Mexico's laws permit foreigners to reside, work, and even officially immigrate to the country after a certain period of time. If you have come to retire, telecommute, or in any way live from savings or a foreign source of income, it is easy to solicit a visa that allows you to live in Mexico, either as an official immigrant to the country or a nonimmigrant resident. If you plan to work or open a business, the process is slightly more complicated but not excessively difficult; many foreigners are able to successfully solicit the paperwork they need for a job. Generally speaking, applying for any type of visa is a bit time-consuming but otherwise easy, straightforward, and free of corruption.

Immigration and Visas

The Mexican government has a well deserved reputation for painstaking bureaucracy, so it's natural to feel a bit intimidated by the idea of applying for legal immigration documents. In reality, the process is not as complicated as you might expect. Yes, you'll stand in some long lines and fill out a few forms in triplicate. You'll have to gather documents, make some Xerox copies, and pay fees at the bank. However, Mexican immigration processes are actually fairly streamlined. If you plan to stay in Mexico long-term, maintaining the correct legal status is generally worth the relatively minimal cost and effort.

TOURIST CARDS (FMM)

To enter Mexico, foreign citizens must have a valid passport. Otherwise, no special visa is needed. For citizens of most countries, six-month travel permits, officially known as the Forma Migratoria Multiple (FMM) but unofficially referred to as "tourist cards," are issued at the point of entry. If you enter Mexico by plane, you will pass through immigration as soon as you land, where your tourist card will be ratified. If you enter by car, it is necessary to stop at an immigration office (most are located close to the border crossing).

Hold on to your stamped FMM form; you must return it to the airline or to an immigration official before leaving the country. Alternatively, if you apply for a resident visa, you will need to turn in your FMM at an immigration office to have it replaced by your new immigration form. If you happen to lose your tourist card while you are in Mexico, you can report it at an immigration office and pay a fine to replace it, or you can wait and pay the fine at the airport. Leave a little extra time if you've lost your FMM and plan to visit immigration before your flight.

WHO NEEDS A RESIDENT VISA?

Not everyone needs or wants to be an official resident of Mexico, even if they spend extensive time in the country. If you travel frequently or maintain a residence elsewhere, it may not be necessary for you to legalize your status in Mexico. FMMs only provide 180 days of permission for Mexico; however, if you leave the country and come back, immigration will provide you with a new FMM every time. If you plan to spend just a season in Mexico or if you frequently return to your home country, you can do so with a series of tourist cards. However, you cannot own a business or work legally with an FMM, nor can you open a Mexican bank account. If you bring a car with you on an FMM, its permit expires along with your tourist card; you must return the car to the border within six months to maintain its legal status.

If you will be living in Mexico for an extended period of time—even if you don't plan to work—resident visas have a few key advantages. First and most importantly, a resident visa allows you to remain in Mexico for longer than the allotted 180 days for an FMM, without penalty. Once awarded, resident visas give you the right to a one-time import of your household possessions without duty. The FM3 visa type will also give you the right to have a foreign-plated car in Mexico, for as long as your visa is valid. Visas allow you to open a bank account in Mexico and can be used as identification for other official processes. Finally, if you are planning to take a job or even open your own small enterprise, you will need to apply for a visa. Both FM2 and FM3 visa types can come with or without the right to work.

APPLYING FOR RESIDENCY

Applications for all visa types are reviewed and processed by the Instituto Nacional de Migracion (INM), or National Immigration Institute. Visa applications must be submitted through their website (www.inm.gob.mx). After that, you collect all required paperwork, including black-and-white front and profile photos, and submit it to your local immigration office. You will receive forms to pay your fees; all immigration fees are paid at the bank—never directly at the INM—where you will receive a receipt with a confirmation number. Once the application is processed and approved, you will receive your visa in the form of a plastic card with your photo.

As long as there is nothing particularly complicated about your application, the whole process usually takes a few weeks. During the interim period when your visa is being processed, you will receive a letter from INM explaining your status. This letter will serve as paperwork for any official purposes, but it cannot be used to enter or leave the country. It is best to apply at a time when you are not likely to leave Mexico since you are not permitted to leave the country without the appropriate immigration documents. If you do need to leave unexpectedly, you will need to request a *permiso de salida y regreso* (permission to leave and return) at the immigration office where you applied for the visa. Generally, these permits cannot be issued at the airport.

There are frequent changes to immigration policy, and some immigration offices have slightly different requirements than others. Before you begin the paperwork, stop by your local INM office, where they can provide you with an updated list of requirements. The INM website (www.inm.gob.mx) also has information about the visa application process, predominantly in Spanish.

NONIMMIGRANT VISAS (FM3)

Far and away the most popular visa option for residents of Mexico is the Forma Migratoria 3, or FM3. There are several categories of FM3, but all of them classify holders as nonimmigrant residents of Mexico. FM3s are the type of visa issued to most

The heavily trafficked United States embassy in Mexico City is located on Paseo de la Reforma.

retirees, employees, and business owners. FM3s are renewed annually and good for up to five years, after which you must apply for a new visa.

The benefit of an FM3 is that it allows you to come and go from Mexico as you please, and there is no minimum residency requirement. You also have the opportunity to import your household items one time without duty, and you may legally own a foreign-plated car as long as your visa is valid. These benefits are extended to any FM3 holder, no matter what type.

To apply for an FM3, the applicant must submit a proof of citizenship (passport), proof of residence, three months of bank statements, five color photos measuring 2.3 by 3 centimeters (three looking directly at the camera and two in profile), and proof of income. If you are applying to work legally in Mexico, you will need to include additional information about your qualifications for employment. The following are the most common FM3s.

FM3 for *Rentistas*

Mexican law allows foreign residents with a foreign source of income to live in the country permanently as a *rentista* (renter). Most retirees will fall under this category. Those who principally telecommute to a job overseas should also apply for an FM3 as a *rentista*.

CONSIDERATIONS FOR SNOWBIRDS

Summer at home, winter in the sun: It's a pretty unbeatable combination, and many people achieve the enviable "snowbird" lifestyle by living half the year in Mexico. Following the sun, part-time residents of Mexico have plenty of advantages, but dividing your time between two countries has a few additional considerations and costs. When weighing the possibility of splitting time between Mexico and your home country, keep the following in mind.

BUDGET

The budget for a part-time resident will be a bit different than for a full-time resident of Mexico, and likely a bit more expensive. If you plan to buy in Mexico, you will have to maintain two residences and all that goes with them, like cars, car insurance, home owner's insurance, and utilities. Even if you plan to rent your home in Mexico, don't rely on rental income as a mainstay of your financial plan. Though you may be able to offset costs through a rental, make a sound budget, accounting for the cost of living in both places.

IMMIGRATION

Mexico welcomes visitors without a visa for stays of up to 180 days per year. If you only plan to live in Mexico part time, you can skip a visa altogether (you do not need a visa to rent or buy a home). However, there is no residency requirement for a "nonimmigrant" FM3 holder, so many part-time residents prefer the flexibility of having a resident visa for their time in Mexico, which allows them to open a bank account or stay a little longer than the allotted time. Note that "immigrant" FM2 holders must live in Mexico full time and cannot be outside the country for more than 18 months over the course of five years.

TAXES

When you live part time in two countries, you are likely to owe money to both governments. Quite a headache! It is likely you'll continue to pay your taxes the same

To apply for an FM3 as a *rentista,* you only need to submit the required paperwork and supporting documents, plus proof of a minimum income from a foreign source. According to immigration law, a foreigner residing in Mexico must earn or receive 250 times the minimum wage; in the past few years, that number is equal to about US$1,200 per month. For a spouse and for each dependent, the income requirement rises another 50 percent.

The income requirement is almost always illustrated with three months of bank statements, showing deposits equal to or higher than the minimum amount. These bank statements are not excessively scrutinized, nor does IMN require pay stubs, canceled checks, or letters from your employer. As long as the minimum amount of money is deposited into your account each month, you qualify for an FM3.

Like all FM3s, *rentistas* must renew their visas annually. Although you

way at home (as a part-time resident, you will not lose your residency status), but seek the advice of a tax professional in Mexico. In most cases, part-time residents will be considered "nonresident aliens" of Mexico and will therefore only owe taxes on Mexican-based income or assets, such as property, rather than worldwide income.

MEDICAL INSURANCE

Maintaining health care can be one of the more difficult aspects of splitting your time, particularly for U.S. citizens. You may be obliged to pay your year-round premiums on health care at home if you carry independent insurance and are not old enough to qualify for Medicare. Many international medical plans require their holders to live in Mexico full time, even if they do offer coverage to those visiting their home country. It may be most efficient to do the majority of your doctor's visits at home, paying out of pocket for services in Mexico, though you should also check into temporary international plans.

RENTAL INCOME

If you are going to be leaving your home for several months each year, you can plan to rent your home in Mexico during the time you are away. In areas where there is robust tourism or a large expatriate community, there are often companies that will help facilitate the rental, though they also claim a percentage of the rental price. Talk to rental agencies early in the game so you can make good choices when buying and decorating your home.

PETS

If you will be traveling between Mexico and the United States or Canada, it is generally easy to bring your pet aboard an airplane or in the car. However, the animal will need to have a health check at the veterinarian before every international trip, in or out of Mexico. Vaccinations, too, must always be up-to-date in order to travel with an animal.

will not have to supply all the paperwork and photos, you must submit a copy of your proof of income each year. Remember, the minimum income requirement slowly increases annually along with the minimum wage.

FM3 for Self-Employment

Foreign professionals living in Mexico can apply for permission to work for themselves or to set up their own business with an FM3. This visa type is appropriate for someone who wants to give private lessons in English or teach yoga or art. It is also appropriate for someone who wants to open a shop, hotel, restaurant, or gallery. Even though you are applying for the right to work, you must submit all the same paperwork for the FM3 for *rentistas* and meet the same minimum income requirement.

The key difference between this visa type and the FM3 for *rentistas* is the right to perform "lucrative activities." In order to solicit this right, you must include a letter in your application explaining what you plan to do, and show immigration that you either have money to invest in the country or a skill that is unusual in the general Mexican population. For many U.S. and Canadian citizens, tutoring English might be deemed acceptable, and a college diploma from a college or university will often prove an applicant's eligibility.

Setting up a business obviously involves more than just getting a visa (the visa will simply give you the right to work for yourself or to work at your own company). If you are planning to open your own business, you will need the assistance of a *notario publico* (notary public), who will help you fill out the paperwork, register your company name, and file the draft deed of incorporation. You will also need the help of an accountant, who can help you file and pay your taxes. (Note that investors may open a business without working at it and therefore do not need a work permit.) Foreigners who work for themselves must also declare and pay taxes annually.

FM3 for Employees

If you land a legal job in Mexico, you can be sponsored for an FM3 with permission to work through your company. This FM3 will allow you to work legally in Mexico (and also obligate you to pay annual taxes) and voids the necessity to provide proof of income outside the country. To get a visa for employment, you will need: a job offer in writing, demonstrable skills to perform the job you are being offered, and proof that the company for which you are working needs to specifically hire a foreigner to fill that position.

Your company will provide you with a letter to present to immigration, documenting your employment and their own employment needs. In general, Mexico's immigration authorities approve employment for foreigners with a special skill not generally found in the Mexican population. For Americans or Canadians, that skill is often native fluency in English. For example, as a native English speaker, you may be uniquely eligible to teach English or to work in the hospitality industry.

In addition to your company's letter, you are responsible for providing certified documentation that you have special skills to perform the job you are being offered. In this case, a certificate like the TOEFL (Teacher of English as a Foreign Language) can be useful, though many immigration offices will also accept American, Canadian, or British teachers of English if they have a college diploma. Note that these documents must be certified with an apostille (a certificate authenticating the documents) from your home country, as well as an official translation. If you plan to apply for jobs in Mexico, consider getting an apostille before you leave home. It is much quicker and more inexpensive to get an apostille at home than to send for one through the consulate in Mexico.

In some cases, your employer will pay the cost of the visa, either up front or after you have completed a year of employment with the company. At other companies, covering the cost of the work permit is up to you. Remember, FM3 work permits are nontransferable; they only authorize you to work for one employer performing one activity. If you get another job, you will need to return to the immigration offices to request a change of employer and, depending on your new position, a change in authorized activities.

Student Visas

Students who will be in Mexico for fewer than six months can use a tourist visa for the length of their stay. No special visa is required. Those planning to study in Mexico for a longer period of time may need to apply for a student visa, which is a variation of the FM3 (application procedures are roughly analogous). In most cases, students should arrive in Mexico with an FMM and then apply for a student visa within 30 days of arrival. Like FM3s for *rentistas,* students must show proof of income, though it is only required to be about half as much as is required for *rentistas*. Students must also present a letter of admission from the university at which they will be studying.

IMMIGRANT VISAS (FM2)

Immigrant visas, or FM2s, are designed for those who plan to live permanently in Mexico. FM2s, like FM3s, are renewed annually, and, after five years, the holder can become an official "immigrant" to Mexico. Those thinking long-term will receive some serious benefits to holding an FM2; specifically, they have the right to purchase restricted property without a foreign trust, thereby avoiding U.S. taxes. The FM2 also creates a pathway toward citizenship; after five years of holding an FM2, you can apply to naturalize. However, there are also stricter requirements placed upon FM2 holders. Specifically, you must live the majority of your time in Mexico: To maintain an FM2, visa holders must not spend more than 18 months outside of Mexico during a five-year period. Unlike FM3 holders, you cannot own a car with foreign plates if you have an FM2.

The application process for the FM2 is identical to the FM3, though the proof of foreign income is higher, equivalent to 400 times the minimum wage (around US$2,000). Just like FM3s, FM2s come in a variety of flavors, depending on your needs. You can get an FM2 as a "*rentista*" if you have a steady source of foreign income. You can also get an FM2 with the right to work. After holding an FM2 for five years, you can have your status officially changed to "immigrant," or you may apply for citizenship. If you choose to apply for immigrant status, you will have many of the same rights as citizens. Immigrants can hold any type of job, buy property anywhere in Mexico (including restricted zones), and open and run a business. Immigrants do not have the right to vote or to carry a Mexican passport unless they naturalize.

RENEWALS

The first time you apply for a resident visa is the most complicated; every year thereafter for the next five years, you only need to confirm the information you submitted in your original application. Generally, the immigration office will ask you to submit the following: a letter in Spanish requesting an extension of your visa (use this letter to explain a change of address), an application form, receipt of fees paid, and proof of income. After five years, you must apply for a new FM3, which is renewable every year for the next five years. If you have an FM2, you can adjust your FM2 status after five years to "immigrant," which does not need to be renewed every five years.

EXPIRED VISAS

Visas are generally good for one year (and renewable for up to five). You must renew all visas and immigration paperwork at your local immigration office in Mexico. You can renew your FM3 for the following year up to a month before the document expires. If you let the date pass, you can usually renew your FM2 or FM3 up to 30 days after it has expired without penalty. If you have passed the grace period, you will likely pay a fine to renew your paperwork. The longer you wait, the more complicated the renewal will likely become. Stay on top of your anniversary dates!

If you are out of the country when your FM3 expires, you can generally reenter the country with the expired document, as long as you do so within 60 days of its expiring. You must renew your visa within 30 days of returning. If you have let more than 60 days pass, you are probably going to encounter fewer problems by soliciting a new tourist card on your return to Mexico and applying for a new resident visa.

If you are leaving the country permanently or do not intend to renew your visa, you technically have 30 days after its expiry to leave Mexico, and you must turn in your documents with immigration upon exit. If you have exceeded the 30-day limit, you may have to pay a fine. Either way, go to the airport early as these processes can often take time at the immigration offices.

CITIZENSHIP

Mexican law allows permanent residents of Mexico to become citizens by fulfilling a combination of residency, cultural requirements, or family relationships. The Secretaría de Relaciones Exteriores (SRE)—not the immigration office—oversees the naturalization process.

Anyone born in Mexico can petition for citizenship using their birth certificate. For those married to a Mexican citizen and residing in Mexico, SRE offers the opportunity to naturalize after just two years of residence. Similarly, anyone born to Mexican parents or grandparents can petition for Mexican citizenship after just two years of legal residency with an FM3 or FM2. To apply based on marriage, you need a valid marriage certificate (with an apostille if it was issued anywhere outside Mexico), and to apply based on family relationships, you need proof of your relative's Mexican citizenship.

While having Mexican family may speed up the process, anyone residing in Mexico for an extended period of time may be eligible for citizenship. When you have been living in the country with an FM3 or an FM2 for five years, you may choose to apply to naturalize rather than renew your visa. As a requirement, you cannot have left the country for more than 180 days in the two years preceding your naturalization application. To apply, you submit an application directly to SRE, including your FM2 or FM3. You pay a fee, SRE reviews your paperwork, and, if the outcome is favorable, you receive a naturalization card and may apply for a passport. Thereafter, you should always refer to yourself as a Mexican citizen (and use Mexican ID) when in the country and when entering Mexico. (When returning home, it is likely best to use your home country's passport.)

Becoming a citizen of Mexico affords numerous rights that are not extended to permanent residents, including the right to vote, the right to buy restricted property, and the right to carry a Mexican passport. However, nationality through naturalization can be taken away; if you live outside of Mexico continuously for more than five years, you may lose your citizenship.

Dual Nationality

Mexico recognizes dual nationality with any other nation. Whether or not a foreigner can become a dual citizen of Mexico depends on the laws in his or her home country. The United States officially allows dual citizenship with Mexico. As a part of the naturalization process, new Mexican citizens must declare allegiance to Mexico. In the past, this declaration created a conflict with U.S. laws, which prohibited declaring allegiance to another country. It is no longer the case; dual citizenship is now fully recognized.

EXPERT ASSISTANCE

Filling out visa paperwork isn't rocket science, and many people successfully complete the entire process unassisted. However, it can be helpful and wonderfully time saving to get some assistance with the process, especially if you do not speak Spanish. In places where there is a large community of expatriates, such as Guadalajara and Lake Chapala, Mexico City, Puerto Vallarta, and San Miguel de Allende, immigration experts can help you write your letter of intent, fill out the paperwork, and properly present your bank statement; many will even complete some of the busy work, like paying bank fees and waiting in line for immigration. If you are applying for an FM3 with permission to engage in lucrative activities, an immigration expert can also help you assemble the appropriate application materials. Unless you have a very complicated case, you will rarely need the help of a lawyer. However, there are immigration lawyers available to help foreigners with paperwork, if necessary.

Moving with Family

If you are moving to Mexico with your family, every family member must apply individually for a resident visa. If you are moving to Mexico with your spouse, you will complete the visa process together. Income requirements for married couples are lower than they would be for two individuals, though some couples find it easier to apply separately nonetheless. In

© CARLOS MEADE

Mexico's family-oriented culture is a draw for families with young children.

order to apply as a couple, you will need a copy of your marriage certificate, with an apostille.

Children must also carry visas, like adults. In order to apply for an FM3 on behalf of your children, you will need to prove your relationship with their birth certificate. For each dependent, adults must meet an income requirement that is 50 percent higher.

ENTRY REQUIREMENTS FOR MINORS

In order to combat human trafficking, minors entering Mexico must be accompanied by both parents. If one parent isn't present, the other must present a notarized letter from the absent parent giving permission for the trip. If neither parent is accompanying a minor, the child must travel with notarized consent from both parents.

Moving with Pets

Taking a cat or dog to Mexico is a relatively easy process—and once they're there, no paperwork or visas are required!

CATS AND DOGS

Mexico, the United States, and Canada share land borders, and therefore, as long as a cat or dog is in good health, there are no quarantine requirements

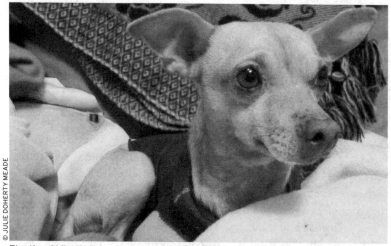

© JULIE DOHERTY MEADE

The tiny Chihuahua is among the most popular breeds of dog in Mexico.

A CHILDHOOD IN MEXICO: MELANIE HARRIS DE MAYCOTTE

Melanie Harris de Maycotte is a gallery owner and artist living in San Miguel de Allende. She moved to San Miguel from New York City in the early aughts, though she had already lived there long before, as a child. Moving to a foreign country can be a wonderful experience for a child, but it isn't without its challenges. If you are thinking about bringing your family to Mexico, here's some of Melanie's firsthand advice.

When did you arrive in mexico for the first time? How old were you?

I was seven when I first moved to Mexico, back when foreigners couldn't have a job. My mom couldn't work, and so we could only live here for five years, and then she had to go back to the United States. I moved back again at 25 and have been here for the past nine years.

As a kid, did you experience culture shock? What was different about life in Mexico?

Yes! I cried every day for the first two months. Kids are mean anywhere you live, but I didn't speak a bit of Spanish, and they really had fun with me. Since San Miguel was a much smaller town back then, everyone knew each other, and I was the new girl, and therefore an easy target.

The differences were instantly felt: the clean air, the walk to school, the new and tangy *tamarindo* candies, the playing in the streets. It was easier to make friends with the kids on my street than it was with the snobby kids at my private school.

How quickly did you learn Spanish?

If I remember correctly, I think in about six months I was pretty good. I still think I could learn the language better, even now, but a child is a sponge, so expect six months.

What was it like growing up in San Miguel? Is Mexico a good place to be a kid?

Growing up here was marvelous. There was an adventure around every corner...randomly stumbling upon a cock fight; exploring the surrounding neighborhoods, which each have their own flavor and fiestas; sneaking into the tent of traveling circus shows. The lights, the fireworks, the playing in the street – it was all truly magical!

Mexico has got to be the best place to be a kid. The neighbors all

between the countries. If you are bringing a cat or dog to Mexico, the animal must be accompanied by a certificate of health, issued by a licensed veterinarian no more than 10 days before arrival in Mexico, and proof of a current rabies vaccination. The certificate must include the name of the pet, the name of its owner, and their residence, as well as confirmation that the animal is in good health and has been treated for worms and parasites. Rabies vaccinations must be issued at least 15 days before entry but can be no more than a year old. It is also advisable to bring a copy of your pet's vaccination

look out for you, but you can play on the streets and feel free to explore with little worry about something bad happening. We never kept our door locked, nor did the neighbors. Nowhere in the world is 100 percent safe, but here you have a community looking out for you.

When did you return to the United States? And what was that like?

I returned to Texas in 1990. It was sad to leave San Miguel and also strange to be in a place so disconnected from each other – always in a car, no playing in the street, no festivals, everything so seemingly perfect. In school I was ahead of everyone in math and science but behind in U.S. history, of course. Since I always went to a bilingual school and since my maternal language was English, that wasn't an issue.

What brought you back to Mexico?

Mexico is pure magic to me. It tugs at the heartstrings and beckoned me "home." I love being part of the community, always learning about the vast traditions, and walking down a colorful, cobblestone street. The imperfections just seem so much more natural and connected with what life is all about.

Obviously, San Miguel is like home to you, but are there things about living there that specifically appeal to you as an adult?

As an adult, the intrigue is still there. It is a constant learning experience living here. It has taught me patience and pathos. It is a reminder that life isn't all about work, and that family is still the most exciting and wonderful part of living. If there is a fiesta for a saint, may as well go enjoy it even if I am an atheist...it is an opportunity to feel connected to people.

Looking back, any advice for parents who are considering moving to Mexico with their family?

Do it! Don't be afraid to put your child through uncomfortable situations...life is full of them, and they may as well get used to it now. With Internet and phones (which we didn't have as a kid), it is easy to stay connected with family and friends back home and maybe even learn some Spanish before starting school. I look at the life of my American friends who didn't have this opportunity, and I do kind of feel sorry for them. Your kids will survive and be better for it!

DAILY LIFE

record; customs may request it. If your pet does not meet health standards, it may be detained at the airport or at the border until it can be examined by a veterinarian.

Keep in mind that the rules and regulations for importing a pet to Mexico may be different than the rules required by an airline. Check with your airline before you fly. Although it is relatively easy to bring a pet to Mexico by plane, most buses do not accept animals, unless they ride in the luggage compartment under the bus (not a very comfortable option for Fido!). If you plan to bring your animal on a flight, your best bet is to arrange ground transportation through a private company or via rental car.

If you are bringing an animal with you via car, you'll find few hotels that accept pets. Again, plan ahead to guarantee you'll have places to stay en route.

OTHER ANIMALS

In Mexico, only dogs and cats are considered pets. Therefore, importing other animals can be far more complicated, though technically legal. Birds and reptiles are particularly difficult, though tenacious pet owners with no fear of paperwork will be able to get some bird species across the border. In many cases, you will need to work with the U.S. Fish and Wildlife Service, as well as the Secretaría de medio ambiente y recursos naturals (Secretary of Environment and Natural Resources), or SEMARNAT, in Mexico.

What to Take

Moving all your worldly possessions from one country to another—even the country next door—can take some careful planning. Whether you choose to move your household down south or purchase everything in Mexico will likely depend on your situation. Are you keeping a residence in the United States or Canada? Can you afford to buy everything you need again, or will a move be more economical? Are you moving to a city where there are plenty of shopping options, or are you heading somewhere remote, where you'll have a hard time finding things you need?

Before making a decision, it's worth evaluating the cost of shipping versus the cost of purchasing. Even if you don't decide to move your entire household, you may wish to bring some more expensive items—computers, television, lamps, sofas—along with you. When trying to decide what to bring with you and what to buy in Mexico, you will probably weigh each item individually, considering cost, ease of shipping, quantity, and, of course, sentimental value. Overall, standard household items cost roughly the same in Mexico as they do in the United States, though some items cost a bit more or a bit less.

If you have decided to make a substantial household move, you will need to solicit a resident visa in order to legally import your personal effects. The visa can be an FM2 or an FM3, both of which afford the opportunity for a one-time import of household items. Those traveling on a FMM, or tourist card, are only permitted to bring what is necessary for a short trip. Usually, a couple suitcases are considered the limit, though you may or may not have your luggage reviewed by customs.

Remember that Mexican laws strictly prohibit entering the country with firearms, ammunition, or illicit drugs. The penalties for violation of these laws are incredibly strict.

IMPORTING YOUR HOUSEHOLD EFFECTS

If you have an FM3 or an FM2, you are entitled to a one-time duty-free import of household items from the United States to Mexico. To do so, you will need a copy of your immigration paperwork, a proof of residence in Mexico, as well as a typed list of everything you are importing, stamped by the consulate. At the top of the list, you must indicate your address in the United States and how long you lived there, as well as the address to which you are moving in Mexico; at the bottom, leave space for the consular seal. You must list everything you are importing, including the brand and serial number of all electronic appliances, and the list must be written in Spanish.

Household items may include furniture used in the household, clothing, computers, books, bookshelves, musical instruments, and art (not intended for exhibition), as well as scientific instruments for a laboratory or art materials. Everything must be yours and intended for personal use. It is better to avoid buying new items, since you may have to answer more questions or pay a duty on new products. If you do buy something new, remove it from the factory box or remove the price tags.

Once you have decided to import your things, you can drive your household items over the border yourself or hire movers to help you with the process. (Either way, the approved list must accompany your things.) Many shipping companies will help you with this process and provide you with an estimate before you make the move. Shop around to find the best deal with a recommended moving company.

WHAT TO BUY IN MEXICO

For many people, it ends up being more cost-effective to buy most of their household items new, rather than import them. In any big city, you'll find big-box supermarkets and items such as furniture, electronics, cooking supplies, and mattresses. International chains like Costco, Walmart, Sam's Club, and Home Depot have branches throughout Mexico, offering familiar products at similar prices. If you need to buy anything new, you should do so in Mexico (household import rights only apply to items that belong to you, not new items).

© ARTURO MEADE

bustle on the street near the artisan market in Puebla

You can find most household basics at relatively similar prices to the United States. However, some items, such as electronics, stereo equipment, computers, and brand-name clothing can cost quite a bit more in Mexico. If you are a multimedia person, you might want to weigh the costs of shipping computers, televisions, and other electronics, rather than purchasing them in Mexico.

There are some items that you would be particularly well advised to seek out south of the border. In particular, Mexico produces a wide range of artisanal products, which are often significantly cheaper and more beautiful than industrial designs. You can buy inexpensive hand-painted flatware and planters, traditional wood furniture, light fixtures, bedspreads, rugs, copper pots and pans, hand-blown glasses and pitchers, and other handmade items in Mexico. The lovely and economical leather-and-wood *equipal* furniture from Guadalajara is very popular with both Mexicans and foreigners for its durability and comfort. The benefits of buying artisanal products are manifold. Not only are these products more inexpensive than industrial items, they support local cottage industry and centuries-old craft tradition. Plus, there is nothing more beautiful and appropriate for a Mexican home.

SHIPPING OPTIONS

If you decide you want to import some or all of your household items to Mexico, there are a couple of different ways get your stuff across the border. If you are planning to bring your car, the first and simplest plan is to simply pack your vehicle with the most important items and drive it over the border yourself. Make sure you have your immigration paperwork and a typed and stamped list of your belongings. In some cases, you may be asked to pay a small duty. In some cases, you may not be checked at all.

If you are planning to bring more than you can fit in your car, you will probably need the assistance of a shipping company, which can do the heavy lifting and facilitate the process at the border. For this, you have two options. One is to use an international moving company, which will handle the entire move. There are numerous Mexico-based moving companies that offer international moving services, many of which are located in popular destinations like Ajijic and San Miguel de Allende. UPS also offers door-to-door freight shipping from the United States to Mexico, with customs brokerage included. The other option is to ship or drive your household items to the border yourself, then contract a Mexican shipping company to pass through customs and take your things over the border. If you have a cheap and trusted mover in the United States (or you can move your things yourself), the second option can be more economical. Costs depend on the distance traveled and the size of your load, however making an international move is generally a pricey proposition.

HOUSING

When moving to a foreign country, finding a place to call home is often the most important step in the process. In most parts of Mexico, renting a home is easy and inexpensive, though many foreigners also choose to invest in real estate. Building or renovating a home usually costs far less than it would in the United States, Canada, or other parts of the industrialized world. It can be an exciting process, though it also comes with its share of challenges!

The real estate market in Mexico varies by region. Beachfront property can cost you a considerable sum, especially in and around popular beach resorts. However, you might travel down the coast a few miles and find rock-bottom prices in a small seaside village. In off-the-beaten-track communities, you can find old and inexpensive fixer-uppers with lots of history, while colonial-era houses fetch a much higher price than newer constructions in Mexico's famous cultural capitals.

The process for buying real estate in Mexico is a bit different than what you find in other countries. Professional real estate brokers can be an enormous help, but you should also take the time to talk to other buyers and acquaint yourself with the process on your own. Occasionally, you hear horror stories about expatriate real estate deals gone awry. Arming yourself with the correct information is the smartest way to avoid real estate problems. While mishaps and catastrophes can happen, most foreigners are able to get the right advice and make good choices about housing.

Renting

Renting a home in Mexico is generally easy and affordable. Since most Mexican families also rent their homes, those who plan to rent will find plenty of options, from small bungalows to fully furnished houses. Renting can be a good choice if you eventually plan to buy, but you want to get to know the local community and real estate market first.

As in any country, rental markets in Mexico vary distinctly by region. In some cities, there is ample housing for rent at a range of price points. In others, you'll have a harder time finding a place that is appropriate and affordable. Depending on where you look and what type of housing you need, rental properties could cost anywhere from US$200 for a small apartment to a US$4,000 for a multibedroom luxury home. A simple two-bedroom rental averages around US$400 per month in Mexico, though prices vary tremendously by region (as well as by type of property).

FINDING THE RIGHT PLACE

Looking for a place to live in Mexico is a pretty straightforward process. Generally, you browse listings in the newspaper or online, you make an appointment with the owner or a broker, and you go to visit the property. If you like it, you sign a lease, pay a month's rent and deposit, and move in.

Throughout Mexico, you will often see For Rent signs in the windows of homes and apartments. If you find a neighborhood you like, spend a few days wandering the streets to see if you find any rentals. Bring your cell phone along, and make a call as soon as you see a place you are interested in. Often, an agent or doorman will be available to show you the apartment immediately.

Word of mouth can also be an important tool in Mexico. Stop into corner stores in neighborhoods you like and ask the proprietors if they know about any rental properties. Make sure you let any friends or acquaintances know that you are looking for a place.

The Rental Market

There are two very different (but slightly overlapped) rental markets in Mexico. One rental market is principally focused on vacationers who would prefer to stay in a house than stay in a hotel. Usually, these rentals are meant for short-term stays, so the monthly rates can be a bit higher than a long-term rental. However, you may be able to negotiate a better deal if you want to rent long-term. Most vacation homes are fully furnished, have telephone and television service, and are equipped with kitchen supplies. They may also have maintenance or cleaning staff. However, not all vacation rentals are necessarily luxury accommodations. You may be able to find a basic and simply furnished place designed for inexpensive short-term rental.

Often, the best way to find a rental property is to walk through your favorite neighborhoods looking for signs in the windows of vacant homes or apartments.

In addition to vacation homes, the much larger and more ubiquitous rental market covers local long-term rentals—principally unfurnished houses and apartments. In general, you will find listings for rental properties in the local paper or in the window of the property for rent. The owner may handle the process, or the property may be represented by a rental agent. Foreigners can rent from Mexican or foreign landlords without any restriction.

Furnished vs. Unfurnished

The standard unfurnished rental in Mexico can feel a bit bare-bones by U.S. standards. Of particular note, unfurnished houses and apartments rarely come equipped with kitchen appliances, and some will even come without kitchen cabinets, shelves, or countertops. (If the rental ad says *cocina integral,* that indicates that there are kitchen furnishings, like shelves and cabinets, already installed.) Throughout Mexico, the tenant is responsible for buying a refrigerator and stove, and they will likely also be responsible for other basic items like window dressings, mirrors in the bathroom, or even doors on the closets.

If you don't want to invest in appliances or furniture right away, you can rent a furnished home. A furnished rental may run the gamut from barely furnished (just kitchen appliances and some basic bedroom accessories) to fully decked out, with art on the walls, cable television, and a telephone line. Often, the most lavishly furnished rentals will be called *suites*. You'll save more with an unfurnished rental, but you should be ready to invest in some basics when you sign the lease.

RENTAL AGENTS

Owners will often list their homes directly in the newspaper, but many also use rental agencies or real estate offices to help promote properties. Rental agents show the property, perform any necessary background or financial checks on the tenant, oversee the signing of the contract, and collect the deposit. Most rental agents receive a commission for their services—usually a month's rent—though some receive a monthly commission for overseeing the full duration of your rental. If you are directed to pay your monthly rent at the agency, it is likely the latter. (Needless to say, this arrangement includes a rather substantial markup of your monthly rent.)

Overall, there is little advantage or disadvantage to working with an agent, as long as he or she is receiving a one-time fee. In Mexico City, a few large rental companies represent hundreds of properties. Oddly, the situation may not always streamline the process for the renter. Often, different agents from the same company will represent different properties; you may have to make an individual appointment with each.

NEGOTIATING THE RENT

Rental prices in Mexico are often, surprisingly, negotiable. If you have found a place you like, you can let the rental agent or landlord know that you were looking for something a bit more inexpensive and ask if the price is flexible. Often, and especially in a less competitive rental market, the owner will be willing to drop the price US$100 or so. It is not considered rude or unexpected to ask if a rental price is flexible.

RENTAL CONTRACTS

Mexican rental agreements are similar to what you'd find elsewhere, with clauses describing the terms of the rental, its duration, the cost, late payments, notifications, and the security deposit. In many cases, landlords will use a boilerplate contract they've purchased at a stationery store, possibly modifying certain clauses. The rental terms tend to last for one year, with an option to renew (along with an option to increase the rent) after the first year. Renters are usually expected to return the home in the condition in which they

HOME ON WHEELS: RVS IN MEXICO

For Americans and Canadians planning to spend a season or two down south, driving a recreational vehicle into Mexico is a popular option. There are many RV parks and facilities in Baja California and along the Pacific Coast, which are easily accessible from the United States. Many RV parks have full hookups, as well as Internet connections, pools, and even housekeeping services. While many parks are aimed at tourists, they may also permit long-term residents.

Just like cars, RVs can enter Mexico on a temporary vehicle permit. To bring an RV into Mexico, you need a passport, a valid driver's license, and a registration for the vehicle. Technically, you should also purchase insurance for your vehicle. You may or may not be asked about insurance at the border. Finally, you will also need a valid credit card to leave as collateral (if you don't have a credit card, you will need to post a bond for your vehicle, which is a slightly more complicated process). At the immigration office, these documents will be reviewed, you will pay a fee, and the office will provide you with a sticker permit. If you are entering the country on an FMM or tourist card, you and the RV must leave the country within six months. If you have an FM3 (or convert your FMM to an FM3 once you are in Mexico), you can have your RV in the country for as long as your visa is valid. Keep all your paperwork.

On the road, RVs are usually treated as two-axle trucks, so tolls can be up to double the cost of a car. Some parts of the country are more prepared for RVs (visiting cities can be more difficult, for example), but most parks and campgrounds offer very affordable rates.

rented it. All major changes to the property must be approved by the landlord, though occasionally, the owner will agree to split or fund improvement projects if you suggest them.

Rented houses and apartments should be rented in good condition, usually with a new coat of paint on the walls, functional plumbing and electrical appliances, and working locks. Both the tenant and the landlord should note any defects in the apartment at move-in. If you find something wrong when you first move in, let the landlord know right away. Thereafter, unless explicitly stated, you as the renter will be responsible for all minor upkeep, like plumbing or gardening or painting.

It is not unusual for landlords to ask for proof of income, especially if you are renting in a big city, like the capital. They may request pay stubs or, if those are unavailable, copies of your bank statement. To cover the cost of any damages to the home or apartment, most owners also request a deposit in addition to the first month's rent. Sometimes, landlords will also request an additional deposit for the telephone line, since calling can be so expensive in Mexico and tenants occasionally leave large debts behind. In some cases (such as for brand new houses), the owner may request a double deposit, though this is unusual. Generally, the landlord will review a property when it has been vacated and will subtract costs from your deposit. Even small damages may be deducted, so be prepared to sacrifice some of your deposit to the wear and tear of daily living.

The *Fiador*

Mexico's laws aggressively protect the rights of renters; for that reason, many landlords feel the need to aggressively protect their own interests. To do so, some owners will ask for a cosigner on your lease, known as a *fiador*. The *fiador* must live in the same city you are renting and, in most cases, must own a property there, with no mortgage owed. *Fiadores* are commonly requested in Mexico City—and they are fairly consistently requested there! In other parts of the country, they are far less common. This pesky requirement can be particularly difficult for foreigners, who may not have an acquaintance willing to cosign their lease. Sometimes, your Mexico City employer may be able to fulfill the *fiador* requirement. If you don't work at a large company, it may be easier to look for the elusive apartments that do not request cosigners or offer to put a trust in the bank. Outside Mexico City, foreigners can usually talk a landlord out of a *fiador* by offering to pay a larger deposit.

Utilities

Unless you have a full-service rental or vacation home, you will likely be responsible for paying all the utilities on your rental property, including water, electricity, and gas. Both water and electricity bills, if not overdue, can be paid at a local convenience store or bank. Mexico does not have public gas service, so if your home needs gas, you will have to purchase it from a private company (prices, however, are fixed by the government). Many houses have *gas estacionario* (stationary gas tanks) on the roof with readable meters; you can call the gas company and refill the tank when gas runs low. If you do not have a stationary tank, you will need to buy cylinders of gas, which you hook up to your home's main gas line. When the cylinder runs out of gas, you call up the gas company and request a refill (cylinders, unfortunately, do not have meters, so you'll either have to wait until gas runs out or use multiple tanks to avoid running out).

Telephone service is the most complicated and expensive utility. For that reason, many rental homes do not come with ground lines, and those that do may ask for an additional deposit (phone bills can run hundreds of dollars if international calling is involved). If your rental home doesn't have a phone, it may be possible to solicit a new line. To do so, you will need to visit Telmex to check availability and buy a new line in your name. Once you move out, you should cancel the associated address; you can transfer your line to a new place or sell it.

Buying

Buying a property in Mexico is more complicated than renting, but it can be an excellent investment—especially if you plan to live in Mexico long-term. If you spend a little time checking out the market, acquainting yourself with the buying and selling process, and finding a good agent and notary, you will likely have a smooth and easy experience purchasing a property in Mexico.

That said, buying real estate in Mexico can be a minefield for uninformed newbies. Real estate transactions are complicated, official paperwork is written in Spanish, and the purchasing process includes steps that might not be familiar to American and Canadian buyers. In addition, brokers and real estate agents aren't legally licensed in Mexico, so the wrong real estate agent can lead you astray. Be careful, but also remember: Thousands of Americans, Canadians, and other foreign residents have successfully brought property in Mexico without incident.

The average price for a two-bedroom home in a nice neighborhood is around US$200,000, though costs vary tremendously by region and by the type of home you are buying. You can buy land for an average of US$50–75 per square meter, depending on the location of the property and the services available. Cost of land, too, varies widely by region and can be far pricier on the coasts.

FINDING THE RIGHT PLACE

Once you have decided where in Mexico you want to live, you can start looking for the right home. Obviously, all the essential factors are in effect: budget, size, location, and investment potential. However, houses can be a bit different in Mexico (both in design and functionality), so it's worth taking the time to shop around.

In general, you will have a good experience buying property if you do your research, talk to people who have successfully purchased homes, work with a trusted broker, and shop around until you find the best deal. Ben Calderoni, a real estate agent for more than 30 years, has spent more than a decade representing buyers in San Miguel. He says the biggest mistake that new buyers make is "trusting their real estate agent without really checking out the market." It's worth the extra effort to follow Ben's advice and have a good look at what's available in your area. If budget is an issue, you may be able to save a few pesos by looking in more outlying neighborhoods, in smaller towns, or at properties that need some renovation. Many buyers also like the idea of purchasing a piece of land and building a house from the ground up. No matter what you choose, it's worth investing a little time and effort into the process.

Many expatriates purchase historic and colonial-era properties, which often have a great deal of character.

Houses

You will find houses for sale by owner in any part of Mexico, with rather large and hopping real estate markets in Mexico City, Guadalajara, Puerto Vallarta, Cabo San Lucas, and other beach resorts. In most cases, the owner will list the property with a real estate company—and sometimes with several (exclusive listings aren't particularly common in Mexico). Note that house listings may include patio and outdoor spaces as a part of the total square footage.

Typical Mexican houses are often a bit different than what you'd find in the United States and Canada. Even if they aren't historic, many houses take a cue from traditional Spanish design, with central patios or courtyards around which the rooms of the house are arranged. You may also notice that front yards are not particularly popular; residential streets are usually lined with tall and impenetrable walls. To see what a house is really like, you need to peek behind the doors. Often, you'll be surprised to see what's on the other side!

For many foreigners, the biggest difference in Mexican housing is the more fluid relationship between indoor and outdoor space. Because the climate is more generally agreeable in Mexico, many homes have drafty uncovered hallways, central patios, or even open-roof living areas. Many foreigners—used to more control over the indoor climate—feel the need to remodel houses with lots of outdoor area, sealing up the windows and hallways so they can run air-conditioning or heat.

Land

Buying land and building a home can be a good investment, as well as a rewarding experience. There are plenty of skilled architects, contractors, and builders who can help you realize your project, and building your own house

REAL ESTATE TERMS IN MEXICO

When checking the paper, talking to real estate agents, going over paperwork, or signing a lease, it's a good idea to know the basic vocabulary.

- agent: *agente*
- appraisal: *avalúo*
- attorney: *abogado*
- bathroom: *baño*
- bedroom: *recamara*
- certificate: *certificación*
- community land: *ejido*
- cost: *costo*
- credit check: *verificación de crédito*
- deed: *escritura*
- deposit: *depósito*
- escrow: *depósito de confianza*
- floor: *piso*
- for rent: *se renta*
- for sale: *se vende*
- furnished: *amueblado* or *amueblada*
- furniture: *muebles*
- installed kitchen: *cocina integral*
- insurance: *seguro*
- interest: *interés*
- land: *terreno*
- lease: *arredamiento*
- loan: *préstamo*
- mortgage: *hipoteca*
- mortgage loan: *préstamo hipotecario*
- neighborhood: *vecindad*
- notary: *notario*
- price: *precio*
- purchase contract: *escritura de compraventa notarial*
- purchase option: *opción de compra*
- purchaser: *comprador*
- real estate: *bienes raices, inmueble*
- registry: *registro*
- rent: *alquiler, rentar*
- roof: *techo*
- room: *habitación*
- seller: *vendedor*
- sublet: *subarrendar*
- surveyor: *topografo*
- tax: *impuesto*
- term: *plazo*
- title: *título*
- transfer: *traspaso*
- transfer tax: *impuestos de traspaso*
- trust: *fideicomiso*
- value: *valor real*
- well: *pozos*

© ARTURO MEADE

Traditional Mexican houses are built around a central patio or garden, sometimes used for alternate purposes like laundry or parking.

gives you more control over the property and its design. It is, however, a more complicated process than buying a house directly.

You may be able to find an empty lot in the center of a city, but there are far more available in suburban neighborhoods and throughout Mexico's countryside. Some lots are sold as part of a general development, where each parcel is already equipped with electricity, water, sewer hookups, storm drains, and access to paved roads. If you are looking at lots outside a city, one of the primary considerations is its access to utilities like water and electricity, as well as access and maintenance of roads. Places off the beaten track may not have electrical hookups, and it may not be a quick or simple process to connect to the grid. If you do not have water on the land, it is possible to dig a well; however, the cost of a well is determined by how deep you have to dig. It can quickly add up if water is a long way down; do your research and consider the cost of installing utilities in the total cost of a property. At the same time, lots without utilities can be far cheaper, presenting an opportunity for those interested in building in an ecofriendly way. Just be ready for the challenge!

In addition to privately held land, Mexico has a system of *ejidos,* or communal land, that was established after the Revolution of 1910. *Ejido* land is not private property, but communally owned territory that is designated for use as residence, common land, and farmland. Until recently, *ejido* land could not be bought or sold. However, in 1992, during the presidency of Carlos Salinas, the New Farm Act discontinued the *ejido* system. Today, *ejido* land can be sold, but it must be converted to private property first. To do so, the entire community designated as "owner" must agree to the sale. If all owners are not notified, the sale could be annulled. For Mexican nationals, the buyer can become a member of the *ejido,* to whom the land will eventually be transferred when the property becomes regularized. For foreign nationals, it is necessary to find a *prestanombre*—a Mexican national who will stand in for the buyer. The buyer, in the meantime, has no rights to the land. *Ejido* land is often far more inexpensive than private property, so some foreigners risk the investment. However, there is no entirely safe way to buy communal land without running the risk of losing control of the property. Anyone looking at *ejidos* should use caution and assume the associated risks.

Lynn Rawden and her husband purchased *ejido* land on the coast of Oaxaca. She explains:

> We have a presta nombre – our friend in San Miguel offered to put the land in her name, and in return we are offering her a small portion of it. And the ability to visit our house (when we have one!) anytime she wants. It was ejido land, so our plot was cheap but well supervised by the community. It still is risky in the sense that we have heard several stories of nullified documents and debated land rights. But so far, we have been lucky. We have had to visit the site every year at least once, meet with the communitario [the community council] there, and maintain relations with them. We are expected to "improve" the land constantly, by clearing it, posting it, and putting up some basic structures. This ensures our ownership as well as signifies our dedication to the project, and most importantly employs the local people.

Resort Communities and Condominiums

Those looking to make a quick transition without worrying about remodeling, refitting, or building a new place can buy into a development. In many beach towns, as well as in colonial cities, there are large residential communities that are built and overseen by a single company. Many offer diverse living arrangements (with similar design), and some even provide furnishings in the total cost—a good pick for those who don't want to go through the hassle of moving their household items.

Many developments offer the opportunity to invest in a condo before the development is complete. The rates for prepurchased houses may be significantly lower. These places may also have finance plans.

© ARTURO MEADE

Inside many Mexican homes, there is a fluid relationship between indoor and outdoor spaces.

Restricted Zones

Foreign citizens are permitted to buy property anywhere in Mexico with the permission of the Mexican Foreign Affairs Ministry, with the exception of the restricted zones. When registering their purchase, foreigners must agree to adhere to Mexican law and waive any right to foreign intervention. When selling a property, foreigners are permitted to sell at a profit to either national or foreign buyers.

According to Mexican law, foreigners cannot buy a simple title for any property located within 100 kilometers of an international border or within 50 kilometers of the coast. However, there is a legal pathway through which foreigners can secure all rights of the owner, even in a restricted zone. In these cases, foreigners can establish a *fideicomiso* (trust) at a Mexican bank or credit union, and then purchase the property through the trust. The trust can be purchased for up to 50 years, with the option to renew when the original term is up. In this case, the beneficiary (or the foreigner) has all rights to the land—including resale for profit.

REAL ESTATE AGENTS

Most buyers work with a real estate company when looking for and purchasing a property. Generally, real estate agents will show properties for sale and help broker the contract when you find a place you like. Because the contracts are all created in Spanish and because the buying process is different in Mexico than elsewhere, it is important to find a trustworthy real estate agent with a good understanding of the buying and selling process.

In Mexico, not all real estate agents are created equal. Here, there is neither government oversight of the real estate market nor any official licensing for real estate agents. In fact, anyone with a piece of land to sell can set up a real estate agency. Not surprisingly, plenty of entrepreneurs will try their hand at representing buyers and sellers. You'll see a proliferation of agents in booming real estate markets, like San Miguel de Allende.

That said, there are plenty of great brokers who can help you find the right place, make an offer, and close on a sale. Real estate agents can be a great source of advice; they can often help you learn a bit more about the local market and make informed choices. The Asociación Mexicana de Profesionales Inmobiliarios (AMPI), or Mexican Association of Real Estate Professionals, is an independent organization that outlines rules, regulations, and ethics for real estate agents and the sale of real estate. If possible, it is best to choose a broker who is a member of AMPI, if you don't have a personal recommendation.

MAKING AN OFFER AND CLOSING

When it comes to buying and selling in Mexico, getting the paperwork right is incredibly important for foreign buyers. At this point in the process, you will need the help of a trustworthy *notario publico,* or notary public. Unlike a notary in the United States, a public notary in Mexico is a highly trained, government-appointed lawyer who is responsible for overseeing all contract terms and the transfer of assets. Generally speaking, the notary should be able to handle all aspects of the transaction; you do not need another lawyer.

First, the notary will help verify that there are no title disputes or liens against your property. Before making any purchase, you must ascertain that the current owner can present the *escritura publica* (public deed) to the property, as well as the *certificado de libertad de gravamen* (lien certificate). In uncommon but serious cases, foreign buyers have been duped into buying properties from someone who isn't the legitimate owner. In addition to these steps, you may also want to get a property map and check it against the actual property. It may be a bit smaller or larger than advertised, which you may use to bargain the price.

Once you are satisfied with the legality of the property, you must work with the notary to make a written offer, known as the Promise to Purchase and Sell. The promise includes terms for a deposit on the property and is usually accompanied by a check for part of that amount. There is no escrow in Mexico, so a paid deposit can be difficult to recover, if the deal does not go through. Always conduct all financial transactions through the notary. Remember, although notaries are responsible for creating a valid contract, they are not responsible for insuring the title to the property. Foreigners do have the option of investing in title insurance to protect their investment. Under any circumstance, be sure to include a clause in the contract that specifies the date that the title will be transferred to the new owner.

Finally, before the final transaction, all foreign residents must register their purchase of property with the Ministry of Foreign Affairs, where they must agree to adhere to Mexican law and waive any right to foreign intervention. Once all of these steps are complete, closing usually takes between 30 and 180 days.

FINANCING

Until recently, Mexican banks extended very little credit, and it was difficult for both national and foreign buyers to borrow in pesos. In the past, foreigners had to borrow against their current home, pay directly, or finance a purchase through a Mexican bank at incredibly high interest rates.

Today, things have changed. Mexican banks—most of which are foreign owned—have larger lending and mortgage programs, allowing nationals and residents to borrow in pesos at a reasonable interest rate. You can also finance a property in Mexico though a collateral mortgage company in the United States, many of which even cover the cost of up to 80 percent of a property in restricted zones. Many of these companies will process all the financial documents in the United States, and some require title insurance to process your mortgage. Your real estate agent should be able to recommend a good international mortgage company.

Even if you are financing, you should still be prepared to pay between 20 and 30 percent up front. Generally, the buyer also covers all closing costs, some of which differ in Mexico. Thereafter, you can expect adjustable or fixed interest rates at roughly between 9.75 and 12 percent, usually with 15- to 25-year terms.

BUILDING AND REMODELING

Low labor costs and ample open space make building your own home affordable in Mexico. Many expatriates prefer to oversee their own design project rather than purchase a prebuilt home. To do so, you will need the assistance of an architect and a reliable contractor. Even if you have experience building, an architect can be a valuable asset to your project by helping you secure the proper building permits and plan the construction. For a contractor, ask around for recommendations and work together with the architect to create a detailed estimate for the construction, as well as a payment schedule for the construction team. Construction costs vary by region, and, as anywhere, they tend to go up as the project progresses. Work with the contractor to fix a price for the project. If you want more savings, consider visiting suppliers to see what types of materials you can purchase at a discount.

It is best to be available to the crew while construction is taking place so you can attend to any last-minute details or decisions, and to make sure the project remains on schedule. Once the construction is complete, you need to present a manifestation to the local property tax department. The manifestation includes, among other items, the plans for the house, the deed to the property, and costs paid to construction workers. This document will serve as the basis of tax calculations if you eventually sell the property—and it will save you lots of money to do it at the right time.

This house in Mineral de Pozos in Guanajuato was constructed with a collection of irregular stones.

© ARTURO MEADE

SELLING YOUR HOUSE

Foreign owners of Mexican property are free to sell at any time. If you purchased your home through a *fideicomisco,* you retain all rights to sell the home at a profit. In order for you to sell your home, all utilities and fees must be paid up to the date of closing. If you have lived in your home for fewer than five years, you will also pay capital gains tax, around 30 percent of the net profit.

Setting Up Your Household

ANNUAL PROPERTY TAXES

It is common practice for the buyer to pay the acquisition tax and all related closing fees, including the notary fee. Thereafter, property taxes—or the *predial*—are typically very low in Mexico, usually accounting for less than half of 1 percent of the value. Most people pay just a couple hundred dollars per year. The government stipulates that you must pay taxes on the selling price of your property or the official appraisal of your property, whichever is higher.

UTILITIES

Once you've moved in, you will need to set up your utilities. If you are living anywhere "on the grid," you can set up an account with the Comisión Federal de Electricidad (CFE), the Federal Electricity Commission. If your home does not have electricity, you can easily get a new service contract if there are already electric poles on your street, an electric post is located within 35 meters of your home, and the home has an installation to receive the energy cable and meter. Water service is provided by different regional companies. Both water and electricity bills can be paid at their respective offices, or, if not overdue, at banks and certain convenience stores.

Contrary to popular belief, Mexican tap water is treated before it is pumped into your house. Nonetheless, it is generally considered unsafe as drinking water. Therefore, most households order large water jugs, called *garafones,* for drinking water. Alternatively, you can make tap water safe for consumption by boiling it for three minutes or treating it with iodine, chloride, or colloidal silver. Purifying drops are sold at most supermarkets and corner stores. Note that these techniques do not remove metals and additives, only bacteria.

Unlike water and electricity, gas is not managed by the government but by private companies. There are no public gas lines. For gas at home, you must install a tank on your roof and call a gas company to refill it periodically. If you do not have or cannot install a stationary tank, you can buy cylinders of gas from the gas company and call to have them replaced when they run out. Gas trucks generally circle through the city center, playing a song as advertisement; even if you haven't specifically called them to ask for more gas, you may be able to flag them on the street.

TELEPHONE, INTERNET, AND TV

Mexico's largest telephone company, Telmex, owns more than 90 percent of the country's telephone lines (as well as most of the cellular telephone service). In most cities, it is fairly easy to solicit a ground line for your house if it doesn't already have one. To do so, go down to your local Telmex office. In many cases, a line will be immediately available in any property that previously had a phone line. You simply sign the paperwork and pay a rather hefty fee to have the line installed.

If your property never had a phone line, the process can be easy, or it can be complicated. If you live in a very small town or far outside a city center, Telmex may not already have run local phone lines. In some cities, Telmex also runs out of new lines. If your town does not have any new contracts available, you can be asked to be placed on a wait list for a new telephone number when one becomes available. This process can take a few months.

Residential Internet connections are inexpensive and easy to install. Anyone with a phone line can immediately set up a DSL connection with Prodigy through Telmex. Telmex will provide you with a cable or wireless modem; there is a small surcharge (around US$20) for Internet service. You can also get a cable connection to the Internet through your cable company. Usually, the company will sell you a full package that includes cable television, Internet, and possibly telephone. In some cases, you may be able to set up just an Internet connection.

In most places, you can get several basic television channels by plugging your set into the wall and using an antenna. However, you'll get much better reception if you use a cable. For cable television, there are several Mexican companies that offer basic digital cable and "on demand" television service, as well as high-definition television. Basic service generally includes programming in English; the more comprehensive option you choose, the more English-language options you will have. You can also get SKY satellite television for far more diversity of English-speaking programming, including movie channels. Though these are the two most popular options, there are several other cable television companies operating in Mexico.

In general, if you have a basic telephone plan, including local calls and some national long-distance, your telephone bill will likely run between US$60–120 per month, depending on your usage and how often you call cell phones or lines in other area codes. Costs for other communication tools depend on where you live and what companies provide service to your area. In most places, cable costs around US$30 for basic service. Internet is usually bundled into telephone or cable packages, and costs an additional US$25 per month on average. On its own, the cost will be a bit higher.

HOUSEHOLD HELP

It is inexpensive to hire household help in Mexico, and many foreigners find their budget is sufficient to include a housekeeper, and possibly a cook or gardener. Most household laborers—including housekeepers, child-care workers, cooks, and gardeners—work for a daily wage. Costs vary depending on location, but are generally very low compared with most industrialized countries, ranging from US$25–60 per day for housekeepers, and US$35–85 per day for cooks or gardeners. (Foreigners should check with other people in the local region and pay a fair wage to their employees.) When you hire someone for the home, ask for their daily rate and hours. You should be prepared to offer a raise to any household employees every one to two years. If your housekeeper also cooks or performs child care, you should be prepared to pay more for his or her services.

Labor Laws

Unfortunately, there are few laws that protect the rights of household workers in Mexico. However, many people work in the informal household economy, and foreigners should make every effort to comply with the highest standards. If you can afford the luxury of household help, treat your household employees with the same rights and respect as you would at home, even if they aren't "on the books." Even though you may have the opportunity, do not hire anyone to work in your home who is under the legal age limit of 16 (and anyone under 18 must have permission from their parents to work). For blue collar labor, the average work week is six days, 48 hours.

As the foreign employer, you must also be responsible for treating your household employees with the same rights as they could expect in the workplace. If your employee's regular shift falls on a national holiday, like Independence Day or Christmas, you should always give your employees a paid day off. If your employees request a day off for religious or personal reasons (a birthday, the anniversary of the Virgin of Guadalupe), it is up to you whether you simply want to grant him or her the day off or pay for the day. During the winter holidays, it is also customary to give an *aguinaldo,* or Christmas bonus, to every employee. Generally, this bonus should be roughly equivalent to a month's salary for your employee. For newer employees, it is acceptable to give a bit less for the first few years, but no less than two weeks' salary. In the case that you need to dismiss a household employee, give ample notice and a severance package that is equal to at least several months of pay. Legally, Mexico requires three months plus 20 days of severance pay for any employee who is laid off for no fault of his or her own.

Aside from these necessary rights, you should make an effort to be a responsible employer. If your employees are not enrolled in the public health program, Instituto Mexicano de Seguro Social (IMSS), you should consider helping with medical costs or, at the very least, prescriptions. Medical services are relatively inexpensive in Mexico, and most foreign employers can make some contribution. If you hire someone to work in your home who is under 18 years of age, consider offering assistance with schooling or coursework.

LANGUAGE AND EDUCATION

Spending time in Mexico is a learning experience in itself. Whatever you come to do, you will certainly learn from the culture, from the food, and from the way of life. You'll likely pick up some Spanish, become more proficient in Mexican geography, and learn to use the metric system. And, if you want to take a more formal approach to education, there are plenty of opportunities to study—for students of any age.

Learning the Spanish language is far and away the most popular reason people come to study in Mexico, though you can also get an education in many other areas, too. For college undergraduates or adult students, many Mexican universities and private schools offer courses in Mexican history, art, and culture. Throughout the country—and especially in cultural havens, like San Miguel de Allende—artists and writers give workshops in English and Spanish. Foreign children also have positive experiences enrolling in Mexican schools, where they can receive a strong (and sometimes U.S.-accredited) education while also learning the language.

Learning the Language

Many people hope that moving to a foreign country will automatically rewire their brain for high-speed language learning. Just a few months in Mexico, and you'll be chatting casually in Spanish with your next-door neighbor! Unfortunately, learning to speak a foreign language isn't so easy for most of us. Learning Spanish takes time, patience, and practice. If you are starting from scratch, you'll probably need to take classes, spend some serious time repeating your verb conjugations and practicing grammar, and tuck away your initial self-consciousness as you practice your halting Spanish on (hopefully) understanding strangers.

Most people come to Mexico with the intention of learning or improving their Spanish. The biggest stumbling block for most well-intentioned foreigners is the prevalence of English spoken in Mexico. Because the country's gross domestic product (and many local economies) relies heavily on tourism, most people in the service industry speak at least conversational English. Many of Mexico's primary and secondary schools are bilingual (and those that aren't usually require English classes), so even those who don't work in the tourist industry are likely to know a little bit of English. Among the educated classes, speaking English is almost universal, and many people take frequent trips to the United States. Especially in social situations, it's tempting to simply chat in your native tongue rather than plow slowly through verb conjugations.

For the same reason, learning to speak Spanish isn't a necessity in Mexico. Plenty of foreign residents live in the country for decades but have never moved beyond the basics required to order food in a restaurant or direct a taxi to their home. Many of these people love Mexico, have Mexican acquaintances, and have taken beginning language classes. However, most of these people would tell you that they're missing out by not being able to use the language.

Yes, it takes some work, but the rewards are well worth the effort. Learning to speak Spanish will offer you a much richer and more fluid experience in Mexico. To begin with, Spanish is the official language used in all contracts and official documents. Being able to understand and read a bit of Spanish will help you navigate immigration paperwork, housing negotiations, and daily chores without making too many mistakes or hiring someone to help you. Despite the prevalence of English in Mexico, you may still find yourself in a position where you absolutely need to explain something to someone— say, an immigration official at the airport—in Spanish. For anything official, it helps to have some ability with the language.

Socially, speaking Spanish will open up the possibility of creating friendships in the local community without being limited by your language skills. Speaking only English does not preclude the possibility of having Mexican friends, but it certainly limits you to English-speaking people and functions. Finally, learning to speak Spanish is a matter of respect. Anywhere in the world, immigrants are expected to learn the basics they need to communicate with locals. And, just like anywhere else, Mexicans wonder at people who live a long time in their country without learning to speak Spanish.

The good news is, Mexico is an excellent place to learn Spanish. People in Mexico are generally friendly and patient when newcomers are practicing the language. Despite some regional accents, most Mexicans speak clear and easy-to-understand Spanish, with nice phonetic pronunciation. You might also notice that Mexicans often tell stories with animated hand gestures, which can make it all the easier to follow the course of conversation. Best of all, there are many inexpensive and high-quality language schools throughout the country where you can get excellent Spanish instruction at any level.

LANGUAGE SCHOOLS

Mexico is a popular place to study Spanish. There are hundreds of Spanish-language schools throughout the country, many open for years. Depending on your goals and availability, options include intensive two-week programs, laid-back introductory courses in small groups, and one-on-one tutoring sessions.

When deciding where to study, consider your learning goals, your time commitment, and your living situation. Are you looking for course credit or a semester-long program, or do you prefer a flexible schedule to accommodate travel and personal time? Do you want cultural activities and field trips to accompany the curriculum? Are you looking for an academic curriculum, or a place that will focus on conversation skills? There are as many different Spanish-language programs as there are diverse students to fill them. Unless you are living in a place with only one school, shop around. You'll find there is quite a variety in offerings and approach.

Private Language Schools and Tutors

There are excellent and inexpensive private language institutes throughout Mexico. Cuernavaca, Oaxaca, San Miguel de Allende, Guanajuato, Guadalajara, and Mexico City are some of the most popular places to study, though you're likely to find a Spanish school in any sizeable city or tourist-friendly town. If you'd like to do your homework while listening to the crash of ocean waves, you can even study Spanish at the beach.

The most popular option for foreign students, private language academies usually employ local teachers for small group or individual classes. Most offer flexible class schedules, allowing new students to start every week or two. Each school has its own approach to pedagogy. Some have proprietary curriculum, while others use major textbooks. While some programs are more leisurely, others offer the opportunity to earn college credit for study. In short, there is a wide variety in quality, cost, and method, so check websites and read student reviews before choosing a school.

For greater flexibility and more one-on-one attention, private tutors are also a popular option—especially for foreigners who want to acquire a very specific vocabulary. Many private schools will provide experienced tutors, though they take a commission on each class. It can be a bit cheaper to find someone on your own; check the classifieds in a local paper.

University Programs

Many of Mexico's public and private universities offer intensive Spanish-language classes to foreign students. In many cases, the credit from these classes can be transferred to a U.S. or Canadian college. Among the most noted programs, the prestigious Universidad Nacional Autónoma de México's Centro de Enseñanza Para Extranjeros (Center for Instruction for Foreigners), or CEPE, offers blocks of intensive introductory, intermediate, and advanced Spanish-language classes. In Guadalajara, the same acronym stands for the Centro de Estudios Para Extranjeros (Center for Study for Foreigners) at the University of Guadalajara, a special language institute for foreign students. You will also find language programs at some regional universities, including the Universidad de Guanajuato.

University programs tend to be more rigorous and less flexible than programs you'd find at a private language school, often following a semester system. Many also offer related cultural and art history classes in Spanish. In some cases, the university can help you find local housing; plan in advance if you don't have a place to stay.

Immersion Programs

As many a forlorn expatriate can tell you, it can be far more difficult to learn Spanish in a place where everyone seems to speak a little bit of English. A few hours of class a day can help you learn the basics, but if you want to ramp up your language skills quickly, the best bet is full immersion in the Spanish language. The more hours you spend thinking and speaking in Spanish, the more quickly your brain will start learning to use the language. There

VOLUNTEERING

Many expatriates are involved in long-term volunteer projects, which are a great way to get make friends in the local community, help refine your Spanish, and make a positive difference in your adopted home. Often, language schools will offer volunteer opportunities through partner organizations. You may also find that the local expatriate group sponsors a nonprofit or two.

There are a wide range of nonprofit organizations in Mexico, though you will most often find foreigners volunteering with environmental conservation groups, in children's services, or in health care. Some work directly with the community, while others use their professional skills to plan fund-raising events, coordinate volunteers, or contribute graphic or Web design. If you are interested in volunteering, the following are some of the many organizations operating in Mexico (their full contact information is listed in *Resources*).

- **Habitat for Humanity** (www. habitat.org) is a U.S.-based organization that builds affordable housing in communities in need. They operate long-term international volunteer programs (usually requiring a time commitment of 6-12 months), as well as short-term volunteer projects.

- **WWOOF Mexico** (www.wwoofmexico.org) is part of the World Wide Opportunities on Organic Farms movement, which matches willing volunteers with small organic farms throughout the country; farms provide volunteers with food and lodging in exchange for their assistance.

- **Global Exchange** (www.globalexchange.org) is a multifaceted nonprofit organization based in San Francisco, California, which focuses on human rights internationally, including activist campaigns against violence in Mexico.

- **Amigos de las Américas** (www. amigoslink.org) is an international nonprofit that matches high school and college students with community-based projects throughout Latin America, including Mexico.

- **CASA,** San Miguel de Allende, is a multifaceted nonprofit organization that provides health services, social services, and health education to rural families. They also operate a traditional midwifery school.

- **Centro Ecológico Akumal** (www. ceakumal.org). Located in the small Caribbean town of Akumal, CEA operates a sea turtle protection program in addition to conducting environmental research.

- **Playa de los Tortugas** (www.playalastortugas.com) near Puerto Vallarta needs volunteers to help patrol the beach at night during sea turtle egg-laying season.

For even more opportunities, check out the following online databases:

- **Idealist** (www.idealist.org) offers a searchable database of nonprofit jobs and volunteer opportunities throughout the world, including extensive listings for Mexico.

- **Go Abroad** (www.goabroad.com) is another youth-focused volunteer database, with searchable listings in Mexico.

are intensive immersion programs throughout Mexico, which usually combine ample classroom hours with a home stay with a local family. If you haven't already rented or bought a home, a home stay can be a great way to practice Spanish conversation in a more informal setting, while giving you the opportunity to speak Spanish almost around the clock. Many adult students and even seniors participate in home stays in Mexico. If you don't want to stay with a family, you can still participate in time-intensive language study. Numerous schools offer summer programs with intense classroom schedules.

© ARTURO MEADE

an art school and cultural center in San Miguel de Allende

ART, COOKING, AND CULTURAL STUDIES

In addition to language, Mexico is a popular place to study art, cooking, and culture. Like language schools, there are many options in these fields, from one-day workshops on making salsa to U.S.-accredited master of fine arts (MFA) programs. If you are taking cultural classes through a university or through a language institute, instruction will likely be in Spanish (a great way to improve your comprehension). However, there are also many programs and teachers who instruct in English, especially in more tourist-friendly cities.

In San Miguel de Allende, there are several art schools (one of which offers a U.S.-accredited MFA), as well as dozens of working artists who give classes in painting, printmaking, drawing, photography, weaving, ceramics, and other disciplines. Foreign students may also find opportunities to study art in Oaxaca, a major art center in Mexico and home to numerous art schools and cultural centers.

The Education System

The Secretaría de Educación Pública (SEP), or Secretary of Public Education, administrates the Mexican public school system. Public education in Mexico is free for all citizens. Foreign students may be permitted to enroll in Mexican public schools if there is space available; however, they will likely pay tuition. In most cases, foreign families send their students to private schools, of which there are abundant options.

Public education is largely overseen by state governments. It is divided into three general phases: primary, secondary, and high school. Education is compulsory through secondary school, though national graduation averages still fall a bit below that benchmark.

PRIMARY AND SECONDARY EDUCATION
Basic Education

Public schooling begins with preschool. Often referred to as *kinder* or *jardín de niños,* public preschool is free but not compulsory. All students must begin school in the *primaria,* or primary school, which spans grades 1–6, for students aged 6–11. *Primaria* is followed by *secundaria.* Roughly analogous to junior high in the United States, *secundaria* covers grades 7–9. In order to reach more rural students, the government also offers a program called *telesecundaria,* which offers instruction via television, combined with live instruction. Currently, the average Mexican completes schooling up to the second year of

School children in Cholula gather on the steps of a historic church during a class field trip.

© ARTURO MEADE

secundaria, or about eighth grade. Students in Mexico City have the highest annual graduation rate, with an average of 10.5 years completed.

Public schools in Mexico are often stretched a bit thin on resources. Student achievement is lower than what you find in most industrialized countries, especially in mathematics. To accommodate the large student population, most schools use their facilities for three daily turns: morning classes, afternoon classes, and evening classes (called *matutina, verspertina,* and *nocturna,* respectively). Usually the best students are assigned to a morning time slot. Generally, public schools do not have after-school sports or other extracurricular programs in Mexico, though students may participate in those types of programs in their neighborhood.

There are *colegios,* or private schools, for both *primaria* and *secundaria,* as well as schools that run from primary school through high school. *Colegios* are often bilingual or offer comprehensive instruction in English. Many also have art or sports programs that you won't find at public schools.

Preparatoria

After compulsory education, students have the opportunity to continue their schooling in the *preparatoria* or *bachillerato,* which is roughly analogous to high school in the United States. To be placed in public high schools, students must usually pass an entrance exam. *Preparatoria* is designed to prepare students for college; in the second two of the three years, students specialize in certain subject areas, like humanities or sciences. You can graduate from a Mexican *prepa* and then apply for admission to a U.S. or Canadian university; however, students must follow admissions requirements for their prospective college, which usually includes standardized testing, a test of English as a foreign language, and a college preparatory curriculum.

Certain well-regarded *preparatorias* are specifically affiliated with universities, such as the Escuela Nacional Preparatoria and the Colegio de Ciencias y Humanidades, which are affiliated with the Universidad Autónoma de México in Mexico City. These schools do not guarantee admission to the university, but they help students prepare for the entrance exams and usually boast very high admission rates.

International Schools

For students (both foreign and national) who want to attend college outside of Mexico, there are a number of bilingual international schools, many of which are accredited in the United States. The Association of American Schools in Mexico (ASOMEX) is an organization of 18 U.S.-accredited schools located in Guadalajara, Mexico City, Querétaro, Puerto Vallarta, and other large cities. Many of these schools operate K–8, as well as college prep high schools. The U.S. Embassy also maintains a list of bilingual schools in the capital, including British schools.

In addition, there are numerous private schools throughout the country that employ international teaching methods, including Montessori and Waldorf schools.

COLLEGES AND UNIVERSITIES

After finishing the *prepa,* students may pursue an undergraduate degree at a university, technical institute, or technical university. There are both public and private universities in Mexico, though public options far outnumber private schools. To be admitted to a university, students must pass an entrance exam. Admission is granted based on test scores.

In addition to undergraduate degrees, most universities offer graduate and doctoral programs, though many Mexican students pursue their graduate degrees overseas. Medical and law degrees are taught at the undergraduate level in Mexico, not as graduate programs. The Universidad Autónoma de Guadalajara offers an international graduate medical school program, which recruits students from the United States, Canada, and Puerto Rico. Graduates are licensed to practice in the United States and match in the U.S. residency program.

Some of the best universities in Mexico are public schools. The country's largest and most selective university is the prestigious Universidad Nacional Autónoma de México (UNAM) in Mexico City, with a combined undergraduate and graduate student body of more than 300,000. UNAM is widely respected for its programs in the humanities and medicine, among many other fields. Also in Mexico City, the excellent Instituto Politécnico Nacional (National Polytechnic Institute) offers respected programs in engineering and the sciences. This

the entrance to the Department of Philosophy at the University of Querétaro

© ARTURO MEADE

UNAM: THE NATIONAL AUTONOMOUS UNIVERSITY OF MEXICO

The Universidad Nacional Autónoma de México (National Autonomous University), or UNAM, is the country's preeminent educational institution. With an enrollment exceeding 200,000 (most of which are undergraduates), UNAM is a free public school, though its administration is totally autonomous from the Mexican government. Students must pass rigorous entrance exams to be accepted, and most study at the school's massive main campus in the south of Mexico City (the school also operates six satellite campuses across the country). Alumni include many of the country's most illustrious names and political leaders, including numerous presidents of Mexico, Nobel laureate Octavio Paz, journalist Carmen Aristegui, writer Carlos Fuentes, businessman Carlos Slim Helu, and Nobel Prize-winning chemist Mario J. Molina, among others.

In 2010 UNAM celebrated its 100th anniversary. With the decline of Jesuit and other Catholic institutions during the liberal reform movement of the 19th century, many of the country's longstanding universities closed. Founded in 1555, the Royal and Pontifical University of Mexico – renamed University of Mexico after independence – was the country's most prestigious institution until its closure in 1867; UNAM was founded as its secular alternative in 1910 by Minister of Education Justo Serra, who envisioned a school administration operating outside government control. By the 1920s, the school had gained status as *autónomo* (autonomous) of the government.

The school grew rapidly throughout the 20th century, establishing itself among the best universities in Latin America. In addition to its prestigious academic programs, UNAM has long maintained a reputation for political activism and social movements, with strong leftist ties. During the 1960s, it was the site of massive student protests; the school was occupied by the Mexican military before the Olympic games of 1968, leading to a confrontation between soldiers and students, which culminated in the famous Massacre of Tlatelolco. When the school's rector announced a tuition increase (from less than a dollar to US$150 per semester) in 1999, the school was shut down for nine months by student protests.

UNAM is also bastion of modern thought and the arts, contributing a great deal to Mexico City's overall culture, as well as to the country at large. The school's Orquesta Filarmónica (philharmonic) is the oldest symphonic group in Mexico City, performing at the school's lovely concert hall, Sala Nezahualcóyotl. In addition to that venue, the campus is home to a gourmet restaurant, an expansive public sculpture garden, and a beautiful contemporary art museum. Its campus was inducted into the World Heritage program along with Mexico City's *centro histórico* and the Xochimilco neighborhood. Not to mention, the school's football team, Las Pumas, is consistently among the best clubs in the country, playing in a stadium originally constructed for the Olympic Games of 1968.

school was established by President Lázaro Cárdenas when he nationalized Mexican oil. Throughout the country, state universities are often the best local options. Several universities, such as the University of Veracruz and Jalapa and the University of Guanajuato in Guanajuato are well respected throughout the country. A number of these schools offer exchange programs with foreign universities or programs designed for foreign students.

Though public colleges are far more numerous, there are also many private colleges and technical institutes in Mexico. Generally, public colleges are far larger and more widely recognized than smaller private schools, though not in every case. Tecnológico de Monterrey in Monterrey, and Universidad de las Americas in Cholula, are two of the most recognized private colleges in the country, and both offer exchange programs for foreign students.

STUDYING ABROAD

Many U.S. and Canadian high schools and colleges offer overseas exchange programs in conjunction with Mexican institutions. If your school does not offer preapproved programs in Mexico or you cannot find one that suits your interests, there are numerous other options for summer programs and study abroad in Mexico.

High School Study Abroad

There are several programs designed for high school students who want to spend a year in Mexico or who wish to spend the summer studying Spanish. Several year-long programs run through private schools in various parts of Mexico. In addition, many language institutes offer intensive summer programs for high school and college students. These programs usually entail a home stay with a Mexican family, meals, language classes, and frequent field trips or cultural components.

In addition, there are various educational volunteer programs that combine Spanish-language learning with hands-on volunteer work. One of the most popular is Amigos de las Américas, an international nonprofit that places students in rural communities throughout Latin America, including Mexico.

University Programs

The Universidad Nacional Autónoma de México's CEPE program for foreign students attracts pupils from across the world. The school offers eight levels of intensive Spanish coursework, as well as university-level coursework in history, literature, and art. Students may earn credits at foreign colleges. Most CEPE courses are taught at the main university campus, though there is also

© ARTURO MEADE

The main campus of the University of Guanajuato lends a lot of spirit and color to the city's downtown.

a branch for Spanish-language study in the Polanco neighborhood. There is an additional CEPE campus in Taxco, Guerrero. Similarly, the Universidad Autónma de Guadalajara operates the Centro de Estudios Para Extranjeros, also called CEPE for short. In Guadalajara, students can also earn course credit for culture and language classes with other foreigners.

In the city of Puebla, the Universidad de las Americas offers an accredited student exchange program through affiliated universities in the United States, Italy, and France, as well as dual degree programs. For students interested in attending the school but who do not attend an affiliated university, Universidad de las Americas also allows students to enroll as visitors. Classes are taught in both English and Spanish. In addition to these popular options, there are similar exchange programs offered through other public and private universities, including Tec de Monterrey in Monterrey, Nuevo León, and the University of Guanajuato in the Guanajuato.

Other Student Programs

For students who would like to spend time in Mexico, there are numerous other summer and volunteer programs. Those interested in spending time in Mexico might work as a volunteer English teacher, as a child care assistant, or with animals. There are ecological schools and volunteer programs for students who want to spend a few weeks (or a few months) studying Mexico's wildlife.

HEALTH

The availability, cost, and quality of health care in Mexico has made it an attractive destination for many expatriates. While the Mexican government still struggles to deliver adequate health care to rural citizens, foreigners living in most parts of the country will find the health system is generally accessible and affordable. Throughout Mexico, there are modern hospitals and clinics staffed by highly trained doctors, nurses, and techs. For the aging population, home care is far more inexpensive in Mexico than in developed nations, and there are a plethora of alternative therapies available, from acupuncture to homeopathy.

Living in Mexico can also be a healthy lifestyle choice for those looking for a slower pace of life, less stress, and more sunshine. Mexico tends to have a positive effect on both the physical body—as well as the psyche—though in big cities you will certainly suffer from a few negative environmental factors, like poor air quality and traffic. At the same time, urban dwellers benefit from the many hospitals and doctors available in Mexico's major metropolitan zones. Most of the best facilities are located in big cities.

© CARLOS MEADE

INSTITUTO MEXICANO DEL SEGURO SOCIAL

Health Care and Insurance

Mexico's health system is a blend of public and private services. Most of the country's health care professionals are highly trained, and care is modern and up-to-date. There are some excellent medical schools in Mexico, as well as some renowned hospitals with active medical research programs. From routine physicals to heart transplants, Mexico supports a full range of medical services.

Thanks to the low price of health care, most Mexicans do not carry private medical insurance (millions are enrolled in public programs), though there are some very good national and international plans available for those who prefer an insurance model. Foreigners can also take advantage of Mexico's public health programs, but, for a blend of reasons, most choose to use private care. In most cases, Mexico's private health care services are significantly more inexpensive than medical services in the United States or other developed countries.

PUBLIC HEALTH CARE

Through the secretary of health and as guaranteed in the country's constitution, all Mexican citizens are entitled to health care. More than 50 million people are covered by the Instituto Mexicano de Seguro Social (IMSS), or the Mexican Social Security Institute, which covers gainfully employed Mexican citizens and residents. IMSS is paid into by employers and employees, and highly subsidized by the government. IMSS offers comprehensive care to its members, covering doctor's visits, diagnostic testing, lab work, surgeries, basic dental care, and all prescription medication, as well as all emergency services. IMSS clinics and hospitals vary in quality and service, and they can be rather bureaucratic in many places. Even if you have an appointment, you will often experience a long wait to see the doctor, and referrals can take several months to be processed. Prescription drugs, though included, are often more limited than at a private pharmacy and occasionally understocked.

In addition to IMSS, social security manages Instituto de Seguridad y Servicios Sociales de los Trabajadores del Estado (ISSSTE) hospitals and clinics specifically for state employees, which covers around 17 million people.

Over the past two decades, the government has been making an effort to bring health services to the most marginalized and underserved communities. In 2004, the government made a commitment to provide universal coverage to its citizens, introducing a new voluntary public program called the Seguro Popular. The program has enrolled tens of millions and provides a range of basic medical services and medication to people who are not covered by IMSS

LA CRUZ ROJA MEXICANA

Throughout the world, the Red Cross is known for their important work in disaster relief, humanitarian campaigns, and medical support in war zones. The Mexican Red Cross – or Cruz Roja Mexicana – has also played a vital role in response to hurricanes, floods, earthquakes, and other natural disasters. However, unlike other Red Cross organizations, the Cruz Roja Mexicana plays a fundamental role in primary health care and emergency response throughout the country.

The Red Cross was first introduced to Mexico in the early 20th century, and the organization received its international charter in 1923. Originally founded to assist the Mexican military in disaster response, its role rapidly expanded. During the past century, the Cruz Roja opened hospitals and clinics throughout Mexico. Today, the Red Cross is responsible for providing primary health care to rural communities, with hundreds of clinics serving populations that would otherwise have no access to basic medical services. The Red Cross hospital in Mexico D.F. is among the biggest and best facilities in the city, attending to indigent patients in emergency cases. Just as importantly, the Cruz Roja is Mexico's principal first responder in the case of emergency. In fact, when you dial the emergency telephone line 065, it is the Cruz Roja that will answer the call and come to your aid. Throughout Mexico, almost all ambulance service (and especially those serving public hospitals) are operated by the Cruz Roja.

As a nonprofit, nongovernmental organization, the Cruz Roja is entirely dependent on volunteers and donations, and their charter prohibits them from receiving any government money. Learn more about the Cruz Roja, donate, or volunteer your time at www.cruzrojamexicana.org.mx.

or ISSSTE. At the same time, public health programs have faltered in servicing poor and rural communities. While health programs expand, millions of people have little more than basic needs met. Many also rely on the services of volunteer organizations like the Red Cross, as well as other nonprofit and nongovernmental groups.

Foreigners and IMSS

Foreigners may enroll in IMSS programs by paying a low yearly premium. Annual fees are calculated based on age but run under US$350 annually, even for the oldest age group. After enrolling, all care is covered, including drugs. IMSS works like an HMO in that you are assigned a primary care physician, and all care flows through your primary doctor's referrals to specialists. Note that you cannot choose your primary physician.

Foreigners can apply for IMSS coverage during several time windows each year. The process is rather slow and bureaucratic; it is possible to hire an agent to help you with the paperwork if you do not speak Spanish. If you want to enroll in IMSS, you cannot receive treatment for certain preexisting illnesses, such as cancer, HIV/AIDS, liver disease, and heart disease. There is a 10-month waiting period for prenatal services and maternity care, as well as a waiting period for certain surgeries, such as gynecological surgery.

IMSS is a public program aimed at Mexico's working class, so its functions and services aren't always well matched to foreign clientele. Of particular note, most IMSS doctors and health care workers speak only Spanish, especially in the first level of care. If you do not speak Spanish, you may need to bring someone along to help you at the mandatory introductory appointment.

It is further worth noting that although IMSS does offer services to foreigners, its primary function is to provide health care to Mexico's working class. The system can handle the addition of some foreign users, but it was not designed to offer health care to a large population of expatriates. Considering that IMSS already suffers from long wait times and massive patient loads, the system would be aversely affected if too many foreigners were to begin heavily using its services. If you have the financial means, choose private health care so that IMSS can maintain its focus on Mexican families. Many expatriates enroll in IMSS for emergencies and use private care for their day-to-day needs.

General Hospitals

General hospitals and clinics are public facilities operated by the Ministry of Health. They are open to anyone, regardless of their ability to pay, and many have emergency services. Foreigners may use general hospitals, which, in a small town, may be the best option for an emergency. However, these facilities are generally intended to serve the country's poorest citizens. If you go to a general hospital in an emergency, consider transferring to a private facility for ongoing care.

The quality of general hospitals vary by city, but many are excellent for emergencies. Since the inception of Seguro Popular, the government has also opened women's hospitals and mobile clinics, as well as new facilities in rural communities. Generally, these rural clinics address basic care like vaccines, flu shots, and hydration. Unless there are no other options, foreigners should seek health care elsewhere.

Military Hospitals

Mexico's strong system of military hospitals is principally designed to treat military families. However, many will also accept the public at low cost and on a space-available basis. Members of the American Legion or those who have a background or family in the military may be able to qualify for special rates at military hospitals. Many of the military's facilities are excellent.

PRIVATE CARE

Most foreigners (and Mexicans with sufficient income) pay out of pocket for private care, even if they are entitled to IMSS benefits. Private doctors and hospitals often have shorter wait times, nicer facilities, and a more time for their patients. In addition, by using private care, foreigners avoid taxing a health care system that is principally designed for working class people. Those who can afford it will often enroll in IMSS but only use it for emergency cases.

Private hospitals and clinics run the gamut in terms of cost and care. Some private hospitals offer basic clinical facilities with few frills. Other private hospitals are gleaming, spalike, and luxurious, with free coffee in the lobby and views from the bedrooms. You can get great care in all types of facilities; the key is finding a good doctor.

In addition to basic care, Mexico's private health services include many elective and state-of-the-art treatments, which have begun to attract medical tourism from the United States and beyond. In Mexico City, Monterrey, Guadalajara, and other big cities, brand new cutting-edge hospitals offer cheaper alternatives for these services.

Clinics and Doctors

There are a wide range of clinics, hospitals, and doctors in Mexico, so the patient is in a position to shop around. If you are looking for an inexpensive option, there are many basic clinics and hospitals that offer acute care, surgery, and other services. You can find an excellent doctor at even the most basic clinic, though service can be bare-bones; in many places, family members are expected to stay with a patient and help out postsurgery.

© ARTURO MEADE

Many foreigners are pleased with the quality and cost of health care in Mexico.

ALCOHOLICS ANONYMOUS

Mexico is a wonderful place to live a healthy and sober lifestyle. Many people in Mexico, both foreign and local, do not drink alcohol, and there are plenty of alternatives to tequila when you're out at a restaurant or in a social setting, from the ubiquitous *limonada* (limeade) to *aguas frescas* (fruit drink). Plus, there is a strong, highly visible, nationwide network of Alcoholics Anonymous organizations, with numerous English-speaking and Spanish-speaking meetings throughout the country.

Currently, English-language AA groups meet in Mexico City, Guadalajara, the Lake Chapala area, Puerto Vallarta and vicinity, Manzanillo, Zihuatenejo and Troncones, Acapulco, Oaxaca, Playa del Carmen, Cozumel, Cabo San Lucas, San Jose del Cabo, Alamos, Todos Santos, Loreto, and many other locations. A partial list includes:

- **Mexico City:** http://sites.google.com/site/aamexicocity
- **Lake Chapala Area:** www.aalakechapala.org
- **San Miguel de Allende:** http://12stepsanmiguel.com
- **Acapulco:** www.alcoholicsanonymous-acapulco.com/
- **Puerto Vallarta:** www.recoverpv.com
- **Cozumel:** www.aacozumel.org
- **Playa del Carmen:** www.aaplayadelcarmen.org

For those groups that do not have websites, it is easy to locate an AA group once you are on the ground. Mexico Mike (www.mexicomike.com) maintains a list of English-speaking AA meetings in Mexico. In addition, English speakers are welcome at Spanish-speaking AA meetings. You can find a nationwide directory of Spanish-speaking groups at Alcohólicos Anónimos (www.aa.org.mx).

Finding a good doctor in Mexico is usually a matter of asking around. There are many excellent general doctors and specialists in private practice, as well as working in private hospitals. Many speak English, and some have done training in the United States, Canada, or other countries. In a smaller town, expatriates tend to visit the same doctors, so it is easy to get a recommendation. In big cities you'll have more options, and costs can vary tremendously.

If you don't have anyone to ask for a personal recommendation, the U.S. Embassy maintains a list of English-speaking doctors in Mexico City who have serviced government employees. Consulates may keep similar lists of regional doctors and hospitals. If you have health insurance, your provider may also have a list of covered doctors; in this case, you can begin your search with them.

Costs and Payment

Although costs for private care are higher than IMSS, they are significantly lower than in the United States or other industrialized countries with no public health programs. Most procedures will cost you 50–75 percent less than they would in the United States, including maternity care and surgeries. A routine consult can run US$20–40, nudging up a bit for a house call. Most drugs are also affordable. Generally, private hospitals do not accept foreign insurance, though there are several national and international insurance options for those who prefer coverage.

© ARTURO MEADE

Though most expatriates opt for private health care, there are public options available, too.

In almost all cases, private health care hospitals, clinics, and doctors expect patients to pay up front or to have a valid credit card to cover the costs. If you show a foreign credit card when you check in to a hospital, you will usually be admitted without a problem. In the case that you are admitted in an emergency but cannot pay your bill, the hospital will likely stabilize your condition and then transfer you to a public facility.

In Mexico, it is often possible for middle class families to pay for health care out of pocket. Although most Mexican families aren't insured outside the public system, health insurance plans are available, both national and international, and have been growing in popularity. However, some expatriates find that the cost of health care is so reasonable that they prefer to forgo insurance altogether and pay out of pocket for health care.

Malpractice and Liability

On the whole, seeking recourse for medical malpractice is not as common in Mexico as it is in the United States. Doctors generally carry less malpractice insurance, so you will have less compensation in the event that something goes wrong. Furthermore, you cannot seek recourse in a foreign court for anything that happens to you medically in Mexico.

INSURANCE

The health insurance industry is very small in Mexico. Most middle class Mexicans are able pay for their health care needs out of pocket, or else they are covered by IMSS. Many use a combination of coverage, visiting private doctors for their day-to-day health care needs but keeping their IMSS coverage for emergency services.

To cover costs, there are options for foreigners to purchase Mexican medical insurance packages (often at low cost) or international packages, which will cover them both at home and in Mexico. However, not everyone decides to buy medical insurance in Mexico. The cost of visiting a doctor or even having a routine medical procedure is often low enough in Mexico that expatriates can pay their expenses out of pocket. Depending on your health care needs, the cost of the premium, and the coverage you want, it may be more cost-effective to do the same.

Originally from California, Pamela Thompson is a health care consultant who has been living in Puerto Vallarta for more than 20 years. With regards to Mexico's health care systems, she offers this advice:

> It is very important that foreigners know there is no such thing as "free medical care" here. It is important to have insurance that will cover major medical. Insurance is rarely ever accepted for outpatient services (consults, medications, diagnostic services), and payment must be made out of pocket and turned in for reimbursement. The plus side of this is that prices are quite low for these types of services. People should look for policies that are accepted at a private facility and that the insurance company will pay directly to the hospital (for inpatient services).

International Insurance Coverage

There are numerous international insurance packages that cover care in Mexico, as well as abroad. While there are short-term international plans (designed for travelers or those who will only be overseas for a year or two), there are also many long-term renewable health insurance plans that offer lifetime coverage if you apply before a certain age.

Generally, you set the parameters of your coverage, and the insurance company will adjust your premium accordingly. For example, many plans will offer the opportunity to be insured in both Mexico and the United States (Mexico must be your primary residence) or just Mexico, or they may include medical evacuation for U.S. citizens and Canadians who want to be treated at home in the case of a major emergency. You can also adjust your deductible, coverage limits, and treatment options to affect the cost of the premium. HCC Medical Insurance Services, Allianz, BUPA Group, and IHI Danmark are some of the popular companies offering international insurance. In addition, there are a few companies (like SkyMed) that offer medical evacuation services in event of emergencies.

Short-Term Plans and Travel Insurance

If you are going to be in Mexico for a short period of time but you would like to be covered for unexpected medical expenses, you can purchase short-term international or travel insurance. Most insurance plans aimed at travelers cover unexpected illness and injury rather than preexisting conditions. Many will also cover the cost of medical evacuation so that you can return to your home country for treatment. The Atlas plan from HCC Medical Insurance is one option. When comparing plans, be sure to ascertain how you will get care and contact the insurance company in the event of an emergency; any company offering travel insurance should have a toll-free number that you can call from Mexico.

U.S. Health Insurance

Mexican doctors and hospitals will generally not accept U.S. insurance in lieu of payment; however, some U.S. carriers will reimburse medical expenses in Mexico on a limited basis. Usually plans do not reimburse any costs for preventative medicine, and you may only be permitted to use certain hospitals or facilities. If you are heading to Mexico and have a plan in the United States that you would like to maintain, call your provider to see about their Mexico policy.

Currently, U.S. Medicare benefits do not extend to Mexico, so those wishing to use this will have to travel back to the United States to get health care. There is a small but growing movement of people who are trying to extend coverage south of the border. Proponents insist that extending Medicare to Mexico would save the U.S. government money in the long run.

Canadian Health Care Coverage

Full-time residents of Mexico from Canada may choose to declare nonresident status for tax purposes, or the Canadian government may determine that they are "nonresidents" if they have been living away from Canada for an extended period of time. Being a nonresident of Canada means you forfeit provincial health care benefits (though these benefits can be reinstated if you return to Canada, usually after a short waiting period). In order to maintain their public health benefits, many Canadians have a residence in both Mexico and Canada; though it varies by province, most Canadians must reside in Canada around 165 days out of the year if they want to maintain their health care coverage. In some provinces, you may be able to file for a leave of absence if you only plan to be away from Canada for a year or two.

DENTISTS

Dental care in Mexico is abundant, high quality, and inexpensive. Like doctors, getting a recommendation is the key to finding a good dentist. You will have plenty of options in big cities, border towns, and beach resorts.

Like doctors, dentists in Mexico cost much less than they do in the United States, with pricey procedures like crowns or tooth extractions costing as little as a third of the price as at home. In addition to expatriates, many U.S. citizens specifically plan to visit Mexican dentists while on vacation south of the border (or they make a special trip to see a Mexican dentist).

HAVING A BABY

While some return to their home country, many expatriates choose to have a baby in Mexico, securing dual citizenship for their child after he or she is born. Most insurance plans, including IMSS, enforce a 10-month waiting period before coverage begins for prenatal care. If you want to be covered during your pregnancy, you will have to plan ahead. That said, prenatal care and obstetrics are much more inexpensive in Mexico than in the United States.

In most hospitals in Mexico, the birthing experience is still traditionally allopathic. Women are routinely given pain medication during labor, husbands may not be allowed in the birthing room, and doctors frequently induce labor if the baby is overdue. Most importantly, families committed to having a natural birth experience will have to shop around. A staggeringly large percentage of births end in C-section; the national Cesarean rate is estimated around 45 percent (with some estimates for private hospitals reaching as high as 70 percent nationally), as compared to the 15 percent Cesarean rate suggested by the World Health Organization. In many cases, the doctor will present preplanned Cesarean as a birth option for mothers.

Big cities offer more options for families, with some hospitals in Mexico City offering alternatives like water birth or large birthing rooms where the father can sleep. If you are planning to have a baby in Mexico, don't get discouraged if you don't immediately find the right doctor or environment. Keep looking until you find a doctor who will help you plan the birthing experience you want.

MEDICAL TOURISM AND ELECTIVE PROCEDURES

The low cost and high quality of health care in Mexico has attracted notice from the north. For U.S. citizens with no health coverage or for those with a high deductible on their insurance, having surgery in Mexico can be a far more affordable option than in the United States. In addition, elective procedures that may not be covered in the United States, like Lasik eye surgery or plastic surgery, are generally much more inexpensive in Mexico. Depending on the procedure, costs can be 50–75 percent cheaper.

Hospitals in many big cities offer good care; there are also numerous clinics and hospitals along the U.S. border that specifically cater to the American market. Even in the interior, places like Guadalajara, where there is both a large expatriate population and tourism, hospitals and clinics may specifically cater to foreigners and medical tourists.

Pharmacies and Prescriptions

Pharmacies are abundant and well stocked in Mexico. In all large cities, there are many pharmacies that operate 24 hours; in smaller towns, at least one pharmacy will stay open all night (in some cases, they coordinate different nights when each will stay open).

Because of the high cost of health care in the United States, many Americans drive across the border to purchase prescriptions at a Mexican pharmacy. Generally speaking, most medications and prescriptions do cost less in Mexico, but in some cases they can be the same price or more expensive.

PRESCRIPTIONS

Most medication in Mexico does not require a doctor's prescription or *receta,* including drugs that are commonly prescription-only in the United States or Canada. If you know what medication you need, you can usually ask for it directly at the pharmacy. If you can, bring a packet of your current medication with you so the pharmacist can check the drug and dosages; frequently, Mexican medications are sold under different brand names and in different dosages than in other countries. If you have a necessary prescription, the best bet is to bring a few months' supply with you when you move, then consult a local doctor.

In some cases, a pharmacist will also help diagnose and recommend a course of treatment, especially for minor conditions like stomach upset, eye infections, or contraception. Often pharmacists will sell you antibiotics (which

© CARLOS MEADE

Prescription medications can only be dispensed with the authorization of a Mexican doctor, though fewer drugs require a prescription in Mexico than in the United States.

don't require a prescription) for stomach trouble; antibiotics are widely used in Mexico to treat all forms of illness. Needless to say, you will likely get a more accurate diagnosis from a doctor, and unless you know exactly what medication you need, you will do better to visit a doctor before going to the pharmacy. For anything that does require a prescription, the prescription must come from a Mexican doctor. Prescriptions from foreign doctors are illegal.

If you have chronic pain, schedule II pain medication can be extremely difficult to purchase in Mexico. Because of their potential for addiction and abuse, these substances are heavily regulated throughout the country. If you need OxyContin, Percocet, morphine, or other schedule II pain medication, you will need to see a doctor who specializes in pain treatment. Bring recent medical records to help your case. In small towns, there may not be a doctor licensed to prescribe these drugs, and, even in hospitals, there may only be one doctor on the staff with the appropriate credentials. Most pharmacies won't have more than one box in stock.

Generic drugs manufactured by the national chain Farmacias Similares can be much more inexpensive than regular brand-name pharmacies. However, there have been reports of contraband and lower standards within generic products. If you are considering using generics, talk to your doctor.

BRINGING MEDICATION WITH YOU

Generally speaking, you will have no problem bringing in a small amount of prescription medication with you for personal use, as long as you are not carrying schedule II narcotics. Customs authorities will generally consider the dosage appropriate if it covers a few weeks to a few months. Leave all medication in its original packaging. If you are planning to live in Mexico full time, you should meet with a doctor or pharmacist to determine a course of treatment using local drugs.

Almost everything you might need is available in Mexico, though occasionally newer drugs are not yet approved or on the market. If you are taking a necessary medication that is not available in Mexico, you must solicit permission to import from the Comisión Federal para la Protección contra Riesgos Sanitarios (Cofepris). A customs broker can help you with the process for a fee.

OVER-THE-COUNTER MEDICATION

Most over-the-counter medication available in the United States is also sold at a similar price in Mexico. Basic pain relievers, antidiarrhea medication, cough syrups, cold medicines, antihistamines, and antacids are all readily available, so there's little reason to purchase these at home and tote them down south. Note that ephedrine and pseudoephedrine (including the brand-name drug Sudafed) are illegal in Mexico, and they aren't sold in pharmacies. If you're caught with a bottle of Sudafed from home, it can cause some problems.

Preventative Measures

There are few serious health risks for visitors to and residents of Mexico, and there are no required vaccinations for travel. With a balanced lifestyle and reasonable precautions, most people live active, safe, and healthy lives down south. At the same time, there are a few special health considerations for those relocating to Mexico.

SHOTS AND VACCINES

Children in Mexico are vaccinated with the same series of routine immunizations common to most countries, including measles, mumps, rubella, and polio. For adults, there are no required vaccines for travel to Mexico. However, depending on where you will be living and traveling, you may want to talk to your doctor about immunizations. Generally speaking, there are more health risks in rural and remote areas than in cities or tourist resorts.

Improperly handled or undercooked food and untreated water are the source of most common health problems in Mexico. In most cases, foodborne illnesses

TEMAZCAL

Temazcal is a traditional herbal steam bath or sweat lodge with roots in Mexico's pre-Columbian era. Ritual steam baths were widely practiced throughout the Americas, and there is evidence of traditional *temazcal* steam rooms in ruin sites throughout Mesoamerica. In Mexico, *temazcal* is believed to have been a part of therapeutic treatments to promote health, as well as religious ritual. The word comes from the Nahuatl term *temazcalli* (bathhouse).

Temazcal is usually performed in a low, dark, domed stone chamber (often, it is necessary to crawl through the door on your hands and knees). Once everyone who is receiving the steam bath is arranged inside (usually seated on the floor and draped in a sheet or in minimal clothing), the room is slowly heated by pouring water over hot rocks and fragrant herbs. Often, the herbs are medicinal, and the aromatherapy aspect is complemented by the use of copal incense. The chamber becomes increasingly hot as the steam bath progresses, with temperatures reaching well over 100°F. The combination of intense steam and heat provokes profuse sweating. In some practices, the person leading the *temazcal* will beat your body with herbs or perform ritual chants to complement the mental and spiritual aspects of the cleansing.

Temazcal is a popular therapy and relaxation treatment throughout Mexico, in everywhere from low-key hippie settings to high-end spas. Each *temazcal* is a bit different: Depending on where you go, you'll have access to a different style of bathhouse, varying degrees of heat and steam, and a unique blend of herbs. Some *temazcal* are purely performed for relaxation, while others incorporate the traditional series of rituals called the "four doors," meant to heal the physical body. Along the Caribbean coast, *temazcal* may incorporate more aspects of Mayan cosmology.

While *temazcal* is generally a gentle treatment, some people with existing health conditions should avoid it. For example, anyone with epilepsy, hypertension, heart disease, or other cardiovascular problems are generally advised against *temazcal* or any other type of sauna or steam bath.

DAILY LIFE

are not particularly serious; with rest and over-the-counter medication, they will clear up on their own. In more serious cases, hepatitis A can be contracted from food or water infected with fecal matter. Hepatitis A affects the liver, and symptoms may resemble the flu, though they are more severe and can last up to several months. There is a vaccine for hepatitis A, often recommended for travel to Mexico. You can also avoid infection by eating in trusted places and correctly preparing your food at home.

Another serious foodborne illness, typhoid, is caused by the *Salmonella enterica* bacteria in contaminated food. Typhoid does occur in Mexico; it can be very serious and occasionally fatal, with very high associated fevers. There are two types of typhoid vaccinations, which are 50–80 percent effective in recipients.

Generally, typhoid vaccinations are not recommended for Mexico unless you will be traveling to remote areas; discuss the option with your doctor. Because typhoid is contracted through contaminated food, you can also reduce your chances of getting it by being aware of proper food safety and hygiene.

Though it is uncommon, there is some instance of malaria in low-lying, remote areas of Mexico, including the state of Chiapas as well as more isolated parts of Nayarit, Oaxaca, and Sinaloa. It is often necessary to begin antimalarial medication 4–6 weeks before traveling to an area where malaria is a prevalent; plan ahead and talk to your doctor about the risks.

Although H1N1 is no longer a major health concern, some foreigners may also wish to get flu shots before visiting Mexico.

INSECT-BORNE ILLNESS

Though there are a number of creepy crawlers in Mexico, the mosquito is the insect that most commonly causes illness. In addition to malaria, mosquitoes are carriers of dengue. Since 2001, there has been an increase in dengue outbreaks in Mexico, including the more serious hemorrhagic form of the illness. In response, the government has launched an extensive campaign against mosquito proliferation, which includes periodic checks of residences and their water storage systems, as well as insecticide spraying along public streets (it usually takes place at night to avoid spraying humans directly).

The best way to prevent dengue and other mosquito-borne illness is to avoid mosquito bites altogether. In areas with high concentrations of mosquitoes, you can prevent bites by wearing long-sleeved shirts and using DEET-based insect repellent (there are also natural, plant-based varieties of insect repellent; experiment to see which are most effective). Stay indoors or use mosquito screens at dawn and dusk, when mosquitoes are most prevalent. Sleep in air-conditioned or well-screened rooms, and consider draping your bed with mosquito netting. In addition, it is important to have proper water storage systems. Mosquitoes breed in standing water, so make sure you have functioning drainage around your home, as well as a sealed rooftop water tank.

ALTERNATIVE THERAPIES

Foreigners are generally pleased with the cost and quality of health care in Mexico, but allopathic medicine isn't your only option. Alternative therapies are immensely popular throughout the country and across demographics.

Among the most ubiquitous health-care options, *homeopatía* (homeopathy) is practiced throughout Mexico, both in big cities and small towns, and many Mexicans prefer it to traditional allopathic medicine. Homeopathy was originally introduced to Mexico by the Spanish in the mid-19th century, and the first homeopathic school opened in San Miguel de Allende not long thereafter. In the following century, many more homeopathic schools, pharmacies, and clinics were founded, including the Hospital Nacional Homeopática, or National Homeopathic Hospital, which opened in 1893 and is still in operation today. *Acupunctura,* or acupuncture, is also very popular, with both foreign and Mexican acupuncturists practicing throughout the country. Though practitioners aren't overseen by a licensing body, both homeopathy and acupuncture are highly regarded and rigorous forms of medicine in Mexico. Even the prestigious Instituto Politécnico Nacional (National Polytechnic Institute) includes homeopathic medicine as a part of their general medical department, and acupuncture is a recognized medical specialty at IPN.

In addition, Mexico has traditions in herbology that span back centuries. Certain herbs have been cultivated since the pre-Columbian era, and there is a growing interest in reclaiming the medicinal plants used by Mesoamerican cultures. One of the most popular healing traditions with pre-Columbian roots, *temazcal* is a traditional herbal steam bath that has mental and physical healing properties.

There is a general openness to alternative therapies and healthy living in Mexico, prevalent in both the national and international community. In many cities and even small towns, you can find practitioners of naturopathy, chiropractic, Feldenkrais, therapeutic massage, ozone therapy, Bach flower remedies, and Reiki, among other more unusual practices. Meditation, yoga, Pilates, and other healthy lifestyle options are also popular throughout the country.

Seniors

Many people come to Mexico to retire and stay in the country through old age. With its warm climate and friendly, family-oriented culture, it can be a wonderful place for seniors to live. Many foreigners note that Mexican society is not as deeply stratified by age as other countries are. Seniors, like children, are valued members of society and are generally treated with kindness and respect. Add in the lower cost of home health care and nursing homes, and Mexico can be a great place to spend your later years.

ASSISTED LIVING

Mexican families typically stay close throughout their lifetimes. As a matter of both cost and tradition, children usually care for their elderly parents at home. As a result, nursing homes and assisted-living facilities are not particularly common in Mexico. However, the growing number of baby boomers retiring to Mexico has created a new and rapidly growing demand for retirement communities and assisted-living facilities, especially in areas near large American and Canadian retirement destinations, including Baja California, San Miguel de Allende, and Ajijic.

Currently, assisted-living facilities in Mexico are not regulated by the Mexican government or any other governing body, so there is a wide variety in what's being offered. As more North Americans choose Mexico for retirement, AMAR, the Mexican Association for Assisted Living, is taking charge of the regulation and oversight of assisted living, and this organization can be a good resource. If you are looking for a place to retire, check out all your options. Many are clean, comfortable, and staffed by competent health professionals; others offer very basic facilities and staff without special training. A full-service facility, including meals and medical care, can often run half the price of a similar facility in the United States.

HOME CARETAKERS

Hiring a home caretaker can be inexpensive and practical in Mexico. Many expatriates find a housekeeper or cook is within their budget, and for seniors with limited range of motion, hiring someone to help with shopping, cooking, and cleaning is an affordable option. Most caretakers receive daily wages for services. Explain your needs to potential candidates.

Most household help will likely speak predominantly Spanish. If you need additional assistance, there are many bilingual Mexicans and expatriates who can be hired to make appointments, pay bills, or accompany you on a doctor's visit or to the hospital. If you need someone with a professional medical background, it will cost a bit more for home care.

Finding a home caretaker is usually best accomplished by word of mouth, or by placing an advertisement in the local paper and interviewing candidates. In some popular retirement communities or border towns there are services that can help connect you with a home health aid.

Environmental Factors

As many expatriates will tell you, living in Mexico is likely to improve your health. There is more open space, more sunshine, and a more relaxed atmosphere than most places in the world. Many find it is easier to be active in Mexico, whether it's swimming in the ocean or ambling along cobblestone streets.

However, there are a few environmental factors that can negatively affect your health and well-being in Mexico. Some new residents experience mild illness from food or water quality. There are also incidents of infectious disease and crime. With reasonable precautions, most people live healthy, safe, and comfortable lives in Mexico.

AIR QUALITY

In many of Mexico's large cities—and especially in Mexico City and Guadalajara—emissions from automobile traffic and industry have created high levels of air pollution. It is particularly noticeable during the dry season, from January to May. Air pollution can cause lung and heart problems, eye trouble, and asthma, and can be particularly difficult for the elderly and children.

Mexico City, located in a valley that traps air just above the city, is most notorious for its poor air quality. There have been strong city programs to reduce traffic and related air pollution by limiting the number of days a driver can be on the road. The program has had a positive impact on the environment, but pollution can still be a problem during the drier months.

© ARTURO MEADE

Bottled water is delivered to clients via a bicycle carrier.

DAILY LIFE

WATER QUALITY

Mexican tap water is treated, but it's generally considered unsafe for drinking in most parts of Mexico. Most people buy purified water in bottles. If you are living in Mexico long-term, you can have large plastic jugs delivered directly to your house. In addition, grocery stores sell water purification droplets, which can be added to tap water to sterilize it (though some add a slightly unpleasant taste). You can also make tap water safe for drinking by boiling it for several minutes to kill any bacteria or parasites, though this process does not remove any additives or chemicals.

In restaurants, you will rarely be served anything made with tap water, including ice. Most Mexicans do not drink tap water themselves, and they do not serve it in their restaurants or bars. Bottled water, like all bottled beverages, is always safe for drinking and is available almost everywhere.

FOOD SAFETY

Visitors to Mexico may experience gastroenteritis, a mild stomach upset that is usually called traveler's diarrhea. Diarrhea can be caused by bacteria, a virus, or a parasite, and it usually derives from contaminated food. It can also be caused by simple excess (a few too many margaritas one night) or a change in diet and water source. Over time, your stomach will likely adjust to the new water and diet in Mexico, and you will likely be able to expand your eating.

In most cases, you do not need to see a doctor about diarrhea. Symptoms should clear up with a few days of rest and hydration. You can help avoid stomach upset by properly handling food, frequently washing your hands, and eating in places where hygiene is taken seriously. Some travelers also carry small tubes of alcohol-based hand sanitizer to use in markets and street stalls.

When eating raw vegetables and some fruits in Mexico, it is best to disinfect them before consumption. In some cases, leafy vegetables, berries, and herbs may contain residual bacteria from watering or handling. For raw consumption, supermarkets sell several varieties of food sanitizer, the most common of which are made with chloride bleach or colloidal silver. If you plan to cook your vegetables, you do not need to disinfect them; the heat will kill any potentially harmful substances.

There is always more risk associated with food stands located outdoors or in marketplaces, where hygiene is more difficult to maintain. Many people are able to comfortably eat anywhere in Mexico, while others become ill after eating in markets or on the street. Use your discretion and introduce new foods into your diet slowly.

SMOKING

In most parts of Mexico, smoking indoors has been prohibited, including most restaurants and bars. In some places, bar owners are more lenient about enforcing smoking laws; however, in Mexico City heavy fines have almost entirely eradicated smoking indoors. Throughout Mexico, fewer people smoke than in the past, though it is still a more common and more inexpensive habit than in the rest of North America.

ALTITUDE SICKNESS

Most of north and central Mexico is situated atop a massive plateau, which can reach as high as 7,000 feet above sea level. Many of Mexico's most popular cultural destinations are located at a high altitude, including Mexico City and San Miguel de Allende, both located at more than 6,000 feet above sea level. Depending on where you are visiting, you may experience mild altitude sickness when you arrive. As most Mexican cities don't have a particularly alpine atmosphere, many people do not recognize the symptoms of altitude sickness, mistaking it for food- or water-quality issues. Symptoms of altitude sickness include nausea, dizziness, fatigue, headaches, or trouble sleeping. In most cases, rest and hydration can alleviate the problem, and symptoms generally abate within a few days as the body acclimatizes. If symptoms are severe or persist, see a doctor.

INFECTIOUS DISEASE

Mexico has witnessed several outbreaks of dengue fever, a serious (but rarely life-threatening) mosquito-borne illness. Dengue is a flulike sickness, most common in tropical and low-lying areas along the coasts, where mosquitoes are common. In 2009 and 2010, there were outbreaks in Guadalajara and Puerto Vallarta in Jalisco, and in the states of Nayarit, Veracruz, and Hidalgo, among others. The best form of Dengue prevention is to avoid insect bites. Wear pants and long sleeves in the evenings, and sleep in screened rooms. To combat dengue and other mosquito-related illness, the Mexican government frequently sprays insecticide within cities and townships. The government has also been sending representatives to inspect water tanks and water drainage in private homes, where mosquitoes often breed.

Typhoid fever is uncommon in Mexico but does occur in rural communities. Typhoid is contracted through contaminated food or water, and it causes severe diarrhea, as well as its namesake high fever and abdominal pain. It is usually diagnosed through a blood or stool test. Generally, typhoid is not a

DAILY LIFE

recommended vaccine for travelers to Mexico; however, if you will be traveling somewhere that is particularly rural or remote, you can discuss the possibility of inoculation with your doctor.

H1N1, or swine flu, was a major health concern during the 2009 flu pandemic. The virus first made an appearance in Veracruz, spreading to Mexico City, where more cases were reported, including fatalities. The World Health Organization eventually declared swine flu a global pandemic as it spread to the United States and Asia. Since then, news of H1N1 has disappeared almost entirely. You may still notice hand sanitizers at the entryways of restaurants, and, of course, it is always best practice to wash your hands before eating. However, swine flu is no longer a major health concern.

Malaria is a parasitic infection also born by mosquito. It is far less common in Mexico than in other developing countries, though there are malarial mosquitoes in the deep jungles along the border with Guatemala. There is no malaria risk in Mexico's resort towns.

Disabled Access

According to the government's statistics bureau, Instituto Nacional de Estadística y Geografía (INEGI), almost six million people in Mexico have some form of *discapacidad,* or disability. Across the country, both public and private institutions are becoming increasingly aware of the need for better services, specialized health care, and access for the disabled; however, there is still a long way to go in making Mexico an accessible country.

Living in Mexico today can be more challenging for the disabled, especially those with limited mobility. Very few buildings have ramps, and most public transportation does not have any access for people in wheelchairs. Simple topography can make parts of Mexico particularly challenging: Many of Mexico's cities were constructed during the 17th and 18th centuries, so streets are narrow and often lined with uneven cobblestone. If you use a wheelchair or have limited mobility, you will have the best experience in larger cities or in popular tourist destinations, where there will be more accessible facilities as well as private transportation services.

On the upside, people with disabilities are generally treated with respect and rarely patronized. Mexicans are usually courteous and polite, and it is easy to ask for help if necessary. In addition, those who require additional assistance will find the cost of at-home care is very reasonable in Mexico. Overall, it may take some special planning, but disabled people can live comfortably in Mexico.

PUBLIC PROJECTS

The Consejo Nacional para el Desarollo y la Inclusión de las Personas con Discapacidad (CONADIS), or the National Council for People with Disabilities, was established in 2005 by the federal government with the objective to oversee increased access for disabled people, as well as attend to disability-related health issues. At the department's behest, wheelchair ramps were installed in public schools and government buildings, which are now about 90 percent equipped. Hospitals are also being staffed with sign-language interpreters. In several larger cities, like Oaxaca, there are audio-enabled crosswalks. Private companies and parking lots have also begun to offer more handicapped parking spaces. (Unfortunately, it is common to see nondisabled people occupying handicapped parking spaces.) Though public transportation is still a problem in most places, as is access to most privately owned buildings, there is much greater awareness about accessibility in Mexico today.

OTHER ORGANIZATIONS AND SERVICES

In addition to public programs, there are several organizations that help the disabled visit and live in Mexico more comfortably. Based in Puerto Vallarta, the company Accessible Mexico will help arrange travel plans, as well as set up home care and other medical services, for people visiting or moving to the region. Adapta runs accessible tours to Mexico, with a focus on Cancún and the Riviera Maya.

In addition, there are numerous Web resources and organizations for travelers with disabilities, handy for anyone planning to relocate to Mexico, such as Ability Trip (http://abilitytrip.com). In addition, the U.S.-based organization Society for Accessible Travel and Hospitality, SATH (www.sath.org), provides news and information about traveling overseas with disabilities.

DAILY LIFE

Safety

Since 2006 there has been a lot of media attention focused on Mexico's drug wars. As a result, safety has become a major concern for people considering a move south of the border. While the drug-related violence is very real, it is important to understand that it is principally isolated to specific areas where there is major cartel activity. With reasonable precautions, most foreign residents of Mexico experience little threat to their safety.

POLICE

There are several levels of law enforcement in Mexico. The *policía federal* (federal police) are overseen by the Secretaría de Seguridad Pública, or the Secretariat of Public Security, in Mexico City. Federal police patrol interstate highways and respond to crime and emergencies. They have also been highly involved in the government's war against drug cartels. In addition to federal police, each state maintains a police force, as do most municipalities. Municipal police usually focus on traffic and smaller infractions, like theft or break-ins. In Mexico City (and some other tourist-friendly cities, like San Miguel de Allende), there are police officers on horseback—some dressed as *charros*—who can answer questions and give directions, while also generally ensuring the safety in central areas.

Police corruption is a real problem in Mexico, with many officers involved in crime and gang- or drug-related activities. There are also widespread problems with police brutality, especially in large protests where the people and law enforcement clash. Foreign residents are unlikely to have problems with police corruption, extortion, or violence, though it is important to note that the police are generally mistrusted in Mexico. That said, law enforcement, like many aspects of life in Mexico, is variable by region. As you get to know

Three policemen stand in front of a newsstand in downtown Mexico City.

© ARTURO MEADE

your local community, you will gain greater insight into local law enforcement; in certain areas or in smaller communities, police officers are more frequently trustworthy.

In addition to police, you may note the presence of paramilitary troops in some parts of Mexico. These groups are usually a part of federal and state operations against crime, and rarely attend to civilian problems.

CRIME

By and large, visitors and expatriates have a safe and comfortable experience in Mexico. Like anywhere, the type and frequency of crime depends on the region, with bigger cities experiencing more crime and greater dangers than small towns. In most Mexican communities, petty theft and break-ins are not uncommon. Take sensible precautions: Lock your doors, avoid traveling alone at night, don't carry excessive amounts of money in cash, and remain aware of your surroundings. In addition, there has also been a recent spate of ATM cloning, where a user's PIN number is stolen and money is extracted from her account. Although you can often have the money reimbursed by a bank, you are best to use ATMs that are part of a bank branch, rather than freestanding. Keep an eye on your account, and call your bank if you notice suspicious activity.

Foreign citizens may be tried and held accountable under Mexican law for any crimes committed in Mexico. In the case that you have been arrested for a crime in Mexico, contact your embassy. (International law requires that the Mexican government contact a foreigner's embassy at his request.)

EMERGENCIES

As anywhere, it is best to be prepared for an emergency in Mexico by having the proper telephone contacts. The Secretaría de Seguridad Pública (Secretary of Public Security) in Mexico has rolled out a number of nationwide, direct-dial emergency telephone numbers. For general emergencies, including medical, fire, and police, you can dial 066. You can also dial 065 for medical emergencies.

In addition to these numbers, you should research the numbers for first responders in your area and make note of their direct telephone lines. Look up the contact information for local ambulance services, police department, and emergency lines for local hospitals and clinics. In addition, the Cruz Roja Mexicana, or Mexican Red Cross, is a vital first responder, in addition to their work in disaster relief. Throughout Mexico, the Red Cross responds to medical emergencies and provides ambulance transport to local hospitals. In some

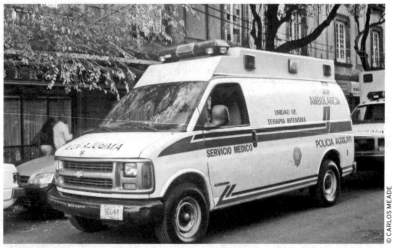

A majority of Mexico's ambulance services are operated by volunteers from the Red Cross.

cases, it is the only option available. The Red Cross responds to the 065 calls, but it is a good idea to have the local Red Cross number on hand.

You can reach the fire department by calling 068. Note that the fire department, or *bomberos,* only respond to fires, not medical emergencies.

THE DRUG WAR

Since 2007, the violent conflict between rival drug cartels and the Mexican government has created an upsurge of violence and instability in Mexico. The violence has received a great deal of media attention internationally, though it is generally isolated to specific regions, specifically the border states, plus Sinaloa, Michoacan, and Guerrero. The U.S. Department of State maintains information on their website related to drug-related dangers, as does the U.S. Embassy's website. Although the violence is unlikely to affect most visitors, take the time to familiarize yourself with the political and social situation in modern Mexico.

SAFETY FOR WOMEN

Many women live alone in Mexico or travel on their own throughout the country. Generally, Mexico is safe for women, as long as you take the common-sense precautions you would take in any country. Avoid walking alone at night, stay alert when interacting with strangers, and use good judgment with regards to drinking. Those living in the country for an extended period of time will find that Mexico is a largely provincial place, which can be advantageous for women. Once you have settled down in your neighborhood, you will likely meet your neighbors, as well as the local shopkeepers.

Women, especially young women traveling alone, may be the recipients of unwanted attention from men in some parts of Mexico. It is not uncommon for men to call out to women walking on the street alone; however, these exchanges very rarely result in any actual interaction. You can answer back, but most women—both Mexican and foreign—tend to stride right past without so much as a glance. In some instances, unwanted attention can be uncomfortable, especially in big cities. Outside of beach resorts, revealing clothing will often attract attention. Stick to more conservative attire if you want to avoid notice.

ROAD SAFETY

Practice defensive driving while on the road in Mexico. Traffic accidents are a major cause of death throughout the country. Although most toll highways are well maintained, you may find smaller roads are more patchy or have unexpected potholes. Seat belt and speeding laws are rarely enforced, and drunk driving is not uncommon. Outside of the city, it is not unusual for livestock to wander onto the road.

If you plan to drive in Mexico, buy Mexican auto insurance. Premiums are inexpensive, and the insurance company will help you navigate the bureaucratic system in the case that you are in an accident. If you are at fault for an accident, you may spend some time in jail if you do not have insurance.

EMPLOYMENT

Mexican law allows foreign residents to legally work in the country when they are offered a job and can demonstrate an appropriate skill set. Immigration law also allows foreigners to invest in Mexico by opening a business or working for themselves, though people in both these categories must also prove a small amount of foreign income to qualify for the appropriate visa.

Mexico's economy is not as robust as the economy in the United States, Canada, or other developed nations, which can have both positive and negative consequences for those who plan to work south of the border. Even though foreigners often receive a higher wage based on their unique skill set, salaries tend to be lower in Mexico. On the flip side, those relocated to Mexico by an international company may find their salary stretches much further down south, while entrepreneurs will find start-up costs are far lower in Mexico than in their home country. For those with savings, who plan to telecommute, or who work for themselves, a smaller income in dollars can stretch a lot further south of the border.

© JULIE DOHERTY MEADE

Unless you are moving to a community with many foreign residents or you plan to teach English, you will likely need to learn some Spanish in order to take a job in Mexico. Although English is widely spoken, business transactions and contracts are almost always written in Spanish.

Self-Employment and Business Ownership

There is an entrepreneurial spirit throughout Mexico, and small business is fundamental to the country's culture and economy. From corner shops and ice cream stands to restaurants and galleries, there are millions of small business owners working in Mexico.

Taking a cue from the local culture, many expatriates in Mexico work for themselves or set up a small business. Working for yourself is permitted by law and is, in some cases, easier than finding a sponsored job. Likewise, starting a small business in Mexico is not excessively complicated, and it can be lucrative; however, you will need a good idea, some capital, and some expert advice to get your project off the ground.

INDEPENDENT CONTRACTORS

If you have a professional skill that you can market in Mexico, you can apply to have your FM3 benefits cover self-employment. As a resident with the legal right to work, you can bill clients, create invoices, and pay taxes. In general, immigration does not grant work privileges for any profession; you must plan to work in a field that is uniquely suited to a foreigner or for which you have a special skill. As such, self-employed foreigners are likely to work as foreign language teachers and tutors, art teachers, translators and interpreters, writers, yoga or fitness instructors, tour guides, lawyers, photographers, and graphic designers. When you apply for your FM3 or FM2, you will need to show evidence of your skill or expertise. The evidence may be a TOEFL (Teacher of English as a Foreign Language) certificate, a university diploma, or, for artists, a portfolio of work. Approval for these visas is routine; if you have the correct paperwork, you should be granted permission to work.

Once you have the appropriate immigration paperwork (either an FM2 or FM3 with permission to work), you will need to *darse de alta* (legalize your status) with an accountant so that you can declare income and pay income taxes. If you are an independent contractor, you will be classified as a *persona física* and will have a Registro Federal de Contribuyente (RFC), or a personal tax identification number. You can use your RFC to invoice clients, who will withhold your taxes from the payment and send them to the tax authority (the ability to create legal invoices will be a huge asset to your clients; larger companies may only be willing to work with you if you can provide the correct invoicing paperwork). If you receive income from other sources, it is your responsibility to withhold and pay your taxes. Even if you weren't able to wrangle up any jobs, you must file your taxes with the government at the end of the year, even if you are declaring no income.

STARTING A BUSINESS

Starting or investing in an existing small business in Mexico can be rewarding, fun, and, if well executed, lucrative. Like anywhere, you need to have a good idea, a product that is in demand, and plenty of dedication to make a new venture work. Not all foreign business owners—no matter how many ideas or how much money they have to invest—are able to launch successful businesses. Many foreigners have sunk time and money into bars, restaurants, and other service industries only to shutter their businesses a few years later.

Before you get started, do your research and come up with a solid, marketable business idea. Though start-up costs are much lower in Mexico, you still need a good product, a marketing and advertising plan, and a projected customer base. There are plenty of opportunities for industrious and creative investors, and many foreigners open restaurants, cafés, hotels, bed-and-breakfasts, galleries, shops, design businesses, real estate agencies, and small-scale manufacturing companies, to good effect.

There is some paperwork involved in starting a legal business, and the best thing to do is seek the assistance of an experienced accountant. Unless you live in a city where English is widely spoken, you should also have basic Spanish under your belt or a trusted person to assist you with the paperwork.

© ARTURO MEADE

Many foreigners open their own businesses or get involved in community projects, like farmers markets.

Both legal residents and nonresidents can own a business in Mexico, but you will need the right visa if you also plan to work in your business rather than employ others.

If you are planning to invest in a large or international corporation, you will need the ongoing help of seasoned professionals. The information in this section refers to small business, one with fewer than 50 employees. Even for a small business, there are several different options for setting up a legal corporation, and it makes sense to solicit professional advice when deciding which is right for you.

Sole-Ownership Companies

For a sole-ownership corporation in Mexico, you must be legally registered to perform *actividad empresarial* (business activity). For very small businesses, the Servicio de Administración Tributaria (SAT), Mexico's federal tax board, offers a designation called *pequeños contribuyente,* or small contributor, which is exclusively available to businesses owned by a sole individual. In most cases, if you make fewer than 1.5 million pesos per year (about US$120,000), you will qualify. *Pequeños contribuyentes* have simplified tax filing rules and pay a low flat-rate tax on their profits. Generally, the benefits to registering as a *pequeños contribuyente* are great, but there are some restrictions to the designation. For example, small contributors cannot purchase property under their business name.

Forming a Corporation

In Mexico, the majority of business owners apply to open a limited liability stock corporation, or Sociedad Anónima (S.A.), for a fixed capital company, or Sociedad Anónima de Capital Variable (S.A. de C.V.) for a variable capital company. Corporations in Mexico are similar to corporations elsewhere in the world.

The other option is to open a limited liability company, which receives the designation Sociedad de Responsabilidad Limitada (S. de R.L.) for fixed-capital companies, or Sociedad de Responsabilidad Limitada de Capital Variable (S. de R.L. de C.V.) for variable capital companies, with members liable only for the amount of their investment. These are legal entities with associated rights and obligations. When determining what will best suit your business, you may want to work with a consultant, the American Chamber of Commerce, or other trusted contacts.

If you are planning to open any form of corporation, the first step is to solicit a permit from the Departamento de Relaciones Exteriores (Department of

PATRICE WYNNE:
A SMALL BUSINESS OWNER

Patrice Wynne moved to San Miguel de Allende, Mexico, from Berkeley, California, where she was the longtime owner of an independent bookstore and cultural center called Gaia. She came to Mexico at a time of great personal change but says, "I love small business; I love giving back to the community...it's just an innate value that I have." So of course, it was only a matter of time before she found a way to get involved in her adopted home.

Today, Patrice is the businesswoman and creative force behind **San Miguel Designs** (sanmigueldesigns.com), a community-based clothing and design company, for which a group of local seamstresses creates colorful, Mexican-themed aprons, ties, kimonos, handbags, and pajamas, in addition to other merchandise. She explains, "Anything the seamstresses can make, we can start a product line."

After getting her product line launched, Patrice opened her own store in San Miguel. She named it **Abrazos** (Embrace) in honor of the Mexican people who had embraced her and her new life. Here, Patrice shares some insights on life, business, San Miguel de Allende, and Mexico.

ON DECIDING TO
RELOCATE TO MEXICO
San Miguel is *divino* – it's just divine.

It's so beautiful; it's so inspiring just by its very essence; it's glorious. When I first closed the bookstore I was actually very sad; it was a big loss in my life and in the community's. Also my marriage ended at the time, so there were a lot of changes. I thought: I could stay in Berkeley and be very sad for a long time, or I could let Mexico work its magic, because I've loved that country since I was a child, and I speak a little Spanish.

WHY SAN MIGUEL
DE ALLENDE
San Miguel is just gorgeous. It's one of the most beautiful places you could ever visit. It's a colonial town that's very well preserved; it's a UNESCO World Heritage Site, so there's been a lot of investment in the infrastructure; it's easy to navigate. It's a town that takes care of itself.

Some people say, "Oh San Miguel, so overrun by Americans." Not true! If you believe that, you're hanging out in the wrong place...I often say that San Miguel is slow and sweet and sensuous and sophisticated... It's got art galleries, and this documentary film festival, and lots of interesting people you can meet really easily.

ON OWNING A BUSINESSS
If you want to learn the language

Exterior Relations), which receives your company name and checks it against existing companies. Once your name has received approval, you must work with a *notario* (notary) to draw up the articles of incorporation and enter your business name into the Registro Pùblico de Comercio (Public Registry of Commerce). Before you can sign the deed of incorporation, you must have a draft of the company's bylaws and charter; a notary public can help you

© ARTURO MEADE

Patrice Wynne in her store, Abrazos, in San Miguel de Allende

ates lots of opportunities to give back to the community.

HER BIGGEST CHALLENGE

The biggest challenge facing any of us who have businesses in Mexico right now is the propaganda and the focus on Mexican crime, which is not really *the* story. It is *a* story, but it's not *the* story. The story is the amount of expats who are moving to Mexico because of the outstanding quality of life that you can have there, the marvelous people who you get to know, and the reduced cost of living, dramatically, on almost every count. So people are finding they have a higher quality of life for a lot less.

I think it's a very great public relations and public image problem that's affecting small businesses at every level...There are areas in Mexico that are dangerous – the borders have some degree of concern, of course – but it's like there's a war in Texas and Europeans aren't coming to New York City.

ON HER FUTURE IN SAN MIGUEL

I love it. I love it. I love it. It's where I want to grow younger. It's where I want to continue the rest of my life. I don't see myself moving back [to Berkeley]. I have a wonderful house; I have a fantastic staff running my business.

and you want to understand the Mexican people and the Mexican culture, the best way to do it is to start a business, as I did when I opened Abrazos. I have had more interesting conversations, and more understanding of Mexican society and Mexican ways of being, by working in the store and talking to Mexicans who travel there. And also donating your time and energy and knowledge to nonprofits and other organizations in town, which San Miguel abounds in, cre-

with these documents, though fees can be substantial, so get a recommendation and agree to a price before you start working. Remember that notaries in Mexico are highly trained, government-appointed lawyers; their costs can be high, but finding the right person can be well worth the cost and effort. Once the articles of incorporation have been included in the public record, you must solicit your tax registration number or RFC, which you will need to issue invoices. (Official invoices must be generated with your RFC number from special printers.)

Finally, if you plan to hire employees, the company must register with Instituto Mexicano de Seguro Social (IMSS) and Instituto del Fondo Nacional de la Vivienda para los Trabajadores (INFONAVIT) for all employees, as well as with the local tax authorities. Remember, just because you own a corporation in Mexico doesn't mean you are legally allowed to work there; if you plan to open a business, talk to your notary about appropriate work permits.

Income Taxes

Anyone earning money in Mexico must pay federal taxes, no matter how little they earn. Tax evasion is not uncommon, particularly among small single-person businesses, but any foreigner planning to earn money from self-employment or their own business should be prepared to file and pay taxes annually. (If you are hired permanently by a Mexican company, they should deduct your taxes from your earnings.) For small business owners, tax liability will depend on your business type. The federal corporate tax rate is 30 percent; small contributors and independent contractors pay a very low flat rate with simplified filing.

Unfortunately, you aren't home free once you cross the border: The United States has a tax-treaty relationship with Mexico that allows the IRS to exchange information with the tax authorities in Mexico. If you are a U.S. citizen and are running a business in Mexico, the IRS expects you to pay taxes on any earned income. However, you may be able to waive some or all of your tax liability under the foreign-earned income exclusion, which allows exemptions of around US$90,000 on foreign-earned income. For full information on your tax liability in the United States, Publication 54 *Tax Guide for U.S. Citizens and Resident Aliens Abroad* is available on the IRS website. If Mexico is your main source of business, the IRS grants you an extra month to file.

VAT Taxes

Certain goods and service are subject to a value-added tax (VAT) of 10 percent, including rents and imported goods. Corporations that have paid taxes on business-related purchases may usually credit those taxes against the tax due on their own profits.

TELECOMMUTING

Earning dollars and spending pesos is a winning formula, and, for some, it can be the basis of a more permanent lifestyle. Through the Internet, many foreigners are able to earn in their home country while living in Mexico. Some foreigners are lucky enough to arrive in Mexico with ongoing contracts in their home country and use Mexico as a home base for their work. Others are able to slowly build up their business by applying to jobs online. However, some employers are reluctant to work with people overseas; it can take time and persistence to find telecommuting positions. If you are thinking about telecommuting from Mexico, start making contacts right away and talk to other people who have successfully made it work. Often, foreign residents will combine telecommuting with freelance work in Mexico.

Writing, graphic design, and Web programming are some of the most popular industries for telecommuting. If you are able to pull together enough jobs, you can use this income to qualify for a resident visa as a *"rentista,"* and Mexico—considering your foreign income as an investment in the country, not direct income—will not charge you any fees or taxes beyond the small cost of your immigration paperwork. When it comes to the paperwork, you will likely need to maintain a bank account in your home country (as well as a permanent address) and declare and pay taxes at home.

The Job Hunt

Finding a good job in Mexico is tough, but not impossible. Generally speaking, there are more opportunities (both legal and under the table) for expatriates in cities with a large foreign population or a robust tourist industry. There is also a large job market in Mexico City, with a substantial need for English-speaking employees. At the same time, you cannot come to Mexico expecting the same diversity of career opportunities as you'd find in your home country—nor will you likely receive a similar salary. For most people, choosing Mexico is more about lifestyle than career. Living in a foreign country, interacting with a new culture, and benefiting from Mexico's more laid-back attitude are good reasons to spend some time working down south.

Generally speaking, Mexican immigration does not grant work permits to foreigners if they are taking a job that a Mexican citizen would be qualified to fill. Therefore, your employer will need to demonstrate a need for your services, while you will have to document your specific skill set. There is also a limit as to how many foreign employees a company can hire, based on their size and market. In most cases, if an employer is advertising for native English speakers, they are prepared to assist you with the immigration paperwork.

BUSINESS ETIQUETTE

Maintaining positive and respectful relationships with your business partners, employers, and employees is fundamental to any professional endeavor in Mexico. Here, people value their relationships, and email and telephone, though ubiquitous, aren't enough to sustain a professional association.

Adhering to business etiquette is important, but not difficult. Overall, business practices in Mexico don't differ greatly from what you'd find in the rest of the world, though it is important to note that Mexico's is a generally formal and polite culture.

when addressing a business partner, associate, or boss, unless they indicate that you may do otherwise. It is also considered polite to address people with the appropriate title, such as *señor* for a man, *señora* for a married or older woman, and *señorita* for a young woman. When speaking with a professional, Mexicans may also use the person's professional title, such as *doctor* or *doctora* (doctor), *arquitecto* (architect), or *ingeniero* (engineer), in addition to the ubiquitous *licenciado/a*, a respectful title denoting a college graduate.

LANUAGE

Spanish is the official language for all business transactions and contracts in Mexico. Although many Mexicans speak English well, don't assume a business meeting or interview will be conducted in English. Before going to a meeting, double check that all parties speak English. In addition, learning a few polite greetings and phrases in Spanish can communicate both respect and friendliness, even if you'll be speaking in English.

If you do not speak Spanish, you may want to consider asking a Spanish-speaking employee or associate to accompany you to a business meeting. Any printed or marketing materials (including a résumé to accompany a job application) should be printed in both Spanish and English.

GREETINGS AND FORM OF ADDRESS

A handshake is the appropriate greeting in any professional situation in Mexico, and you should always use the formal *usted* form

DRESS

In Mexico's cities, the workplace is still rather formal, especially in the corporate environment. Business-people generally wear a dark suit to the office, and, even in casual settings, they dress conservatively when dealing with their business partners. For teachers or other professionals outside the corporate environment, business-casual attire is generally appropriate, though you should tailor your dress based on your workplace. For example, if you teach English to employees at a corporate office (not uncommon in Mexico City, for instance), you will need to dress more formally to match the company's culture. Polo shirts and slacks are generally appropriate for real estate brokers or rental agents.

Outside major cities, Mexico is a far more casual country. In small towns, you will rarely see anyone dressed formally, though shorts are generally not worn outside the beach zones. If you are meeting in a warm climate or at the beach, you can dress in lighter clothing

© ARTURO MEADE

Formal dress is still important in a business setting; in cities, a suit and tie is standard professional dress.

ally considered unprofessional in Mexico.

NEGOTIATIONS

Building strong, friendly relationships is important to doing business in Mexico, and Mexicans are often reluctant to give a negative response or impart unpleasant information. As a result, a Mexican may initially say "maybe" or refuse to give a direct answer if he is concerned his response will be poorly received. For that reason, foreigners occasionally perceive Mexicans as evasive or even dishonest, but the intention is to avoid unpleasantness, not to deceive. Likewise, it is considered a bit abrupt or rude to deliver a definitive "no" in a meeting; deliver news softly.

MEALS

It is not unusual to hold a business meeting over a meal in Mexico, usually breakfast or *comida* (the midday meal). When eating out with people you work with, arrive on time and don't start eating until everyone's food has arrived at the table. Generally Mexicans do not split a bill. If you are the person who suggested the meal, you should be prepared to pay the entire bill.

SOCIAL ENGAGEMENTS

If you have been invited to a business associate or employer's home, always bring a small gift, such as a bottle of wine or flowers. You can dress more casually, but stick to more conservative clothes nonetheless. It is appropriate to arrive a little bit tardy – usually, about a half hour – to social engagements in someone's home. If you aren't sure when to arrive, ask another invitee.

when meeting with business partners or clients, though avoid sandals or T-shirts.

BUSINESS CARDS

Even in the electronic era, business cards are still a popular tool in Mexico. As you'll quickly find, business cards can be particularly handy if you are an independent contractor, small business owner, or job seeker who may make an unexpected professional contact at a social event or elsewhere. Business cards are generally cheap to print at local *papelerías* (stationery stores); print them in both English and Spanish.

PUNCTUALITY

Although Mexico has a deserved reputation for running a little more slowly than the rest of the world, it is essential to arrive punctually for business meetings, interviews, or the workday. Tardiness is gener-

EMPLOYERS AND INDUSTRIES

For those looking for employment, the types of jobs available depend largely on where you live. Throughout Mexico, teaching English as a second language is the most perennially popular career choice for English-speaking expatriates. There are numerous language institutes throughout the country, including some larger organizations like Harmon Hall, a Mexican-owned language company, and Berlitz, an international language institute. In addition, there are hundreds of independent language schools throughout the country. In bigger cities (especially Mexico City), many independent language schools cater to executives, giving individual and small group classes at corporate offices.

Private language schools are often hiring teachers, as turnover can be high. If you can make a longer-term commitment, you can also look for positions at primary and secondary schools, high schools, and even preschools. There are many bilingual schools in Mexico, and English education often starts early. If you have an undergraduate or masters degree in English, or you hold a TOEFL certificate, you may even be able to find work in a university, which is often better paid and less demanding.

Teaching English is not the only opportunity open to foreigners, although it is the most common. At the beach and in other tourist towns, hotels, shops, restaurants, bars, and other tourist-related industries have a need for English-speaking staff in a customer service capacity. Often, these types of businesses will be willing to hire a foreigner under the table or for a season. Service jobs can be a good choice for those looking to extend their Mexican vacation or those who want to get their footing while looking for a more permanent position. In some cases, small businesses are also to willing to go through the paperwork to hire foreign staff, but usually if you are willing to make a long-term commitment.

The growing number of foreigners moving to Mexico has also created a demand for English-speaking real estate agents, as well as English-speaking time-share representatives. Many Mexicans work in the real estate industry, but in cities like Ajijic, Puerto Vallarta, Playa del Carmen, Cabo San Lucas, and San Miguel de Allende, you'll find lots of American and Canadian representatives as well. Many foreigners also oversee vacation rental companies, or manage properties for home owners who are in Mexico part time.

In addition, there are a limited number of jobs in creative industries, like media and communications, available to English speakers with special skills. Currently, there is more demand for technological skills and creative services in Mexico than can be filled by the local populace. In addition to independent contractors, it may be possible to find a paying job in advertising and creative services. For those who speak very good Spanish, translation is also an option; you can pick up freelance projects from time to time, which may augment a regular job.

WHERE TO LOOK

In most cases, you will have better luck finding a job once you have arrived in Mexico rather than looking for something from home. If you want to get a jump start on the process, start looking at job postings and classified ads online, and do an Internet search for schools, companies, and publications in the city where you are planning to relocate. Even if they aren't actively hiring, you might send introductory emails to schools or local organizations in order to get a feel for the local job market.

Once you've touched down, there are several ways to find a job. If you have just arrived in Mexico, check the classifieds in the local newspaper for listings. The Web hasn't become as important to the job search as it has in other countries; however, you may still be able to find a job through websites, specifically the websites of local publications and newspapers. The American Chamber of Commerce of Mexico also maintains a job bank with open positions at its member institutions. You may also get in direct contact with private language schools, which are often hiring new teachers on a rolling basis. If you have a special skill set or are looking for an executive position, you will likely want to work with a recruitment agency or headhunter. Most positions for executives or upper management will be located in the capital or in another large city.

While you can certainly find a job in Mexico through traditional channels, the best way to do so is often through personal contacts. Throughout many parts of Mexico, there is a demand for educated and English-speaking people to assist with sales, real estate, and media and communications. If you spread the word in the local community that you are looking for a job, you will likely get some tips. If you are new in town, chat with restaurant owners and shop attendants; sometimes you will be approached directly with an offer for employment.

QUALIFYING FOR A JOB

The ability to speak English (or another foreign language) fluently can open up many employment opportunities in Mexico. Public and private schools, universities, and language institutes throughout the country are constantly in need of native English speakers. Plus, tourism is a billion-dollar industry in Mexico, and there is always a need for native English speakers to help in the service industry.

In addition, undergraduate and graduate degrees are highly regarded in Mexico, where a small percentage of the population goes on to study at the university level. Foreigners with a college diploma will be able to qualify for higher paying or professional positions. If you are planning to apply for jobs in Mexico, bring a copy of your college degree along with its apostille—an international certificate that proves the document's validity.

Interviews

Interviews are generally required during an employment application. In many cases, the personal connection will be a deciding factor for a job, especially if you are applying

If you need a quick polish before a big meeting, there are shoe-shine stands throughout Mexico.

for a people-oriented position, like teaching. Although Mexico is generally a casual country, business is run with a bit more formality. In preparing for an interview, it is best to dress formally for any professional position. For a teaching or service position, business casual attire is appropriate for an interview. As anywhere, bring along a hard copy of your résumé.

HOURS AND SALARY

In general, salaries in Mexico are much lower than they are in the United States, Canada, or other developed nations. A middle-class salary will cover the basic costs of rent and food, but luxuries like eating at restaurants or taking vacations aren't necessarily accessible to most middle-class Mexicans. Although foreigners may earn a bit more than locals, many foreigners working in Mexico find they must live more simply on a Mexican salary or augment their earnings with freelance work, telecommuting, or savings. Fortunately, the cost of living is much more inexpensive in Mexico as well.

In very broad strokes, college graduates usually earn a middle-class salary of US$1,000–2,000 per month for a full-time position, though salaries for highly trained professionals and management positions may be much higher. In a private language school, English teaching positions are usually paid by the hour (and rarely add up to a full-time schedule), with hourly wages ranging around US$12–25 in most regions. If you get a position in a pricey private school, you may be able to earn more money.

Foreigners working in an entry-level position in a school, at a hotel, or in another service-related position may expect salaries in the standard middle-class range, adjusting for regional differences. In sales positions, salaries are often much lower, but employees are paid a significant commission on their sales. Even in small shops, commission may be a large part of your earnings.

Most companies pay their employees every 15 days. In addition, permanent employees receive an annual bonus at the end of the year, called an *aguinaldo*. The *aguinaldo* can be anywhere from four to six weeks of pay. For foreign workers, some companies will also cover the cost of the resident visa when the employee reaches a year of employment.

Business Hours and Holidays

Standard business hours are 8 A.M.–6 P.M. Monday through Friday, with lunch breaks taken between 1 and 3 P.M. Banks are usually open 9 A.M.–5 P.M. Monday through Friday, though hours may be longer (and include Saturday) in a big city. Though lunch breaks are common in a corporate environment, many small business owners will work in their shop from morning to night without so much as a coffee break. At the same time, the pace of business can be much slower in many parts of Mexico. For many small business owners, family life, holidays, and other personal matters can take precedence over business.

Labor Laws for Employers and Employees

Established after the Revolution of 1910, federal labor law governs all employee-employer relations, though enforcement usually takes place on a state level. Mexican labor law is designed to protect workers' rights, including the right to form unions and to strike, the right to a safe workplace, and the right to equal pay for equal work. Both employers and employees should be aware of the laws when offering and accepting employment.

In each Mexican state, there is a court that handles labor disputes. Employees with a claim against their employer can get free help from federal or local representatives. If you are planning to hire employees for your business, be sure to carefully review labor law and workers' rights. Employers should be aware, for example, that it is very difficult to dismiss an employee, and unlawful firing can lead to court cases and fines. It is best to be well-informed before you begin the hiring process. All workers in Mexico are protected by the country's labor laws, even if they work in your home. Likewise, you are entitled to fair treatment in a Mexican company, even if you aren't employed "on the books."

HOURS AND WAGES

The minimum wage in Mexico is set as a daily rate (rather than by hour) and fluctuates slightly by region, but it hovers around US$5 per day nationally. In reality, very few working people are paid so low a wage, so it should not be used as a benchmark. (For benchmarks, the American Chamber of Commerce of Mexico publishes an annual survey of salaries for dozens of job types, available for a fee of about US$250.) By law, the workday is eight hours long, and any additional hours must be compensated with overtime pay. The maximum workweek is 48 hours (or six days), and most Mexicans are accustomed to working those hours. However, schools, banks, and some other industries will limit the week to five days or 40 hours.

Annual Bonus

As mandated by law, all employees are entitled to an annual bonus, called an *aguinaldo*. The *aguinaldo* is equal to 15 days of pay, with a slowly increasing payment with each year the employee works for a company.

© ARTURO MEAD

Commuters ride the subway in Mexico City.

BENEFITS

Employers are obligated to provide their employees with benefits through Mexico's public health and housing programs. For a very small business, you can hire employees as independent contractors, which negates the obligation to provide benefits. Otherwise, all employers are required to register their employees with IMSS, a comprehensive state-run health care program that covers the country's workers. For each employee, employers must make a financial contribution to the system, depending on the job's risk factors.

If you are working for a Mexican company, you may be eligible for IMSS. Mexico also offers employers the opportunity to pay into a pension plan for their employees, though foreign workers are rarely extended this benefit.

Vacation

After the first year of employment, all employees are entitled to six days of vacation. Thereafter, the number of vacation days increases by two days for each year for three years, until the employee reaches two full weeks of vacation. After that, the employee receives two additional days of vacation for every five years with the same company.

There are seven official holidays in Mexico, for which all employees are granted the day off: New Year's Day (January 1), Constitution Day (February 5), Benito Juárez's Birthday (March 21), Labor Day (May 1), Independence Day (September 16), Revolution Day (November 20), and Christmas (December 25).

Maternity Leave

Employees are entitled to six weeks of maternity leave both before and after the birth of their child. IMSS assists employers with the costs with subsidies.

JUST DISMISSAL AND LAYOFF

In Mexico, workers are entitled to just dismissal. You cannot be fired at your employer's discretion, though firing for just cause is permissible. Make sure your employee's hours are properly recorded, and have your accountant keep a tab on all money paid to the employee. In the case that you have a problem with your employee, document the problem in a letter and have the employee sign the statement. If you must lay off an employee, severance benefits must cover an employee for 90 days after one year of employment, plus 20 days for each additional year with the company. If you fire an employee with reason, the severance obligation is reduced. Employees who have been with a company for more than two years may sue for reinstatement.

FINANCE

Mexico's economy has grown slowly but steadily since the beginning of the 20th century, though its upward trajectory has been punctuated by moments of accelerated growth and unexpected dips. Most recently, Mexico was hard hit by the worldwide financial crisis of 2008, though the economy made a swift recovery thereafter. Today, the World Bank ranks Mexico among the top 15 biggest economies internationally.

With numerous free-trade agreements, abundant natural resources, and a large and able workforce, the country has a lot of potential for big growth in the future. Since the introduction of the North American Free Trade Agreement (NAFTA) in the 1990s, Mexico has become an incredibly popular place for American and Canadian companies to invest and do business. In addition to large corporations, many investors, real estate developers, and small-business owners have been able to make meaningful investments in Mexico.

Despite the economy's generally rosy outlook, wealth is unevenly distributed throughout Mexico, with a large percentage of the population still living below

© CARLOS MEADE

the poverty line. Accordingly, the cost for basic services, like food, housing, and health care, is affordable throughout the country. If you have savings or receive retirement benefits, it is relatively easy to live a comfortable and fulfilling life in Mexico for far less money than in the United States or Canada.

Cost of Living

The lower cost of living is one of the major reasons many expatriates first consider relocating to Mexico. Relatively speaking, it is much more inexpensive than the rest of North America, and, for many, a combination of income and savings make Mexico an appealingly low-cost place to live. Nonetheless, the cost of living in Mexico depends largely on where you live and your lifestyle. Some expatriates keep costs low by renting modest but comfortable homes in traditionally Mexican neighborhoods, buying fresh food at local markets, cooking at home, and spending their free time taking walks in the park or along the beach. In addition to basic costs, most expatriates spend a little extra on cable television, Internet, an international telephone plan, a cell phone, and occasional trips home or around Mexico. You might also want to own a car, which means adding maintenance, gasoline, and insurance to your budget. Even with a few extras, though, you can whittle down your cost of living to far less than what you'd pay to live in the United States, Canada, or other developed nations.

For most expatriates, however, the appeal of living in Mexico isn't necessarily spending less, but getting much more for your money. You will likely be able to afford a nicer or more spacious home in Mexico. You may be able to afford the luxury of a housekeeper, babysitter, or gardener—a surprisingly inexpensive option throughout the country. Many expatriates enjoy the relatively low price of restaurants and bars; eating and drinking out is a favored social activity in most expatriate enclaves. Plus, it's always easy to spend a few more pesos on a bottle of aged tequila, an international magazine subscription, a slice of imported cheese, or a satellite dish for your rooftop. Mexico may offer the basics on the cheap, but there are plenty of luxuries and pleasures to accommodate a very comfortable lifestyle down south.

While the cost of living is considerably lower in Mexico, it is important to understand that it isn't a shoestring destination. In the regions and cities where most expatriates live, the cost of living might run about 25 to 50 percent cheaper than in the United States or Canada. In very small and remote places, you might be able to attain an even more inexpensive lifestyle, but that would take some serious planning and budgeting. Finally, with all this talk of "bang for your buck," it is important to note that Mexico is inexpensive for those who are spending in dollars, rather than pesos. If you have savings, social security benefits, or a telecommuting job, your dollars will almost certainly stretch further in Mexico than they would in the developed world. However, for those who depend on a Mexican source of income, the cost of living can be high relative to your salary. In absolute terms, Mexico costs less than the United States, but in relative terms, the standard of living in the United States is higher for the majority of its citizens.

BASIC EXPENSES

Although Mexico is one of the world's biggest economies, there is still widespread poverty throughout the country. The gross domestic product per capita is less than US$14,000 (as compared to $47,000 in the United States and $39,000 in Canada), and the highly uneven distribution of wealth means that a substantial percentage of the population lives in poverty. As such, most basic expenses are still very affordable.

At the same time, the economy varies regionally, and the single biggest factor in determining your cost of living will be where you choose to live. For example, a middle-class lifestyle in Mexico City will run you 30–40 percent less than in Los Angeles, while the lifestyle in San Miguel de Allende will likely run about half the price of a major U.S. city. In popular beach resorts like Cabo San Lucas, prices can be significantly higher than many parts of the United States, while less-trafficked beach communities, like those along the coast of Oaxaca, are decidedly budget destinations.

In very broad strokes, the basic cost of living for most middle-class expatriates usually falls between US$1,500 and US$3,000 per month, with some spending much more and others spending a bit less. Within that framework, you will likely be able to afford occasional treats, like going to the movies or eating dinner out, without decimating your budget. At the same time, with a minimum wage of around US$5 a day, many Mexicans live on far, far less. If you watch your pesos, you can live in Mexico for less than US$1,000 per month (or even lower in inexpensive areas, like the southern states of Oaxaca and Chiapas), especially if you are willing to live a basic, traditionally Mexican lifestyle. If you want to rent a luxury penthouse apartment in Mexico City or a beach-view home in Los Cabos, eat at great restaurants, drive a nice car, have household help, and all around live it up, you could spend anywhere between US$6,000 and US$9,000 per month, depending on where you live.

Housing and Food

The cost of housing depends on numerous factors: location, size, neighborhood, and whether you rent or own. In many parts of Mexico, housing costs about half what it would cost for a comparable property in the United States or Canada. However, if you want a major upgrade—views, beach access, or a prime downtown location—remember that these assets come at a premium in Mexico, too. You'll definitely pay more to overlook the Pacific, but the cost of a coastal Puerto Vallarta home will still likely be lower than a waterfront condo in Miami. Again, there are major regional differences in the real estate market. In more expensive areas, such as Mexico City or Cabo San Lucas, you should expect to pay more than in less-touristy or smaller communities, like Ajijic or Oaxaca.

Food is inexpensive and abundant in Mexico. Even though Mexico exports a great deal of its produce to the United States, you will still find a bounty of domestically grown produce, with tomatoes, onions, chili peppers, bananas, mangos, melons, guavas, potatoes, carrots, mushrooms, radishes, lettuces, cilantro, basil, and many other fresh fruits and vegetables grown throughout the country and sold at extremely accessible prices. Domestic meats, milk, cheese, eggs, tortillas, Mexican beer, soft drinks, and national brands of pasta, canned goods, and prepackaged foods are all inexpensive. On the other hand, certain products and imported items cost a bit more in Mexico. Luxuries like dried cranberries, almonds, tahini sauce, sushi rice, or Parmesan cheese can be far more expensive in Mexico than at home, and likewise less available. If you are on a budget, you may have to adjust your eating habits to match local offerings.

When shopping, you will always find the best prices at traditional markets, where there is little markup on fresh produce. There are markets throughout Mexico, in both small towns and big cities, and, in addition to produce, most sell dry

© ARTURO MEADE

Basics are inexpensive in Mexico; a grocery bag full of fresh produce can cost less than US$5 in some parts of the country.

goods in bulk (like beans, rice, and nuts), cheese, tortillas, eggs, and other products. Tomatoes may cost as little as MXN$6 for a kilo (or about US$0.50 for two pounds), while fresh mangoes and guavas in season can go as low as US$0.25 per pound. In inexpensive places, like Oaxaca, you can easily buy a week's worth of fresh produce for less than US$10. Add a third more for more expensive areas, like Mexico City, or nonagricultural zones, like Los Cabos.

In addition to traditional markets, most major cities and popular tourist towns have large and inexpensive supermarkets, as well as smaller, local food shops, known as *abarrotes*, which sell dry and packaged goods, like pastas, breakfast cereals, and canned food, as well as cheese, deli items, milk, and eggs. They usually also include a bakery. Most items produced nationally are lower priced than their imported counterparts; if you stick to national brands, food can be 30–50 percent less expensive in Mexico than the rest of North America.

Utilities

Most utilities in Mexico are inexpensive, though costs may be higher or lower depending on the region in which you live. Water service is incredibly inexpensive throughout the country. In most areas, water use is billed every other month and will rarely cost a household more than a few dollars per month for normal usage. Drinking water is sold in large 20-liter jugs, called *garafones*, and can be delivered to your home or picked up at the store. Drinking water costs can vary widely by region, ranging from under a dollar for a *garafon* in cities like Oaxaca to US$5 in Mexico City.

Overseen by the Comisión Federal Electricidad (CFE), electricity is more expensive than water and also a bit more variable. Bills come bimonthly and tend to fluctuate month to month (even if your usage seems relatively stable). Generally, you can expect to spend anywhere between US$35 and US$100 on electricity for two months of use, depending on where you live (obviously, the size of your house will make a difference). Fortunately, Mexico's temperate climate means that most people won't spend a bundle on heat or air-conditioning, reducing overall energy use. Those along the coast will likely use air-conditioning during the summer, though.

Natural gas for cooking and heating is purchased from private companies and delivered to your home (there are constantly trucks circling the city streets if you want to flag one, though you can also call to request a delivery). Some homes use individual cylinders, which are hooked up to the gas pipes. Others have a stationary tank on the roof, which can be periodically filled. Stationary tanks are more expensive to install, but overall they provide a more economical option for buying gas over the long term. A cylinder costs around US$30 (the price is regulated by the government) and will generally last about three weeks before it needs to be replaced.

Telephone service through Telmex is among the most expensive in the world, with basic phone plans starting above US$50; adding long-distance or international service can cost quite a bit more. Internet lines can be purchased through the phone company or the cable company, usually as a part of a package deal. Usually, service costs around US$30 a month when part of a package with other services, like telephone or cable.

Household and Clothing

Most basics are inexpensive and accessible in Mexico. Kitchen appliances, mattresses, building supplies, furniture, bedding, and other household necessities are available throughout the country and usually cost less or are roughly comparable to their cost elsewhere in the world. However, foreigners are often surprised to find that not everything is cheaper in Mexico. Electronics, computers, video games, and brand-name clothing can be more expensive in Mexico than in the United States, and big blowout sales are virtually nonexistent. (In fact, many Mexicans go on major shopping sprees when visiting the United States, where discount clothing and super sales are more common. You'll never find something with an 80 percent discount in Mexico.) A few international retailers, like the Spanish chain Zara, have been able to set up business in Mexico. However, most similar clothing chains from the United States have no Mexican presence. Many foreigners do their clothes shopping at home, both for cost and variety.

In big cities, you'll find international chains like Home Depot, Walmart, Sam's Club, and Costco, in addition to massive Mexican supermarkets like Comercial Mexicana, Mega (a larger version of the Comercial Mexicana), and Soriana. In addition, most sizable cities have multiple malls anchored by large department stores, like Liverpool and Palacio de Hierro, which both sell designer clothes, shoes, makeup, and fragrance. In smaller cities and towns, locally owned businesses traditionally cater to the local market, especially in the downtown district. However, as Mexico modernizes, big box stores are cropping up throughout the country, often building on the ring roads right outside of colonial towns and smaller cities.

Currently, self-service laundromats are not common in Mexico. If you do not have facilities at home, you can send your clothes to be laundered. Most Laundromats charge per kilo to wash and dry your clothing, usually starting at around US$1 per kilo and up.

© ARTURO MEADE

There is always a buzz of commerce in the *centro histórico* of an old Mexican city.

Public Transportation

If you are using public systems, transportation costs are very low. Within city limits, buses rarely cost more than MXN$4 for a crosstown ride (about US$0.35). In Mexico City, the famous and far-reaching metro charges just MXN$2.50 (about US$0.20) per ride and connects the entire *distrito federal* from north to south and east to west.

Most people augment public transport with occasional taxi rides to take groceries home or to visit places off the grid of public transport. In Mexico City, taxis run on a meter and are generally inexpensive. Elsewhere, they charge a flat rate for service, which may be around US$2–3 in a small town and US$5–10 in a larger city. Prices go up the longer the distances traveled.

Health Care

Health care and health insurance have become increasing concerns for U.S. citizens, and many find Mexico is much easier on both their pocketbook and peace of mind. Even if you pay out of pocket, health care costs are significantly cheaper in Mexico than in the United States, often far less than half the cost. Doctor's visits might cost anywhere from US$30 to US$80, while a night in a hospital could run just a few hundred dollars.

OPTIONAL EXPENSES

Beyond basic expenses, you'll likely add a few more items to your budget.

Car

If you have a car, transportation will cost a bit more than if you rely on public transportation. Despite the nationalization of oil, gas prices aren't as low as you might expect, since most crude oil from Mexico must be refined overseas, coming back home with a higher price tag. Although the cost fluctuates according to the market, it usually runs more than MXN$9 per liter of regular unleaded and more than MXN$10 per liter of premium (around US$2.90 and US$3.10 per gallon, respectively). Maintenance costs are a small consideration in Mexico, as basic mechanic services are generally inexpensive, as are common car parts like batteries or tires. Do bear in mind, however, that certain makes of cars manufactured in the United States and Canada have never been produced in Mexico (such as Volvo or Lexus), and therefore, getting parts for these cars can be more costly.

Car insurance is inexpensive, generally running a couple hundred dollars per year (it is slightly cheaper for American or Canadian cars that have a temporary import permit). If you bring a car from abroad, you'll have to keep up with your registration at home.

Finally, new cars can be a bit more expensive in Mexico than they are in the United States. If you plan to buy a new, Mexican-plated car (or even a used recent model), you should expect to spend around 15–30 percent more. Shop around for better deals.

Household Help

Many people in Mexico can afford to hire household help. Housekeepers, cooks, gardeners, and nannies are all inexpensive cottage industries in Mexico; industrious self-employed women and men make themselves available for these jobs, and most middle-class families avail themselves of their services. The cost to employ someone in your home depends entirely on where you live; in smaller towns, a housekeeper will be much cheaper than in a big city, possibly costing as little as US$35 per day. Cooks and gardeners run a bit higher. For those with kids, Mexico is a great place to hire a nanny; babysitters generally cost more than housekeepers but are still incredibly affordable.

Communications

Internet, international telephones, and cell phones can add US$50–200 to your monthly budget.

Entertainment

There are plenty of entertainment options in Mexico—movies, books, magazines, cable television, restaurants—most at good prices. Those who reside in big cities may also want to see concerts or attend the theater.

U.S. SOCIAL SECURITY

Many U.S. citizens rely on social security benefits to cover the costs of life in Mexico. In most cases, social security checks are lower than the aforementioned costs in this chapter, but industrious retirees can carve out a comfortable lifestyle with social security checks. Others also have another form of income or savings to augment standard social security. Is it possible to live on just social security? It is, and people do.

Banking

Mexico remains a largely cash-based culture. Most people have bank accounts, but they are more likely to pay for their goods and services in cash (called *efectivo*) rather than checks or credit/debit cards. If you will be taking a legal job in Mexico, it can be advantageous to open a Mexican bank account, so that you can deposit checks from your employer and save money. (If you work off the books, your employer will likely pay you in cash or with a check made out to the holder.) It can also be convenient to have a bank account so you can write checks in pesos, receive checks in pesos, and receive deposits. For many expatriates, however, it is easiest to simply maintain their foreign bank account and use ATMs for cash.

Mexico's central bank, the Banco de Mexico, oversees the country's financial and banking systems. There are many major banks operating in Mexico, and most are foreign owned. Currently, the biggest are Citigroup subsidiary Banamex, British-owned HSBC, and BBVA (Banco Bilbao Vizcaya Argentaria) from Spain. Canadian-owned Scotiabank, European giant Santander, and Mexican-owned Banorte are also major players in the banking industry. In addition to these options, Lloyd Bank caters to foreign residents in Mexico by offering deposit service for checks mailed to their address in the United States. There are branches in the Chapala area and San Miguel de Allende.

CURRENCY

Mexico's currency is the peso. It is denoted with same symbol ($) used for the dollar. Pesos are divided into 100 cents, or *centavos,* and they come in $1, $2, $5, and $10 coins, and $20, $50, $100, $200, $500, and $1,000 bills. There

CHANGE!

Any seasoned Mexico traveler already knows that changing larger bills can be a tall order, especially in taxis, at the market, or in very small businesses. In some cases, you will simply be unable to purchase something small, like a bottle of water, because the correct change is not available at the store. It can be frustrating for those with a fistful of MXN$500 notes fresh from the ATM, but it is important to understand the reasons why change is so often unavailable.

In many cases, small business owners or single-person enterprises (like taxis or ice cream vendors) begin the day with no capital at all. Leaving the previous day's earnings at home, these small business owners head out with empty pockets, slowly accumulating change as they make sales throughout the day. You will find that change is often particularly tight in the morning.

If you want to avoid the constant back-and-forth about change, make an effort to carry change with you. Use big bills when you visit a large retailer or grocery store, where they are more likely to have a register full of pesos, saving the small change for markets, street vendors, taxis, and small businesses. If you take money out of the ATM and it comes in only $200 or $500 notes, you can go inside the branch and ask them to change the money into smaller bills.

are also a smaller number of $20 coins in circulation, which look similar to the $10 coin. In addition, there are 5, 10, 20, and 50 centavo coins minted, though you will rarely see or use coins with a value lower than 50 centavos.

With the exception of the border region and major tourist destinations, pesos are the only universally accepted currency in Mexico. Occasionally, department stores will allow you to pay for something in dollars; however, they generally offer poor exchange rates.

Exchange Rates

On the international market, the peso is a free-floating currency. Therefore, exchange rates fluctuate slightly due to supply and demand. If you are changing foreign money, you will usually get the best exchange rates at banks, though you can compare the daily rates posted outside banks and exchange houses if you want to get the best deal. Some people get very involved in following exchange rates, waiting to change money at a time when the peso has lost a bit of value. Generally, though, the peso is a stable currency, with few fluctuations against the dollar.

Changing Money

The easiest way to obtain pesos is to withdraw directly from your bank account using an ATM. You can also change foreign currency to pesos in banks and *casas de cambio* (currency exchange houses). There are ATMs and *casas de cambio* in almost all international airports and in any sizable town or city. In most cases, banks and currency exchange houses do not charge a commission on money exchange; instead, they make money on the difference between the rate they buy and sell pesos. Usually, you can see the difference in the two rates posted outside the teller window or in the doorway of a bank.

If you need to change cash into pesos, you will be better off visiting a *casa de cambio* rather than a bank. In some cases, banks will only exchange cash money for existing clients. In recent years, Mexico has placed tighter controls on changing foreign currency in cash, especially in large amounts. To change any amount of cash, you are usually asked to show picture identification and proof of citizenship (bring along your passport). Usually, no more than US$1,000 in cash can be changed during a single month.

Changing Checks

In some parts of Mexico, there are boutique financial institutions that offer the option of changing checks from American dollars into pesos. You must be registered with the institution before you can have a check changed, and you must have a proof of address and valid immigration paperwork on file (a tourist card or a resident visa) with the company. You will be required to update that information annually. Canadian checks are more difficult to cash.

Credit Cards

Banks charge a high percentage on sales paid with a credit card (around 7 percent in most cases), which makes credit card machines impractical for many small businesses. You will not have the same ease of payment as you do in the United States and may be surprised to find that many restaurants, bars, shops, and even art galleries are cash-only establishments. (Generally, hotels, high-end restaurants, and most gas stations will take credit cards, especially in tourist-friendly areas.) In the case that you are paying with a card, ATM cards can be used as credit cards; you will rarely, if ever, be asked to enter a PIN number to use an ATM card in a business or restaurant.

OPENING A BANK ACCOUNT

To open an account at most Mexican banks, you will need proof of residency in Mexico (an FM2 or FM3 of any type), proof of address, and a passport. Most banks charge account holders a monthly fee or ask you to maintain a minimum balance. You can open a simple deposit account, which gives you

© CARLOS MEADE

a branch of Banorte, the only major Mexican-owned bank in the country

the ability to deposit and withdraw money with an ATM card or at a cashier's window. You can also open a checking account, which includes a checkbook; these usually come with a slightly higher fee or with higher balance minimums than basic deposit accounts. Today, most of Mexico's big banks offer online banking services, where you can check your balance and pay bills. Some have rather elaborate password-protection systems; ask about the online options when you are opening your account if you will need to access your bank statements remotely.

In addition, banks can issue credit cards. Usually, you must already be a bank customer and must meet a minimum balance requirement before you can qualify for a credit card, though rules vary. Although credit has become more accessible in recent years, credit cards in Mexico generally offer much higher interest rates than in the United States and elsewhere.

USING A FOREIGN BANK ACCOUNT

Unless you need to write checks or deposit pesos, you can continue to use a foreign bank account while living in Mexico. It is easy to get pesos via your ATM card, and foreign credit cards are accepted as easily as national ones. The major drawback to a foreign account is that you will be charged withdrawal fees at Mexican banks when you use the ATM, as well as any fees your bank may charge.

LOANS

You do not need to be a Mexican citizen to borrow money from a Mexican bank, but until recently, credit was very restricted throughout the country. Today, banks will lend highly rated customers money for homes, cars, or business investments. As credit becomes more widely available, foreigners may look into the option of borrowing money from a Mexican bank. Generally, interest rates remain incredibly high, so foreign buyers will often choose to make their purchases in full or to work with a foreign lender. For example, there are some U.S.-based lenders that specialize in long-term mortgages for properties purchased in Mexico.

Small business still fuels the Mexican economy, especially in small towns like Ajijic.

© JULIE DOHERTY MEADE

To qualify for a bank loan, you must be a legal resident of Mexico (holding either an FM2 or FM3), present proof of income, and offer a credit reference from your home country.

If you do take out a loan with a Mexican bank, there are a couple things to keep in mind. First of all, Spanish is the official language for all legal documents in Mexico. Even if the bank provides a translation of the documents, it is the Spanish-language contract that will be enforced under the law. In addition, there are often fees and service charges associated with a new loan contract. Be sure to get the full details on these; some can be quite high. In addition, all bank fees and charges are subject to the Impuesto del Valor Agregado (Value Added Tax), or IVA.

MONEY TRANSFERS

Millions of Mexican citizens living in the United States and Canada send millions of dollars back to their families at home. If you have a bank account in the United States, you can wire money to a Mexican bank via wire transfer. Banks usually charge a flat fee for wire transfers—around US$40–50—so it makes more economic sense if you are going to be sending larger amounts of money. To make these types of transfers, you need the ABA or SWIFT code for the receiving institution, plus the account holder's name and account number. Some banks will allow you to perform the transaction online. With the correct information, bank-to-bank transfers are secure, though they usually require a few days of processing time.

For smaller amounts of money and quicker service, an "over-the-counter" money wire service is often the easiest and most inexpensive option. Companies like Western Union and Money Gram will transfer money using a credit or debit card to a pick-up point in Mexico (Banamex, for example, is a Western Union pick-up location, as is the electronics chain store Elektra). You can send money through them online, via telephone, or in person at an office. You will need to give the name and location of the person who will be picking up the money (that person must arrive with the confirmation number and identification). Fees are based on the amount of money you send; they also make a profit on the exchange rate. If you want to send money from Mexico to the United States, you can follow the same procedure; however, the flow is so rarely in that direction that the services may be more inefficient.

If you are not in a hurry, you can also purchase an international postal money order at a U.S. post office (you specify the currency it will be converted to) for very low fees. The post office then mails the money order—made out to the recipient—to Mexico, where it can be paid out at a bank. Sometimes, there is a waiting period before the recipient can cash out the money.

Bank Transfers

It is worth noting that, in Mexico, it is common practice for people to deposit money into someone else's account as payment for goods or services. Banks are used to this type of request, and you should not be surprised if someone asks you to deposit money directly into their account as a form of payment (producing the deposit receipt will serve as confirmation of the transaction). To transfer money to a Mexican bank account, you can simply go to the bank of the person to which you are depositing, present their name and account number, then hand over the cash to the teller. You will receive a receipt.

Taxes

The Servicio de Administración Tributaria (SAT) is Mexico's federal tax board, similar to the IRS in the United States. Many foreigners live in Mexico without paying any taxes, though many others do pay into the system through employment or other income. Your tax liability depends on where you are making your money and if you are already paying taxes on that income. For any foreign resident, Mexico taxes worldwide earned income, though it also gives tax credit for any income for which you paid taxes in another country. Therefore, if you've already paid taxes on your U.S.- or Canada-based income at home, you won't have to pay again in Mexico. Any money you've earned in Mexico, however, you will owe taxes on.

Income taxes are paid to the federal government; state and local governments have a far more limited ability to tax, though they may extend some taxes on paid salaries and property.

INCOME TAXES

Anyone legally working in Mexico is required to pay income taxes on their salary, which includes wages, overtime, benefits, bonuses, and indemnities and other income. There is no tax on the first MXN$125,900 (around US$9,700). From MXN$125,900 to MXN$1,000,000, the rate is 15 percent. Anything in excess of MXN$1,000,000 is taxed at 30 percent. If you are a salaried worker, your employer should withhold taxes from your earnings. Fees for doctors, artists, designers, or any other professional services are taxed at a rate of 25 percent, with no standard deduction.

Foreigners who don't work may still have tax liability on other Mexican sources of income. For example, renting your home to vacationers while you travel would be considered income made in Mexico, and all citizens and residents must pay a 25 percent tax on all income from rental properties of leases. If you are running any sort of business in Mexico, no matter how small, meet with an accountant to determine your tax liability.

PROPERTY TAXES

If you own a home, you will also owe property taxes. Fortunately, property taxes are shockingly low in Mexico, costing most homeowners just a couple hundred dollars a year. Do note that you will pay high capital gains taxes if you sell your home within five years of buying; selling thereafter will not incur particularly high fees.

OFF THE BOOKS

Like anywhere, many foreigners in Mexico initially find employment "off the books" in Mexico. It is often hard to procure a work permit for casual jobs, like working at a bar or restaurant. Plus, business owners will often pay cash to employees in service positions, whether or not they are Mexican, making it easier for a foreigner to come onboard. Even some language schools will take on a few employees without legalizing their status, especially if they only need a part-time teacher or if they already have numerous legal employees on the books and don't have permission to hire more.

Working under the table is not particularly uncommon, and it is not frowned upon in Mexico as it often is in the United States. Many of the under-the-table jobs that foreigners are offered would likewise be paid in cash to an employee, so there is little concern about tax evasion. Plus, many business owners feel a native English speaker could be a great asset to their business, even if they don't have the time or resources they need to legalize a foreigner's immigration status.

Needless to say, there are risks associated with working under the table. Immigration officials do occasionally check local businesses to make sure employees have the correct paperwork (and they will respond to a report that someone is working illegally at a Mexican company, too). In most cases, the punishment for working illegally is deportation, and there can be associated fines for you or your employer (though this is less common if you are working in more casual setting). In the case that you are caught working under the table, don't panic: Many foreigners are able to work with immigration so that they may legalize their status in the country. At the same time, it may be worth a preventative trip to immigration before you meet them unexpectedly; there are plenty of ways for foreigners to legally work in the country, so if you've found a job you like, it may be worth the effort to get your visa.

FOREIGN TAXES

Whether you continue to pay taxes at home depends on the laws in your home country, as well as your employment situation. If you are still receiving income from your home country in the form of rental property, pensions, dividends, or any other source, you will likely owe money. Fortunately, Mexico will not tax you on these earnings, so you are only paying one set of taxes on foreign income.

United States

No matter where they live, citizens of the United States are required to pay income taxes, as long as they meet the minimum income filing requirement (around US$400). The IRS expects American citizens overseas to pay taxes on their foreign-derived income, even if that income is already taxed in Mexico.

If you are a U.S. citizen and are running a business in Mexico, the IRS expects you to pay taxes on any earned income. The United States has a tax-treaty relationship with Mexico, which allows the IRS to exchange information with the tax authorities in Mexico. However, you may be able to waive some or all of your tax liability under the foreign-earned income exclusion, which allows exemptions of more than US$90,000. For full information on your tax liability in the United States, Publication 54 *Tax Guide for U.S. Citizens and Resident Aliens Abroad* is available on the IRS website. If Mexico is your main source of business, the IRS grants you an extra month to file.

Canada

Moving away from Canada does not absolve you of your tax liability, and in many cases, Canadians living overseas will be required to pay taxes to the Canadian government. If you are planning on making a permanent move to Mexico, you will need to inform the Canadian Revenue Agency of your plans, and your residency status will be determined. If you still have strong ties in Canada—family, a permanent residence—you will likely be liable to pay taxes. At the same time, retaining your status and paying your taxes can also help you maintain your health care coverage. (Most Canadians must reside in Canada around 165 days out of the year if they want to maintain their health care coverage; being a nonresident means you forfeit provincial health care benefits.) If you live in Mexico but still have a Canadian source of income (rental properties, a pension, etc.), you will be liable to pay taxes on this income.

Investing

Mexico is a massive recipient of foreign investment, on the very smallest to the very largest scale. The United States is far and away the biggest source of investment money coming into the country, and there are many U.S.-owned companies doing huge business south of the border. Mexico's economy is expected to grow annually into the future, so well-chosen investments in the country may well pay off in the long run. Although it doesn't boast the massive growth of emerging markets in China or India, Mexico is considered by economists to be a stable investment for an emerging economy. Among other promising indicators, Mexico's government is expanding the country's infrastructure, and the country has a large number of free-trade agreements. In addition, Mexico is strategically located just south of the

United States, the world's largest economy (which also buys 80 percent of Mexico's exports).

MARKETS AND THE MEXICAN STOCK EXCHANGE

Mexico presents many investment opportunities. It has the most foreign direct investment of any country in Latin America and a steadily growing currency. Though it was strongly affected by the worldwide financial crisis in 2008, the Mexican stock market made a strong recovery thereafter, outpacing the U.S. markets.

Overseen by the Mexican Securities Market Act, the Bolsa Mexicana de Valores (Mexican Stock Exchange), or BMV, is Mexico's only stock exchange, and it's a private company located on the Paseo de la Reforma in Mexico City. The BMV calculates 13 indexes, with the Índice de Precios y Cotizaciones, or IPC, as its benchmark. A little over 150 companies trade on the BMV, including all of the country's largest and most profitable corporations.

Industries

About 30 percent of direct foreign investment goes to the manufacturing sector. Manufacturing costs are still low, and since 2003, the country has seen an average annual growth of 5 percent in manufacturing. Television sets, cars and trucks, car parts, telephones, electrical wires, and computers are among the country's most exported goods.

Manufacturing is among the most robust industries, but it's not the only sector for investors. For more information about Mexico's exports, international investments, and economy, there are ample statistics presented by the government at ProMéxico (www.promexico.gob. mx), which also publishes a multilingual magazine called *Negocios* (Business).

ARTURO MEADE

The Mexican Stock Exchange is located on Paseo de la Reforma in Mexico City.

How to Invest

Foreign nationals who wish to invest in pesos on the Mexican Stock

DAILY LIFE

Exchange may do so through an authorized brokerage firm in Mexico. Brokerages usually charge a commission of around 1–1.5 percent on sales. While most of Mexico's largest companies trade only in Mexico, a few prominent companies also have ADRs (American Depository Receipts) on the New York Stock Exchange (NYSE), including Grupo Televisa (Mexico's largest television broadcaster), Cemex (the world's largest cement company), and Telefonos de Mexico, or Telmex (one of the world's largest telecommunications companies). Americans can buy shares of these companies through the NYSE; there are also investment funds in the United States that focus on Mexican companies.

REAL ESTATE

The most common form of foreign investment in Mexico is purchasing real estate. Mexico's economy has been growing consistently, and, as a result, appreciation on real estate can be extremely high, especially in high-demand areas.

Although there are no official incentives for foreigners to buy property in Mexico, the country's low property taxes make investing very attractive. In most cases, you will only pay a few hundred dollars per year on your property. However, it is important to note that real estate is a long-term investment; you will pay capital gains tax if you sell the home in fewer than five years after purchasing it.

Investing in real estate can be a great idea, but it also can be a minefield. Take advice from Jeff Levy, a seasoned businessman who got in too deep in Cabo San Lucas:

Around 1997, I took a second vacation trip to Los Cabos (the first being in 1994 right after the hurricane). I had recently sold my interest in the final remaining telecommunications business and decided to try retirement again or find something less demanding of my time. Cabo San Lucas was in a growth phase at the time, and the future of development there looked rosy. I had participated in some commercial development previously, and venturing into the high-end residential real estate market seemed like a no-brainer.

Wow! Was I ever wrong. I jumped in head first by purchasing five lots in one of the premier gated communities of Cabo San Lucas with the intent of building high-end spec homes for the gringo second-home market. After a year of construction nightmares, I concluded that spending a week a month to keep things under control was not going to cut it. I ultimately gave into the idea that I needed to be on-site full time in order to complete the three projects that I had insanely undertaken simultaneously in order to get out of the situation I found myself in. I was lucky to come out of this venture with a slightly positive monetary return after building and selling the three homes and dumping the remaining two lots back on the developer just prior to our global financial crisis. It can best be summed up as "a tremendous learning experience on how not to do things."

COMMUNICATIONS

Mexico's media and communications have long been dominated by a few large corporate conglomerates. The results have not been particularly positive for consumers, who have suffered from less choice in the media and higher prices in communication systems than most of the world. The market is slowly diversifying, though a truly competitive market is still a way's off. Nonetheless, Mexico has good infrastructure and services, making it relatively easy for foreign residents to comfortably keep up with friends and family at home. While telephone service is expensive, it is generally efficient, and Telmex has begun to offer more deals and packages for households making calls overseas. Internet is widely available and generally inexpensive across the country, and most people are able to set up broadband accounts at home. As a result, foreigners have been able to reduce their communication costs through VoIP and other Internet-based communication technologies, in addition to using the Internet for email and Web browsing.

Media, too, makes it easy to feel close to home. Cable television offers

© ARTURO MEADE

worldwide programming, so you'll never miss your favorite TV shows or long for the latest news. Magazines and other media are widely available in Spanish and, to a smaller extent, in English.

Telephone Service

Standard ground-line telephone service is more limited and far more expensive in Mexico than it is in most developed countries, though prices have been getting better as the market opens to competition. Cellular phone service has become increasingly popular as an alternative to landlines (though largely operated by the same telecommunications company). Costs for a cellular phone are also relatively high, though more akin to world prices.

LANDLINES

Landlines are becoming increasingly uncommon in Mexico, as many people switch to the relative ease and lower up-front costs of cellular telephones. Still, standard telephone lines are indispensable for certain businesses and residences, and the calling rates can be much lower if you sign up for the proper plan. You may be surprised to learn that not every house in Mexico comes equipped with a telephone line. If you have bought or rented a place that doesn't have a telephone line, you will need to solicit a landline through Telmex, the country's largest phone company. Depending on the availability of lines in your area, you could have a phone installed immediately or be asked to wait a couple months. If you already have a line installed, Telmex is the only option for basic telephone service. However, in some cases you may be able to use an alternate company for your long-distance service.

Telmex

Mexico's largest telecommunications company, Telefonos de Mexico, or Telmex, was originally founded as a private entity in the 1940s, when Mexican investors bought foreign-owned telephone companies and consolidated service into a single corporation. In the 1970s, the Mexican government bought Telmex, operating it as a public entity with a full monopoly on the telephone market. It was privatized again in 1990, when it was sold to Carlos Slim and a group of investors. As of 1991, the Mexican government holds no interests in the company.

Competition was introduced into the telecommunications market as a prerequisite of Mexico's acceptance into the World Trade Organization, though

© ARTURO MEADE

Although there are now several phone companies in Mexico, Telmex remains the biggest player in the telecommunications market.

Telmex continued to maintain a virtual monopoly on the market. Slowly, other companies have been able to shave off small slices of Telmex's consumer base; today, Telmex controls around 80 percent of the country's ground lines (and through Telcel, its subsidiary, more than 70 percent of its cellular phone service). Outside the country, Telmex controls numerous cellular companies, ground line service, and pay-per-view television channels. It is the largest telecommunications company in Latin America.

In Mexico, Telmex has wide-reaching and well-developed service, which includes local and long-distance service, as well as dial-up and DSL Internet connections. In most locations, you will have no option but to contract your telephone line through Telmex, especially for local calls. However, you may be able to purchase long-distance service through another provider.

Other Phone Companies

A few telephone companies have stepped up to play David to Telmex's Goliath. Monterrey-based Axtel is the second-largest phone company in Mexico, offering ground lines and Internet service to a growing number of subscribers. Their services are available in most major cities, and, like Telmex, they offer packages for local and long-distance calling along with Internet service. Alestra is another major Telmex competitor, though it principally focuses on business clients.

Telmex is also seeing increasing pressure from other large media and communications companies. For example, cable companies like Cablevision are offering telephone service via cable line in conjunction with their television and Internet packages. If you already plan to get cable and the service is available in your area, these plans may save you money.

COMMUNICATIONS AND CARLOS SLIM

Almost every time a phone rings in Mexico, it's another peso in the pocket of multibillionaire Carlos Slim Helú, a telecommunications mogul who in 2010 surpassed Bill Gates and Warren Buffett to become the world's richest man. Although he is the owner of a sundry and lucrative assortment of retail, food, construction, tobacco, and mining companies, none is more famous than his stake in Mexico's largest phone company, Telmex. Through Telmex, Slim and his investment group hold a virtual monopoly on the country's telecommunications and Internet service, controlling more than 80 percent of the country's landlines. An early mover in the mobile market, Slim's cellular companies also cover at least 70 percent of mobile service in the country.

It seems improbable that an investor from a developing nation would become the world's richest person, but intelligence, luck, and excellent personal connections have worked in the multibillionaire's favor. Slim began his career in the 1960s with real estate, later investing in and acquiring Mexican construction companies. By the 1990s, his investment group, Grupo Carso, was large enough to go public. Not long afterward, Slim won the bid to buy Mexico's public telephone company, Telefonos de Mexico (Telmex), from the government. Now in control of the country's telephone lines, Slim continued to invest heavily in telecommunications throughout Latin America and the United States. His wealth ballooned as Mexico's basic phone service remained among the most expensive worldwide.

In 2010, Slim officially outpaced other megabillionaires to take the top spot on the *Forbes* list of the world's richest people, with a net worth estimated at more than US$5.3 billion. In Mexico, he is the owner of the Sanborns department store chain, El Globo bakeries, and OSTAR Grupo Hotelero, among many other holdings. As the owner of América Móbil, he has vast holdings in the telecommunications industry throughout Latin America, and his investments include a more than 7 percent stake in the *New York Times* and a controlling 16 percent stake in the American department store chain Sak's Fifth Avenue.

Like many multibillionaires, Slim is an interesting character. In addition to being an enthusiastic New York Yankees fan, he has a strong interest in the fine arts. In 1994, he opened the fine art museum Museo Soumaya in Mexico City. Several years later, he founded the Fundación del Centro Histórico de la Ciudad de México, a part of his greater philanthropic organization, Fundación Carlos Slim, and began investing heavily in the purchase and renovation of properties in downtown Mexico City, in addition to social and educational programs. He has received many awards for his commitment to social service, just as he has received widespread critique for his continuing monopoly on Mexico's telecommunications.

As impressive as Slim's story may be, the monopoly on telephone service has made this basic service far more expensive in Mexico than in most developed countries. The Mexican government has long supported Slim's endeavors, but he has lately become less popular with regulators, who have begun to chip away at Telmex's dominance.

Costs and Billing

Compared to the United States, Canada, and Europe, telephone service in Mexico is expensive. However, Telmex offers a range of telephone plans and promotions that may undercut costs for those who know what types of calls they plan to make. Many users opt for Telmex's communications packages, which usually cover the monthly telephone service fee, a set number of local calls (they are billed at a flat rate, no matter the time spent on the phone), Internet service, and a limited number of long-distance minutes for a flat rate, not including international calls. After exceeding those limits, users are charged

© ARTURO MEADE

Some Internet cafés still operate long-distance calling booths, though they have become less prevalent.

for calls per minute. Alternatively, you can sign up for individual local, long-distance, or international plans, which will be billed individually in addition to the monthly service rate.

When it comes to long distance, rates vary by city, by distance called, and by the time the call is placed. If you will be making international calls, ask a Telmex representative about promotions that lower the cost of calls to certain area codes in the United States and Canada, or to certain phone numbers. Again, alternative phone companies may offer lower rates for long-distance or international calls.

Generally, the cost of calling ground lines (whether local or long distance) can be mitigated with the right package or plan. However, it is important to note that Mexico's cellular phone service operates on a different system, called El Que Llama Paga (whoever calls, pays). There are high surcharges for calling a cellular telephone, especially when the phone is in a different area code. Even if the phone you call shares your area code, you will billed at a long-distance rate if the user is in another city. If you are concerned about the costs of calling long distance or calling cell phones from your ground line, you can ask Telmex to restrict your phone service to local calls only.

As long as it isn't past due, you can pay your telephone bill at most banks and convenience stores, as well as directly at a Telmex office. Generally, clients

DIALING

Making telephone calls in Mexico isn't always a straightforward business. Here's a basic primer for dialing around the country and internationally.

LANDLINE TO LANDLINE

To dial from landline to landline within a city, you only need to dial the seven-digit number. If you are calling long distance, dial 01 + *lada* (area code) + seven-digit phone number.

CALLING MEXICO CITY, GUADALAJARA, AND MONTERREY

Phone numbers in Mexico City are eight digits long, rather than the standard seven digits used throughout the rest of the country. However, the area code for these cities is just two digits, so the full number is the standard 10 digits long.

When calling Mexico City from anywhere outside the city, you must dial the area code, 55, followed by the eight-digit number, for a total of 10 digits. Guadalajara and Monterrey's area codes are 33 and 81, respectively.

FROM LANDLINE TO CELL PHONE

To call a cellular phone from a landline in the same city, you must dial 044 before the phone number. If you are calling a cell phone in another city (in other words, long distance), put 045 before the number. If you are calling a cell phone from a pay phone, you do not need to use any prefix.

FROM CELL PHONE TO LANDLINE

To call a landline from a cell phone, dial area code + phone number, even if you are dialing from within the same city.

FROM CELL PHONE TO CELL PHONE

To call one cell phone from another, dial 1 + area code + phone number, even if you are dialing from within the same city.

DIALING THE UNITED STATES AND CANADA

To reach the United States or Canada, dial 001 + area code + phone number. There is no required country code.

DIALING ELSEWHERE INTERNATIONALLY

To call any country other than the United States or Canada, dial 00 + country code + area code + phone number, for a total of 14 digits.

FROM OVERSEAS TO MEXICO

Mexico's country code is 52. To call Mexico from the United States or Canada, dial 011 + 52 + area code + phone number. If you are calling a Mexican cell phone from overseas, you usually must add a 1 before the area code and after the country code.

receive about 10 days' notice on a bill; shortly after your balance is due, Telmex will cut off your ability to make outgoing calls until the bill is settled. (You can still receive calls for about a month before that service is also disconnected.)

INTERNET AND VOIP PHONES

The easiest and most inexpensive way to work around the high costs of the Mexican phone system is to use Internet communication tools or install a Voice Over Internet Protocol (VoIP) telephone. Skype is the most popular Internet-based communication tool, which allows you to speak for free with other Skype users or to call telephone numbers for a small charge per minute. Google also offers a video chat feature for registered users, though you cannot make phone calls through this service.

VoIP phones are very similar to regular telephones. With VoIP technology, an Internet connection is routed through a telephone headset. To use VoIP telephones, you must buy a router and telephone in the United States or Canada, then connect them directly to your modem in Mexico. Once registered, you will be assigned a Canadian or U.S. phone number, where you can make and receive calls for a monthly fee. Vonage is the most popular VoIP option, though several other companies offer this service. Another hardware-based option is MagicJack, a USB plug-in that allows you to connect a telephone to your computer and make calls to the United States or Canada for a very low annual charge. You need to purchase the equipment, but the yearly fee is inexpensive.

Clearly, the major drawback to any Internet-based telephone is that it is only available to users who have high-speed Internet connections. Since neither Telmex nor Cablevision offers complete coverage, some users will not be able to take advantage of Internet communication tools.

CALLING CARDS

The introduction of Internet-based telephony has made international and long-distance calling cards less popular than in the past. However, those who do not have access to high-speed Internet connections can save money on calls by buying prepaid calling cards. Stationery stores, airport kiosks, and other convenience stores will often carry lines of prepaid cards; ask the cashier. In most cases, these cards provide you with a local 800 access number. You call that number and then enter the unique PIN on your card. If you are using a calling card from a hotel room, always check that the access number is toll free before dialing.

PAY PHONES

As everywhere, pay phones are on the decline in Mexico, where widespread cell phone usage has negated their usefulness. You can still find them in airports and bus terminals, public parks, or other frequented places, though many are broken and out of service. When you first arrive, using a pay phone may be the easiest way to communicate. It is also among the most economical options for local calls.

With very few exceptions, public telephones aren't coin operated in Mexico. To use one, you must buy a prepaid Ladatel telephone card with MXN$20, MXN$50, or MXN$100 of credit. These cards are usually for sale in corner shops or convenience stores (look for the Ladatel ad in the window). As you talk, a small screen above the keypad will tick off the cost of your call. Some people also bring prepaid international calling cards to use from pay phones, though this option has become less popular.

CELLULAR PHONES

There are more than 83 million cell phone users in Mexico. In fact, there are far more mobile phone users in Mexico than ground line subscribers. For many, a cell phone is easier and more inexpensive to set up than a ground line, in addition to offering all the convenience of mobility. In fact, getting a cell phone is so easy and economical that it can be a practical purchase for short-term visitors to Mexico.

Service Providers

Mexico has several competing cellular phone companies. Telcel, a subsidiary of Telmex (and which has now grown larger than its parent company), is the far-and-away leader in the cellular phone market in Mexico, covering about 70 percent of cellular users. In large part, it has maintained its dominance by charging higher rates when a non-Telcel telephone dials a Telcel customer, putting non-Telcel users at a serious disadvantage. The situation is currently being reviewed by Mexico's Federal Competition Commission.

While they are still far from catching up with Telcel, Spanish-owned Movistar has made a major leap in sales, signing up more new users than Telcel over the past few years. An early mover in the cell phone market, Iusacell is the third-largest cellular phone provider in Mexico, with coverage in more than 90 percent of the country, including the capital. It is owned by Grupo Salinas, another large media conglomerate that also owns TV Azteca.

Buying and Registering a Mexican Cell Phone

Getting a cell phone in Mexico is quick and easy. There are literally dozens of cell phone retail outlets in every city, with Telcel leading the pack in ubiquity. (Sometimes, one Telcel store will be right across the street from another.) Franchised operations, these small shops usually represent just one of the major cell phone carriers, so you'll have to walk between different shops if you want to compare plans and prices. Phones range from very inexpensive to pricey and high-tech, including smartphones.

When you purchase a cell phone, you will be given a handset with a chip that contains your telephone number and the phone's memory (specifically, your address book). This chip can be transferred to another phone manually if you want to upgrade your hardware. You will need to register your phone and number at the time of purchase; if you lose your phone or chip, you can report it to the company to recover your phone number.

Pay-Per-Use

The vast majority of Mexican cell phones operate without a payment plan. Users simply buy credit for their cell phones, which is used up as they make and receive calls and send text messages. (Note that you must have some credit on your telephone in order to receive a long-distance call, and that call does incur a small charge.) There are two options for buying credit on your cell phone. You can buy a prepaid phone card of MXN$100, MXN$200, MXN$300, or MXN$500 value, call the access number, and enter the card's ID number. These cards usually come with bonus credit for values more than MXN$100. Alternatively, many pharmacies and convenience stores (including the ubiquitous OXXO) allow you to recharge the credit on a Telcel telephone for any amount, paid up front—a convenient option if you only want to buy MXN$30 of credit, for example.

The balance on most cellular phones has a limited lifespan, usually three months. If you haven't used your minutes by then, they will be erased from your balance. From a Telcel phone, you can dial #109 to check your balance via text message, or dial #333 to have your balance read to you in Spanish. Note that there is a small charge for these calls.

While prices have come down, owning a cell phone in Mexico can be expensive, especially when you use your cell phone to make long-distance calls. For plans with minimal minutes, you can pay as little as MXN$300 a month, though plans work better for heavy users (those who don't use their cell phone often or don't talk for long will be best off using a prepaid credit). As an alternative to phone calls, text messages are enormously popular in Mexico because they provide a more inexpensive alternative to phone calls (with most carriers, text messages cost less than a peso).

Monthly Plans

In addition to prepaid phone cards, all of Mexico's major cell phone carriers offer flat-rate monthly plans—generally called *planes de renta*—which include minutes, texts, and data. Monthly plans can also be more economical if you have a general idea of how many minutes you use and, not to mention, less of a hassle since you don't have to worry about running to the drugstore every time your credit runs low. Those with smartphones will almost certainly benefit from a monthly plan, which includes air time, texts, and data transfer. Internet use and data transfer can be very expensive on prepaid cards.

In general, cell phone companies offer monthly plans that charge a flat rate for a certain number of air time and text messages, usually accompanied by unlimited talk to certain frequently called telephone numbers in the same mobile network. Depending on your budget and needs, you can adjust these parameters. For more money, you can also buy Web access for Internet-enabled phones. For iPhones, there are also numerous levels of data transfer and voice plans, some starting as low as US$40 per month for small number of minutes.

Unfortunately, choosing a cell phone plan is far from simple and straightforward; each cell phone company offers dozens of plan options at different price points. Plus, you'll have to speak directly to representatives of each company in order to compare costs and benefits. Fortunately, most offer the details of their phone packages online.

El Que Llama Paga

As mandated by Mexican law, Mexico employs an El Que Llama Paga program (he who calls, pays). In other words, only the person placing a call is charged for the minutes spent talking. If you call a cell phone from your ground line, the call will be charged on your monthly statement. If you call a cell phone from your cell phone, it will be deducted from your credit.

Generally, you do not need to have any credit on your cellular phone to be able to receive calls. However, there is one small but important exception: You often cannot receive long-distance phone calls if you have no credit on your phone. Sometimes, the phone company will notify you that someone out of the area is attempting to call you; other times, you will not have any idea that you are missing calls.

Smartphones

Smartphones, including iPhone and Blackberry, are available through Mexican carriers. Plans are paid monthly and usually include a discount on the hardware when you sign a one- or two-year contract. Unlike the United States, iPhones in Mexico are unlocked and include chips, which means you can switch carriers on the same hardware. All three major carriers, Telcel, Movistar, and Iusacell, offer iPhone service, as well as iPad service. Telcel, for example, offers a range of data and airtime packages from around US$45–130.

Foreign Cell Phones in Mexico

Considering the high costs of domestic telephones and cellular service, it is not surprising that roaming charges can be particularly high for foreign cell phones in Mexico. U.S. cell phones are generally locked to their carrier, so you will have to stick with the same company if you plan to use your U.S. cell phone in Mexico. Canadians have the option of buying unlocked phones and may be able to transfer their service to Mexico by buying a chip with a cellular carrier.

Some people are able to work with their foreign carrier to receive international cell phone service in Mexico. Several cellular phone companies offer North America plans, which allow unlimited calling on the continent for a monthly fee. These plans can be more expensive than regular single-country calling plans, but they are considerably cheaper than paying roaming charges or calling a foreign country from a Mexican cell phone.

When checking into international coverage for a smartphone, you must purchase an international data plan in addition to an international talk plan. Applications like Google Maps can use a lot of data, so be sure you understand the parameters of your coverage before you head south. Consider resetting your usage meter so you know how much data you are using, as well as connecting via free wireless connections in cafés or restaurants to save money. You can also turn off "data roaming" so that your smartphone will not automatically connect to the Internet to download email. Finally, if you decide to keep your smartphone in Mexico, you can often save money by using Skype (or another Internet-based telephone service) rather than your smartphone's long-distance package.

Internet

Mexico is wired. Internet service is available and inexpensive in almost all of Mexico, and there are an estimated 30 million Internet users in the country. Though you may not find everything online yet (conveniences like online bill pay are still a way's off in Mexico), most people are extremely fluent in the virtual environment, with email, chat, and social media all widely popular.

RESIDENTIAL AND COMMERCIAL SERVICE

Telmex acquired the Internet service provider (ISP) Prodigy Communications in the 1990s, and it offers Internet service packages under the Prodigy name, both as residential dial-up and DSL connections. As an ISP, Telmex controls 80 percent of the market in Mexico; in many cases, Telmex is the only option for residential service.

Through Telmex, Internet service can be purchased together with telephone service. You can choose between different bandwidth, but even the smallest package is fairly swift. If you subscribe to their broadband service, called Infinitum, you can use your computer, smartphone, or iPad to connect to the company's wireless networks, which are set up in airports, universities, and other public places in Mexico. Note that Telmex does not offer broadband service to every residence, even if that residence has a ground line.

Aside from Telmex, there are several other ISPs in Mexico. One of the most

© CARLOS MEADE

There are inexpensive Internet cafés throughout the country.

prominent options is Axtel, a Monterrey-based communications company, which offers residential and commercial Internet service (as well as telephone service). Cablevision, Mexico's biggest cable company, offers Internet connections via cable for home and offices. In some areas, Cablevision will only provide Internet service to cable subscribers who purchase Internet as part of a package. In others, they will simply run a cable line for Internet and charge only for that service. When contracting Internet service, installation is usually charged, but the modem is included in the cost. A wireless modem may cost extra.

INTERNET VIA CELL PHONE COMPANIES

Most people get their home Internet connections through telephone or cable service. However, those who live in more rural areas (even if they live near a city) may not be able to install either cable or phone lines at home. Telmex, Iusacell, and Movistar all offer the option of connecting to the Internet via the satellite network. You buy a special plug-in, which connects to your computer's USB port, and then pay for a monthly access plan, priced according to the amount of bandwidth you request. Those who use this service say it can be erratic but generally works well.

INTERNET CAFÉS

For many visitors—and even residents—the easiest way to check your email, fax, scan a document, or print is by visiting one of the multitude of Internet cafés, also called *cibercafes*. These outfits charge hourly or by-minute rates to use their computers, and per page for printing. Many *papelerías* (stationery stores) also have Internet service.

Postal Service and Shipping

Correos de México, Mexico's national postal service, is infamously erratic and slow. It can be reliable, if sluggish, for simple communications like postcards. However, larger and more valuable items are at risk of loss or seizure; packages often disappear without recourse. If they do arrive, months of delay are not uncommon. Sometimes, mail will arrive quickly and without incident, inspiring a momentary trust in the mail system; your next encounter with the post is likely to erase that good impression, though.

While it is certainly possible that the postal service will successfully deliver your package or letter, it isn't a particularly reliable way to communicate. If something absolutely must arrive in the hands of the recipient, you must pay more for a private service.

POST OFFICE

© ARTURO MEADE

In 2008, Correos de México rolled out a new image, which included a hot-pink logo depicting a passenger pigeon with a letter in its beak. Pleasing as that image is, the new look hasn't done much to win back customers or improve service. The Mexican post remains a very limited and unreliable operation. Generally speaking, the post office is most reliable when sending mail within a city. If you want to send mail to other parts of Mexico, the chances of it arriving decrease. International post is even less reliable.

Mexico City's central post office is a historic building with gilded cashier's stations.

If you own a business, you can use the post for mass mailings or promotions—anything that isn't particularly time sensitive. Avoid sending valuables or sensitive materials through the mail. No matter what you send, expect a substantial wait time. Even though you can occasionally receive a letter quickly, mail can sometimes, inexplicably, take months to arrive.

MexPost

Within the post office there is a more expensive and more reliable mail service called MexPost, which allows you to send registered envelopes and packages throughout Mexico, as well as overseas. MexPost is operated by Mexico's postal system, but it is a guaranteed service. They can usually provide you with a fairly accurate estimate of when a letter or package will arrive, especially nationally.

SHIPPING COMPANIES

In most cases, you will have better luck shipping with private companies, and there are several that offer more reliable (though also more expensive) service for letters and packages. Within Mexico, DHL, UPS, FedEx, and Mexican-owned Estafeta all offer national and international expedited shipping. In some cases, these companies will not be as reliable in Mexico as they might be at home (in other words, give yourself some buffer time if you need a package to arrive right away); generally, however, they are reliable and fast, if a bit pricey.

INTERNATIONAL MAIL FORWARDING

For expatriates, there are several regional companies that offer mail forwarding services to and from the United States and Canada. In the popular expatriate enclaves of San Miguel de Allende and the Lake Chapala region of Jalisco, several companies offer Texas-based mailing addresses; mail is then brought down to Mexico and available for pickup. Many residents receive their regular post, plus magazines and newspapers, via these proxy addresses. In Guadalajara, Mail Boxes Etc. offers similar services to residents of that city. There are also several international companies that offer mail forwarding services worldwide, such as USA2Me.

CUSTOMS

Anything sent to Mexico from overseas is subject to import duties. Even if sent through a mail forwarding service, contents must be declared and may be searched by a customs agent. Fees are calculated based on a item's weight, size, and classification. Generally, books and other paper goods are subject to relatively low import fees. You'll pay a lot more for electronics or computer equipment, which may negate the higher costs of simply buying the item in Mexico (duties can run around 17 percent).

For large or expensive items (goods that will be used in a business, for example, or furniture), it may be necessary to use a customs broker. Companies like UPS will provide customs brokerage as a part of their international shipping services, or you can choose a broker yourself and then have a Mexican freight company pick it up at the border. (The second option may be more inexpensive if you have a trusted shipping company in your area.)

Media

Several large conglomerates control most Mexican media, though there are also sufficient independent communications channels (often operated in conjunction with universities) and publications.

NEWSPAPERS

Daily newspapers are popular throughout Mexico, with numerous high-quality periodicals produced in the capital and other large cities. The vast majority of these are written in Spanish, though many pick up translated stories from the AP, Reuters, and other news wires, in addition to Mexico's wire service, Notimex. For English speakers, there is a more limited selection of print publications, though you'll likely find something worth reading in your area.

Spanish-Language Newspapers

Many of Mexico's most important periodicals are published in the capital. The most well-known daily newspapers, including *El Universal, Reforma,* and *Excélsior,* are based in Mexico City and cover national news, sports, travel, and entertainment. These papers are widely distributed throughout the country, in addition to publishing local editions in several big cities, like Monterrey and Guadalajara. In the north, the newspaper *Milenio* is based in Monterrey and published in 12 cities.

In addition to mainstream publications, the leftist periodical *La Jornada* is a political news and opinion tabloid favored by Mexico's intellectuals and widely read and distributed throughout the country. *El Financiero* is a serious business and finance-focused paper, also published in Mexico City. All of these papers have a strong online presence in addition to their print editions.

In addition to these national papers, there are many regional news services, which are often important in covering local news, including *Noticias* in Oaxaca, *Correo* in Guanajuato, and *El Informador* in Guadalajara, among many others. Regional papers and tabloids tend to cover local news and politics, in addition to national and international stories. Although a lot of information is available on the Internet, newspapers are still an excellent source of job and housing information in Mexico; larger cities usually have at least one newspaper with a strong classifieds section.

© ARTURO MEADE

Newsstands often sell public telephone cards in addition to magazines and newspapers.

English-Language Newspapers

There are a small number of English-language newspapers in Mexico directed at the expatriate community, many with good local events sections. The most serious of the bunch is Mexico City-based newspaper, *The News,* a tabloid-format newspaper covering national and international news, with a strong focus on the United States. They publish stories from the news wires in addition to doing their own reporting. Once a subsidiary of the Mexican newspaper *Novedades,* it is now an independent publication. In Guadalajara, the *Guadalajara Reporter* covers local, national, and international news, as well as arts and cultural events.

Other regional English-language publications cover local news but focus more seriously on culture and local events, such as *Atención San Miguel* in San Miguel de Allende and the *Gringo Gazette* from Baja California. These papers can be an excellent resource for new Mexico expatriates, and they can be a good way to get a bead on the local community. Seek them out!

Magazines

There are a number of good monthly magazines and weeklies published in Mexico, including the political magazine *Próceso,* known for its crack reporting.

For art and culture, there are several high-quality Spanish-language publications in Mexico. *Artes de Mexico* is a beautiful and well-researched series of magazines covering traditions, craft, architecture, museums, history, film, and other cultural topics. The more academic *Arqueologia Mexicana* is another beautifully photographed and rigorously researched Spanish-language publication covering anthropological study of Mexico's pre-Columbian cultures. *Mexico Desconocido* is an excellent travel magazine, often with an anthropological twist, covering travel, traditions, and environmental attractions in unusual and off-the-beaten-track destinations in Mexico, with excellent insights into national traditions.

You'll also find Mexican-published editions of glossies like *Vogue, Elle,* and *InStyle,* in addition to a bunch of national gossip magazines and sensationalist tabloids.

International Publications

Newsstands in Mexico tend to be limited to national publications, though most airports and some bookshops will carry a wider range of imported titles like *Vanity Fair, Time, The Economist,* and other general interest magazines. In big cities, the department-store chain Sanborns has a large newsstand, with dozens of national titles and many English-language titles as well.

TELEVISION

Mexican television is heavily dominated by a few big players. As a result, it is rather commercial and fairly homogenized, and with the exception of the public channels, it isn't a bastion of innovation. In addition to network television, cable companies offer a range of additional channels to subscribers.

Network

There are six commercial broadcast stations in Mexico, four of which are controlled by media conglomerate Televisa: Canal 5, Canal de las Estrellas, Galavisión, and ForoTV. Run by billionaire Emilio Azcárraga, Televisa controls 70 percent of the free-to-air television audience in Mexico. (Among its many subsidiaries, Televisa also owns the popular club soccer teams Aguilas de America from Mexico City, Necaxa from Toluca, and Atlante in Cancún, so these teams receive good coverage, as well as nice cash infusions from their parent company.) The other two commercial stations are controlled by TV Azteca, another major media conglomerate owned by the Salinas Group, which also controls Banco Azteca, Elektra, and numerous other large financial institutions and national corporations. The group's chairman and founder, Ricardo Salinas Pliego, is ranked within the five richest people in the country.

Channels run by Televisa and TV Azteca broadcast a mix of morning shows, news programs, sports, and American television series (usually dubbed into Spanish), as well as widely popular telenovelas (soap operas), which are limited-run television dramas. For those studying Spanish, the telenovelas' theatrical acting and easy-to-follow plot lines are good for practicing your aural comprehension skills!

Public Television

There are two excellent public television channels in Mexico: the widely viewed Canal Once (Channel 11) and the Mexico City–based Canal 22 (Channel 22). These channels offer special programming on culture, politics, travel, and anthropology, in addition to airing high-quality movies and documentaries. Canal Once is operated by the Instituto Politécnico Nacional (National Politechnic Institute), a prestgious public university in Mexico City. Canal 22 is operated by Conaculta, the Consejo Nacional para la Cultura y las Artes (National Council for Culture and the Arts), the government body that oversees anthropological and cultural projects. Canal Once is principally available in big cities; Canal 22 is limited to the capital.

DAILY LIFE

Cable and Satellite

Through cable and satellite options, Mexican households have access to premium programming, including U.S.-based networks in Spanish, such as CNN en Espanol, as well as English-language sitcoms and dramas from the United States. The providers and availability of cable television vary by region; Megacable and Cablevision are two of the biggest. Most of cable companies will include at least some English-language programming in their roster, though some have more than others.

You will have even more options for English-language programming if you get a satellite dish, including major U.S. networks like NBC and Fox. Small-dish satellite television is available through several different companies, with DISH Network from the United States and Star Choice from Canada leading the pack in English-language programming for central Mexico. In some cases, users report inconsistency with their satellite signal, so ask around before you invest.

RADIO

Radio has a long history in Mexico, and it remains a popular media for news, information, sports, and music. Located in downtown Mexico City, the fabled XEW has been operating since 1930 and has broadcast some of the country's most popular radio personalities over the years. XEW, broadcast at 96.9 FM, eventually spun off to create XEW-TV, Mexico's first television station, now owned by Televisa and operating under the name Canal de las Estrellas.

Local radio stations are still common in most Mexican towns, and they can be a great way for Spanish speakers to learn a bit more about local culture. Some stations allow city residents to buy slots on the air, so programs can often run the gamut from political commentary to local news to opinion.

Mexico's universities often operate popular radio stations, many of which are among the best stations in the country, including Radio UNAM, in Mexico City; Radio Universidad de Guadalajara; Radio Universidad Queretaro; and Radio Universitdad Guanajuato "La Colmena," among others. These channels have diverse programs highly focused on culture and entertainment, and often feature classical music and jazz programs. Most university stations offer streaming radio via the Internet.

TRAVEL AND TRANSPORTATION

Getting to and from Mexico from overseas is generally convenient and affordable, and the country's good infrastructure makes it easy to travel once you're on the ground. There are beautiful toll roads crisscrossing the country and small, scenic freeways connecting smaller towns and beaches. On land, travel can be more arduous in rural areas, but Mexico's highways are generally well maintained and safe.

With the busiest border crossing in the world, there is a constant stream of folks crossing into the country. People enter Mexico in cars and RVs, on cruise ships and sailboats, in the air, or on buses.

© CARLOS MEADE

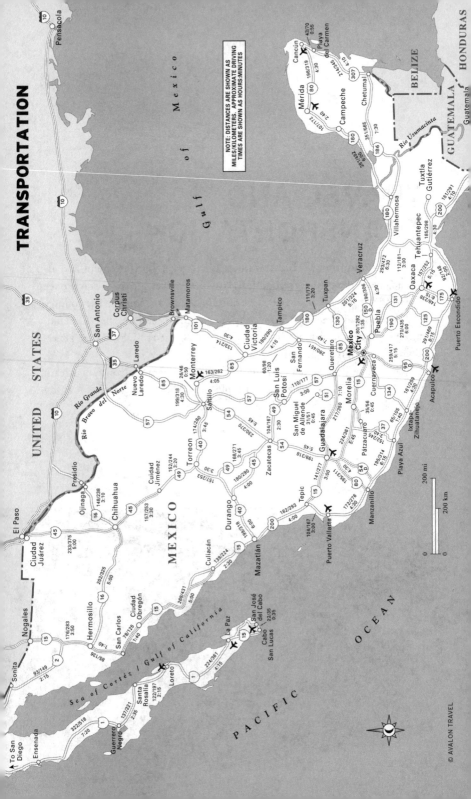

By Air

Since Mexicana declared bankruptcy and ceased operations in the summer of 2010, Mexico has only one major airline, Aeroméxico, in addition to several smaller low-cost carriers that specialize in national routes. For international travel, many major air carriers have service between points in Mexico and the United States and Canada. Aeroméxico, Air Canada, United, Continental, American Airlines, Delta, Alaska Airlines, and US Airways all have daily service from major North American cities to various Mexican cities and resorts. For travel between Mexico and Europe, there are several direct flights from Mexico City to European capitals (like Paris, Madrid, and Frankfurt) operated by both European carriers (like KLM, Air France, and British Airways) as well as Aeroméxico. Heading anywhere else (including South America) can be a bit trickier—travelers must occasionally fly to the United States to reach Pacific destinations.

Air travel is still more limited within Mexico than in the United States, Canada, and Europe, and it's a less-popular option. When traveling domestically, most Mexicans drive or take the bus, which is vastly more affordable than flying. Air travel to regions outside major cities and resorts can be more limited and expensive. Most small airports only have domestic service, with connecting service through the capital.

AIRPORTS

Major cities and important tourist resorts have large airports, where flights arrive both domestically and internationally every day. Mexico City's Benito Juarez International Airport (MEX) is far and away the largest and busiest airport in the country. More than 30 airlines fly into Mexico City from more than 100 destinations. Located right in the middle of the metropolitan region, this intercity airport was expanded to include a new terminal and runways where Aeroméxico, Delta, and several other carriers have their operations. For service to cities near the capital, there are several bus lines that leave directly from the airport for Puebla, Querétaro, Cuernavaca, and Pachuca.

In addition to Mexico City, there are busy international airports in Monterrey, Guadalajara, Puerto Vallarta, Cancún, Cabo San Lucas, León, and Acapulco. (Though, from Europe there are only direct flights to Mexico City and Cancún.) Other airports usually offer only domestic routes, usually to and from the capital, where you can connect to international service.

Though there are direct flights to many U.S. cities from Mexico, Los Angeles, Chicago, Dallas, Houston, and Miami offer the most options. If you are flying from Texas to the capital, the flight is a little more than two hours. From New York City, the flight is about five. From Europe, travel to Mexico takes about 11 or 12 hours from most cities.

International airfares to Mexico are fairly stable, which make them great for budgeting but bad for bargain hunters. The country gets tourists and business travelers year-round, so there is little seasonal fluctuation in prices. You may find promotions for national flights, though, especially to less well-known beach resorts.

AIRLINES

When Mexico's preeminent airline, Mexicana, declared bankruptcy and ceased operations in 2010, it changed the landscape for Mexican air travel. Today, Aeroméxico is the country's biggest airline and the only major carrier. Aeroméxico offers flights between Mexican cities, as well as to numerous international destinations in the United States, Canada, Europe, South and Central America, and Asia. It is joined in international service by dozens of airlines from around the world. From the United States, Continental, United, US Airways, and Delta are among the biggest carriers.

Most domestic flights are handled by national airlines. Aeroméxico connects all major cities, while smaller carriers pick up competing routes to smaller airports. For national travel, there are a few smaller and low-cost lines operating in Mexico. You may not always see these options when you search for flights on the Internet, as some of these carriers may not have code-sharing agreements with other airlines or aren't represented by online booking agencies. A travel agent in Mexico can often book flights on low-cost carriers, or you can consult the airline's website directly.

If you need to fly within the country, try Calafia (for Baja California and the Pacific Coast), Aeromar (for smaller cities), Aviacsa (for Southern Mexico and Monterrey), VivaAerobus (for low cost travel to many major cities), Volaris (for north and central Mexico, as well as Oaxaca and Puebla), and Interjet (for national flights and Guatemala). Aside from Interjet's Guatemala route, the only low-cost Mexican airline to offer international destinations is Volaris, which is based in Adolfo López Mateos International Airport in Toluca. It is currently expanding, with plans to move its hub to Guadalajara.

By Bus

For both expatriates and Mexicans, bus is the most popular way to travel around Mexico. Dozens of private companies offer service to almost every location in the country, with literally hundreds of buses leaving major cities every hour. (The one exception is the Baja peninsula, where there are fewer bus companies operating than in other parts of the country.) Buses are called *camiones*, and bus travel in Mexico is usually affordable, comfortable, and safe. In some cases it is faster than flying, and it is always much more inexpensive.

That said, Mexico is a large country, so it can also be a long haul between distant cities. Often, passengers will undertake their journeys overnight, traveling from Mexico City to the coast from dusk to dawn. If you can spare a few days and want to save money, there are even bus lines that will take you as far north as Chicago. For especially long trips, buses make periodic stops to switch drivers and to allow passengers to get off the bus to stretch their legs and eat.

BUS CLASSES

For any intracity travel of more than an hour or two, first-class or executive-class buses are faster and more comfortable than second-class buses. First-class buses generally offer direct service between major destinations, and most have air-conditioning, reclining seats, and bathrooms. Most also play loud and outdated Hollywood movies in Spanish from overhead TV screens—an annoyance to most passengers, though also a bit folkloric. A major bus line will service almost anyplace in Mexico, with connecting service to small towns.

Second-class buses are more inexpensive than first-class buses, but they rarely offer direct service between two cities. Second-class buses make more frequent stops between cities and usually stop to pick up and drop off passengers along the roadway, slowing travel time. At the same time, second-class buses are more convenient for shorter trips, with many bus lines offering frequent and inexpensive service between neighboring towns.

On major routes, second-class buses are usually comfortable and inexpensive, though they may not have air-conditioning or toilets onboard. Off-the-beaten-path, smaller bus companies (especially in the southern states) may have more rustic units. Though hardly ubiquitous, there are still some "chicken buses" in service.

RESERVATIONS

It is rarely necessary to make bus reservations in advance; however, on big holiday weekends, first-class bus service to popular destinations will fill up quickly. If you are traveling during Christmas, Holy Week, the Independence Day holidays, or any other three-day weekend, buy your tickets a few days in advance. Second-class buses do not have assigned seating and therefore rarely take reservations. Show up to the station early to buy your ticket.

Most first-class bus companies have websites, but it is generally easier to make reservations by phone, at the bus station, or through a travel agent (note that telephone reservations systems are generally Spanish speaking). In Mexico City, Ticketbus is an authorized ticket reseller.

TO AND FROM MEXICO CITY

Mexico City is the country's largest transportation hub, and most people find themselves taking a bus in or out of the city at some point. Most Mexican cities have a single bus station for long-distance travel (or a single first-class and a single second-class bus terminal), but there are four major bus terminals in Mexico City: Terminal Centro Poniente (serving western destinations, like Michoacan), Terminal Central Sur "Tasqueña" (serving southern destinations, including Cuernavaca), Terminal de Autobuses de Pasajeros de Oriente "TAPO" (for eastern and southeastern cities, like Oaxaca and Puebla), and Central de Autobuses del Norte (for northern destinations, like San Miguel de Allende). When planning your travel, you must also determine which bus station offers the most service to your destination.

COLECTIVOS

Public transportation or private bus companies many not offer service to more remote areas, small beach areas, or rural towns. Therefore, transportation is often offered by more informal services, called *colectivos* (shared taxi service) or *combis* (shared vans). Generally, *colectivo* stops aren't marked; you'll need to ask where the van stops (any local should know). Once onboard, you pay your fee to the driver, with the cost usually based on the distance you travel. Along the coast of Oaxaca, there are also pickup trucks that will carry passengers in their beds for a few pesos per ride.

By Boat

Mexico's beautiful coastline, with great sportfishing along the Pacific Coast, can also be visited by boat. Few people enter Mexico with their own vessel, preferring to hire a boat once across the border. However, some people do enter Baja and the Pacific Coast by sea. Ferries between Baja California and the mainland are also an important transport mode, especially for those with automobiles.

FERRIES

Baja Ferries offers passenger and vehicle ferries that cross the Sea of Cortez from Baja California to mainland Mexico. Currently, there is ferry service La Paz–Topolobampo and La Paz–Mazatlan. There is also a ferry farther north, between Santa Rosalia and Guayamas.

Ferries accept passengers, pets, and cars. If you are traveling with your foreign car, you must have all the correct import paperwork for your vehicle; you will officially pass through customs when you board the ferry (Baja California is considered a special trade zone). Car and personal tickets are sold separately, and there are both regular seats and private cabins for passengers.

The trip between La Paz and Mazatlan takes about 12 hours; La Paz–Topolobambo is about 5 hours. Pets must be crated and ride in a designated area. Buy tickets with anticipation; the ferry often fills up and can be especially booked during whale-watching season.

© GABRIELA PEÑA GARAVITO

Boats cram the harbor in Mazatlan.

BRINGING YOUR OWN BOAT

Sailing and fishing are popular activities off Mexico's azure coast, especially along the Baja California peninsula and the Pacific. Most people simply rent boats in Mexico for sportfishing or sailing, though some travel from ports in the United States to Baja California. Bringing a boat to Mexico isn't very different from bringing a car; you need the proper paperwork from immigration to legally dock. Like anywhere, you also need to proper permits to enter and leave marinas, and to fish.

To temporarily import a boat to Mexico, you will need to bring its title, proof of citizenship, and the departure clearance from the foreign port where you set sail. (If you are bringing your boat by land with a trailer, you will also need the title for the trailer.) Once you arrive at your destination in Mexico, you need to solicit an FMM (tourist card) from immigration, and then get a temporary vehicle permit for your boat. With your FMM, the title for the vessel, and an international credit card, you will be granted temporary import paperwork for your boat.

There are also requirements to sail in Mexican waters. Once you have legally entered Mexico, you will still need to get all the legal entry and departure clearances from each port. If you plan to do any fishing (or will have fishing equipment on your boat), you will need to get a fishing license before you leave. Check with the Mexican Fisheries Office.

If you are considering bringing a boat to Mexico, keep in mind that sailing along the Pacific Coast of Mexico is for experienced open-ocean sailors. If you are new to open-ocean sailing, bring along an experienced guide.

Boat Insurance

If you have boat insurance in the United States, you can usually extend the policy to Mexico for a small additional cost. You may also want to purchase Mexican liability insurance in the case you have an accident and cause damage to Mexican property.

Public Transportation

Cars are ubiquitous in Mexico, but public transportation is also widespread, affordable, and accessible in both big cities and small towns. Many people rely entirely on public transit to get from home to their jobs, and the systems are often efficient—if occasionally haphazard. In many places, it can take some time to learn the ropes, since bus schedules are rarely posted—even if they exist.

CITY BUSES

In most Mexican cities, a proprietary system of public buses are the most inexpensive way to get around. Most urban bus lines run from early morning (about 6 A.M.) to late evening (about 10 P.M.). Routes are fixed but rarely published (with the exception of the relatively new MetroBus system in Mexico City). Although you won't be able to get your hands on a map of the urban bus routes, a bus's major destinations are posted on the windshield, so once you locate a bus stop, you can see where the buses are going. Once onboard, you can ask the driver to verify your destination. In a small town, you may be able to use the system quickly; in larger cities, it may take a bit more time. In many ways, learning to use the transport system is best accomplished through some adventurous trial and error.

In most larger cities, *urbanos,* or city buses, connect major neighborhoods. City buses usually offer cheap and frequent service to most major neighborhoods. In smaller cities and towns, especially in Southern Mexico, cities might only have *colectivos,* or smaller vans, that transport passengers across town. *Colectivos* will also have their destinations painted on the windshield; you hail the *colectivo* from the street and can generally ask to be dropped off anywhere along the route.

METRO

Mexico City's famous metro transports millions of people every day. It is the world's second-busiest (trumped only by Tokyo), as well as its cheapest, public metro system. Indeed, at just MXN$2.50 per ride (US$0.20), it is a bargain. The metro is safe and clean. In addition to Mexico City's famous metro, there is also a smaller light rail system in Guadalajara, which connects downtown with neighborhoods like Zapopan—though generally it does not stop at any major tourist destinations.

TAXI

Taxis are an abundant, inexpensive, and popular form of transport

Mexico City's extensive metro system is the world's cheapest subway, as well as the second-largest, after Tokyo's.

throughout Mexico. Painted green, taxis circle around every city in Mexico (and most small towns), and they are generally safe to flag off the street anywhere except Mexico City. In most parts of Mexico, taxis offer a standard flat rate, depending on where you are going. You can ask the driver for the cost before you take off. In Mexico City, some cars also have fare calculators, based on time and distance.

Registered Cabs and *Sitios*

In most airports, as well as some bus stations, there are taxi stands representing a fleet of registered drivers, or *taxis autorizados*. Taxi stands offer a set fare depending on where you are going; usually, you purchase a ticket from the stand, which you present to the driver. Taking registered taxis is a security necessity in Mexico City; elsewhere, it is simply a convenience. If there is a taxi stand, it is prohibited to take a taxi that is not specifically registered for the airport or bus terminal, since the drivers pay a special fee for their license. Some taxi stands have caddies who will help carry your luggage. (If you use their services, offer a tip.)

If you are not at an airport or bus terminal, registered taxi companies are usually called *sitios*. You can call a *sitio* to have a taxi come to pick you up, or you can walk to a *sitio,* where taxis are waiting for passengers. In Mexico City, taxi crime is common, so visitors and residents should always take registered cabs. In other parts of Mexico where it is safe to hail cabs on the street, *sitios* come in handy when you are located in a more remote neighborhood where flagging a cab would be impossible.

Driving

For those who love the romance of the open road, Mexico is the closest thing to paradise. The country is ribboned with picturesque and well-maintained highways, which snake past scenic small towns, open fields, and waving cornfields. Rural roads—especially in areas that suffer from severe weather and flooding—may have mudslides and potholes. Look out for road advisories, and avoid driving in the rain. However, off-the-beaten-track drives can often be the most rewarding way to see the country, offering a glimpse of rural life and serene landscapes.

MEXICAN HIGHWAYS

During the past few decades, Mexico has invested heavily in its infrastructure. Generally, there are two types of highways in Mexico: high-speed toll roads,

Driving through Mexico City can be a challenge; pay attention to the signs!

known as *autopistas* (highways), and lower-speed open roads, usually called *carreteras* or *libramientos*. You will also see toll roads designated as *cuota* (toll) and freeways designated as *libre* (free).

Toll Roads

Generally, toll roads, or *autopistas,* are much faster, safer, and more efficient than free highways, though you won't find a toll road to every destination in Mexico. Toll roads are often privately owned, and their quality can range significantly.

If you are traveling long distances, bring cash. In some *casetas* (toll booths), you can pay with a bank card or credit card; others require cash payments. There are often free bathrooms and snack bars right after each toll booth, as well as gas stations. The cost of your toll includes road insurance, which will cover the cost of damage to your vehicle and medical bills.

Mexican toll roads are patrolled by Los Ángeles Verdes, or Green Angels, a fleet of emergency responders and road mechanics operated by the Mexican Secretary of Tourism. The Green Angels can offer tourist information for visitors, assist with medical emergencies, and attend to mechanical problems 8 A.M.–6 P.M. daily. Dial 078 from a telephone to reach the Green Angels. There are also frequent emergency telephone booths along the roadside; look out for the signage.

Highway Information

You can get updated highway information at the government's Caminos y

DAILY LIFE

HOY NO CIRCULA

Mexico City's Hoy No Circula program has made major strides in reducing automobile emissions in the Valley of Mexico. Both the capital and Mexico state participate in the program, which prohibits cars from driving on certain days of the week based on the last digit of their license plate.

If you will be driving in the capital with a foreign or Mexican-plated car, take care to avoid driving on the days that your car isn't permitted on the road. Cars that violate the Hoy No Circula rules are immediately impounded, and fines for the violation (in addition to the cost of towing and impounding) are incredibly high. There will be no opportunity to claim ignorance; these rules are set in stone, and every driver has the burden of staying aware of the restrictions.

On the days your license number is restricted, you may not drive between 5 A.M. and 10 P.M.

WEEKDAYS

- Monday: licenses ending in 5 or 6 (yellow sticker)
- Tuesday: licenses ending in 7 or 8 (pink sticker)
- Wednesday: licenses ending in 3 or 4 (red sticker)
- Thursday: licenses ending in 1 or 2 (green sticker)
- Friday: licenses ending in 9 or 0, letters only, or temporary plates (blue sticker)

WEEKENDS

- First Saturday of the month: licenses ending in 5 or 6 (yellow sticker)
- Second Saturday of the month: licenses ending in 7 or 8 (pink sticker)
- Third Saturday of the month: licenses ending in 3 or 4 (red sticker)
- Fourth Saturday of the month: licenses ending in 1 or 2 (green sticker)
- Fifth Saturday of the month (when applicable): licenses ending in 9 or 0, letters only, or temporary plates (blue sticker)

FOREIGN-PLATED CARS OR CARS FROM OTHER STATES

Cars with non-Mexico City or Mexico state license plates, or any foreign-plated car, are not permitted to drive on any day, Monday through Friday, between 5 and 11 A.M., in addition to the standard of the aforementioned digit-based restrictions. For example, a truck with a California license plate ending in 2 cannot drive in Mexico City from 5 A.M. to 10 P.M. on Thursday, 5 A.M. to 10 P.M. on the fourth Saturday of the month, or from 5 to 11 A.M. Monday though Friday.

Additionally, pay attention to any advisories issued for Hoy No Circula. In addition to the standard restrictions, the government may occasionally announce changes to the program. You can get more information from Mexico Secretaría del Medio Ambiente (www.sma.df.gob.mx).

© ARTURO MEADE

on the road in Mexico

Puentes Federales website (www.capufe.gob.mx), including toll costs for each highway and road conditions. Check the news for information about inclement weather or violence.

Checkpoints

There are military checkpoints throughout the country, both on free and toll highways. Generally speaking, military checkpoints are designed to stop criminal activity, so law-abiding foreign travelers have little to worry about. Usually, you will just be waved through a checkpoint. On rare occasions, military officials may ask for your immigration paperwork, proof of insurance, or car registration. Even rarer (but still possible), they may ask to review the contents of your trunk. They are looking for drugs or weapons, which you should never carry anywhere in Mexico (and especially not on the road). Be polite and comply with instructions. In most cases, the military has no interest in involving foreigners in problems, and they will likely let you go with little hassle.

RENTING A CAR

There are large international chains and independent companies that rent automobiles and small trucks for daily and weekly use. Renting a car in Mexico is generally easy and inexpensive, though prices may be slightly higher than in the United States. You will usually get the best rates if you book in advance (in smaller cities, availability may also be limited). In most cases, car rental companies require drivers to be older than 25 and have a valid license (it can be foreign, as long as it displays a photo of you). All drivers must be registered with the rental company.

Usually, you will need to leave an open credit card on the account while the vehicle is rented; some companies will also put a sizable hold on your card. Be sure to note all previous damage to the car when you leave the lot; most rental companies have small fleets, and they will charge you for any damage to the automobile. Rental car companies will include insurance in your quote, and it is generally a good idea to take the insurance option. Third-party insurance is also fine. Some renters have insurance fees covered by their credit card; double check before you waive the insurance option.

Note that car rental agencies—even those with major names like Hertz— are generally franchises, so if you need to rent in one location and drop off in another, you will pay a very high fee.

BUYING A CAR

Foreign residents can purchase a car or truck with Mexican license plates in Mexico. If you want to avoid keeping up with your car registration or insurance at home, buying a car in Mexico can be an attractive option. It is permissible to drive a Mexican-plated car into the United States. Plus, Mexican-plated cars can be driven by anyone, not just the registered owner (as is the case with foreign-plated cars). On the flip side, you will pay higher insurance premiums on a Mexican-plated car, as well as taxes if the car is 10 years old or younger.

BRINGING YOUR OWN CAR

Both tourists and visa-holding residents of Mexico are allowed to temporarily import a foreign-plated car to Mexico. Your vehicle is legal in Mexico for as long as your immigration paperwork is valid. That is to say, if you have an FMM, or tourist card, your car permit is valid for the same six months that you are permitted in the country; you must return the vehicle to the border when your FMM expires. If you have an FM3 or FM2, your car may remain in the country as long as your paperwork is valid. You will also need to update your car's permit at a local transit office. However, as long as you keep your visa up-to-date, your car is legal.

One of the major obstacles to owning a foreign-plated car in Mexico is keeping up with registration and insurance at home in Canada or the United States. It is usually possible to arrange waivers of smog checks or other requirements that would necessitate your periodic return to the United States.

VOCHOS: THE LATE, GREAT VOLKSWAGEN BEETLE

For decades, Mexico's most beloved and ubiquitous automobile was the diminutive, sputtering Volkswagen Beetle. Cheap, durable, and easy to repair, Beetles won the Mexican heart during the 1960s and continued to thrive in the country, even as their popularity declined worldwide. Today, Vochos, as the Beetles are lovingly known, continue in rather widespread circulation. If you've got a nostalgic hankering for your own VW Bug, you'll likely find many used versions listed in the classifieds.

Though the first Beetles were imported to Mexico during the 1950s, their sales really took off after Volkswagen opened a plant outside Puebla in 1967. A decade later, production in Puebla had grown enough to begin exporting cars to Europe, and in 1980, the plant had produced more than one million Volkswagen Beetles. It is said that one in three cars sold in Mexico during the 1970s was a VW Bug.

While the Bug's international popularity began to wane with the rise of economy cars from Asia, it remained immensely popular in Mexico. During the 1980s and '90s, kelly green Beetles with the front passenger seat removed were the most ubiquitous model for the thousands of taxi cabs in Mexico City (an estimated 70 percent of the city's cabs were Bugs). While the city has since banned Volkswagen taxis (today, Nissan's Tsuru is the preferred model), you can still see 1970s-, '80s-, and '90s-model bugs of every color (some lovingly retouched and elaborately painted) throughout the city.

In 1996, Volkswagen phased out production of the Beetle everywhere but its plant in Puebla. In 2003, Puebla produced the 21,529,464th Volkswagen Beetle, the very last of the line. Decorated with red, white, and green flowers, it rolled off the assembly line accompanied by a mariachi band. The final car was nicknamed El Rey (the king) and sent to the company museum in Germany.

You can maintain a permanent address with a friend or family member, or with a company like Mail Boxes Etc., which will list your box as an apartment number if you prefer.

Remember, only foreign residents or visitors can have a foreign-plated car in Mexico. If you plan to nationalize, you will give up the right to own a foreign car as a Mexican national.

Border Crossings

There are more than 40 designated border crossings between the United States and Mexico. You can apply for a car permit and immigration paperwork at any of these crossings. Most customs and immigration offices are open 24 hours a day. Note that the immigration offices in Baja California Norte are located in Ensenada.

Car Permits

All foreigners bringing a car into Mexico must request a temporary import permit from the customs office at the border. The permit is good for 180 days. Thereafter, the car must be returned to the United States. Alternatively, the car's temporary import permit may be renewed locally if the car's owner has an FM3 or FM2 resident visa. All cars brought into Mexico from the United States or Canada must be returned with the import permit sticker still attached to the windshield.

To get a permit, you must stop at the immigration and customs offices at a border crossing to request immigration paperwork and a temporary import permit for your car. You must have the car's registration (in your name), a driver's license, and proof of citizenship (passport). You must pay a fee (about US$45) and a deposit, either in cash (deposited into a bank account) or on a Visa or MasterCard. The car's permit will thereafter be linked to your FMM or FM3.

Once you have brought your car into Mexico, you and your spouse are legally allowed to drive it. Another person can drive the car if you or your spouse is a passenger. However, no one else can drive the car alone. If pulled over by transit cops, a foreign car without its owner will be seized and impounded. In some cases, the driver will face legal problems. (It may be easier for another foreigner to explain the situation, but Mexicans are not allowed to own foreign-plated cars and therefore can find themselves in real trouble when driving one.)

CAR INSURANCE

Technically, you are not obligated to insure your car in Mexico; however, it is highly recommended and generally inexpensive to do so. Auto insurance will be a great asset in the case that you are in accident. In general, all drivers involved in a crash are detained until guilt is established. If you have insurance, you are less likely to be held by the police, as your financial responsibility for the accident is already assured.

If you are driving your car to Mexico from the United States or Canada, you can preregister for insurance via the Internet, or you can sign up for insurance at one of the many insurance agents located along the U.S.-Mexico border. U.S. automobile insurance is usually not valid in Mexico. Although most of Mexico's largest insurance carriers will offer reasonable policies on foreign-plated cars, some companies specialize in travel insurance, including Sanborns insurance and Mexico Insurance Services. Some of these plans have a time limit.

The handpainted lettering on the back of this truck encourages drivers to relax.

If you buy a car in Mexico, the cost of insurance is slightly higher. Some of the largest insurance carriers are Qualitas, Seguros Altas, Interacciones, and Grupo Nacional Provincial (GNP), in addition to insurance programs run through banks like HSBC. Many of these companies include roadside assistance in their insurance packages.

DRIVER'S LICENSES

A foreign driver's license is valid in Mexico as long as it isn't expired. Most expatriates do not bother to get a Mexican driver's license; however, if you don't have a foreign license or prefer to have a valid form of Mexican ID, you can apply at the transit office. (Note that the voter card, called IFE, is the most commonly accepted form of ID in Mexico, though a driver's license is also valid in most instances.) To get a driver's license, you must be a legal resident of Mexico (a citizen, or holder of an FM2 or FM3).

Check with the local transit office to see what paperwork you need for a driver's license, as requirements may vary by region. Generally, you will need to present a passport, visa paperwork, and proof of address in Mexico to apply for a license. You may also be asked to take a written test (if you aren't fluent in Spanish, you are permitted to bring a translator with you to the exam). You must also report your blood type (if you don't know it, you will need to be tested before you can get a license).

RULES OF THE ROAD

Overall, Mexicans follow driving rules that are very similar to the vast majority of the world, with a few small but notable exceptions. As long as they

PYRAMID AHEAD! MEXICAN ROAD SIGNS

No deje piedras sobre el pavimiento (don't leave rocks on the highway) implores one ubiquitous Mexican road sign. As a foreigner, you might not have realized that abandoned rocks are a common roadway problem, but it is just one example of the slightly different rules of the Mexican road. Here are the translations of other common road signs.

- *alto:* stop
- *camino sinuoso:* winding road
- *carril izquierdo solo para rebasar:* left lane only for passing
- *cinturon de seguridad obligatorio:* seat belt is obligatory
- *concede cambio de luz:* dim your brights
- *con niebla o lluvia enciende sus luces:* turn your lights on in fog or rain
- *cruce de escolares:* school crossing
- *cruce de peatones:* pedestrian crossing
- *curva peligrosa:* dangerous curve
- *desviación:* detour
- *encienda sus luces:* turn on your lights
- *este camino no es de alta velocidad:* this is not a high speed road
- *glorieta:* traffic circle
- *guarde su distancia:* maintain your distance (don't tailgate)
- *maneje con precaucion:* drive with caution
- *modere su velocidad:* keep speed moderate

conform to the rules of the road and use caution, foreigners will find themselves comfortable driving around Mexico. Before getting behind the wheel, review these safety tips.

Highways and Freeways

In Mexico, you must share the road with much more than cars, pickups, and SUVs. Truck drivers in Mexico work long shifts and often have tight deadlines to meet, speeding along freeways at maximum speed (give them a wide berth). There are often many trucks on the road, in addition to passenger buses. At the same time, ranchers will drive tractors or farm equipment onto highways at dangerously low speeds. With such a wide variety of traffic and few pullouts on Mexican highways, driving can occasionally feel like the Indy 500, with faster cars zipping around slower traffic. When passing any vehicle, use caution.

- *no maltrate las señales:* don't deface the road signs
- *no maneje si cansado:* don't drive tired
- *no rebase:* no passing
- *no rebase con raya continua:* don't pass on the solid line
- *no tire basura:* don't litter
- *permite rebasar utilice acotamiento:* permit passing; use the shoulder
- *poblado proximo:* approaching a populated town
- *prepare su cuota:* prepare your toll
- *puesto de control military:* military checkpoint
- *reductor de velocidad:* speed reducer (speed bumps) ahead
- *respete las señales:* respect the road signs
- *retorno:* return (place to make a U-turn)
- *sanitarios:* bathrooms
- *semaforo:* stoplight
- *si toma, no maneje:* don't drink and drive
- *tope:* speed bump
- *topes a 100m:* speed bumps in 100 meters (slow down)
- *tramo en reparación:* road repairs ahead
- *transito lento carril derecho:* slow traffic in right lane
- *zona de niebla:* foggy zone

On all highways, a car will use the left turn signal to indicate its desire to pass. If you are stuck behind a car or truck, it will often indicate that it is safe to pass by illuminating its left turn signal. The signal is a convenient form of communication; however, it can cause some safety problems when you actually want to make a left turn off a freeway.

On two-lane *autopistas* with a wide shoulder, it is common practice for drivers to pull onto the shoulder and allow faster traffic to pass in the middle, riding along the dotted line between the two lanes. Traffic in the opposite direction will also pull onto the shoulder to allow a car to pass. If you see a car passing in oncoming traffic, slow your speed and pull toward the shoulder.

Safety

The most common advice for drivers in Mexico is to avoid driving at night. Most roads and highways do not have overhead lighting, so it can be harder

© ARTURO MEADE

With its beautiful and well-maintained highways, Mexico is a wonderful place for an old-fashioned road trip.

to see potholes, animals in the road, or other cars without taillights. Roads are also more heavily patrolled during the daytime, so it can be safer for drivers heading into unknown regions or where security is a concern.

Small towns along the highway will often install a series of speed bumps in attempt to reduce the speed of traffic. Called *topes,* speed bumps are usually indicated with road signs at least 200 meters before the bump. However, the speed bumps themselves are often unpainted or unmarked.

Always drive at the speed limit, which is posted in kilometers per hour. The speed limit on *libres* is usually 90 kilometers (about 55 miles) per hour, and the speed limit on *autopistas* is usually 110 kilometers (about 65 miles) per hour.

Choosing Safe Routes

Widespread violence related to the drug trade along the U.S.-Mexico border has made travel through the northern regions more precarious than it was in the past. Throughout the north and around the city of Monterrey, there have been an increased number of illegal roadblocks and carjacking. While drivers should certainly be aware of the hazards of driving through Northern Mexico, many Americans and Canadians continue to drive through Mexico with little problem.

In order to ensure your safety on the road, travel during the day. Whenever possible, choose to drive on a toll road rather than a free highway. Toll roads are well maintained, well lit, and patrolled by police. On most Mexican toll roads, the toll also includes insurance coverage while you are on the highways.

City Driving

As in any city, Mexico's metropolises present their own obstacle course of cars, buses, pedestrians, and bicycles. Road rules are a bit more relaxed than you may be used to at home; stop signs can often merit little more than a slow-down, and cars routinely run red lights.

Cities are often filled with narrow, one-way streets. Be sure to check the flow of traffic before making a turn, and don't be surprised if you see people backing up a one-way street during a lull in traffic. Resist the urge to speed around city buses as they stop to drop off or pick up passengers. Often, people will cross in front of the bus and then cross the street.

Parking Violations

If you park illegally, transit cops will often remove your license plate. You must go to the local transit office to pay a fine and receive your license plate. The hassle is often more frustrating than the cost.

Hoy No Circula in Mexico City

Anyone planning to drive in the capital—even just passing through—must be aware of the rules with regards to Hoy No Circula (literally, today no circulation), a program designed to reduce automobile traffic. Through the Hoy No Circula program, certain cars are not permitted to drive in the capital or the adjoining state of Mexico on a designated day each week, depending on the final digit of their license plate. This law is ironclad. If you are pulled over driving on a day when your car is not permitted on the roads, your car will be impounded, and you will have to pay serious fines.

ACCIDENTS

If you have an automobile accident in Mexico, stay on the scene and phone emergency services; you can reach the Green Angels emergency services by dialing 078. If you are not attending to anyone injured, call your insurance company next. If no one was hurt and the damage was minimal, you may able to reach an agreement with the other drivers. However, if the damage was more substantial or anyone was injured, the police will arrive to investigate.

Once the police arrive, all drivers are detained until the investigation is complete. If you have an insurance plan, you will be allowed to leave after the investigation is complete, and your insurance will cover the damages and any related medical expenses. If you do not have insurance, you may be detained until fault is determined. In the case that there is a fatality, all drivers may be jailed until fault is determined, and the guilty party will likely serve jail time.

If you are at fault in an accident, having auto insurance will likely spare you extended time in custody (usually, guilty parties are held so they can be held responsible for the costs of the accident).

TRANSIT COPS

Interstate highways are patrolled by *federales,* or federal police. Although they have a reputation for extortion, federal officers are well-trained professionals, and they can be a huge asset in the case of an emergency. Within cities, transit cops enforce traffic laws, not federal police (it is outside their jurisdiction). If you are pulled over, remain calm. You will likely be asked for your license, registration, and proof of insurance. If you have committed a violation, you can pay your fine in the local transit office.

Much has been made about the so-called *mordida,* or bribe. Although in some cases a police officer may offer to waive your ticket for a payoff, generally speaking it is not in your best interest to offer a bribe to a police officer. If you suspect a police officer is trying to ask for a bribe, you can either pay the fee if it doesn't seem too exorbitant or insist on being given a ticket to pay at the transit office. Be aware that the fines for violating Hoy No Circula in Mexico City are incredibly high, and you may not avoid them by offering to pay off the cop. If you are pulled over because your car is not permitted to drive, follow instructions.

PRIME LIVING LOCATIONS

© JULIE DOHERTY MEADE

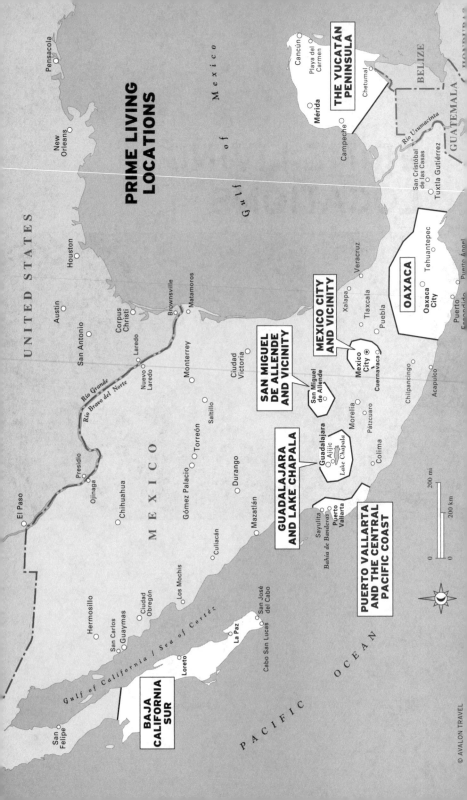

PRIME LIVING LOCATIONS

THE YUCATÁN PENINSULA

OAXACA

MEXICO CITY AND VICINITY

SAN MIGUEL DE ALLENDE AND VICINITY

GUADALAJARA AND LAKE CHAPALA

PUERTO VALLARTA AND THE CENTRAL PACIFIC COAST

BAJA CALIFORNIA SUR

UNITED STATES

MEXICO

GUATEMALA

BELIZE

HONDURAS

Gulf of Mexico

PACIFIC OCEAN

Gulf of California / Sea of Cortez

Pensacola
New Orleans
Houston
Austin
San Antonio
Corpus Christi
Brownsville
Matamoros
Laredo
Nuevo Laredo
Monterrey
Ciudad Victoria
Saltillo
Torreón
Durango
Gómez Palacio
Culiacán
Mazatlán
Chihuahua
Ojinaga
Presidio
El Paso
Hermosillo
San Carlos
Guaymas
Ciudad Obregón
Los Mochis
La Paz
Loreto
San José del Cabo
Cabo San Lucas
San Felipe
Río Grande
Río Bravo del Norte
Campeche
Mérida
Cancún
Playa del Carmen
Chetumal
Río Usumacinta
San Cristóbal de las Casas
Tuxtla Gutiérrez
Tehuantepec
Oaxaca City
Puerto Ángel
Puerto Escondido
Veracruz
Xalapa
Tlaxcala
Puebla
Mexico City
Cuernavaca
Chilpancingo
Acapulco
San Miguel de Allende
Morelia
Pátzcuaro
Colima
Guadalajara
Ajijic
Lake Chapala
Sayulita
Bahía de Banderas
Puerto Vallarta

200 mi
200 km

© AVALON TRAVEL

OVERVIEW

When deciding where to settle down, you won't suffer from a lack of options in Mexico. Foreigners can choose between a wide range of lifestyles, environments, and communities, from world-class beach resorts along the Caribbean coast to tiny colonial towns in the high desert plains. Many foreigners prefer the convenience and camaraderie of living in an established expatriate enclave, while others have made their way off the beaten track, choosing to pursue a more traditionally Mexican lifestyle in a remote village or undervisited city. You will find expatriates living in every nook and cranny of Mexico, and each region of the country offers its share of advantages and disadvantages. The key is finding the mix of culture, community, and atmosphere to match your budget and lifestyle.

That said, many people fall immediately in love with a certain town or region in Mexico, never considering life anywhere other than their beloved destination. Others may have a general idea about the lifestyle they are looking for but haven't zeroed in on the perfect destination yet. Even if you know you'd

© JULIE DOHERTY MEADE

like to live on the coast, for example, you can still take your pick between a Caribbean resort, a desert surf town, or a remote Pacific hideaway, among other options. Those looking for a life off the grid might choose to shack up in coastal Oaxaca, while others love the lively atmosphere in cosmopolitan Los Cabos. While narrowing down the options is a harrowing task, console yourself with the fact that getting to travel around Mexico is one of the best parts about living in the country permanently.

In the following pages, you'll find an introduction to seven destinations in Mexico, with details on the regional lifestyle, culture, and cost of living. These chapters will help you plan your relocation or, if you are still deciding where to hang your hat, offer a perspective on the different options available. The destinations featured in this book are among Mexico's most attractive options, though they are by no means the only places where expatriates happily live. As you research the country, keep your options open. If you like colonial towns like San Miguel de Allende, you might want to visit Taxco, Patzcuaro, or San Cristóbal de las Casas. If you love vibrant, traditional cities like Oaxaca, Michoacan's capital city of Morelia or the university town of Xalapa, Veracruz, might be a good match for you. Beachgoers will find plenty of additional options along the Pacific Coast, including the low-key, old-fashioned resort towns of Manzanillo, Barra de Navidad, or Ixtapa, among other, quieter locales. There's no right way to pick the place; as always, follow your instincts and see where Mexico takes you.

MEXICO CITY AND VICINITY

Maddening and magnetic, Mexico City is the political, cultural, and economic capital of the country, home to an estimated 22 million residents. Those who have been offered a job in Mexico (or are being transferred by their company) are more likely end up in the capital than anywhere else, and, for those who plan to work, Mexico City is far and away the best choice in the country. There are plenty of professional opportunities for foreigners who want to make a living here, as well as those who'd like to set up their own business or telecommute.

From the observation deck of the Torre Latinoamericana—one of the only skyscrapers downtown—the low-lying urban landscape spreads before you in all directions. Covering more than 3,000 square kilometers, the sprawling metropolis never reached the population density of vertical cities like New York or Tokyo. Instead, Mexico City has expanded outward, with an urban map filled with wide avenues, public parks, and towering trees. Living spaces are often surprisingly spacious, too, though the drawback to so much space is the long distances you'll travel to get from one neighborhood to another.

Mexico City grew rapidly during the second half of the 20th century, and this has had some negative effects on the urban environment: Air pollution, traffic, poverty, dwindling water resources, and sprawling shantytowns have blighted the city as it careened into the future. Noise, pollution, traffic, and crowds are a part of daily life, and you may need to develop a thick skin to survive: Poverty and crime can make the city a decidedly tough place to live. Living here isn't necessarily easy, and yet Mexico City is nonetheless an exciting, alluring, and duly rewarding place to call home.

Despite its monstrous size and decidedly urban atmosphere, Mexico City is remarkably attractive, charming, and livable, largely defined by its many discrete and culturally distinct neighborhoods. Throughout the city, you'll find a unique mix of modernity and tradition, with bustling covered markets, old cantinas, old-fashioned ice cream parlors, hipster bars, world-class museums, and a spectacular mix of architecture all coexisting within the same jumbled metropolis. Parks and public spaces take the edge off the energy, and people in the capital are remarkably friendly and laid-back, despite the social challenges that inevitably accompany life in a city of 20-plus million inhabitants.

GUADALAJARA AND LAKE CHAPALA

The beloved capital of the state of Jalisco, Guadalajara is a friendly and livable city with a stately colonial downtown, strong cultural traditions, and a large and longstanding expatriate community. Guadalajara and environs are celebrated for their quintessentially Mexican culture (tequila and mariachi are just two

PRIME LIVING LOCATIONS

© JULIE DOHERTY MEADE

An ice cream vendor chats with his client in the quaint Guadalajara suburb of Tlaquepaque.

of the state's many contributions), yet Guadalajara is also a highly contemporary place, with excellent schools and universities, good health-care facilities, well-managed museums, and modern shopping centers. For those who want the economic opportunities, modern resources, and excitement of a big city but aren't ready to brave the capital, Guadalajara is an excellent option.

Guadalajara's robust economy has made it a great choice for professionals looking to work in Mexico, and the cost of living is reasonable enough that a comfortable, middle-class lifestyle is largely attainable. With many pleasant, residential communities spreading north and northwest from the city center, there are plenty of nice places to rent or buy around town, while also a substantial job market. At the same time, modern life has left its mark on Guadalajara; there's a grittier element to the industrial neighborhoods to the east of the *centro,* and air pollution and traffic have become serious problems in the city.

If you like Guadalajara's character but would prefer a more peaceful environment, the surrounding countryside is rich and beautiful, particularly the string of small towns on the northeastern shore of Lake Chapala. Just an hour outside Guadalajara, Chapala's pretty lakeside communities have been popular with American and Canadian expatriates since the mid-20th century, with many foreigners living in the lovely little community of Ajijic. With tropical vegetation and lake views, these towns continue to maintain an easygoing and traditionally Mexican atmosphere, despite the increasing number of foreign retirees and residents in the area.

The great Guadalajara region is propitiously located in the center of the country, with a busy international airport that connects the city to the United States, Canada, and the rest of Mexico. Of particular note, the resort town of Puerto Vallarta is a scenic, five-hour drive from the capital; *tapatíos* (Guadalajara residents) frequently make the trip to the shore and enjoy fresh seafood throughout the year. Those who love a good climate will be particularly gratified by life in Guadalajara and its environs, which is known for its warm, sunny, and perpetually springlike weather.

PUERTO VALLARTA AND THE CENTRAL PACIFIC COAST

The seaside city of Puerto Vallarta is the heart of the central Pacific Coast, and it's one of Mexico's oldest and most charming resort towns. Its spectacular natural environment and calm, sandy beaches have made the city perennially popular with vacationers, and tourism has introduced plenty of modernity to the region—a busy international airport, movie theaters, modern malls, and hospitals are in town. Nonetheless, Puerto Vallarta manages to retain a pleasingly old-fashioned atmosphere despite its ongoing growth. While there are some high-rise hotels and noisy nightclubs in town, the city itself remains remarkably low-key and charming, with the breezy atmosphere of a small seaside fishing port.

Puerto Vallarta is one of just many options along the central Pacific Coast, which is dotted with fishing villages, coastal hideaways, burgeoning beach resorts, and full-scale tourist towns. Blessed with an abundance of marine life, a warm and balmy climate, and miles of sandy beaches, the region offers many beautiful places to settle down. North of PV, there are expatriates living in the fishing village of Bucerias and the surf town of Sayulita; south of the city, virgin stretches of wilderness blanket large swaths of the coast, sheltering tucked-away communities.

Here, like many places, lifestyle is largely what you make it. For many, Pacific Mexico is a place to unplug from modern life and enjoy the simple pleasures of sea and sand. For others, it's a great place to volunteer, write, practice yoga, or open a business; many expatriates own shops in Puerto Vallarta, write for local publications, work in the tourism industry, or are active in the community in other ways. On that note, you'll find a fairly large group of expatriates living in the area, especially in and around Puerto Vallarta, if you are looking to make friends and gain a foothold in the community.

Most of the homes along this street in San Miguel de Allende have rooftop gardens overlooking the city.

SAN MIGUEL DE ALLENDE AND VICINITY

San Miguel de Allende is a charming, old-fashioned small town located in the rugged high plains a few hours north of Mexico City. In the blocks surrounding San Miguel's central square, the atmosphere is pure romance: Crumbling red and ochre buildings flank narrow cobblestone streets, adjoined by sandstone chapels, gurgling fountains, and draping vines of bougainvillea. Overlooking the floodplain of the River Laja from its hillside location,

PRIME LIVING LOCATIONS

© JULIE DOHERTY MEADE

© JULIE DOHERTY MEADE

Paper flags flutter in front of the *parroquía* (parish) in San Miguel de Allende.

San Miguel seems to be blessed with a particularly soft and beautiful quality of sunlight, which turns to deep pink during the spectacular winter sunsets.

San Miguel de Allende has been a popular destination for artists and bohemians since the early 20th century; today, the expatriate community makes up around 10 percent of the local population. Even so, the San Miguel community retains a rather distinct old-fashioned friendliness. Here, families stroll through the town square on Sunday afternoons, donkeys carry goods to the market, and lost dogs are announced on the radio. It is common to bump into friends on a walk through town, and social gatherings are often casual, spontaneous affairs with a welcoming tone.

Despite tradition, San Miguel de Allende is rapidly changing. Across the region, large supermarket chains are appearing along the outskirts of colonial cities, the highway system is steadily expanding, and burgers and fries are becoming as popular as tacos and hot sauce. Yet change is an essential characteristic of this region, and you'll find little friction between expats and locals in this open and ever-changing area.

OAXACA

The state of Oaxaca is known throughout Mexico for its considerable natural beauty, colonial-era architecture, fascinating history, inventive cuisine, and colorful modern culture, as well as for its rich traditions in handcraft, popular design, and contemporary art. The state's capital, Oaxaca de Juárez (almost always called simply Oaxaca), is a handsome colonial city with a blend of cosmopolitan sensibilities and age-old tradition.

While Oaxaca offers just enough convenience (there are supermarkets and an international airport, among other touches of modernity), living here is a far greater cultural transition than what you might experience in north and central Mexico. Oaxaca is its own very distinct place, and residents will need to learn to adapt to an entirely unique lifestyle. You'll even find that common words can be different here (for example, green tomatoes, or *jitomate verde,* are often called *miltomate* in Oaxaca).

Those really looking to escape the modern world will be well suited to life on the coast of Oaxaca, a remote and largely undeveloped stretch of Pacific shoreline. From the capital, you can cross the coastal sierra to several laid-back and indisputably bohemian beach towns where you can live in the woods and eat from the trees, while also enjoy a small dose of hippie sophistication from the expatriate residents and visitors who have long loved and visited this stretch of shore. These little communities are good for an extended sojourn in the sand and sea, or, in some cases, a whole new approach to living.

BAJA CALIFORNIA SUR

The slender Baja California peninsula extends for almost 800 miles along Mexico's northwestern coast. Bordered by the Pacific Ocean to the west and the Sea of Cortez to the east, Baja is desertic and largely undeveloped. Down at the peninsula's southernmost tip, where the Sea of Cortez meets the open ocean, the resort town of Cabo San Lucas is perched along one of the most spectacular environments in Mexico.

The immense natural beauty is perhaps southern Baja's greatest asset—the iconic stone arch at Land's End is emblematic of the dramatic vistas that abound in the area—though the region's modernity, convenience for international travelers, and wide range of sports and recreational activities are also a major attraction for expatriates. Many foreigners settle down or retire here, others spend part of the year in Baja, while others come down for a season. Prices run quite a bit higher here than in other beach resorts in Mexico, though you'll still find the cost of living is a bit more reasonable than most coastal cities north of the border.

Though the peninsula has always been sparsely inhabited, the Spanish established numerous missions in Baja California, around which many of the current settlements are centered. The town of San Jose del Cabo has the most southerly mission, as well as a pleasant Mexican-style town center. Over the years, Baja has attracted many residents from the other side of the Sea of

a beach on the Yucatán Peninsula

Cortez, and, as a result, the region has a northern Mexican flavor. Culturally, this region also maintains strong links to the west coast of the United States—many Californians vacation in Cabo, just as others buy vacation homes in town. English is widely spoken, and tourism is a major industry.

THE YUCATÁN PENINSULA

The Yucatán Peninsula, which includes the three states of Yucatán, Campeche, and Quintana Roo, is geographically, environmentally, and culturally distinct from the rest of Mexico. Still home to a large ethnic Maya population, the age-old culture here is among Mexico's most interesting, with many traditions in dress, ritual, and cuisine dating back to the pre-Columbian era.

Along the coast of the Caribbean Sea, the peninsula's turquoise seas and white-sand beaches are as close to paradise as you'll find in Mexico. Along the jungle-blanketed coastline of Quintana Roo, tourists flock to the sparkling resort town of Cancún, though foreigners may find a better place to settle down within the mellow beach destinations of Playa del Carmen and Cozumel, as well as smaller ports like Tulum and Akumal. Every year, more expatriates choose this region of Mexico, well connected to the rest of the world via Cancún's busy airport.

To the east, the state of Yucatán is a vibrant cultural region. Though not traditionally an expatriate enclave, the stately colonial city of Mérida has begun to attract foreign residents with its beauty, friendliness, and low-key charms. Though suffering from a hot and humid climate during half the year, it can be a great pick for part-timers or warm-weather enthusiasts.

MEXICO CITY AND VICINITY

Mexico City is the sprawling, chaotic, decidedly urban, and surprisingly charming capital of Mexico, and it's one of the oldest, biggest, and most historic cities in the Americas. Mexico City's long history is reflected in its diverse neighborhoods and varied architecture, from the splendid Baroque churches of the *centro histórico* and French-inspired monuments on the Paseo de la Reforma to glittering skyscrapers in suburban Santa Fe and the makeshift residential neighborhoods that blanket the northern hillsides.

During the 20th century, Mexico City experienced a massive population boom, and today it is the biggest city in the western hemisphere. Growth has slowed since the turn of the 21st century, but it hasn't stopped; year after year, Mexico City continues to attract a slew of new residents who come to partake of the country's biggest job market, the ongoing cultural happenings, and the unrelenting energy of a city of 22 million. Despite the size, the city remains surprisingly provincial, with dozens of distinct neighborhoods each maintaining their own individual character and style.

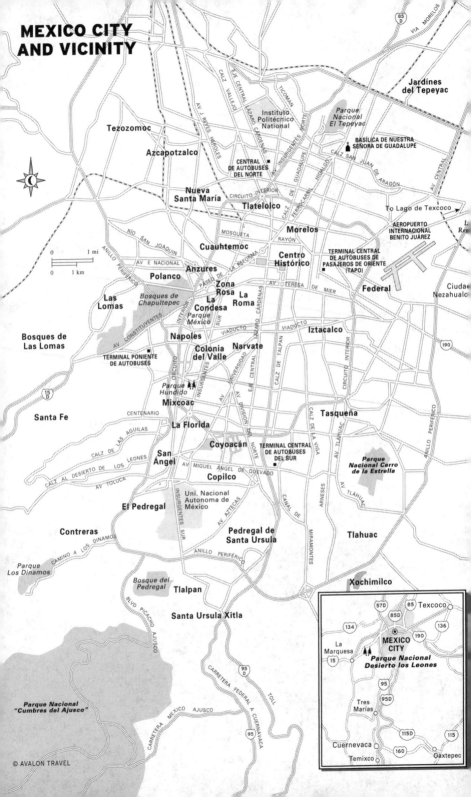

Solely responsible for producing more than 20 percent of the country's gross domestic product (GDP), the capital is the undisputed locus of Mexico's business and economy. Mexico City is the most likely place that anyone involved in business activities will relocate, while academics, teachers, artists, journalists, writers, and other professionals make a good living in the capital. Even if they don't come to Mexico with a job offer in hand, there are many expatriates who choose to live in Mexico City simply because they like the unique and indisputably urban atmosphere.

For foreigners, Mexico City is a wonderful place to live: cosmopolitan and cultural, inexpensive for a city of its caliber, and surprisingly folkloric. There's always another marketplace to explore, an itinerant exhibition at one of the city's museums, or a new café opening on the corner. At the same time, moving to Mexico City can be a challenge. Simply learning your way around this giant metropolis can take months, and dangers and difficulties like crime and pollution make day-to-day life a bit more cumbersome than it is in other Mexican towns. While Mexico City is by no means an easy place to live, the excitement and rewards are manifold for those who are up to the challenge.

The Lay of the Land

Mexico City is located in the Valle de México (Valley of Mexico), a large plain nestled within the transvolcanic mountain range of central Mexico, and flanked to the southeast by twin volcanoes, Popocatepetl and Iztaccihuatl. Perched at more than 7,000 feet above sea level, the valley was once covered in a series of broad, shallow lakes. Today, most have dried up, though a large swath north of the city is still covered in water, a portion of what was once the considerably larger Lake Texcoco. The city itself was built atop the dry lakebed, and the spongy land makes for unstable footing during seismic tremors. It has also contributed to the city's slow sinking: In the *centro histórico,* you may notice old stone buildings are cracked or tilting, some to the point of becoming uninhabitable.

The heart of the metropolitan region is the *distrito federal* (federal district), or Mexico D.F., the capital of Mexico and a distinct political entity (similar to Washington DC in the United States). Though once neatly contained, the metropolitan region now expands far beyond the borders of the *distrito federal,* covering large swaths of the surrounding state of Mexico and enveloping many small communities in the process. Altogether, the entire Mexico City metropolitan area covers more than 3,000 square kilometers.

THE FIRST GREAT CAPITAL: EL GRAN TENOCHTITLAN

A series of large towns stretched themselves along the banks of the lake, out of which still larger ones rose magnificently above the waters. Innumerable crowds of canoes were plying everywhere around us; at regular distances, we continually passed over new bridges, and before us lay the great city of Mexico in all its splendor.

Bernal Díaz del Castillo,
Discovery and Conquest of Mexico and New Spain

In the late 1970s, electric company workers tunneling through the *zócalo* unearthed a massive carved monolith depicting the Aztec moon goddess, Coyolxauhqui. Though anthropologists had long suspected that the ruins of the Aztec city lay beneath the modern capital, there had only been limited excavations in and around the central square. In the following years, anthropologists began to dig in the area adjoining the cathedral, receiving permission to demolish more than 10 colonial-era buildings in the vicinity. Here they uncovered the base of a massive stepped pyramid. Known as the Templo Mayor, this pyramid was once the ceremonial center of the Mexica city of Tenochtitlan, which had spent centuries buried just a few meters below the modern cityscape.

Though the Spanish razed Tenochtitlan during their long and bloody siege on the city, conquistadors like Hernán Cortés and Bernal Díaz del Castillo described the magnificent city in their diaries of the conquest. Through these accounts, excavations and artifacts, and the ongoing study of Templo Mayor and other archaeological sites, anthropologists have been able to largely reconstruct the layout and lifestyle of El Gran Tenochtitlan, one of the largest and most orderly cities on Earth during the 15th century.

Ruled by the Mexica people, Tenochtitlan was built on an island in the middle of Lake Texcoco. The Templo Mayor was the center of the city and was enlarged 11 times over numerous generations of rulers. There were palaces and temples surrounding the Templo Mayor, which were painted bright red and blue. From the center of town, the city spread into several distinct districts, each linked by canals, and covering five square miles of ground. Aqueducts carried water from Chapultepec to the city center, and there was a great market located on the adjoining island of Tlatelolco. As described by Díaz del Castillo, people traveled by canoe, tending to floating gardens around the city.

Though Tenochtitlan was destroyed during the conquest, it remains an indelible part of today's cityscape. Many of Mexico City's downtown churches and pyramids were constructed with stones from the destroyed Mexica temples, and it is believed that the Spanish borrowed from Tenochtitlan's established street plan when building their own city. While the great lake of Texcoco has largely dried up, there are still original canals from the pre-Columbian city crisscrossing the Xochimilco neighborhood in the south of the city. For a vision of the city as it once was, the Templo Mayor Museum contains a full model of Tenochtitlan in the 15th century. For an artist's rendering, visit the Palacio Nacional next door, where Diego Rivera painted detailed murals of Tenochtitlan.

ORIENTATION

Mexico City is so vast, even taxi drivers carry pocket maps in their glove boxes. As any *chilango* can tell you, it is next to impossible to recognize every inch of the capital, but you'll eventually learn your way around your local neighborhoods and get a general idea of the city's layout and transportation systems.

Politically, the federal district is divided into 16 *delegaciones,* or boroughs, which are further divided into more than 250 neighborhoods. Even today, the *centro histórico* is the heart of the city, both culturally and physically, though a good part of the city's business has moved to other neighborhoods, like Santa Fe. From the center of town, massive middle-class residential neighborhoods spread south and southeast. Another important landmark is the city's urban park, Bosques de Chapultepec, which occupies a large swath of land to the west of the *centro.* Most foreign residents and visitors will spend their time in the downtown districts and to the south. The areas to the north of the *centro histórico* are generally less appealing, though there are some interesting places to visit, including La Villa, the site of the original appearance of the Virgin of Guadalupe.

When learning to use the city's public transportation systems, it is good to get a general idea of how traffic flows through the city. There are no freeways passing through the center of town (although there is a perimeter highway, or *periferico,* which runs around the outside of the federal district), so the city has developed a system of *ejes viales* (axes), major thoroughfares that cross the city. In addition to the *ejes,* there are several central avenues that cut crosstown. Of these, the most important are Reforma (which runs northwest–southeast from La Villa to Polanco), Insurgentes (which runs from the north at Indios Verdes past the university in the south), Viaducto Miguel Alleman (which runs east–west through the south-central districts), and the Circuito Interior (a ring road that passes through many of the principal avenues in the city).

HISTORY

With its mild climate, fertile ground, and freshwater lakes, the Valley of Mexico has been home to human settlements for thousands of years. Cuilcuilco, an early city with a central temple-pyramid, was founded on the southern shores of Lake Texcoco somewhere around 800–600 B.C.; today, the archaeological zone is surrounded by the modern city in the borough of Coyoacán. As Cuicuilco declined, the massive pre-Columbian city of Teotihuacan began to grow in the eastern reaches of the valley, flourishing during the 7th and 8th centuries, when its population may have grown as large as 200,000.

By the 15th century, power had changed hands many times in Mesoamerica, but it had once again returned to the Valle de México, where the great Na-huatl-speaking people dominated the region from the tri-city alliance of Tenochtitlan, Texcoco, and Tlacopan; these people are collectively referred to as the Aztecs. The locus of power was Tenochtitlan, inhabited by the Mexica people and located on a island in the middle of Lake Texcoco. Though they originally made peaceful contact, the Spanish sustained heavy losses in their first battle with the Aztecs, known today as the *noche triste* (sad night). They returned with redoubled forces, and after months of siege, the triumphant Spanish vanquished what was left of the city.

Immediately following the conquest of Tenochtitlan, the Spaniards founded the capital of New Spain directly atop the ruins of Tenochtitlan. Using stones from the demolished pyramids and borrowing from Tenochtitlan's preestablished street plan, the Spanish began to construct a city in the European Baroque style. The Spanish came to refer to their city as la Ciudad de México (Mexico City) after the Mexica people who once lived there.

As the Spanish settlers fanned out to settle Mexico, massive silver mines were discovered throughout the country, creating important trading power with Spain. Mexico City became a wealthy metropolis and the center of Spain's empire in the Americas. Today, the fruits of that wealth are still visible in the magnificent downtown district, where beautiful palaces, chapels, courtyards, and plazas were built in the Baroque style.

As silver production slowed, growth also slowed in the capital. After independence, the country was mired in political conflict and was invaded by Americans during the Mexican-American War. During the following conservative rule, the capital did receive architectural gifts under the rule of the French—the short-lived Emperor Maximilian remodeled Chapultepec Castle—and later, President Porfirio Díaz. Díaz was responsible for many of the neoclassical monuments in the city, including the Palacio de Bellas Artes downtown.

After the Revolution of 1910, Mexico City began to grow rapidly. The population shot upward during the 1920s and 1930s, when new neighborhoods like La Condesa were built. Local culture flourished in dance halls and on the radio (the famous XEW began broadcasting in 1930), and Mexican cinema thrived during the Second World War. In the 1950s, the National University's campus began construction, and the city continued its southern expansion. During these decades, the vast residential neighborhoods along Insurgentes Sur were quickly erected as makeshift shantytowns and poorer communities spread across the north.

CLIMATE

Located at a considerable 2,200 meters (7,200 feet), Mexico City's tropical location is tempered by altitude, creating a remarkably pleasant climate year-round. During the spring and fall, daytime temperatures generally hover in the 70s, dropping down to the high 40s and 50s in the evening. The short winter season usually runs between December and February, and the weather is cooler throughout those months, especially at night. You'll get the warmest weather during April, May, and early June, when the temperature slowly climbs until the rainy season begins, sometimes reaching up into the high 80s.

Like most of central Mexico, Mexico City's climate can be divided into two distinct seasons: the dry season, which runs from October to May, and the shorter rainy season, from June to September. During the rainy season, flash floods, furious downpours, and even hail storms pummel the capital, bringing everything to a halt. The rains help to moderate the heat, so the summer weather is mild—rarely too hot.

ENVIRONMENTAL ISSUES

Mexico City is home to an estimated 22 million inhabitants, and their impact on the environment is substantial. Water management is a serious problem in the valley, where the increasing population has put a strain on local water resources.

Automobile traffic in the Valley of Mexico has created considerable problems with air quality in the greater Mexico City metropolitan region. Thanks to the city's location in a mountainous basin, cold air inversion traps smog over the city. You can see the brownish blanket hovering over the rooftops as you descend in an airplane. Generally, the summer rainy season improves the air quality slightly, while the heart of the dry season (November, December, and January) can be the most uncomfortable. People with respiratory problems or asthma may experience some difficulty in the capital.

To help address air quality, the local government has implemented several programs, including vehicle emissions checks and a program to restrict driving called Hoy No Circula. Through Hoy No Circula, cars cannot drive on one day of each week, based on their license plate number. Violations are extremely expensive. (If you have a car or will be driving through Mexico City, you should learn the rules of Hoy No Circula.) Although pollution in the valley continues to be a major problem, these programs appear to have had a positive effect.

THE PARTY OF THE DEMOCRATIC REVOLUTION (PRD) AND POLITICS IN MEXICO CITY

After the Revolution of 1910, Mexico's government coalesced around a single political party, the Institutional Revolutionary Party (PRI.) Originally founded in 1929, the party effectively put an end to post-war unrest and political competition. Its core values, at least in theory, were tied to those of the revolution. Though technically not a socialist party, the PRI was (and remains) an affiliate of Socialist International. Under the PRI's watch, Mexico experienced several decades of strong economic growth, and the party instituted a number of important social and cultural programs during its early years.

Throughout the 20th century, a succession of PRI presidents were elected and the PRI maintained control of federal, state, and local governments. As the memory of the Revolution faded, the long years in power began to chip away at the party's initial leftists tendencies, and PRI politics became more conservative, as well as more corrupt. Due to violent clashes between the Mexican government and student protesters in the 1960s, the Mexican people increasingly criticized the single-party system. After the economic crisis of 1970s, the PRI lost even more supporters in the general populace. Small opposition parties cropped up throughout the country, but most of them were unable to garner enough popular support to affect the balance of power.

In 1987, after openly criticizing the PRI establishment, Cuauhtémoc Cárdenas, a leftist politician and the son of Mexico's revered former president, Lázaro Cárdenas, split from the PRI to announce his candidacy for president against Carlos Salinas de Gotari. He lost to Salinas de Gotari in a suspect election, marred

PEOPLE AND CULTURE

Mexico City has a culture and climate distinct from the rest of Mexico, though as the belly button of the country, it is duly influenced by every region of the greater republic. There is a great deal of ethnic and socioeconomic diversity in this metropolis of more than 20 million inhabitants, with distinct subcultures coexisting in different neighborhoods. There are also many foreign residents from the United States, Canada, Europe, and Asia, working in industries as diverse as high-tech, business, marketing, and education.

Language

Mexico City is a predominantly Spanish-speaking city. Unlike almost every other destination recommended in this book, residents of Mexico City will need to learn conversational Spanish in order to use public transport, work, and have a meaningful life in the capital. In addition, there are large populations of people who speak indigenous languages in Mexico City. Most also speak Spanish, so you will rarely have difficulty

by a reported computer failure. Nonetheless, his ability to stand up against the party galvanized leftist opposition to the PRI.

The following year, Cárdenas and a group of fellow left-wing politicians formed the Party of the Democratic Revolution (PRD), a progressive political party that was quickly joined by other smaller, leftists groups like the Mexican Socialist Party and the Mexican Workers' Party. In the ensuing years, the nascent PRD was unable to take the presidency (Cárdenas lost the election again in 1994, though they made modest inroads in state representation.

Nonetheless, the PRD has had remarkable success in the highly influential region, the Distrito Federal. Running as a PRD candidate, Cuauhtémoc Cárdenas was elected to the position of D.F.'s *jefe de gobierno* (head of government) in 1997, the executive head of the federal district (a position most akin to a mayor in the United States, but with slightly greater power). A majority of the city's borough's repeatedly elect PRD candidates, and the PRD won the election for *jefe de gobierno* in the three elections following Cárdenas's term.

Under the PRD, Mexico City has become a bastion of progressive politics in Mexico, including legalizing abortion for women who are up to twelve weeks pregnant and instituting a no-fault divorce. In 2009, the PRD head of government, Marcelo Ebrard, legalized same-sex marriage in the Distrito Federal, which was followed by the legalization of adoption by same-sex couples. The PRD has also gained widespread support for their urban projects, which include a new rapid-speed bus service, the Metrobús, and a second level of roadway on the *periférico*, the busy freeway that circles the city.

communicating; however, it is interesting to note the diverse fabric of the *chilango* community.

Slang is one of the trademarks of *chilango* speech. If you are learning Spanish, your progress will be much swifter if you learn a couple of key words and phrases (which your Mexico City friends will likely be enthusiastic to teach you). If you've lived elsewhere in Mexico, you may also notice that *chilangos* have their own distinct lexicon.

Chilangos

While *capitaleño* may be the formal terminology, residents of Mexico City are generally referred to as *chilangos*. It's hard to generalize about a population so large and diverse, but *chilangos* do share certain traits: a cosmopolitan energy, a somewhat brusque attitude (compared to Mexicans outside the capital), and a rather pointed affinity for tacos. Outside Mexico City, the term *chilango* doesn't always conjure up positive associations; however, most Mexico City residents are proud of their special status as big-city residents and are surprisingly warm and laid-back for a city so large.

Expatriates in Mexico City

With a strong economy and the largest job market in the country, Mexico City has become a destination for many foreign immigrants. In addition to Americans and Canadians, there is a fairly large population of Europeans throughout the capital, particularly Spaniards, as well as South American expatriates, who have come to work in Latin America's most lively job market. Since Argentina's economic crisis, the tra-

Stray dogs are a part of life throughout Mexico; in the capital, some lucky pooches are cared for and fed by their neighbors.

ditionally large Argentinean population has grown even larger. The city has also become a popular destination for Korean immigrants; several thousand first-generation Koreans live in the capital (check out the excellent Asian grocery stores and delicious Korean barbecue joints near the Zona Rosa).

Despite the myriad influence of foreigners, many get lost in the shuffle of daily life. Here, you'll likely spend time with coworkers and neighbors rather than join up with a large expatriate community. However, if you want to connect with other English speakers or foreigners, there are numerous social and philanthropic groups. Among others, the international Hash House Harriers organizes walking, biking, and running tours with other foreign and Mexican members.

Daily Life

Like any massive metropolis, daily life in Mexico City is energetic, exciting, and often exhausting. With its massive population and sprawling highway system, the city suffers from pollution, traffic, overcrowding, and high costs, and the sheer size of the city can make getting around feel unnecessarily difficult. At the same time, the capital's lively energy and friendly populace make it far more livable than you might expect at touchdown. Once you get used to the city's rhythms, learn your way around your neighborhood, and find some key places to eat, shop, and go out, you can settle into a comfortable lifestyle in the capital.

COST OF LIVING

The cost of living in Mexico City can really run the gamut. Some of the country's richest and poorest citizens live in this enormous metropolis, and you can build a lifestyle appropriate to any budget. Generally speaking, however, Mexico City is more expensive than almost any other part of Mexico. In most Mexico City markets, fresh produce, including tortillas, costs several pesos more per kilo than in smaller cities or in the country. Luxuries, like eating out or hiring household help, can be pricey, and even electricity bills tend to run a bit higher in the capital.

Most capital residents spend the greatest percentage of their income on housing. Rent for a middle-class home or apartment is usually 20–30 percent higher than in a smaller city, like Querétaro or Oaxaca. Depending on the neighborhood, you can find a two-bedroom apartment for anywhere between US$500 and US$2,000 (and even more, if you want to rent a furnished penthouse apartment or a full family home).

At the same time, Mexico City is surprisingly affordable in other ways. For example, the city's metro system is the world's cheapest (at just US$0.20 per ride, it is an incredible bargain), and the numerous small restaurants, called *fondas,* offer shockingly inexpensive meals throughout the city. There are

© ARTURO MEADE

Mexico City is a wonderful place to eat, with diverse and delicious restaurants, markets, and food stands.

parks, public concerts, and other affordable entertainment options, and every Sunday, all government-run museums in the city are free. Many *capitaleños* survive on tiny salaries, and it is very easy to live a thrifty lifestyle if you count your pesos. At the same time, salaries are generally higher in the capital, and foreigners can often earn a decent living in Mexico City.

FOOD AND MARKETS

Almost every neighborhood in Mexico City has its own *mercado* (market), where you can pick up fresh produce, cheese, meat and cold cuts, milk, pasta, dry goods, herbs, bread, and tortillas. Most markets also have casual eateries, where you can get some of the city's most inexpensive meals, in addition to fruit and juice stands. There are also numerous *mercado sobre ruedas* (literally, market on wheels) and *tianguis* (open-air markets) that set up in rotating neighborhoods throughout the city. Some of these pop-up markets are small, selling basics like produce, cheese, and tortillas, while others are mind-bogglingly massive affairs where you can buy fruits and vegetables, imported goods, household products, clothing, electronics, and prepared foods—and choose from dozens of delicious lunch options while browsing! Markets are far and away the cheapest place to buy your food, and they're also a colorful cultural experience. One of the largest in the city, downtown market La Merced offers produce at such low prices that neighborhood fruit stands go there to stock up in the morning.

In addition to the traditional market, Mexico City offers the convenience of many large grocery stores. Mexican-owned chains like Comercial Mexicana, Mega (a larger version of the Comercial Mexicana), and Soriana stock everything you'd expect from a grocery store (produce, bread, pastas, cereal and other dry goods, and dairy), plus household items like ironing boards, mattresses, baby supplies, bedding, pots and pans, and other kitchen supplies. Popular with foreigners, Superama (owned by Walmart) has more specialty and imported foods, as does City Market, Comercial

© ARTURO MEADE

A taco stand prepares a giant spit to make *tacos al pastor*, a Mexico City favorite.

Mexicana's new upscale-supermarket offering, which sells imported products, wines, organic produce, and fancy prepared foods like flatbread pizzas and gelato. Since most Mexicans buy their fruits and vegetables at markets, the selection at grocery stores may be comparatively poor.

There are also a few smaller health food stores and specialty shops. The Green Corner sells organic fruits, veggies, dairy, and other specialty products, with branches in Coyoacan, La Condesa, Polanco, and Cuajimalpa. El Naval is a smaller chain of wine and gourmet food shops, with several branches in Mexico City, including the Condesa. There are also some inexpensive Korean grocery stores in the Juárez neighborhood, just south of the Zona Rosa.

As Mexico City attracts residents from across Mexico, the country's diverse traditions are represented in the local cuisine. Mexico City offers a dazzling array of options for eating out, from simple street carts to fine-dining restaurants. The midday meal, or *comida,* is typically the largest meal of the day. Throughout Mexico City, small restaurants called *fondas* offer cheap *comida corridas* (daily menus) to lunchers. Usually homemade and often tasty, a *comida corrida* consists of soup, rice, and a main dish, plus a fruit drink and, often, dessert. At many popular *fondas,* the volume of diners is so high that a *comida corrida* can cost as little as a few dollars.

SHOPPING

If you need some retail therapy, there are massive malls and modern shopping centers throughout the city, as well as several large department stores (Liverpool and Palacio del Hierro are the largest) that sell designer clothes and accessories, cosmetics, housewares, electronics, and other necessities. For the most upscale shopping experience, head to Polanco's main drag, Presidente Masaryk, where you'll find high-end designer boutiques like Fendi and Tiffany & Co., as well as international labels like Zara and American Apparel.

In Polanco, the Roma, and the Condesa, you will find independent shops that sell furniture, clothes, and home accessories, often featuring work by local artists and designers. Carlos Slim–owned Elektra sells home appliances, including washers and dryers, while the chain Viana sells similar items, as well as furniture sets. The cheapest place to buy clothing, furniture, electronics, or accessories is at the many large *tianguis,* or municipal markets, located throughout the city. While you will certainly get the best deal at a market, remember that you have no guarantee on an item's providence or quality, and, of course, there are no returns. Neighborhood markets may also carry some housewares, depending on their size.

For antiques, the shops surrounding the Plaza de Angel in the Zona Rosa are some of the best spots for vintage furniture, accessories, photographs, and religious artifacts; on Saturday the plaza also hosts an antiques bazaar. You can also find antiques at La Lagunilla, an open-air market right next to the sprawling Tepito (keep an eye on your wallet if you venture into these labyrinthine markets).

For folk art, including ceramic flatware and colorful blown glassware for the kitchen, there are numerous artisanal markets, including the sprawling and abundant La Ciudadela in the *centro histórico.* Some of the finest and most reasonably priced traditional arts can be found at the government-run Fonart; they have several locations, including branches in the *centro,* the Cuauhtemoc neighborhood, and Mixcoac.

There are many excellent bookstores in the capital, and some carry English-language books. The pretty El Pendulo café/bookstore chain (with locations in the Roma, Condesa, and Polanco, among others) has some titles in English. For the largest selection in English, try Libros, Libros, Libros in Lomas.

HEALTH CARE

There are good health care options in Mexico City, including many large and prestigious hospitals with top-notch doctors and facilities. Those enrolled in IMSS—the public health care option—can take advantage of more than 15 IMSS hospitals in the metropolitan region, though most foreign residents use private doctors and hospitals for health care. For private care, the Hospital American British Cowdray (ABC Hospital) in the Las Americas neighborhood and the Hospital Español in Polanco are two of the most well regarded in the city. For more options, the website of the U.S. Embassy in Mexico City maintains a list of English-speaking doctors and clinics. You can visit any private hospital in an emergency, as well as the good but highly impacted general hospital in the Doctores neighborhood.

SCHOOLS

Mexico City is an excellent place to study the Spanish language and Mexican culture, though it is not typically a place that attracts language students. Mexico's most prestigious university, the Universidad Nacional Autónoma de México (UNAM), offers special courses designed for foreign students in Spanish language and Mexican culture on both their main campus and Polanco facilities. The International House also offers Spanish-language courses in both Mexico City and Cuernavaca, southeast of Mexico City. On that note, Cuernavaca is close to Mexico City, but it is a more popular place to study Spanish, with numerous private language institutes.

For parents of school-age children, there is a variety of bilingual or English-language primary and secondary schools in Mexico City. Most foreign parents choose to send their children to a private or religious-affiliated school, where students are more likely to receive some or all of their instruction in English. The American School Foundation, Greengates, Colegio Peterson, and Eton School are a few of the most well-known K–8s in the city. There are also several schools that teach primarily in European languages, including the Alexander von Humboldt School for German and the Liceo Franco Mexicano for French. Some schools are certified baccalaureate schools, others are accredited in the United States, and others have no international certification but may still be excellent. Students entering private schools in Mexico are usually asked to provide a transcript proving their grade level from the United States or overseas.

Mexico City has many universities, though only UNAM offers special programs for foreigners. Nonetheless, foreigners with good Spanish-language skills may be accepted for enrollment at one of the many city colleges, like Universidad Iberoamericana and the Universidad Metropolitana.

ARTS AND ENTERTAINMENT

Mexico City offers a wide range of recreational and entertainment options. An arts capital, the city has numerous world-class museums, notably the Museo Nacional de Antropologia (National Anthropology Museum), which houses a mind-blowing collection of artifacts from all of Mexico's pre-Columbian cultures.

For contemporary art, the Museo Rufino Tamayo in Chapultepec and the Museo Universitario de Arte Contemporaneo (MUAC) on the UNAM campus both host excellent rotating exhibitions. In Coyoacán, Frida Kahlo's childhood home is now a museum in her and Diego Rivera's honor. There are a growing number of private galleries in neighborhoods like the Roma, Polanco, San Ángel, and San Rafael, as well as ongoing musical and dance performances at venues like the Auditorio Nacional (National Auditorium), the Poliforum, and the Palacio de Bellas Artes (Palace of Fine Arts). Amalia Hernandez's world-famous Ballet Folklorico, an artistic interpretation of Mexican folk dances, is performed almost every week at Bellas Artes.

Restaurants range from simple to fine dining, with Mexican food predominating among a mix of international cuisines. For a night on the town, bars, nightclubs, cantinas, and pool halls abound, with options to suit every taste and budget. Whether you like to dance salsa to a live band or prefer to sip cocktails with a view of the city, you'll find what you're looking for in Mexico City.

PRIME LIVING LOCATIONS

Despite its generally contemporary atmosphere, Mexico City is not entirely divorced from traditional Mexican culture. The Independence Day parades brings *charros* and *charras* to the streets, and Día de Muertos (Day of the Dead) is celebrated with a massive display of altars in the *zócalo*.

CRIME AND SAFETY

By and large, the capital has not been deeply affected by the drug-related violence at Mexico's border; however, Mexico City has nonetheless earned a reputation for crime in its own right. In the years following the peso crash, economic desperation led to a surge in crime throughout the city, sometimes involving foreign tourists and residents. Although most people live comfortably in Mexico City, visitors and residents should take reasonable precautions to be safe in the capital.

Most crime against foreigners in Mexico City is economic—in other words, theft, break-ins, mugging, and pick pocketing are the most common problems, with violence usually breaking out when the victim resists. In more uncommon cases, foreigners have been kidnapped and held until their bank account is drained (or a ransom is paid), and sometimes abused or beaten by their captors. Similarly, one of the most troubling crimes in Mexico City are taxi-related muggings or kidnapping. For several decades, corrupt cab drivers have taken advantage of the city's circuitous topography to shuffle unsuspecting passengers down hidden side streets. There, victims are often kidnapped, assaulted, and robbed by organized gangs. Although taxi crime is troubling, it is thankfully easy to avoid. Throughout Mexico City, registered taxis, called *sitios*, are available for hire. There are registered taxi stands in the airport, in bus terminals, and in every major neighborhood, and dozens of safe companies will pick you up anywhere in the city. Most charge a flat rate for their services (in bus terminals and in the airport, you pay in advance), and the cost is more elevated than a regular cab—but well worth it!

Crime can occur anywhere, even in the city's most affluent neighborhoods, but you can reduce the dangers by traveling by day or on well-lit roads, keeping an eye on your wallet in crowded subway cars, carrying a cell phone, and always taking registered taxis. After dark, you should be more cautious, especially when walking through unpopulated areas. The *centro histórico* has become far safer in recent years (and there are many police officers watching over the streets), but it is best to stick to the areas to the west of the *zócalo* and along the Alameda Central. After dark, avoid walking alone through the Doctores, Santa Maria de la Ribera, Tabacalera, Guerrero, and most of the Juárez until you are better acquainted with the city. In the Roma, Condesa, and Polanco, there is less crime in the evening, especially in popular areas where crowds of diners and partygoers make the streets safe for walking. Nonetheless, it is wise to be on guard in the evenings no matter where you are, avoid deserted streets, and not be out at very late hours.

Where to Live

Despite its size, Mexico City is a largely provincial city. Once you learn your way around your little corner of the city, it is remarkably easy to feel at home in this megametropolis. There are numerous interesting and lively neighborhoods throughout the *distrito federal*, and where you live will determine where you shop, where you drink your coffee in the mornings, if you need a

RENTAL REQUIREMENTS AND THE *FIADOR*

Mexico's civil laws are designed to protect the interest of renters, which can make it more difficult for landlords to evict tenants or recover the cost of any damages to the property. As a result, landlords in Mexico City have introduced some surprisingly stringent and remarkably ubiquitous requirements for renting an apartment. As anywhere, renters are required to sign a rental agreement and leave a deposit on the property; however, a majority of landlords also require a cosigner on your lease, known as a *fiador*. In order to meet the cosigning requirement, the *fiador* must own a property in the capital, with no mortgage owed. Along with the rental contract, the *fiador* must provide a copy of the *escritura* (deed) to their property, their last *predial* (tax statement), and a copy of their identification. Needless to say, acting as *fiador* is a hefty favor, and many foreigners are unable to find someone willing to assume such a large risk on their behalf. In some cases, your Mexico City employer may be able to fulfill the *fiador* requirement.

If you find the perfect place but don't have a cosigner for your lease, the first thing to do is speak to the landlord or property manager. If you explain that you are relocating to Mexico from a foreign country and don't have family in the area, the landlord may be willing to accept a bank deposit, or *fianza*, in lieu of a *fiador*. This deposit may be equal to several months of rent, so it's good to have a small cushion of savings if you are planning to move to Mexico City.

Unfortunately, large real estate companies handle rentals in Mexico City, and these people aren't qualified to waive a cosigning requirement and may be reluctant to contact the owner on your behalf. If you don't work at a large company and aren't able to get the *fiador* requirement waived, it may be easier to look for the elusive apartments that do not request cosigners. Speak with other expatriates and look in neighborhoods traditionally popular with foreigners; landlords who have rented to foreigners in the past are more likely to understand the complications of a *fiador* for expatriates.

car or not, and what you'll do on the weekends. Some love the quiet colonial atmosphere in Coyoacán, while others love the energy and history downtown. Before you settle down, get to know the city. As you explore, you'll find each neighborhood has its own character, as well as its pros and cons with regards to transportation, safety, shopping, and nightlife.

HOUSING

There are colonial homes, modern condominiums, large multifamily complexes, small residential apartment buildings, and everything in between in Mexico City. From incredibly cheap crash pads to top-dollar penthouses, there is truly something for every taste and budget in the capital. Likewise, the city's diverse neighborhoods run the gamut from colonial charmers to tough urban landscapes.

In a city so large, location is often just as important as the space itself. It is always a good idea to rent before you buy, but this advice is especially important in Mexico City. Before you permanently settle on anything, give it a test run. When you are ready to buy, housing costs run the gamut and depend on neighborhood. You will find the highest prices in the southern neighborhoods, like San Ángel, Coyoacán, and El Pedregal, as well as in the traditionally up-scale areas of Polanco, Las Lomas, and Santa Fe. In general, there aren't co-op apartment buildings like there are in some U.S. cities, though some newer buildings will sell individual apartments.

MEXICO CITY NEIGHBORHOODS
Centro Histórico and Vicinity

Mexico City's *centro histórico* (historic center) is an unusual mix of grand colonial-era architecture and a gritty urban atmosphere. An old-fashioned-meets-modern mix of cafés, *fondas,* convenience stores, bakeries, clothing shops, newsstands, and cell phone outlets fill the district's stately streets, cramming the doorways of colonial-era buildings; some blocks are charming, while others are downright maddening. During the day, the streets are thronged with pedestrians, and a din of traffic echoes down the avenues. However, as businesses close and people head home, the neighborhood quiets down considerably by evening. Until recently, it was considered fairly dangerous to walk around the *centro* at night. However, the municipal government has hired more police officers to patrol the area, both day and night, and Carlos Slim, Mexico's richest citizen, has begun investing in the area, fixing up many historic buildings. Today, there are new pedestrian walkways lined with bars and cantinas, and plenty of restaurants stay full through evening. Even so,

daily life in Mexico City's *centro histórico*

living in the *centro histórico* is a bit more rough and tumble than the popular enclaves in the south of the city.

When it comes to housing, the *centro histórico* is relatively inexpensive. Most apartments in the area are located in creaky, older buildings; some are well worn but may also be spacious, with high ceilings and interesting details. In addition to the amazing 18th-century architecture, there are also some newer constructions in the *centro,* built in the 1950s and '60s. If you don't mind a little wear and tear, you can find an excellent bargain, with basic two-bedroom apartments renting under US$500 a month. The average cost for a two-bedroom apartment on a safe street is about US$650.

Cuauhtemoc, Zona Rosa, and the Juárez

Heading southwest from the *centro histórico* along the Avenida Reforma, neighborhoods like the **Tabacalera, San Rafael, Santa Maria de la Ribera,** and the northern Juárez can be a bit rough, especially after dark. You can get a good deal on an apartment in these areas (and likely find something with lots of character), though you'll also have to be more vigilant with regards to safety. You can rent a two- or three-bedroom apartment for around US$500.

At the southeast edge of the Juárez, you'll reach the Zona Rosa, an area known for its pedestrian streets, loud boutiques, hotels, strip clubs, dance halls, and somewhat touristy atmosphere. Though few people live in the Zona Rosa proper, the blocks surrounding this area offer some inexpensive, centrally located, and charming options, with nice, unfurnished, two-bedroom apartments renting for around US$600. In the small pocket of the Juárez west of Florencia, between Avenidas Cuauhtemoc and Reforma, you'll find some nice 19th- and early-20th-century apartment buildings, lots of Korean grocery stores, and easy access to transportation, both via metro and bus.

Just north of the Zona Rosa, the American Embassy is located in an area called the Cuauhtemoc, a low-key and largely residential neighborhood known for its streets named after major world rivers. The "rios" can be a great place to live; there are supermarkets, banks, plenty of transportation options along Reforma, and, thanks to its proximity to the embassy, a small local expatriate community. Average rentals run about US$900 and up for a basic two-bedroom apartment; buying an apartment in the Cuauhtémoc will cost around US$150,000, though older homes can be significantly more expensive.

Polanco, Anzures, and Las Lomas

On the northeast corner of Mexico City's largest urban park, Bosques de Chapultepec, Polanco is a historic upscale neighborhood that is perennially popular with well-heeled Mexican families and expatriates. Although most of the capital's wealthiest residents have moved from the city center to the outlying suburbs of Santa Fe and El Pedregal, you'll still see some fashionable old money in Polanco. Here, gorgeous early-20th-century mansions line quiet streets, while along Presidente Masyrk, Polanco's main drag, designer shops, gourmet restaurants, and alfresco cafés give the district a posh, Beverly Hills atmosphere. Throughout Polanco and the adjacent neighborhood of Anzures, there are a variety of housing options, including old family homes, modern condominiums, and apartment complexes. Prices run a little higher here, but those on a budget may be able to find something more reasonable with a bit of persistence. For a two-bedroom apartment, average unfurnished rentals run around US$2,000 a month, though there are options both above and below that number. Buyers should expect to spend an average of US$300,000 for an apartment and US$600,000 for a home, or more for a large or historic property.

Polanco is highly connected to the rest of the city via public transportation, and capital residents have many reasons to visit this pretty area, even if they don't live there. By contrast, the neighborhood Lomas de Chapultepec has a largely suburban feeling. Located above Polanco on the pretty hillsides adjoining Chapultepec Park, the neighborhood is filled with leafy, winding, residential streets that feel far from the busy avenues below. The adjoining neighborhood, Bosques de las Lomas, is a bit farther from the *centro* but shares a similar comfortable, upscale atmosphere to Lomas de Chapultepec. Here, you'll find nice single-family homes, rather than apartment buildings, many with yards or pools. Rentals are a bit harder to come by; expect to spend around US$1,800 for two-bedroom apartments in Las Lomas and vicinity, and double that to rent a house. Buyers will spend anywhere from US$400,000 to US$1,000,000 in these neighborhoods, depending on the size of the property.

Santa Fe

Radical transformations define Mexico City, yet few have been so dramatic as that of Santa Fe. Originally the site of massive sand mines, the area had been converted to landfills and garbage dumps by the 1960s. Over the next several decades, developers slowly transformed the area from industrial to residential, with construction reaching a fever pitch during the 1990s. Today, it is Mexico City's most modern district, with glassy, glittering skyscrapers, massive shopping malls, a large percentage of the city's business complexes and expo centers, and high-end hospitals. Those who live in Santa Fe usually do so because they work there, though others like the modern, big-city environment.

Those looking to experience Mexico City won't have the same access from Santa Fe, which is located on the western edge of the city and is relatively cut off from the larger metropolis. Nonetheless, many prefer the area to the older districts in the center of town; it all depends on your style. Either way, you'll pay more to live here, and you definitely need a car, even if you rarely leave the area (fortunately, most places in Santa Fe have ample parking).

La Roma and La Condesa

The trendy Roma and Condesa neighborhoods lie to the south of the city's central districts but are close enough to keep all of the capital's star attractions at your fingertips. Occupying a mess of streets between Avenida Insurgentes and Bosques de Chapultepec, the vibrant Condesa neighborhood has long been a favorite with hip, young Mexicans and expatriates. Here, the beautiful tree-filled streets are lined with art deco apartment buildings, designer boutiques, and stylish

Beautiful urban parks, like the Parque España in La Condesa, are a welcome respite from the bustling city.

© CARLOS MEADE

PRIME LIVING LOCATIONS

restaurants. The neighborhood also gets some much-needed oxygen from its two attractive urban parks, Parque Mexico and Parque España. The Condesa used to be a family neighborhood, and you'll still get a touch of old-school flavor here; however, as it becomes increasingly popular, fancy cupcake spots, boutique hotels, and expensive wine bars have given the Condesa a posh element, just as they drive the rents higher. Expect to pay around US$900 or US$1,000 for a two- or three-bedroom apartment in one of the Condesa's beautiful deco apartment buildings, and more for a freestanding home. Buyers will find smaller houses and apartments average around US$300,000 or so, but, as in the rest of the city, you could spend three times that amount on a historic home.

To the east of Avenida Insurgentes and adjoining the Condesa, La Roma is another trendy, popular, and livable neighborhood with a variety of housing options. Perhaps a touch more youthful (and a few pesos more inexpensive) than the Condesa, La Roma's stately art nouveau mansions are now packed with bookshops, cafés, and bars. You can rent or buy in La Roma for about the same as the Condesa, though there is a bit more variety, including some larger apartment buildings with more affordable units. Average rents for multiple bedroom apartments run about US$800 per month. It has a great neighborhood market, Mercado Medellin, and several pleasant squares where you can walk a dog or relax on a park bench. Most apartments for rent are located in older buildings with lots of character, but not necessarily with luxury amenities.

© ARTURO MEADE

The Colonia del Valle is one of the capital's many pretty residential neighborhoods.

Colonia del Valle and Napoles

If you like the atmosphere in the Roma and the Condesa, you can save a few pesos (or rent a bigger place) by looking farther south, in the vast residential neighborhoods south of the Viaducto, including the Colonia del Valle and the Napoles, as well as the Narvarte, farther to the east. The Colonia del Valle is one of Mexico City's largest neighborhoods, and it is filled with attractive middle-class apartment buildings and homes. Many have parking, since the *colonia's* major downside is its lack of public transportation (there are only a few metro stops in this giant neighborhood, though those living close to Insurgentes will have access to the MetroBus systems). The Napoles is similar to the Colonia del Valle, with lots of middle-class apartment buildings and some nice places to eat, though fewer upscale offerings than you'll find in del Valle. Neither of these neighborhoods are as hip and trendy as the Roma and Condesa, but, for many, their friendly, low-key ambience is a plus. Average rental and purchase prices are similar here to in the Roma and the Condesa, though possibly just a touch cheaper; plus, you'll likely get a bit more space for your pesos and possibly a parking space.

Coyoacán and San Ángel

Southern Mexico City is swathed with some of the most affluent and beautiful neighborhoods in town. If you are willing to live somewhat far from a metro stop, you will be rewarded by the small-town ambience in the historic neighborhood of Coyoacán. Made famous by former resident Frida

PRIME LIVING LOCATIONS

© ARTURO MEADE

A mosaic mural decorates a public space in San Ángel, an upscale neighborhood in southern Mexico City.

Kahlo, Coyoacán was once a suburban community outside the capital that was gradually engulfed by the larger metropolis. Fortunately, the center of the town has managed to maintain a truly small-town atmosphere. Here, the city streets are filled with old trees, crumbling stucco walls, and overflowing gardens, and the central square boasts old churches and alfresco dining spots. Neighboring San Ángel is another beautiful community, with a weekly art market in its leafy downtown plaza. Like Coyoacán, San Ángel is a fairly expensive area. Many houses are spacious and historic, with price tags to match the luxury, though there are also extensive residential neighborhoods surrounding the historic districts. Renting a two-bedroom home in this general area will likely run about US$2,000 per month or more (apartments are more inexpensive), while buying a similar property will likely cost around US$500,000. Historic homes can cost far more than the average, especially around the quaint central districts of San ángel and Coyoacán.

Around Insurgentes South

Although San Angel and Coyoacán are the most well-known southern neighborhoods, there are many other comfortable, middle-class communities along the southern stretch of Insurgentes. Just beyond the Parque Hundido, at the edge of the Napoles, **Mixcoac** was once a small town that was swallowed by the growing urban sprawl; today, it has some pleasant residential streets and a pretty *centro* near the Universidad Panamericana. Farther south (but before arriving at San Ángel), **San Jose Insurgentes, Guadalupe Inn,** and **La Florida** are a few of the other large upper-middle-class neighborhoods, with quiet streets lined with single-family homes. Average rentals run US$1,500 to US$2,000, and you can buy a home for about US$400,000. Although you won't find much commerce in these neighborhoods (beyond the many shops and restaurants along Insurgentes), they are quiet and comfortable places to live. In most cases, residents prefer to own cars.

Tlalpan

For some people, having the city nearby is a benefit, but living right in the thick of the action isn't a top priority. Some outlying neighborhoods can offer a more tranquil lifestyle while still putting you within striking distance of the capital's many attractions. In the far south, Tlalpan is the name of one of the 16 *delegaciones,* or boroughs, in Mexico City. Like so many of Mexico City's most charming neighborhoods, downtown Tlalpan was once its own discrete community, but it was slowly consumed by the greater metropolis.

In the blocks around the main square, you'll find a charming colonial-era atmosphere, with cobblestone streets, centuries-old haciendas, and a pleasant buzz of cafés, shops, and traditional restaurants. With its country atmosphere, Tlalpan is a wonderful place to feel far away from the city while still living within it. If you will be telecommuting to your job or working in the south of the city, Tlalpan is a mellow alternative to inner-city living. Housing prices in Tlalpan are similar to the rest of south Mexico City.

El Pedregal

Jardines del Pedregal, or El Pedregal, is a beautiful upscale neighborhood just beyond the university. As far south as it is, El Pedregal isn't convenient for those working in the *centro,* or who plan to spend lots of time in the heart of the city. However, it can be a charming and comfortable place to live for those affiliated with the university. Like many of the southern districts, a car is a necessity out here. Housing prices in El Pedregal are similar to the rest of south Mexico City.

CUERNAVACA

Similar to the capital yet offering a mellower, more laid-back lifestyle, the city of Cuernavaca can be a good alternative in the Mexico City region. Less than an hour south of the city, Cuernavaca shares many cultural similarities with the capital. Traditionally, many wealthy Mexico City residents maintained weekend homes here; since the 1980s, many have made the move permanently, giving this medium-size metropolis a pleasant, cosmopolitan atmosphere. Unfortunately, *chilangos* have managed to bring some of their problems with them: Crime, traffic, and air pollution are now problems in Cuernavaca.

Cuernavaca is consistently celebrated for its perfect weather, often claiming to have the best and most springlike climate in the entire country. The climate also gives rise to leafy trees and flowering plants, which, along with the city's lovely colonial architecture, makes for a very charming downtown district. At the very center of the city, the twin plazas Juárez and Morelos adjoin the state government buildings and are often the hub of activity. Today, Cuernavaca, like many Mexican cities, has expanded outward, with modern neighborhoods with a variety of housing options flanking the city center. As in most Mexican cities, homes are more expensive in the central districts of Cuernavaca. On average, you can buy a modern family home for around US$250,000, though pools and gardens can push the price up, as can historic value. You can rent a home for an average of about US$1,200, though there are also more inexpensive options in condominiums, apartments, and smaller properties.

The city has long been popular with expatriates, and there are plenty of services for English speakers, like English-speaking doctors, Hollywood movies, and expatriate groups like the Newcomer's Club of Cuernavaca. Of particular note, Cuernavaca has numerous language institutes, and it is a popular place for foreigners from across the world to study Spanish. On the flip side, it is also a good place to teach English; though you won't find the variety of opportunities in the capital, there are still some jobs in Cuernavaca for foreigners who want to work in the city. Wages here may be a bit lower, but the cost of living is lower, too.

With almost one million residents in the metropolitan zone, Cuernavaca has myriad restaurants, cantinas, museums, theaters, festivals, hospitals, and plenty of other services. Many residents of Cuernavaca are completely fulfilled by the lifestyle in their medium-size city, heading to Mexico City only for the airport or an occasional shopping trip. Others take advantage of the cultural and professional opportunities in the capital.

Getting Around

Getting the lay of the land can be a challenge in Mexico City. A good map is invaluable, and Guia Roji makes the most comprehensive version: a flip-book that covers close to every inch of the *distrito federal*. If you don't get a Guia Roji, Google maps also has a comprehensive online map of the city, which can be helpful to study when heading out or getting a sense of the major avenues and transportation routes. Not to mention, those with smartphones will likely be consulting the Internet frequently as they learn to get around the city.

METRO

Mexico City's extensive underground train, or metro system, is an awesomely extensive, cheap, reliable, and safe way to travel both short and long distances. Most neighborhoods in the city's central districts have at least one metro stop in the vicinity, though the distance between stations can be considerable.

The metro is incredibly easy to use. Color-coded lines run across the city, intersecting at key points, with each stop marked by a visual icon as well as a name. At just MXN$2.50 per ride (or about US$0.20), it is the most reasonable way to get around town. It runs 5 P.M.–midnight on weekdays, 6 P.M.–midnight on Saturday, and 7 P.M.–midnight on Sunday.

METROBUS

Insurgentes was once a traffic-choked artery, jammed with cars, taxis, and an overabundance of buses and *peseros* (minibuses). In 2005, the city government made a radical decision, permanently closing the avenue's middle two lanes to construct an exclusive lane for the city's new bus system. Though construction was painful, the resulting MetroBus—a high-speed bus line—was a major success. The MetroBus runs the entire length of Insurgentes, from the city's northern edge to its southern tip. Travel along Insurgentes has become much more streamlined for public transport passengers, and traffic has reduced now that numerous buses aren't jockeying to pick up passengers. Though the MetroBus can get extremely crowded during rush hour, it is a model of efficiency. The fare for the MetroBus is MXN$5, a flat rate.

After the success of the first MetroBus line along Insurgentes, the city introduced a second line that runs from Tepalcates to Tacubaya along the major east–west corridor, Xola, and a third line from Etopia to Tenayuca.

TAXI

The green Volkswagen Beetle was once the ubiquitous taxi cab of Mexico City. Slowly, and by order of the local government, gold-and-red Tsurus began to replace the Bug, and eventually, the city mandated that all taxis have four doors, effectively eliminating the Volkswagen taxicab. These days, the situation may look a bit more orderly, but foreign residents should still be careful

© CARLOS MEADE

The MetroBus, Mexico City's high-speed public bus system, has helped ease traffic on Avenida Insurgentes and other major thoroughfares.

PRIME LIVING LOCATIONS

when using taxis in the capital. Taxi crime remains a common occurrence, with unsuspecting victims often kidnapped, robbed, and beaten.

To ensure your safety, always use taxis from a registered *sitio* or from a private car service. In airports and bus terminals, *sitios* are well publicized, with tickets you can purchase before heading out to the curb. Taxis must have special registrations to work with bus and airport taxi companies, so it is difficult to err. Throughout Mexico City's residential neighborhoods, you will also find various registered *sitios,* which is safer than hailing a cab off the street.

CAR

Car travel is one of the most popular ways to get around the capital, though you'll need to become fairly familiar with the urban map before setting off on a driving tour of the capital. If you plan to drive, the most important thing to do is learn the system of *ejes viales,* as well as the major thoroughfares. Begin driving around your neighborhood, or ask someone who knows the city well to accompany you. If you get lost, PEMEX gas stations are usually the best place to ask directions.

Once you know where you are going, there is no great challenge to driving in Mexico City. Drivers can be a bit heavy on the accelerator, but they are generally good at handling their automobiles. The worst part may be biding your time in the inevitable, interminable traffic.

GUADALAJARA AND LAKE CHAPALA

Mexico's west-central highlands are the country's verdant soul—a place recounted in ballads and beloved across the republic for its nostalgic atmosphere and rich cultural heritage. With its emerald mountain ranges, sprawling ranches, and sun-baked agave plantations, the state of Jalisco is the distinctly Mexican homeland of mariachi, *charreada* (Mexican rodeo), and tequila. Here, Guadalajara is the star of the show, the state capital and one of the most populous cities in Mexico. Those hoping to learn more about Mexican culture will be thoroughly rewarded in this interesting city, where frequent festivals, a long tradition in the arts, and wonderful Mexican cuisine lend color and folklore to the typical urban lifestyle. At the same time, Guadalajara is a modern city with a quickly growing economy. Over the past few decades, Guadalajara's industry and population have been steadily increasing, along with the size of its long-standing expatriate community. Though it is an urban environment—traffic and air pollution are two concerns for residents—it is much smaller, more inexpensive, and more manageable than the capital in Mexico City.

© JULIE DOHERTY MEADE

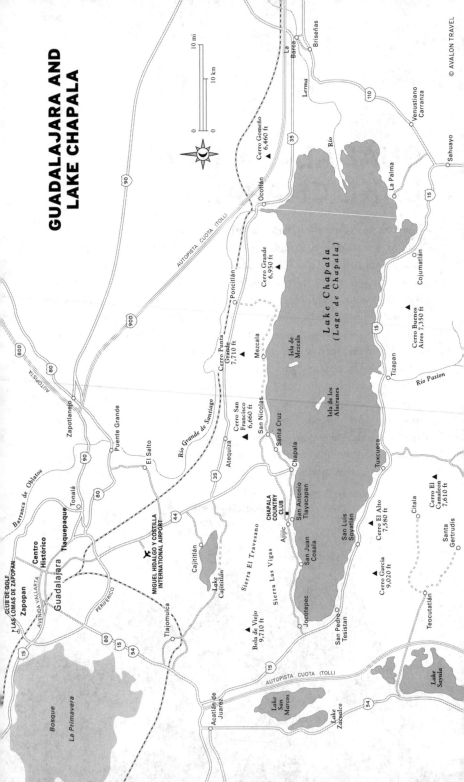

GUADALAJARA AND LAKE CHAPALA

© AVALON TRAVEL

Lake Chapala
(Lago de Chapala)

Just outside Guadalajara, the sunny towns surrounding Lake Chapala have been a favorite with expatriates since playwright Tennessee Williams spent a season in the town of San Antonio Tlayacapan in the 1940s. The sleepy atmosphere, perfect climate, and low prices make these communities popular with retirees, though anyone looking for a slower pace of life will find a good fit in this traditionally Mexican region. Often, a relaxing stroll along the lake's edge is the nicest way to pass a morning, though you can fill your free time with painting classes, yoga, a bridge group, or any number of activities organized by the area's active expatriate population. While offering the tranquility of old Mexico, these charming towns are just a stone's throw away from metropolitan Guadalajara, giving residents access to a top-notch array of stores and markets, health care options, entertainment, and an international airport.

Guadalajara

"Muchacha bonita, la perla más rara de Jalisco es Guadalajara" (beautiful girl, Jalisco's rarest of pearls is Guadalajara) wrote Ernesto Cortázar in collaboration with Manuel Esperón in their popular song, "Ay, Jalisco, no te rajes." Like Cortázar and Esperón, many artists have penned tributes to the city of Guadalajara, a place that seems to capture so much of Mexico's romantic spirit in its bustling avenues and Baroque monuments.

Founded in the 16th century, Guadalajara is an attractive city, though it long outgrew its original *centro histórico,* spreading over several municipalities and growing to almost five million inhabitants. Today, the atmosphere is distinctly urban rather than provincial, yet it still feels manageable, easygoing, and friendly. As evidenced by its fairly large expatriate community, Guadalajara is a great place for foreigners, offering an appealing blend of job opportunities, cultural happenings, a wonderful climate, and a comfortable, fairly inexpensive lifestyle.

THE LAY OF THE LAND

The capital of the state of Jalisco, the city of Guadalajara is spread across in the basin of the mountain-ringed Atemajac Valley in west-central Mexico. At around 5,000 feet above sea level, it is propitiously located in a fertile region with a temperate and sunny climate. There are several active volcanoes just beyond the city, as well as several large lakes, including Mexico's largest, Lake Chapala. With such a beautiful setting, Guadalajara residents have plenty of opportunities to get out of town, taking day trips to the lakeside community of Chapala or tasting spirits in the charming town of Tequila. Even Jalisco's famous coastline is just a four-and-a-half-hour drive from the city, so Puerto Vallarta and the Pacific Coast is a popular getaway.

The original settlement in Guadalajara was established shortly after the Spanish conquest of Mexico and grew slowly over the next several centuries. It was the capital of the province of Nueva Galicia during the colonial era and was named capital of the Xalisco (today Jalisco) state after independence from Spain. The city's *centro histórico* (historic district) is still the seat of the local and state government, as well as the most vibrant cultural district, with Baroque monuments, performance venues, public plazas, shops, and restaurants, and roaring traffic and horse-drawn carriages jamming the busy streets. While the *centro* is still the locus of activity, the metropolitan zone has expanded in all directions, engulfing smaller towns as it grows. The city now blankets seven municipalities and is home to more than 4.5 million people.

With many multinational corporations operating in the city, Guadalajara is a largely industrial town, and much of the city has a gritty, urban feeling. Large swaths of the city to the east and southeast are typically working-class neighborhoods. The western sides are traditionally more affluent, with large, pleasant, residential neighborhoods far from the urban bustle; leafy trees; and wide sidewalks.

History

Guadalajara, named after the Spanish city of the same name, was originally founded in 1532, though the settlement changed locations several times. Though the Spanish had successfully overpowered the native people during the early conquest, Caxcan, Portecuex, and Zacateco people attacked the settlement in 1541, in an episode known as the Mixtón War. The Spanish suffered several defeats before prevailing, moving the settlement again to the city's present-day location. Construction on the city's iconic cathedral began in 1558. It was later named the capital of the province of Nueva Galicia.

Early Guadalajara was small and relatively isolated from the capital of New Spain in Mexico City. The city grew slowly at first, picking up steam as the Spanish expanded their territory westward during the 17th and 18th centuries, establishing ports along the Pacific Coast. The city's first university, still functioning today as the University of Guadalajara, was established in 1791.

During Mexico's War of Independence, Guadalajarans joined with Hidalgo's army to oppose Spanish rule, but the Mexican forces suffered their first brutal loss at the Calderón bridge; the city of Guadalajara was subdued by royalists.

After independence, Xalisco (today Jalisco) was declared a state in the new republic, with Guadalajara named its capital. During the 19th century, Guadalajara continued to grow, becoming the country's second-largest city. It remains one of the largest and most important metropolitan areas in the country, as well as a beloved bastion of traditionally Mexican art and culture.

Orientation

Since the colonial era, the *centro histórico* has been the heart and soul of Guadalajara. Its narrow streets are filled with public plazas, restaurants, shops, theaters, and historic buildings, as well as horse-drawn carriages for hire. The Baroque Catedral Metropolitana (Metropolitan Cathedral) dominates downtown; behind it, a long pedestrian mall runs past the Teatro Degollado, a performing-arts venue, and on to the impressive neoclassical Instituto Cultural Cabañas, which contains impressive murals by celebrated 20th-century artist José Clemente Orozco.

Heading west from the *centro histórico,* Avenida Juárez changes names to become Avenida Vallarta as it heads toward the popular residential neighborhoods of Minerva Chapultepec and Chapalita. At the Minerva, Avenida Vallarta crosses another major boulevard, Avenida Adolfo López Mateos.

© JULIE DOHERTY MEADE

Built in the 19th century, the neoclassical Instituto Cultural Cabañas contains an impressive series of murals by artist José Clemente Orozco.

Continuing northwest, Zapopan is a vast neighborhood and home to wealthy homes and several golf courses.

On the opposite side of the city, the Avenida Avila Camacho leads east toward the communities of Tlaquepaque and Tonalá. Tlaquepaque, with its charming central square and bustling pedestrian streets, feels like a small town within Guadalajara; it is also a craft and shopping capital. If you continue southeast past Tlaquepaque, the highway heads to Lake Chapala and the airport, passing near the craft capital of Tonalá.

Climate

Guadalajara's climate is practically perfect in every way. Warm and sunny year-round, the annual temperature ranges between 52°F and 79°F (11°C to 26°C). December, January, and February are typically the coolest months, dropping down to freezing on some nights. Thereafter, the weather warms up throughout the spring, reaching its high in April and May, when the temperature can reach up to 91°F (33°C).

While temperature fluctuates slightly throughout the year, the seasons are more accurately divided into the rainy season, which runs from June to October, and the dry season, which runs from November to May. During the rainy season, thunderstorms roll over the city in the afternoon, often dropping several inches within a few hours. On average, the city receives more than 35 inches of rain per year.

Industry and Economy

Guadalajara's economy is one of the strongest and most diverse in Mexico, and it has continued to grow over the past few decades. Commerce and tourism account for more than half of the city's jobs, but it also has a large and growing IT and electronics sector, which has prompted some to call it the Silicon Valley of Mexico. After the passage of the North American Free Trade Agreement (NAFTA) in 1994, many international companies relocated to Guadalajara. Today, companies including Motorola, Hewlett-Packard, and IBM have major operations in the city. Many foreigners come to work in the city's high-tech jobs or at one of the numerous well-respected schools and universities in Guadalajara.

Culture

Guadalajara is one of the country's cultural capitals, strongly associated with many of the most typically Mexican traditions. As the largest city in the state of Jalisco, Guadalajara is located in the very heart of tequila country (in fact,

CHARRERÍA AND THE GENTLEMAN COWBOY

Charrería, Mexico's national sport, is a traditional show of horsemanship popular throughout the state of Jalisco. A cousin to rodeo from the American west, *charrería* has its origins in the early colonial era, when Spanish settlers presided over vast cattle-raising haciendas on the country's high plains. Here, local ranchers would show off their equestrian skill during local celebrations. While the competitions were slowly standardized throughout the country, *charreadas* really coalesced as a sport in the 19th century. After the Mexican Revolution, many large haciendas were divided and decentralized, threatening to end the grand tradition of *charros* (Mexican cowboys). Independent *charro* associations were founded to preserve the tradition in both Mexico and the United States (*charrería* is also popular in Texas, where there are more than 100 *charro* associations). Today, many *charros* and *charras* (cowgirls) aren't full-time ranchers, but a privileged class of young men and women who own horses and take lessons to become masters of Western-style horseback riding.

In the modern *charreada*, the *charros* must work as a team to perform a series of nine typical ranch duties, such as roping steer, bull riding, horse-tripping, and horsemanship. Women's stunt-riding events (performed by traditional *charras*, often riding sidesaddle) have also been added to the roster. Culturally, *charros* and *charras* represent more than the event itself, embodying a romantic image of Old Mexico. The *charro* dresses in an old-fashioned aristocratic style, with a brocade suit and short jacket, a butterfly tie, chaps, spurred boots, and a wide-brimmed felt sombrero. Old *charro* outfits, some on display in museums or for sale in antiques shops, often have elaborate hand-stitched embroidery and real silver clasps, as well as thousand-dollar price tags.

During Mexico's golden age of cinema, the *charro* movie brought that romantic image to the big screen in the 1940s and 1950s. Starring universally beloved performers like Jorge Negrete and Pedro Infante, *charro* movies presented a nostalgic vision of Mexico, with the chivalry and codes of old country life. Though there are no more *charro* film stars, mariachi bands continue the tradition, singing and playing exuberant *rancheras* in traditional garb.

If you live in Guadalajara, you will have plenty of opportunities to see *charros* and *charras* in action. There are Sunday shows at the Lienzo Charro de Jalisco in Guadalajara, plus the annual Encuentro Internacional de Mariachi y la Charrería every summer.

PRIME LIVING LOCATIONS

the city of Tequila is just outside the city), and there are probably more mariachi ensembles here than anywhere else. (After all, the famous mariachi band was invented here in Jalisco.) Known to foreigners as the "Mexican hat dance," the Jarabe Tapatío is among the most famous traditional dances in the country. The communities surrounding Guadalajara also create some of the country's most celebrated crafts, including painted ceramics, blown glass, and handmade furniture.

© JULIE DOHERTY MEADE

Horse-drawn carriages are available for hire throughout Guadalajara's *centro histórico.*

Those who'd like to get a full dose of mariachi can attend the city's annual *Encuentro Internacional de Mariachi y la Charrería* (National Mariachi and Charro Festival), which takes place at venues across the city. It's not the only big event in this fiesta-loving town, where national holidays, like Independence Day, are widely celebrated, as are religious festivals and saint's days. During the monthlong *Fiesta de Octubre* (October Fest), the city brims with traditional dance, mariachi, and performance.

In sports, too, Guadalajara is particularly Mexican in its traditions. A quintessential Guadalajara experience is the *charreada* at the Lienzo Charro de Jalisco. *Charreadas* are shows of horsemanship, similar to a rodeo but with pointed focus on the skill of the rider. A role generally reserved for upper classes, the *charro* (gentleman cowboy) and *charra* (cowgirl) dress in the traditional style, with wide-brimmed sombreros and brocade pantsuits. Guadalajara's soccer team, Club Deportivo Guadalajara (popularly known as the Chivas), is also wholly Mexican. Unlike every other club team, which recruit players from overseas, Chivas players are all Mexican born. The biannual face-off with their Mexico City rivals, Club América, is called El Clásico (the Classic) and brings thousands of fans to the stadium.

The Arts

Guadalajara has a long and close relationship with the arts. Many of Mexico's most celebrated artists, writers, and thinkers were born *tapatíos,* including the

LUIS BARRAGÁN IN GUADALAJARA

One of Mexico's most respected 20th-century architects, Luis Barragán was born in Guadalajara in 1902. He studied engineering in college but taught himself architecture, later traveling through Europe, where he was heavily influenced by European modernism. In the 1930s he moved to Mexico City, where, in the following decades, he developed the signatures of his style: clean lines, saturated colors, and natural building materials. Barragán built many residential homes and gardens, but among his most famous work is the Torres de Satélite, a large urban sculpture consisting of five painted towers that marks the entrance to the Satélite neighborhood in Mexico City. Throughout his career, he was repeatedly honored for his originality and vision, and in 1975 he was given a retrospective exhibit at the Museum of Modern Art in New York City.

Most of Barragán's most well-known designs are located in Mexico City, including his former home and studio, now a museum and UNESCO World Heritage Site. However, the architect also designed and built numerous homes in his native Guadalajara. Many of these homes are nestled unassumingly in the Minerva-Chapultepec area, close to the city's downtown district. It's easy to walk between the homes in the neighborhood to get a taste of the architect's aesthetics. You might even live next door to one if you happen to rent in the neighborhood, long popular with foreigners.

famed 20th-century novelist Juan Rulfo, world-renowned architect Luis Barragán, and contemporary filmmaker Guillermo del Toro. Today, there are more than 20 museums in Guadalajara, and throughout the year, the city is host to major exhibitions and performance events, with venues like the Teatro Degollado and the Teatro Diana featuring symphonies, dance troupes, and films.

One of the most important film festivals in Latin America, the Guadalajara International Film Festival, is held in the city annually. A wonderful event for writers and book lovers, Guadalajara's annual Feria Internacional del Libro (International Book Fair) is the largest Spanish-language editorial fair in the world and has attracted guests from Turkey's Orhan Pamuk to Peru's Mario Vargas Llosa.

DAILY LIFE

Though it is a large and bustling city, Guadalajara is far more manageable than the capital, offering most residents a balance of urbanity and tranquility, even in the central districts. In this lively metropolis, there is plenty to keep you busy and entertained, but most live a laid-back lifestyle, where going out is balanced with a pleasant home environment. With a strong economy, beautiful residential neighborhoods, and plenty of entertainment options, it is an obvious choice for many foreigners living in Mexico.

Cost of Living

The cost of living in Guadalajara is reasonable for a city of its size. In broad strokes, a middle-class lifestyle costs about half of what it would in U.S. and Canadian cities, and it is considerably more inexpensive than Mexico D.F. Food is abundant and inexpensive, both in traditional markets and supermarkets. Eating out is both affordable and high quality; a dinner for two in a nice restaurant will rarely cost more than US$30, though there are plenty of casual eateries where you can sit down for a meal of less than US$5. Public transportation is ample, especially in the downtown district and around Minerva Chapultepec, so, for some, it is not necessary to own a car.

Depending on where you choose to live, you could pay between US$500 and US$1,200 for an apartment or private home—more if you want something luxurious. Average homes for sale in residential neighborhoods are listed around US$250,000, with a wide variety both below and above that average. Utilities are inexpensive, as they are in most of Mexico, with the exception of ground-line telephone service. All totaled, a couple can live a comfortable middle-class lifestyle in Guadalajara for around US$2,000 per month, though costs will vary depending on your neighborhood, eating habits, and extras, like a housekeeper or a car.

Food and Shopping

For tourists (as well as locals), shopping is one of Guadalajara's major attractions, with some of the country's most inexpensive and popular craft markets located in the twin suburbs of Tlaquepaque and Tonalá. When stocking your home, do not overlook these beautiful and well-priced shops, where you'll find ceramic flatware and vases, blown glassware, handmade clothing, leather goods, and *equipal* couches, chairs, and tables, made in a traditional manner with natural wood and pigskin leather. Produced in Jalisco, *equipales* are comfortable, inexpensive, and typically Mexican.

In addition to traditional wares, you can shop for clothes, household items, and other goods at the numerous large malls in Guadalajara, including La Gran Plaza on the west side and the large Plaza del Sol, a mall with more than 250 shops located in Zapopoan near the Expo Guadalajara. There is also a large shoe manufacturing industry in Guadalajara; the Galeria del Calzado is a shoe-centric mall near the Minerva, which offers good prices and great variety.

Like most Mexican cities, Guadalajara has traditional markets, as well as large grocery stores. Downtown, the massive Mercado San Juan de Dios (the municipal market) offers three stories of fresh produce, groceries, and food stalls. Shopping for groceries is most inexpensive in traditional markets, where you will find low prices for fruits and vegetables, meat and cheese, tortillas, and dried goods. For imported items, prepackaged foods, bottled drinks, cereals, meats, cheese, and other grocery products, there are numerous supermarkets in Guadalajara, including Soriana, Comercial Mexicana, Superama, Sam's Club, Walmart, and Costco (of these, Soriana and Comercial Mexicana are Mexican owned). In addition to big box stores, small establishments, like Super La Casita and Mercado Alcalde, in the downtown district, stock American products.

Guadalajara's large weekly *tianguis* (open-air market), known as El Baratillo, holds the incredible distinction of being Latin America's largest marketplace. Like most large Mexican *tianguis,* merchants at El Baratillo sell clothing, household appliances, electronics, antiques, fruits and vegetables, breads, and tortillas, as well as prepared foods and tacos.

For a fix of glossies or international news magazines, Sanborns has a large newsstand—with a considerable markup on English-language titles. Sandi Bookstore has a large selection of books in English.

Health Care

As a big city, as well as the home of one of Mexico's best medical schools (at the University of Guadalajara), Guadalajara offers plenty of medical services for expatriates, including many bilingual practitioners, doctors with U.S. medical degrees, and even a few Americans practicing medicine in town. There are English-speaking doctors and staff at Hospital San Javier on Avenida Pablo Casals, Hospital Bernadette on Hidalgo, and Hospital Ángeles del Carmen, among others. Many doctors in private practice also speak English.

Many people from surrounding communities, including the Lake Chapala area, come to Guadalajara for their medical care, especially when they want to see a specialist. In fact, the city is so well-known for its quality medical facilities that many Americans visit the city as "medical tourists," having pricey surgeries or dental care in the city to save the costs of uninsured care or high premiums at home.

Expatriates

Guadalajara has a large and long-standing expatriate community, estimated to number around 50,000 or more. For foreigners, it is a wonderful place to experience Mexico while also maintaining contact with other expatriates. At the same time, although there are many foreigners in Guadalajara, they are sprinkled throughout the city. Unlike the highly visible expatriate communities in small towns like Ajijic or San Miguel de Allende, you may see very few foreigners during your daily life, and your interaction with the expatriate community can be as extensive or as limited as you choose.

For those who would like more contact with other expatriates, the American Society of Jalisco has been in operation since 1945. Members—who do not have to be American to join—have access to networking events and classes, as well as an extensive lending library with books in English. Many of the most active members of retirees, though there are people of every age and profession involved. Focused more on business and networking, the global organization InterNations also has a chapter in Guadalajara. Members come from across the world and usually work in Guadalajara.

An excellent resource for English-speaking foreigners, the *Guadalajara Reporter* is an English-language newspaper that has been in operation for more than 40 years. Serving the state of Jalisco, including Guadalajara, Puerto Vallarta, and the Lake Chapala area, it covers local issues, Mexican politics, sports, and opinion, in addition to offering classifieds, obituaries, and an arts calendar.

WHERE TO LIVE

Guadalajara is a large city with wonderful residential neighborhoods. There are some gritty urban areas in the greater metropolitan region, but most expatriates settle down in the extensive and beautiful neighborhoods to the west of

© JULIE DOHERTY MEADE

A typical residential street in downtown Guadalajara is lined with old homes.

the *centro histórico*. Both renting and buying are affordable options for a city of Guadalajara's size and prominence.

Housing

Housing in Guadalajara is abundant and generally inexpensive. Throughout the central and western districts, there are many lovely residential neighborhoods with quiet and tree-lined streets. You can find a reasonably priced private home or apartment in many of these neighborhoods; there are fewer apartment buildings than you'd find in the capital, but those looking for cheaper digs can look for either an apartment or a casita (smaller house).

Centro Histórico, Minerva Chapultepec, and Chapalita

Guadalajara's *centro histórico* is principally a tourist and entertainment area. Living near the *centro* is a priority for many new residents, especially for those who want to take advantage of nightlife and culture. There are some wonderful old homes and apartments for rent in the downtown area, though you'll find far more options in the residential neighborhoods around Minerva Chapultepec, a district just west of the *centro histórico*. Historic homes will generally sell and rent for higher prices than newer constructions. On average, expect to spend on the higher end of Guadalajara's average housing costs in this area.

One of the oldest communities in Guadalajara, Minerva-Chapultepec grew

© JULIE DOHERTY MEADE

a pretty, residential neighborhood near the University of Guadalajara during the early 20th century as the metropolitan zone expanded west from downtown. Today, it is an attractive and propitiously located residential area, home to the U.S. consulate as well as the University of Guadalajara. Often called the Colonia Americana, Minerva-Chapultepec has long been popular with foreign residents, and it remains so today. Though largely residential, Minerva Chapultepec has become increasingly chic, with lovely garden restaurants set in old colonial homes, fancy bars and nightclubs, and posh houses that emanate a bit of old-fashioned glamour. In addition to the classic turn-of-the-20th-century architecture, there are several homes in the neighborhood that were designed and constructed by renowned Mexican architect (and native *tapatío*) Luis Barragán.

Farther south, Chapalita is another central neighborhood of peaceful, tree-lined streets with wide sidewalks and a smattering of cafés and bookshops. Most of this neighborhood was built in the 1950s and 1960s, with big houses with enclosed gardens. Largely suburban, the neighborhood nonetheless offers all the basics: a neighborhood *tianguis* (market) for food, restaurants, gyms, and, on Sunday, an art fair in the Glorieta Chapalita, the large roundabout that shares the neighborhood's name.

Zapopan

Zapopan is a municipality adjoining Guadalajara to the west. Though once a distinct entity, Zapopan has now been encompassed by the greater Guadalajara metropolitan region. Still, at the center of the district there is a lovely colonial square with the municipal offices and Zapopan's basilica, home of the famous Virgin of Zapopan. Around the plaza, you will find a bit of entertainment and commerce like banks, shops, restaurants, and pharmacies. You'll also find the city's largest malls, a few growing industrial parks, and plenty of supermarket and shopping options. However, Zapopan's real appeal lies in miles and miles of quiet, tree-lined residential streets, which have been referred to as the Beverly Hills of Guadalajara.

Expatriates are scattered throughout Zapopan's many lovely and upscale neighborhoods, such as the northern areas around Colomos Park and near the Zapopan Country Club (where you'll also find the American School Foundation of Guadalajara, for English-speaking students from preschool through high school). You can get to know Zapopan best in a car, and be aware that living here will also require a set of wheels in order to get around and shop.

An average home in Zapopan will likely cost around US$300,000, though there are more luxurious properties and country club villas that cost double that and more. Simple homes and apartments are available for less than US$100,000. Near the American School or the country club, homes generally rent for about US$2,000 a month.

Tlaquepaque

The municipality of Tlaquepaque is located just southeast of the municipality of Guadalajara, though they are both part of the larger Guadalajara metropolitan region. One of the most tranquil and attractive neighborhoods in the city, the central district of Tlaquepaque boasts wonderful restaurants, quaint pedestrian streets, and a sleepy small-town atmosphere. With a unique selection of craft shops, it is also known as one of the country's best shopping destinations.

Despite the surrounding city, Tlaquepaque's center still feels like a small town. The community is dominated by El Parián, a plaza filled with popular cantinas and located just beside the town square. From the square, pedestrian streets lined with restaurants and shops are great for strolling and window shopping. In the evenings, the area is thronged with mariachi musicians.

Tlaquepaque was once an independent city, which was slowly swallowed up by the larger city. Most new residents considering Tlaquepaque will want to look along the quiet, residential blocks around the main plaza. Here you'll find mostly older homes with creaky colonial charm. However, once you start looking beyond the central zone, the area becomes grittier and less attractive.

PRIME LIVING LOCATIONS

© JULIE DOHERTY MEADE

Every evening, mariachi musicians gather in the town square in Tlaquepaque.

GETTING AROUND
Air

It is easy to get to and from Guadalajara and vicinity. Libertador Miguel Hidalgo International Airport (GDL) is located along the Chapala–Guadalajara highway, just 30–40 minutes from downtown. Many major airlines offer national and international flights daily. As a hub for Aeroméxico Connect and Volaris, it serves as a common connection point for travel to and from the United States.

Car

On the ground, Guadalajara is well connected to the rest of the republic by highways; from Mexico City, it takes about 6–7 hours to drive to Guadalajara, passing through the state of Michoacan. From there, modern highway links Guadalajara to the city of Colima, as well as the beach towns of Puerto Vallarta and Manzanillo. A boon for residents, Vallarta is only three hours from Guadalajara.

Most middle-class residents of Guadalajara prefer to get around by car, as many of the large residential neighborhoods aren't serviced by bus or metro.

Public Transportation

Many residents find it is useful to have a car in Guadalajara, but you can get to most major points without one, especially if you live near a major artery.

BUS

A system of city buses links the downtown area to all of Guadalajara's suburbs. Most run along the city's major arteries, departing the *centro histórico* along Avenida Juárez/Avenida Vallarta to the east and west, and along Calzada Independencia to the north and south. The system seems a bit confusing at first, but once you get the hang of it, it is fairly simple. Look for the signs in the window, which indicate where the bus is going. The nicest city buses are run by Turquesa, which are marked TUR on the outside; they have air-conditioning and only carry seated passengers.

SITEUR

Guadalajara has a very small but efficient underground light rail system called the SITEUR (Sistema de Tren Eléctrico Urbano). It has two lines, one heading north and south from the *centro* and the other running east from the *centro*. If you are lucky enough to rent or buy a home near one of the SITEURs, it can be a very reliable form of transportation, especially when you want to head downtown. However, most people in Guadalajara end up owning a car or using public buses, which have a more extensive reach.

Taxi

Taxis circle the central districts of Guadalajara and can be hailed from the street or phoned in advance. Most taxi drivers know the major sights, though it is always a good idea to have an idea of how to arrive if you are traveling into residential neighborhoods. Taking taxis is a generally safe and inexpensive way to travel around the city, though most don't have meters, so ask for the price before you depart if you want to assure the lowest fare.

Lake Chapala

Life continues peacefully along the sparkling shores of Lake Chapala, an hour southwest of Guadalajara. Ringed by small towns, fringed with verdant vegetation, and blessed with truly idyllic weather, the Chapala region has long been a popular destination for weekending *tapatíos* and sojourning foreigners. Though it remains a quintessentially Mexican place, the region's low cost and great weather have attracted a rather sizable community of American and Canadian expatriates. Today, there are tens of thousands of foreign residents living on the lakeshore, many splitting time between Mexico and their hometown farther north.

Despite its mellow, off-the-beaten-track atmosphere, the region is well connected with the cosmopolitan city of Guadalajara via highway, a major advantage to living lakeside. Most residents take advantage of this auspicious position, taking trips to Guadalajara for culture and recreation, medical care, and shopping, as well as for travel via the international airport.

LAY OF THE LAND

Lake Chapala is located about 30 miles southwest of metropolitan Guadalajara along the Chapala–Guadalajara highway. The largest lake in Mexico, Chapala is vast—extending about 50 miles east–west and 12 miles north–south—but shallow, at only about 12 feet deep, on average. There are two small islands in the middle of the water, Isla de los Alacranes and Mezcala, which you can visit on a tour boat from one of the lake's many docks.

There are towns circling the lake on all sides, though most foreign residents gravitate toward the beautiful string of villages on the northeastern edge, which are jointly called the Chapala Riviera. If you drive to the region from

© JULIE DOHERTY MEADE

The small towns along the shore of Lake Chapala have been popular with expatriates for decades.

Guadalajara, the first town on the lake is Chapala. Continuing west along the highway, you will pass San Antonio Tlayacapan and the Chapala Country Club, Ajijic, San Juan Cosala, and, finally, Jocotepec. Some foreigners like the camaraderie of these communities' downtown districts, while others prefer the tranquility of the surrounding mountains, where views of the lake's glassy surface is the perfect mirror to many spectacular sunsets.

Climate

Like Guadalajara, Chapala's practically perfect climate is touted for its year-round sunny, springlike weather. The lake's location in the tropics is abundantly reflected in the verdant vegetation and flowering plants along the shoreline, yet altitude tempers the heat, and a cool breeze off the lake's surface can take the edge off warmer days. You will rarely, if ever, need heating or air-conditioning in a Chapala-area home. Again, Chapala's seasons are divided into wet and dry: From November to May it barely rains, while the summer brings thunderous storms and cool evenings.

Environmental Issues

The Río Lerma runs from Toluca in the state of Mexico to Jalisco, where it empties into Lake Chapala. Agricultural runoff and improper waste disposal have contaminated the river and, as a result, the lake. Since the turn of the 21st century, clean-water programs have helped improve the situation; today, Lake Chapala is safe for water sports and fishing. The lake's tributary has been dammed in 11 places; fortunately, abundant rain during the wet season has also helped to build the lake's water levels.

Nonetheless, water quality and waste treatment remain a concern for lakeshore residents, in addition to common problems associated with human development, including deforestation and soil degradation. Because the region is crucial for migrating birds, it is also an important cause for environmental organizations. SEMARNAT (Secretary of Environment and Natural Resources), Mexico's environmental protection agency, has set goals to improve conditions in the lake and its surrounding communities. The lake is a member of the international Living Lakes program, and the annual Chapala Alive! Festival seeks to raise awareness and money for the cause.

DAILY LIFE

Beautiful views of the lake, an abundance of flowering plants, and sparkling blue skies make the Chapala region one of Mexico's most idyllic hideaways. Most pueblos in this area are family oriented, friendly, and religious, with an old-fashioned, easygoing pace of life. At the same time, the large expatriate community in the Chapala Riviera has also given rise a pleasant assortment of restaurants, shops, hotels, and galleries. Many expatriates are involved in charity or social groups, or gather at popular restaurants or watering holes to spend the evening with friends.

Despite the quiet countryside atmosphere, you can find all the most important necessities along the lakeshore. There are several local clinics, which can attend to most medical problems, including Clinica Ajijic in Ajijic, San Andrés Clinic near La Floresta, and Clinica San Jose de la Ribera in Chapala. (For surgeries or more complicated health conditions, many residents get their medical care in Guadalajara.) For food, flowers, and crafts, there is a traditional market on Wednesday in Ajijic, and Super Lake, a popular store on the highway near San Antonio Tlayacpan, sells groceries and imported foods (some specifically for "north of the border" customers). Also in San Antonio, there is a Walmart Super Center, and at the Plaza Bugambilias in Ajijic, there are shops and a small movie theater.

When it comes to recreation, many prefer the simple pleasures of spending time with friends or relaxing with a book, but the region also boasts a small country club and a racquet club with tennis courts on the way to San Juan Cosala. San Juan Cosala is also the site of natural hot springs, with several thermal pools open to the public. In addition, the local expatriate community is constantly organizing events and activities.

You'll likely know pretty quickly if the Chapala region is a good match for you, though it's worth spending some time in town before making the move. Real estate broker and Ajijic resident Kevin Collins of Collins Real Estate advises potential residents: "Schedule a recon visit for a least 10 days. You'll either love it or leave wondering what all those people see in the place. No one seems to be wishy-washy about the area." He continues, "A good thing to remember is that all the people you meet here love it. The ones who didn't like it went home; you won't meet them. It's not Ohio with better weather. It's Mexico, and some people can't handle living in a different culture."

Expatriates

Since the early 20th century, there has been a small community of foreigners living in the Lake Chapala region, though their numbers began to increase during the 1960s and '70s. Today, an estimated 7,000 foreign residents, mostly from the United States and Canada, make their home along the lakeshore, with even more residing here part time. The town of Ajijic and the surrounding neighborhoods have typically drawn the largest crowd of expats, though new communities along the lake have become more popular as the expatriate community grows.

Throughout the area, the atmosphere is decidedly Mexican, yet the presence of so many expatriates has an influence on the local culture, too. From Scrabble clubs to writers' groups to English-language yoga classes, there are literally dozens of ways to fill up your days and to get to know other expatriates. With more than 3,500 registered members, the Lake Chapala Society (LCS) is the most active expatriate group in the area. The LCS maintains a calendar of events, operates a mail service for U.S. post, and hosts an ongoing lecture series. The LCS lending library contains more than 20,000 books and 4,000 DVDs, available to society members.

WHERE TO LIVE

If you want to live within walking distance of shops and restaurants, look in the downtown area of Ajijic or Chapala. Alternatively, you can find lakeshore homes in quiet residential neighborhoods all along the shoreline. Higher up, the mountains that ring the basin often boast beautiful views of the lake, including the famous Chapala sunsets. Although the communities along the lake are culturally similar, you will get a bit of a different atmosphere, as well as slightly different real estate prices, depending on where you decide to live.

Housing

In the Lake Chapala area, most places to rent or buy are single-family homes, though there is a great variety of options within that framework. There are small and simple houses that could work well for a solo person or a couple, large Mexican-style villas, and modern homes that have been designed or remodeled recently. The cost of your property will depend on its location, though in many communities, you can purchase a comfortable family home for less than US$200,000. For luxurious digs on a large private property, you could pay as much as US$700,000, though houses in this price range or above are uncommon. Roughly, you can expect to pay US$500–1,000 a month to rent a two-bedroom home.

Where there is a preponderance of people buying homes, there is always a preponderance of brokers. There are tons of real estate agents in the Chapala region, including branches of some big-name companies like Century 21 and Coldwell Banker. When you are getting ready to purchase a place in Ajijic, Chapala, and the surrounding region, check in with various real estate agents, but also get to know the area on your own. Driving down the side streets and poking around the various lakeside communities will give you a good idea of where you want to live.

Chapala and San Antonio Tlayacapan

Founded in the 16th century, Chapala is the oldest and most populous town along the lake's shore, and the commercial center of the region. Chapala's downtown overlooks the water, with an old pier and *malecón* (promenade) where you can hire a boat to take you out on the lake, or wander through craft shops. Between the lake and the city's main plaza, about three blocks away, you'll find shops, banks, pharmacies, coffee shops, and other commerce. Chapala is a predominantly Mexican town, which still receives a great deal of tourism from Guadalajara on the weekends. However, it has also received a bit of expatriate spillover from Ajijic, with some foreigners preferring the bustling Mexican atmosphere in Chapala. In addition to homes around the center of town, there is a newer, gated community called Nuevo Chapala, adjoined by the Vista del Lago neighborhood to the northwest.

Just west of Chapala along the lake's shore, the communities of **Chula Vista** and San Antonio Tlayacapan have been popular with expatriates for decades. In fact, Chula Vista was one of the first places that Americans began to settle in the region. Here, you'll find the quiet atmosphere of a traditional small town, though there are also a number of gated communities just surrounding the central region, some of which have pools or tennis courts. Above the city, the Chula Vista Country Club is a nine-hole golf course with beautiful views and well-kept greens. Even if you choose to buy in a private community, both Chapala and San Antonio Tlayacapan are generally a bit more inexpensive than Ajijic.

Ajijic

Ajiijic is a lovely little town with a laid-back atmosphere, a large expatriate community, and a charming downtown district. The town is nestled along the edge of the lake, where a paved promenade curves along the shoreline. Downtown, there is a surprisingly wide variety of restaurants, including Argentine, Italian, and French, in addition to Mexican. Just a few blocks from the water, you'll often find locals gathering in the plaza downtown, which is adjoined by the 16th-century San Andrés Church. Despite the obvious influence of American expatriates, Ajijic maintains traditional Mexican customs, including annual Catholic fiestas.

For those looking for a cozy and welcoming expatriate community, Ajijic is the best choice among Chapala's communities. Since everyone lives nearby, there is a great sense of camaraderie among expatriates in Ajijic, and many people feel immediately at home in this small and friendly town. The long-standing Lake Chapala Society is based in Ajijic, and the city is home to a wide range of social groups, clubs, and educational activities, including Spanish classes, knitting groups, yoga, and English-language theater troupes. What distinguishes Ajijic from other expatriate communities in Mexico is that the town itself is not a tourist destination. Although you'll certainly see many foreigners in the area (and plenty of menus printed in English), almost all these foreigners are full- or part-time residents.

Homes in Ajijic are the most expensive along the Chapala Riviera, but real estate is nonetheless affordable by U.S. or Canadian standards. There are many brokers in town who can help you locate properties for sale. Just east of central Ajijic and not far from the downtown district, La Floresta is a gated, tree-filled residential community, which

Ajijic's 16th-century San Andrés Church

© JULIE DOHERTY MEADE

Ajijic is located on the shores of Lake Chapala, the largest freshwater lake in Mexico.

boasts a yacht club and horse rental, as well as impressive vegetation and picturesque cobblestone streets. Riviera Alta and Lomas de Ajijic are two other gated communities with neighborhood pools and gathering spaces. To the west, Villa Nova is another lovely residential district, with some views of the lake. Generally speaking, these communities all offer a similar, relaxed environment; the key is finding a home that matches your needs and budget.

San Juan Cosala

Heading west, the village east of Ajijic is tiny San Juan Cosala, best known for its natural thermal springs. Fewer expatriates live here than in neighboring Ajijic, though some have settled in this traditionally Mexican community. There aren't gated or big residential neighborhoods in San Juan Cosala, but you will find some properties for sale, some at lower prices.

Jocotepec

Few expatriates venture as far as Jocotepec, the westernmost community at Lake Chapala. A traditional Mexican pueblo, Jocotepec has a pleasant town square and a small beachfront promenade.

GETTING AROUND

The communities around Chapala are spread out and suburban, so many lakeside residents like to own a car, which can be handy for getting around the area, grocery shopping, and visiting Guadalajara. However, depending on where you live, you may not need to use your car on a daily basis. In these small communities, the best mode of transport is often your own two feet.

Bus

There are several bus lines connecting the towns along the Jocotepec–Chapala highway. Large and slow-moving city buses will take you right through the town square of each community, while the newer and faster buses run frequently between Jocotepec and Chapala along the highway, though these will not take you all the way to the center of town (generally, though, it's a short walk from the highway to the lake). Between towns, the cost depends on how far you are traveling; it is about US$1 to ride the entire stretch from Jocotepec to Chapala, and about US$0.60 if you are going from Ajijic to Chapala.

To reach Guadalajara from Ajijic or other lakeside communities, you can flag a bus along the main highway (they don't necessarily stop at appointed places, so be sure to wave your hand to the driver if you see the bus you need). Look for the signs in the window that indicate the bus's destination. The trip takes about 45 minutes and costs about US$3.50. From downtown Guadalajara, second-class buses depart the Camionera Antigua for the lakeside towns until around 9 P.M. From Guadalajara's bus station, there are frequent first-class buses to destinations throughout Mexico.

Air

With daily flights to the United States, as well as various national destinations, the Guadalajara International Airport (GDL) is convenient to the Chapala region, located along the Guadalajara–Chapala highway about a half hour from the lakeshore.

PUERTO VALLARTA AND THE CENTRAL PACIFIC COAST

An emerald fringe of tropical jungle blankets the coast along the Bahía de Banderas, a tranquil and expansive bay along the Pacific Coast of Mexico. Here, nestled between the coastal mountains and the sea, the city of Puerto Vallarta is one of Mexico's oldest and most charming resort towns. Look beyond the string of nightclubs and souvenir shops that line Vallarta's boardwalk, and you'll see a wonderfully vibrant and livable city with fine restaurants, a distinctly Mexican atmosphere, and a large community of foreign residents. Many come to vacation here for a week or two, then decide to buy a part-time residence. Others find it so compelling, they settle down permanently.

Unlike other Mexican resort towns, Puerto Vallarta was constructed long before a preponderance of high-rise hotels and multinational cruise ships arrived at its golden shores. As a result, the city's central district, known as Old Town, retains a distinctly old-fashioned atmosphere, with a colonial-era

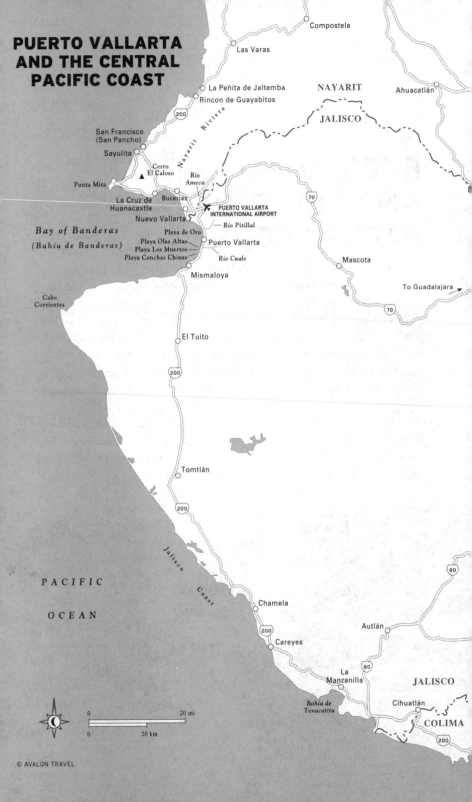

church, cobblestone streets, and leafy green trees. Here, you'll find a pleasant mix of galleries and boutiques, seafood restaurants, and craft shops adjoining the city's *malecón,* a long, palm-fringed promenade dotted with public sculptures by local artists.

As one of the most attractive and modern cities along the Pacific Coast, Puerto Vallarta is a natural pick for expatriates looking for a blend of comfort, convenience, and natural beauty—not to mention first-rate beaches and recreation. Many love the convivial atmosphere in PV, but those looking for a quieter, more rustic, and even more inexpensive option might head north up the coast of Nayarit, where several small beach towns have attracted a modest community of foreign residents and laid-back vacationers. Though not far from the many shopping, dining, and health care options in Puerto Vallarta—including the international airport—the Nayarit coast feels decidedly quiet and remote. If you really want to get off the beaten track, head south from Puerto Vallarta to the remote Jalisco coast, a wonderful place to visit and, for adventurous expatriates seeking a truly mellow environment, possibly settle down.

The Lay of the Land

The city of Puerto Vallarta is nestled between the green slopes of the Pacific mountain range and the sparkling waters of the Bay of Banderas. One of the world's largest and deepest harbors, the Bay of Banderas is known for its abundance of marine life, including pilot, gray, and humpback whales; spotted and bottlenose dolphins; black marlin; Pacific sailfish; manta ray; porpoise; hammerhead shark; snapper; sea bass; and many other marine species. In the surrounding sierras, rivers and waterfalls cut through tropical deciduous forests filled with unique flowering plants and trees. In this lush environment, it is not uncommon to see green parrots in the trees overhead or an iguana sunning itself by your pool.

The Bay of Banderas spans two states, with Puerto Vallarta and the southern stretches of the bay pertaining to the state of Jalisco; north of the River Ameca, the bay and its surrounding communities pertain to the state of Nayarit. Note that the state line also delineates the change in time zones; though right next door to each other, Jalisco adheres to Central time while Nayarit's clocks are set one hour later, in Mountain time. On the northernmost tip of the bay, Punta Mita, Nayarit, is home to The Four Seasons resort. Heading north from Punta Mita, the sleepy Pacific beach towns along the coast are known as the Nayarit Riviera. This region is well connected to Puerto Vallarta by highway and has become popular with low-key, independent travelers. Heading south from Puerto Vallarta, the bay's southernmost tip, Cabo Corrientes, is almost entirely undeveloped. Here, the coastal highway heads inward, leaving this stretch of coastline totally undeveloped, reachable largely by boat or rustic back roads. Between the point and the old beach town of Barra de Navidad, there are miles and miles of largely undeveloped coastal land, often called the Costa Alegre.

Though some Americans began to visit Puerto Vallarta in the 1950s, it was during the 1960s that the city established itself as a resort destination. It gained notoriety (and a touch of Hollywood glamour) when Richard Burton and Elizabeth Taylor shot the movie *Night of the Iguana* in a small town just south of the port. Shortly thereafter, the Mexican government began to invest in infrastructure, making Puerto Vallarta more accessible to the rest of the country. The resort grew rapidly in the following decades, expanding northward toward the River Ameca; new beachfront luxury hotels sprang up along the coast, and the marina was developed. Today, there are around 350,000 residents in the city, yet Puerto Vallarta's Old Town retains the pleasant atmosphere of a traditional pueblo, with narrow stone streets, breezy plazas, and an old parish church rising above the skyline.

Due to the modern expansion, colonial charms melt into modern luxury as you head north along the Bay of Banderas from Old Town. Puerto Vallarta's Zona Hotelera (hotel zone) is principally designed for vacationers, and that's where you'll find rows of high-rise hotels, massive swimming pools, private beaches, fancy restaurants, and nightclubs. Beyond these central districts, there are large residential areas in the surrounding hillsides, from low-key and inexpensive working-class communities to chic hilltop neighborhoods with bay views.

CLIMATE

Mexico's Pacific Coast has a consistently warm and humid climate. Average daytime temperatures hover in the mid-80s throughout most of the year, dropping just 10°F or so in the evening. The warmest months are June, July, August, and September, when the rising temperature and intense humidity create torrid conditions; tourism generally slumps during the summer, while locals head to higher altitudes or northern latitudes. Fortunately, the heat is tempered by the summer rainy season; on many days throughout the summer, clouds roll over the coast in the afternoons, often releasing rain. Slightly cooler and less humid, winter is the tourist high season all along the Pacific Coast.

ECONOMY AND TOURISM

Tourism is fundamental to Puerto Vallarta's identity and economy. More than 50 percent of the city's residents are directly involved in the tourist industry, and the seasons are just as defined by the ebb and flow of foreign visitors as they are by the weather. For those looking for an exuberant, beachy lifestyle, there's plenty of stimulation in Puerto Vallarta. If a tourist town is not your thing, you can easily avoid the high-traffic areas while still benefiting from the great shopping, restaurants, and conveniences of a large resort town. Needless to say, the farther you stray from Puerto Vallarta's central districts, and especially the Zona Hotelera, the less tourism you will see.

As the worldwide economy took a serious downturn in 2009, Puerto Vallarta suffered the consequence of fewer dollars, and, with a dearth of customers, many shops, restaurants, and galleries were forced to close. At the same time, the port's perennial charms continued to attract national tourists while international tourism gradually increased; in 2011, the city began a renovation of the *malecón,* which was designed to create more public space for pedestrians and tourists along the waterfront. Outside of hotels, restaurants, and sailboats, the Pacific Coast's economy is largely based on agriculture (fruits like bananas and mangoes thrive here), livestock, and fishing.

CULTURE

Puerto Vallarta manages to unite small-town ambience, beachy fun, and big-time luxury into one rather charming seaside city. Though it is well-known as a tourist destination, this old seaside resort is far from the stereotypical spring break party spot. You'll find your share of loud nightclubs, high-rise hotels, and time-share hawkers along the waterfront, but you'll also find rope bridges swinging over the gurgling River Cuale and bright green banana trees scatted throughout Old Town's narrow streets.

Puerto Vallarta has long been known for its artistic community, and there are numerous fine-art

Puerto Vallarta's Old Town retains the charm of an old-fashioned Mexican town.

PRIME LIVING LOCATIONS

galleries, specialty boutiques, and high-end craft shops scattered throughout the downtown district. In the evenings, there are often traditional Mexican dance performances along the boardwalk. Throughout the year, but especially during the winter season, the city hosts many annual events, like the International Film Festival and the Gourmet Festival. Puerto Vallarta has also developed a strong reputation as a progressive and gay-friendly destination, drawing significant numbers of national and international tourists for that reason.

Despite the cosmopolitan feeling in Puerto Vallarta, the vibe becomes remarkably relaxed just a few miles up or down the coast. Along the surrounding Pacific corridor, sleepy beachfront bars and casual taco stands are emblematic of local culture. Here, old-fashioned beach resorts and hippie surfer towns like La Peñita and Sayulita, are principally dedicated to sand and sea. Residents will likely travel to Puerto Vallarta to get their share of culture, shopping, and nightlife.

EXPATRIATE COMMUNITY

Most of Puerto Vallarta's American, Canadian, and European expatriates are highly involved in the community, socially and professionally. Not surprisingly, there is a large community of retired foreigners, though you'll also meet many people who have come to work and run businesses in the region. With the area's low unemployment rate and generally consistent tourist market, there are foreigners working as writers, teachers, translators, photographers, shop and restaurant owners, real estate brokers, massage therapists, doctors, and time-share sales representatives. Others are highly involved in the expatriate community, recreational activities, or volunteer organizations.

Many foreigners appreciate the camaraderie within the foreign community, though hanging out with other expats isn't a requirement. For those who'd like to connect, there are various expatriate groups in Vallarta, which plan social and volunteer events, as well as specialty groups like Democrats Abroad and English-speaking Alcoholics Anonymous. Many expatriates are also involved in local charities and nongovernment organizations.

Daily Life

The Pacific Coast is the perfect place to snooze away the afternoon in a swinging hammock, but most expatriates find the lifestyle offers a lot more than simple relaxation. Many foreigners work or open businesses, and in and around Puerto Vallarta, you'll find plenty of social and cultural events, including concerts at the Teatro Vallarta, ongoing tennis and fishing tournaments, benefits for local charities, and social gatherings arranged by the local expatriate community. For a special night out, you can take an evening cruise on the bay, or you can take it easy by heading to the movies (plenty of big Hollywood films come to Puerto Vallarta's multiroom cinemas). There are lots of restaurants and bars that feature live music, from rock to salsa, and wonderful restaurants, both casual and fancy.

COST OF LIVING

With its tropical climate, sandy beaches, world-class restaurants, and myriad entertainment options, Puerto Vallarta is a thoroughly desirable place to live. Many people spend the whole year saving up to visit this beautiful coastline for a week of vacation, so the town's luxuries obviously come at premium. From fine dining to full-service spas, Puerto Vallarta will certainly provide you with plenty of ways to spend your pesos.

Even so, the cost of living in Puerto Vallarta isn't as high as you might expect. Like anywhere, your budget will depend entirely on the lifestyle you pursue. Those looking for a simple home in a residential neighborhood can find reasonably priced and spacious properties for less than half the cost of most U.S. cities. If you buy groceries, cook at home, and enjoy simple pleasures like reading and walks on the beach, you can live in Vallarta for far less than a beach town in Florida.

Want more luxury? That's easy

Puerto Vallarta's street-side vendors prepare fish tacos, shrimp cocktails, and other tasty seafood snacks.

PRIME LIVING LOCATIONS

GARY THOMPSON: CREATING A LIFE IN PUERTO VALLARTA

"On the first day of school when I was around 12 years old, when by custom that day was devoted mostly to meeting fellow students and learning everyone's summer activities, a classmate showed up with a slide projector and his dad as the operator. They showed images and talked about the two-month road trip they had just taken throughout Mexico, coast to coast and border to border, seemingly missing nothing featured in their guidebook. I was like the mahimahi they showed being caught in Mazatlan – that is to say, hooked and brought to submission. It was a life-changing event, and Mexico never totally left my consciousness after that.

Upon graduating from Washington State University, my present to myself was to drive to Guaymas with a buddy, soaking up as much of Mexico as possible in a week. I'd probably have stayed had it not been for work commitments and then a military obligation that eventually resulted in my being a First Lieutenant in the U.S. Army in Vietnam, a second life-changing event, but one that would eventually tie in with the first.

The sunny tropical climate with palm trees and the thick jungle in the area where I was assigned somehow struck a chord deep inside me, as did being in a culture I didn't understand while bonding strongly with other Americans going through the same experience, something I called "concentric circles of confusion." Those feelings came back to me when I first discovered Puerto Vallarta and Yelapa a couple of years after getting out of the army. I'd already spent most of the winter studying Spanish and Mexican history and culture in Guadalajara, as well as traveling around the country for several weeks to places like Cuernavaca, Oaxaca, Puerto Escondido, Acapulco, Barra de Navidad,

enough, but you'll also raise the cost of living with each step up. A very basic apartment might rent for US$400–600 a month, and simple homes and condos can be found on sale for as little as US$150,000. For US$300,000–400,000 you can get a place in a high-rise condo with views of the ocean or a private home with several bedrooms in nonwaterfront areas. Few central Vallarta homes draw close to the million-dollar mark, though those in upscale neighborhoods like Conchas Chinas, which often have spectacular views, pools, and multiple bedrooms, frequently push that number.

FOOD AND SHOPPING

A city of more than 350,000 residents, plus perpetual tourists, Puerto Vallarta offers plenty of modern shopping options. The largest mall is Paradise Plaza in Nuevo Vallarta, where you'll find a supermarket, banks, and Internet cafés. For groceries, there is a Comercial Mexicana in the Plaza Marina (in Marina Vallarta) and Soriana in the Plaza Caracol, and like almost everywhere in

and Mazatlan, so I had some basis of comparison.

Whatever conscious and subliminal forces were at play, the end result was that when I left the Vallarta area in the late spring, I already had plans to return in the early fall to spend 4-5 months in Yelapa, a practice I continued for five years. Throughout those initial winters in Yelapa, I had segued into spending progressively more time in Vallarta and became a full-time resident when I entered the art gallery business here, something I had originally aspired to do in the United States but had never accomplished.

When I opened Galeria Pacifico in the fall of 1987, I had already been a partner in another gallery for nearly five years and later had also owned the first coffee shop in Vallarta, ironically across the street from where Starbucks is located today. In opening my own gallery I vowed to myself that the gallery would focus primarily on Mexican artists, and I've kept that promise; 75 percent of the current group is Mexican, mostly from Guadalajara, Mexico City, and San Miguel de Allende, although several have relocated to Puerto Vallarta and smaller towns nearby. Just as Gauguin was attracted to Tahiti, many talented artists have moved to Vallarta, and it is now recognized as one of Mexico's primary art centers. But beyond these factors, there is still a small-town friendliness and ambience here that have persisted despite the growth and changes that have occurred.

At this point I've been living in Puerto Vallarta for more than three decades, half of my life until now. I'm still amazed at that, and sometimes I wonder if maybe the gravity might be stronger than normal here. Whether the attraction is magnetic or just some kind of subliminal magic, I still feel it, even though the village I first visited has become a bustling city and has changed in many ways."

Mexico, both a Walmart and a Sam's Club near the center of town. There is also a Comercial Mexicana near Bucerias in Nayarit, and convenience stores (selling beer and water, aspirin, snacks and other basics) scattered throughout the town.

In addition to basics, Puerto Vallarta is a good place to buy art, clothing, and crafts. In Old Town, you'll find beautiful craft shops, galleries, cafés, and bookstores, some with English-language books. Vallarta's boutiques range from low-key beach shops to upscale stores with imported European clothing, and most are concentrated in Old Town. There is also a craft market along the River Cuale where you can find traditional Mexican wares, T-shirts, and leather goods.

In addition to what you can buy at the market, dining is one of Vallarta's high points, with options ranging from street-side fish-taco stands to fancy fine dining. In fact, there are many upscale places to eat, some of which are considered among the best restaurants in the country. Seafood takes center stage at many local joints, with local catch like *huachinango* (red snapper), *camarones* (shrimp), and marlin served in both formal and informal restaurants.

HEALTH CARE

For a medium-size city, there are good health resources in Puerto Vallarta, including several hospitals and clinics (both public and private, though most expatriates will use private options), emergency and ambulance services, evacuation services, and numerous English-speaking doctors in private practice. For seniors or the infirm, there are a number of agencies that will help arrange home care, meal services, and nursing care, both on a short- and long-term basis. Like many of Mexico's large cities and resorts, Puerto Vallarta also boasts a modest market for medical tourism, principally for cosmetic surgery and dentistry. If you are looking for a general doctor, hospital, or specialist, talk to other expatriates, post to foreign message boards, consult with the local American or Canadian consulate, or work with a referral service.

Those living anywhere along the central Pacific corridor will likely come to Puerto Vallarta for most health care needs; however, there is a hospital in San Francisco, Nayarit, that can attend to emergencies. In addition to hospitals and clinics, there are many other ways to maintain a healthy lifestyle in Puerto Vallarta and environs. There are Pilates and yoga studios in the city (as well as in many of the surrounding beach communities), spas with an emphasis on holistic treatments and therapeutic massage, meditation resorts, and English-speaking therapists and psychologists. Not to mention, there are tons of great ways to get outdoors and exercise.

RECREATION

Puerto Vallarta would not be known as a world-class resort town if it didn't offer a thousand and one ways to have fun. With its warm ocean waters and sandy shores, you can spend your time sunbathing, snorkeling, swimming, sailing, Jet-Skiing, diving, whale watching, and fishing. On land, there are wilderness hikes throughout the surrounding jungle (some lead to waterfalls!), and the 20-acre Vallarta Botanical Gardens offers a lovely preserve to commune with the natural environment. Golfers can also take their pick among seven local golf courses, while surfers can head north to the town of Sayulita, where there is a beginning beach break. For those on a budget, eating out is a lot of fun in PV, and there is even a bowling league for those who want to knock down pins with a bunch of pals.

Where to Live

Puerto Vallarta and environs has a definitively beachfront style, and anywhere you live, you'd be hard-pressed to forget the Pacific Ocean is right outside your window. Tropical beach paradise aside, there's a lot of variety here. You can find a beach bungalow or a multiroom villa, an air-conditioned condo or a simple apartment. Budget will likely be the main limiting factor in your housing decision, as Puerto Vallarta and the Pacific Coast offer almost every imaginable option.

PUERTO VALLARTA
Housing

Puerto Vallarta's real estate market has been steadily growing for decades, but it really began to boom after 2000. Within the city proper, there are condominiums, luxury apartments, gated communities, bungalows, and simple family homes, among other options. You might pay US$200,000 for a beachfront condominium or a multibedroom home in an outlying neighborhood. Depending on what you want, there is likely a range of options within your budget.

If you are considering Puerto Vallarta, the best bet is to rent a furnished apartment while you look for more permanent digs. Thanks to the horde of vacationers, there are plenty of well-equipped short-term rentals available (for a bargain, consider coming down during the low season) throughout the city.

A street in central Puerto Vallarta leads to the Pacific Ocean.

© ELENA ELISSEEVA/123RF

PRIME LIVING LOCATIONS

RELOCATING TO PUERTO VALLARTA: ADVICE FROM A REAL ESTATE AGENT

Originally from Canada, Charlie Rondot has been living in Puerto Vallarta since the 1990s. He has spent many years working as a real estate agent, currently with Coldwell Banker La Costa. Here, he shares some solid advice for those considering a move to Puerto Vallarta.

What makes Puerto Vallarta and environs a great place to relocate?

Puerto Vallarta offers a beautiful, varied setting, with all desired services easily available. There are many flights daily from most major airline hubs, with more carriers coming onboard, such as Virgin Atlantic. A key advantage is the local population. The citizens of P.V. are warm and kind, and enjoy sharing their culture and traditions with new residents.

Do you have any advice for new residents who are just getting to know the area? How would you choose a neighborhood among the many options in and around P.V.?

The best way for new residents to find a location is to come down for a good period of time, and then drive about to see what appeals to them most. It isn't always possible, but renting down here to "try it on for size" provides more time to visit various areas and select the one that offers the best fit. In this way, a prospective buyer also experiences the culture and lifestyle.

Any advice for folks who'd like to buy a lot and build a home?

Anyone wishing to buy a lot and build should keep a few things in mind. The location, of course, has to suit their desires and budget. As anywhere else, the closer it is to the water, the more valuable the land. Hillside locations are generally available at a lower price than flat land, but they also require a different type of construction, which is often more costly.

Once you've found the land, a very important step is to find an architect who can design the structure according to your criteria. The style of finishes must be determined: granite counters, marble floors, type of carpentry, and so on. The price per square foot or meter can then be calculated, giving the buyer hard numbers to consider.

Is the cost of living lower in Puerto Vallarta than in the United States or Canada? Is it a good place for someone on a budget?

The cost of living in P.V. is generally lower than up north, but as it is a tourist area, some costs are higher as a result. Food costs can be close to prices back home, but that is where getting to know the shops and local markets come into play. Labor costs are much lower, so residents can easily afford housekeepers and gardeners. Property taxes are extremely low, a few hundred dollars per year, which is very attractive to all those paying thousands per year back home.

If you are planning to rent long term, get a year lease on your place; many month-to-month rentals will increase their prices during the high season.

Costs run the gamut, but on the lower end of the scale, those willing to shack up in a simple home in a residential neighborhood can rent something for as little as US$500 a month, though you'll likely nudge that price up a few hundred dollars to get more space, a better bathroom, or a nicer location. Real estate prices can also be much lower in suburban neighborhoods, though residents should still plan to spend at least US$150,000 if planning to buy. Heading north or south along the coast might get you a little more bang for your buck, but prices will generally start in the same range.

Old Town and Environs

Puerto Vallarta's Old Town, also known as the Zona Romantica, is stretched along the verdant hillsides that flank the River Cuale. There's a lovely Mexican atmosphere in this bustling district, with cobblestone streets crammed with corner shops, boutiques, restaurants, cafés, and galleries. Living here feels a lot like living in a small town, with everything you need within walking distance. There's even a weekly farmer's market in the town square. While the area certainly draws its share of tourists, you'll find plenty of foreign residents in Old Town, too. Just a few blocks above the town's church and central square, **Gringo Gulch** is a popular place with expatriates (not surprisingly, given the name), and it's a nice place to wander among beautiful private homes. Gringo Gulch has a long history as an American enclave; among the many mansions in the area is Elizabeth Taylor's former home on Zaragoza Street.

Despite its popularity, you might be surprised to learn that properties in Old Town and environs really run the gamut, with more affordable properties located to the east of the downtown district (you'll get better deals the farther from the *centro* you go, though you'll also get fewer sea breezes).

Conchas Chinas and South Vallarta

The curving roads that wind into hillsides south of Old Town have some of the most breathtaking ocean views in the area. Here, several small neighborhoods, including Conchas Chinas, **Amapas,** and **Punta Negra,** shelter some of the most upscale homes in the area. Cloaked in lush vegetation, homes here offer plenty of quiet and privacy, though they also come with a higher price tag. If you want to buy here, multilevel condominiums are the most accessible option, though they generally run US$200,000 and above; private homes run from US$500,000 to well over a million dollars. Here, you'll also need to have a car for transportation, as there's little more than winding roads and verdant jungle in the surrounding neighborhood.

Zona Hotelera and Marina Vallarta

North of Old Town, Marina Vallarta and the Hotel Zone are where you'll find many of the city's poshest hotels, like the Meliá Puerto Vallarta and the Westin, their towering facades adjoining a wide stretch of sand. Aptly named after its large marina, Marina Vallarta is where yachts and sailboats come to dock (with many available to rent, both short- and long-term). One of several golf courses in the neighborhood, the Marina Vallarta Golf Club operates 18 holes right on the beach. As these details attest, both the Zona Hotelera and Marina Vallarta are upscale, and many condominium owners are part-time residents who rent their property when they aren't in town. The community was planned as a resort destination, so it doesn't offer a characteristically Mexican atmosphere, though residents will enjoy a comfortable and even swanky lifestyle.

North Vallarta

Just east of the Zona Hotelera and Marina Vallarta, there are several nice residential neighborhoods that offer good prices on homes and lots, as well as easy access to the city and the beach. Among these, **Versalles** is a modern, flat, residential neighborhood with paved, tree-lined streets of Mexican-style homes. Just to the east, the **Las Gaviotas** neighborhood is a pretty residential area with traditionally Mexican family homes and wide cobbled streets. These neighborhoods are incredibly close to the beach and downtown Vallarta but feel far more low-key and residential. Above the rooftops, the peaks of the sierra are visible throughout the area.

Those looking for a laid-back atmosphere and slightly lower prices should check out rentals and real estate in more outlying suburbs, such as the low-key communities of **Pitillal** and **Coapinole.** Home to around 50,000 people, Pitillal and its surrounding communities retain the feeling of a small Mexican town, with a central square, old stone church, and low-priced traditional markets for shopping. The area is generally untouched by tourism, but some expatriates have been able to find good deals and a comfortable lifestyle in Puerto Vallarta's suburbs; homes here will generally be basic, though some have yards, mountain views, and spacious rooms, with prices as low as US$100,000 for a simple home. Though you won't get a water view, the beach is just a 10-minute drive from downtown Pitillal.

North Vallarta can be a great, affordable alternative for those who prefer a

ARTURO MEADE

There are many quiet coves and beaches along the Nayarit coastline, north of Puerto Vallarta.

residential neighborhood to a condominium. Single-family homes in North Vallarta's residential communities generally sell for an average of US$200,000. Typical unfurnished family homes rent for around US$800–900 per month in this area, though you can find a simple home for several hundred dollars cheaper per month, or pay a bit more for a pool or garden.

THE NAYARIT RIVIERA

North from the River Ameca, the string of small beach towns along the Bay of Banderas and the Pacific Coast are collectively known as the Nayarit Riviera. Once a string of quiet fishing villages, the coastal towns of Nayarit have become popular with tourists, surfers, and expats.

Housing

Most housing options along the central Pacific Coast are laid-back, simple, beach-ready bungalows and family homes, often built of concrete and boasting open spaces and patios, sometimes with shared or private pools. Outside Puerto Vallarta, there are fewer luxury condominiums and gated housing developments. Most expatriates will rent or buy a freestanding, unfurnished home in a residential community or near the beach.

Nuevo Vallarta

During the 1990s, Puerto Vallarta grew rapidly, spreading north along the Bay of Banderas, over the River Ameca, and into the neighboring state of Nayarit.

For all practical purposes, Nuevo Vallarta is a part of the larger Puerto Vallarta metropolitan region, though it is also the first beach town in the state of Nayarit and therefore the first stop on the Nayarit Riviera. Much like Marina Vallarta, Nuevo Vallarta is an upscale area with several golf courses, a marina for yachts and sailboats, numerous gated communities and condo developments, beautiful sandy beaches, and some lovely luxury hotels.

Most of the properties here are luxury, high-rise condominiums and country clubs, though there are some private, luxury villas in gated communities (price tags on these can often run more than US$1 million). Many Nuevo Vallarta lodgings are vacation homes, purchased as an investment and rented out when the owner isn't there, but the area can also be a nice place to comfortably settle down.

Bucerias

Past Nuevo Vallarta along the coastal highway, the mood mellows considerably as you head north. Driving along the corridor, it might be easy to breeze right past the small seaside community of Bucerias, once a fishing village and now a casual vacation town about 12 miles from Puerto Vallarta. Just off the highway, Bucerias's quiet, cobbled streets adjoin a sandy and uncrowded beach on the Bay of Banderas, surprisingly close and yet entirely disconnected from the row of luxury hotels that rises along the distant coastline. It's a quick drive to the city, so Bucerias residents can shop, eat, or go out in Vallarta, though everything they need can be found in the surrounding area, too. There are low-key nice restaurants, seafood joints, and bars along the beach and around the center of town, and even yoga classes and a few nice shops and galleries. You won't find many luxury homes here, though homes have a beachy, comfortable feel and often have shared or private pools, yards, or patios.

Sayulita

North of Bucerias, the coastal highway slowly transforms into a winding, scenic, two-lane road, covered by a canopy of leafy trees and draping vines. Bunches of fresh bananas swing from the roof of makeshift fruit stands, while sandy turnoffs lead to small, palm-fringed beach towns.

Just 25 miles north of Puerto Vallarta, the laid-back surf community of Sayulita is the most popular destination for vacationers along the Nayarit coast. Though the community is home to just a couple thousand permanent residents, there is an ongoing influx of families and vacationers flocking to Sayulita's long sandy beach, most of them from overseas. Sayulita boasts a good break for beginning and intermediate surfers, and the waters can get

the main beach in Sayulita

pretty crowded during the high season. For peace and quiet, you can walk over the southern hillside to the relatively secluded beaches along the coast. In the town's tranquil main square (just a block from the beach), you'll find an appealing collection of coffee shops, taco bars, and pizza joints; nothing too fancy, but there are some good places to breakfast on banana muffins or sink your teeth into local seafood tacos. In the surrounding hillsides, many foreigner residents have bought or constructed homes, some with views of the sea. There are also markets, pharmacies, beach shops, and a money exchange house (there is only one ATM in Sayulita, and no banks).

Though Sayulita is on the up and up, it's still fairly rustic and decidedly cheaper than Puerto Vallarta. Houses may come with a palm roof or without glass on the windows, but the benign tropical climate allows for less hermetic surroundings. Prices for food and other basic necessities are slightly lower along the Nayarit coast than in Puerto Vallarta and environs, though real estate is roughly comparable, with many homes selling in the US$250,000–350,000 price range. However, there are a number of million-dollar villas along the coast, for those looking for secluded oceanview luxury. Long-term rentals can be affordable, so those considering buying or building in the Sayulita area might want to start by renting a place and getting a feel for the town. Budget at least US$600 per month for a simple rental.

San Pancho and La Peñita de Jaltemba

Heading north along the coast, there are several other beach communities along the Nayarit Riviera, including the tiny community of San Francisco, popularly known as San Pancho. Though it boasts a long stretch of sandy shore, San Pancho hasn't been as thoroughly discovered as its neighbor, Sayulita. It has, however, begun to attract its own community of Americans, Canadians, and other expatriates. Along the main drag, there are restaurants and taco stands (most featuring fresh seafood), and you'll even find yoga and a sea turtle sanctuary in town. San Pancho is also, improbably, the site of the Nayarit coast's only hospital. Most of the homes in town are simple concrete abodes, though some foreigners have constructed more luxurious residences, with multiple bedrooms, private pools, or beach views. As in Sayulita, many homes are available for long-term rental, so prospective San Pancho residents should consider renting before making the move.

The twin towns of **Rincón de Guayabitos** and La Peñita de Jaltemba are located about an hour north of Puerto Vallarta alongside the Bay of Jaltemba and have traditionally been popular destinations for Mexican families on vacation. With a joint population of around 10,000, Guayabitos and La Peñita offer a bit more modernity and convenience than other Nayarit towns; there are more banks, pharmacies, and supermarkets here, though you'll still likely visit Puerto Vallarta for errands or shopping trips from time to time. There are some inexpensive hotels and restaurants along the beach, but the vibe here is low-key, principally attracting expatriates looking for an inexpensive and relaxing lifestyle.

The cost to buy a home in small towns like San Pancho and La Peñita averages around US$150,000, though newer properties with pools, major square footage, or beach access can run higher.

THE JALISCO COAST

Often called the Costa Alegre (the happy coast), the undeveloped stretch of shore between Puerto Vallarta and Barra de Navidad is beautiful and remote. On this stretch of virgin land along Highway 200, you'll find those fabled hidden beach towns, colonies of pelicans, and barely visited tropical jungle. Beachgoers and ecotourists are the main travelers who make their way down the Jalisco coast, though some enterprising foreigners have also settled down out here, opening small bed-and-breakfasts or building rustic dream homes. Living here is a small challenge; basic services like electricity and running water are not easily obtained outside main towns. Even if you build (or fix up) a modern home, you'll still need to get by with a more limited array of local goods and produce, likely heading into Puerto Vallarta for grocery shopping, the airport, or a bit of culture from time to time. The upshot is the natural beauty, the peace and quiet, and the unique landscape you'll call home.

Exploring this region will take some time, and you may want to seek a home base in Vallarta or, alternatively, to the south in Manzanillo while scoping land and locations. There are many small fishing communities and hidden beach resorts along the coast, with a few larger and more well-known towns. Most of these little towns are little, indeed, and very inexpensive. Not to mention, there isn't much to spend your money on!

Housing

This largely undeveloped region feels far from the resort atmosphere in PV. While there are some vacation rentals available, you won't find a plethora of condos or fancy apartment complexes along this coast. Most rentals or real estate for sale are simple, concrete, family homes or empty lots for development. (Although it is often available at low prices, foreigners should take care when buying *ejido* land in this area.) You can also find a small selection of larger properties with multibedroom homes for sale, many of which are owned by foreigners.

The real estate market along the Jalisco Coast is small, so rentals are more scarce and buyers will likely spend some time looking around at their options. Empty lots are the most abundant properties available, with beachfront property commanding the highest prices—1,000 square meters (or about 3,200 feet) on the beach averages around US$150,000, with similarly sized non-beach properties selling for well under US$50,000. Prices fluctuate greatly based on location, proximity to a city and the highway, *ejido* status, and available utilities.

El Tuito

About 30 miles south of Puerto Vallarta, the 16th-century settlement of El Tuito is set in the mountains above the coast and filled with lush vegetation. It is known for its mescal, a spirit made from maguey, like tequila. One of the main highlights of this area is that it is close to the virgin coastline along Cabo Corrientes, the southern tip of the Bay of Banderas. A few expatriates have made their way to this region, though it's definitely best for those who want to get away from it all.

Chamela

Farther south, the Chamela Bay is a protected stretch of sandy coast, which shelters nine small islands. The small community of Chamela is perched on the bay's southern end, though you'll only find basic supplies at the town's truck stop. There are a couple of low-key accommodations, some vacation homes, and a few casual bars and seafood joints to choose from. Just eight miles south, there is a beach resort in **Careyes,** and just below it, **Playa Careyes.**

La Manzanilla

On the beautiful Bay of Tenacatita, the community of La Manzanilla is located toward the southern edge of the Costa Alegre. Along the protected shores, there are several lovely beaches and a small, one-street town. While off the beaten path, La Manzanilla and the surrounding areas have already begun to attract a burgeoning expatriate community. There are some vacation rentals, a smattering of new homes, and even a few galleries in the main area.

Getting Around

PUERTO VALLARTA

Puerto Vallarta's Lic. Gustavo Díaz Ordaz International Airport (PVR) is located just north of the city, on the highway toward Nuevo Vallarta. Millions of visitors pass through this small but busy airport annually, and during the peak season, more than 70 percent of the airport's traffic is international. Aeroméxico, Air Canada, American, Continental, Interjet, Northwest Airlines, United, and Volaris are among the airlines that offer routes to Puerto Vallarta from Mexico and overseas. From Los Angeles, Puerto Vallarta is a three-hour flight. From the airport, you can take a taxi into Puerto Vallarta or catch a bus just outside the terminal.

For those coming to Vallarta on land, the bus station—or Central Camionera—is located just a few miles north of the city on the coastal highway toward Tepic. If you arrive in Puerto Vallarta by bus, you can take a city bus or taxi into town from there. There are also smaller bus lines that offer service to the Riviera Nayarit and to the Costa Alegre from the main bus terminal.

For getting around town, the best way is via city bus, taxi, or car, though many things are close enough to be reached on foot from Old Town. Taxis do not use meters, instead charging per ride based on established zones fixed by the taxi union. Most rides are pretty reasonable, but ask your driver when you get in if you want an idea of the cost.

TO AND FROM THE NAYARIT RIVIERA

Buses leave from Puerto Vallarta to the Nayarit coast from downtown and from the airport. Most will drop you off on the highway, and you will need to walk into town from there. You can also take a taxi to any of the small towns along the Nayarit coast from Puerto Vallarta's airport or from the city's downtown. It costs around US$50 to take a taxi to Sayulita. There are also shuttle services, which offer round-trip rides to Sayulita from the Puerto Vallarta airport. These same companies will also drive you to and from Puerto Vallarta for shopping or nightlife. For many people, taking a shuttle is easier than renting a car, because once you've arrived in Sayulita, San Pancho, or Bucerias, everything is easily accessible on foot.

TO AND FROM THE JALISCO COAST

The Jalisco coast is principally accessible by car, and those traveling there should considering renting or buying a vehicle. Buses do run between smaller towns, though they'll likely leave you on the highway (and you'll have to slog your stuff into town). The second-class bus line Flecha Amarilla and the first-class bus line Primera Plus both offer service to the Costa Alegre from Puerto Vallarta, as does Transportes del Pacifico.

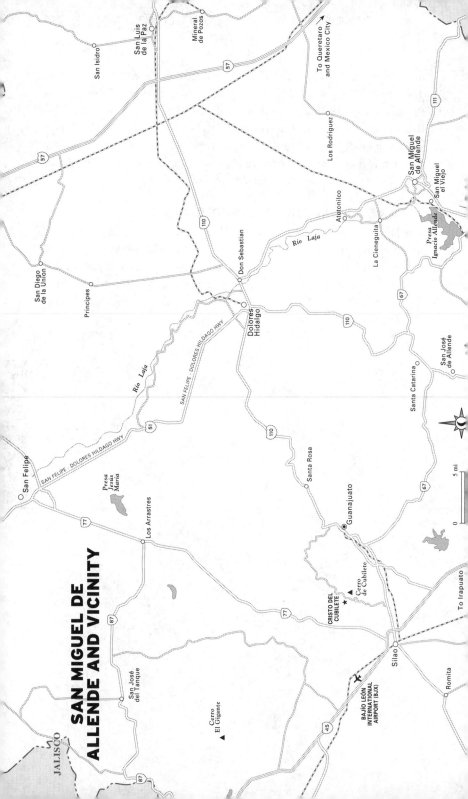

SAN MIGUEL DE ALLENDE AND VICINITY

JALISCO

San Felipe

San José del Tanque

Cerro El Gigante ▲

San José de la Unión

San Diego de la Unión

San Isidro

San Luis de la Paz

Mineral de Pozos

Principes

Los Arrastres

Presa Jesús María

SAN FELIPE - DOLORES HILDAGO HWY

Río Laja

Don Sebastian

Dolores Hidalgo

Santa Rosa

Guanajuato

CRISTO DEL CUBILETE ★

Cerro de Cubilete

Silao

BAJÍO LEON INTERNATIONAL AIRPORT (BJX)

Romita

To Irapuato

Santa Catarina

San José de Allende

Río Laja

Atotonilco

La Cieneguita

Presa Ignacio Allende

San Miguel de Allende

San Miguel el Viejo

Los Rodriguez

To Queretaro and Mexico City

57

57

110

51

77

87

87

45

110

110

67

67

111

0   5 mi

SAN MIGUEL DE ALLENDE AND VICINITY

San Miguel de Allende is a small and splendid city located within the rugged highlands of central Mexico. During the early years of New Spain, San Miguel became an important protective settlement along the colonial silver route, which connected the northern mines to the capital in Mexico City. The town grew wealthy throughout the 17th and 18th centuries, and prominent families invested lavishly in their private homes and religious projects throughout town. Today, that legacy has left behind one of Mexico's loveliest towns: The blocks around the city's central square are a charming mix of crumbling Spanish-style houses, sandstone fountains, and nicely restored Baroque churches. San Miguel's legendary beauty, as well as its blessedly temperate climate, have made it a perennial favorite with cultural tourists and travelers. It is also home to a well-established expatriate community with a distinctly artsy inclination.

A nostalgic town of cobbled streets and a feeling of cozy community, San Miguel still moves at the leisurely pace of another era. Lost dogs are announced

© ARTURO MEADE

© ARTURO MEADE

A parade marches up Canal Street in San Miguel de Allende.

on the local radio, the midday siesta is respected, and mariachi musicians circle the town square each evening. Even today, it is not unusual to see a local
merchant lead a packed donkey through the city center. Despite tradition,
San Miguel is a modern place, largely influenced by its prominent American
expatriate community, as well as the spate of *chilangos* (Mexico City natives)
who call the city home. Today, you can find cranberry sauce and sushi rice in
San Miguel's grocery stores yet still load up on guavas and handmade tortillas
in the traditional market. There are as many wine bars as cantinas, and there
are more yoga studios per capita than most of Mexico can claim. A passion
for the arts ties the community together, and visitors are often surprised by
the wide array of cultural activities around town. Social life is vibrant, and entertainment options range from live theater to ballroom dance classes. Nights
out are often spent lingering over a nice meal, with local restaurants opening (and old ones closing) every season. For expatriates, San Miguel offers an
ideal combination of stimulation and relaxation: one part Mexican pueblo,
one part American college town.

At the same time, things are changing in San Miguel and in the surrounding communities. Large supermarket chains have begun to appear around the
outskirts of town, while the highway system is steadily expanding throughout
the region. New luxury hotels and chic rooftop bars have brought an air of
slick modernity to a place that was once defined by quiet alleyways and mom-

and-pop shops. While some bemoan the ongoing modernization, change is an essential quality of this region, where open-mindedness and hospitality are the norm. A mix of tradition and modernity defines San Miguel, and the result is rarely fractious. For most foreign residents, San Miguel is a stimulating, unique, and supremely livable place.

The Lay of the Land

San Miguel de Allende is located in the state of Guanajuato, about 170 miles northwest of Mexico D.F. There are about 62,000 inhabitants in the city proper, though more than double that number reside in the municipality as a whole. Located on the southern portion of the Mexican Altiplano, San Miguel sits at more than 6,300 feet above sea level, though the scrubby, semiarid landscape doesn't offer a particularly alpine atmosphere. Water is scarce in this region, but rock and scrub become fertile ground along the floodplain of the River Laja, which runs past the city. Just east of the city, the River Laja is dammed to create a large reservoir, called the Presa Allende, which provides most of the town's water.

San Miguel is part of a larger geopolitical region known as the Bajío, a vast plain within the southern Mexican Altiplano. Covering the states of Querétaro and Guanajuato, as well as segments of southern Jalisco and eastern Michoacan, the Bajío is an important region to Mexico, both economically and culturally. Since the colonial era, the region has been one of the country's agricultural capitals—a fact amply reflected in San Miguel's bountiful markets. One of the country's most celebrated cultural destinations, the spectacular city of Guanajuato is about 70 miles northwest of San Miguel. To the south, the growing city of Querétaro is also just an hour's drive from San Miguel. An industrial capital, Querétaro has been steadily growing, and it offers an ample range of

In a town known for its distinctive architecture, the parroquía *(parish) is San Miguel's most iconic structure.*

© ARTURO MEADE

PRIME LIVING LOCATIONS

SPOILS OF THE SILVER CITIES: ARCHITECTURE IN SAN MIGUEL

In the decades following the conquest of Mexico, Franciscan friars and Spanish settlers made slow inroads into the vast territories north of Mexico City. During the early colonial era, most settlements in the central highlands were small ranches, missions, or mining outposts, usually rather makeshift and under constant threat from the native population. Though San Miguel was founded in 1542, there are very few remnants of the first settlements in the region, most of which were abandoned, destroyed, or rebuilt in the following centuries.

Thirst for silver and gold pushed the Spanish far into the north, where they discovered rich veins of precious metals along the craggy mountains of Mexico's highlands. By the mid-16th century, silver mines were flourishing in Zacatecas, Guanajuato, and San Luis Potosí, among others. Propitiously located along the silver route from the northern mines to Mexico City, the settlement of San Miguel served as an important protective town for Spanish merchants. As the mining industry began to flourish, San Miguel grew wealthy and opulent. In the colonial era, as today, it was known as one of the country's most beautiful cities.

Most of San Miguel's most important architectural achievements were constructed during the 18th century, backed by wealthy benefactors who donated funds for public spaces, churches, and chapels. At that time, Mexican architecture and city planning followed design trends from Spain; Baroque architecture, which originated in Italy, was the dominant architectural aesthetic during the colonial era, characterized by its elaborate ornamentation and dramatic use of light. However, indigenous artisans did not strictly follow European trends, incorporating their own techniques and interpretations into Baroque themes. Today, San Miguel's city center is filled with a wonderful mix of colonial-era chapels, civil buildings, and plazas in the Mexican Baroque style.

As the mines were depleted and the silver trade became less lucrative, San Miguel's prominence declined. Over the centuries, many of the region's Baroque churches and colonial mansions were gutted and repurposed, while others were allowed to simply wither away. Fortunately, San Miguel de Allende has undergone extensive municipal restoration projects during the 20th century. Today, its architecture offers a unique glimpse into the past splendor of New Spain.

The facade of the Oratorio San Felipe Neri represents a transition from classic Baroque to a Churrigueresque aesthetic.

art, entertainment, shopping, and transportation options, including several museums and an airport.

Like most colonial cities, San Miguel is organized around a central park, known as the *jardín*. The *jardín* is adjoined by the Parroquía de San Miguel Arcángel, the city's pink neogothic parish church—a wildly original structure and the most recognizable landmark in town. As in the 17th century, the blocks surrounding the *jardín* are the busiest district, filled with banks, government buildings, shops, and restaurants, as well as the majority of San Miguel's most popular sights. Outside San Miguel's official historic downtown, residential neighborhoods blanket the hillside and valley.

CLIMATE

San Miguel de Allende and the surrounding region enjoy a sunny and temperate climate throughout the year. Almost every day brings a blissful dose of blue skies and puffy clouds, and the famous Mexican sunshine imbues the town with a golden glow. Through the course of a year, seasonal changes are mild, though notable. December and January are the coolest months, with average daytime temperatures hovering around 70°F (20°C) and nighttime temperatures dropping as low as 30°F (0°C). Evening frosts are not uncommon. The weather gradually warms up during February, reaching its peak in May—the only month of the year when San Miguel de Allende is uncomfortably hot and uncharacteristically humid.

It rarely rains in San Miguel during the long dry season, which runs from October to mid-June. During summer's erratic wet season, rain often falls during heavy thunderstorms in the afternoons and early evening. Downpours usually last an hour or two, leaving a pleasant chill in the air before bedtime. In total, the region receives somewhere around 20–25 inches of rain each year. Storms generally subside in late September or October, leaving behind a blanket of wildflowers.

No matter what the season, the climate in San Miguel is dry and semi-arid. Therefore, evening temperatures are significantly lower than daytime temperatures, even in the warmest months. It's always best to bring along a sweater when going out at night.

LOCAL CULTURE
History and Architecture

In 1542, Spanish friar Juan de San Miguel founded a small Catholic mission on the banks of the Laja River. Propitiously located between the northern mines and the capital city, the settlement of San Miguel became a strategic protective town for Spanish traders on the silver route. During the 17th and 18th centuries, San Miguel's industries began to proliferate, and its population surged. Wealthy *criollo* (Mexican-born of Spanish descent) families built lavish homes around the central square and contributed extravagant funds to erect Catholic churches and monuments throughout the town. Following design trends from the Old World, San Miguel is particularly well-known for its splendid Baroque architecture, an evolution of Renaissance design that originated in Italy. At the same time, native artisans brought a unique and expressive flourish to the work, distinguishing San Miguel's Baroque architecture from similar European traditions.

After the War of Independence, San Miguel was largely abandoned. Having played a central role in the conflict with the Spanish, many of San Miguel's most prominent families and lucrative industries had been wiped out. The town sunk into obscurity, though it never lost its characteristic beauty. In 1923, it was declared a national landmark by the Mexican government. Over the past century, the *centro histórico* has been finely restored, supported by the Mexican government as well as the United Nations Educational, Scientific and Cultural Organization, which declared the historic downtown a World Heritage Site in 2008. Today, San Miguel is a popular tourist destination, known for its beautiful architecture and charming city center.

The Arts

San Miguel has been the backdrop for a lively local art scene for more than half a century. Wander along San Miguel's web of narrow streets, and you'll quickly find a multitude of contemporary galleries, most showcasing work by local artists. In this close-knit community, many amateurs and art students quickly find a piece of wall where they can hang their work, and even coffee shops, bars, and restaurants are known to host an exhibition from time to time.

While most often associated with the visual arts, San Miguel is home to creative types of every stripe. There is an annual English-language writer's conference, which often invites big names in fiction to speak in town. San Miguel hosts a prestigious chamber music festival every summer, and there are jazz festivals and live music throughout the year. There are frequent film screenings and inspirational talks in the Biblioteca de San Miguel (the town's nonprofit library), as well as theater groups in both Spanish and English. For those who appreciate the arts, or who are interested in developing their creative abilities, San Miguel offers a wonderfully low-key place to explore the arts.

Two mariachi musicians rest in San Miguel de Allende's main square.

Holidays and Events

San Miguel is a small town with a vibrant community, the site of frequent holidays, festivals, and fiestas. Famous throughout Mexico, the religious rituals and events during Semana Santa, or Holy Week, are particularly spirited in San Miguel. The pinnacle of the week is Viernes Santo (Good Friday), when the town stages a dramatic reenactment of the Stations of the Cross.

As San Miguel played a crucial role in the early Mexican War of independence, it is a popular destination for Mexico City youth to celebrate Independence Day, annually observed on September 16th. The celebrations for the Día de San Miguel Arcángel (Saint Michael's Day) begin almost as soon as the Independence Day parties end. For these massive fiestas, pilgrims from across Mexico (and from as far as away the United States) come to pay their respects to Saint Michael with round-the-clock dancing, religious ceremonies, and explosive fireworks.

EXPATRIATE COMMUNITY

San Miguel de Allende is home to one of the oldest and most well-known expatriate communities in Mexico. Since the 1940s, Americans, Canadians, and a smattering of Europeans have made their way to this sunlit pueblo, often buying a home and settling down permanently. More recently, San Miguel has acquired a positive reputation for its accessibility and affordability as a retirement destination. Currently, people near retirement age form the largest segment of the expatriate population. At the same time, San Miguel draws people of various ages and backgrounds, including students, families, and young professionals.

San Miguel makes life easy on expatriates, with a slew of services in English and plenty of entertainment and social options. There is an English-language newspaper, English-speaking church groups, and plenty of people who will join you in celebrating Thanksgiving and the Fourth of July. There are even English-language theater groups, if you want to see a play or try your hand at acting. Local businesses have adapted to their diverse clientele, so you'll always find menus written in English or prices listed in dollars.

While foreign influence has certainly affected San Miguel's character, the expatriate community exists comfortably in this small town. There is little friction between foreigners and locals, and most expatriates feel entirely at home in San Miguel. In fact, many expatriates are involved with the local community, often through charity organizations, while others make friends or develop romantic relationships with Mexicans.

Daily Life

For most foreign residents of San Miguel de Allende, daily life boasts many of the conveniences and comforts of life in the United States, complemented by the color and culture of central Mexico. The town is still rather small, with most services and shops concentrated in the downtown district. Today, there is a bit more traffic than befits a city of 60,000; otherwise, most people find getting around, running errands, and enjoying life to be blissfully simple.

COST OF LIVING

San Miguel de Allende is a bit pricier than other towns of comparable size in Mexico. The large American community, as well as the annual influx of foreign tourism, has raised prices throughout downtown, as well as in the most affluent neighborhoods around the *centro histórico*. However, relative to the cost of living in most cities in the United States and Canada—and even compared to Mexico City—San Miguel is very affordable. In broad strokes, around US$1,200–1,800 a month is enough to sustain a basic middle-class lifestyle, including rent, food, transportation, and some entertainment or travel. Those with a little more income can live quite well. In San Miguel, luxuries like eating out and going to the movies are surprisingly inexpensive. Many expatriates also have cooks or housekeepers, comforts that likely wouldn't be affordable at home.

ARTISTS AND EXPATRIATES

At the dawn of the 20th century, San Miguel de Allende was little more than a quiet outpost in the central highlands, only accessible by train. Though it was once among the most prominent and beautiful cities in New Spain, its population had dwindled, and many of its historic buildings were left in ruin. Nonetheless, it remained one of the most romantic and beautiful spots in Mexico. In 1926, it was declared a national monument by the Mexican government. Shortly thereafter, some artists and intellectuals from Mexico City began to take an interest in the town, buying property or gathering for parties and readings in town.

In 1938, Peruvian intellectual and art historian **Felipe Cossío del Pomar** arrived in San Miguel. Working with the government of President Lázaro Cárdenas, he founded a fine-arts school, La Escuela Universitaria de Bellas Artes, in a former 18th-century cloister downtown. Cossío de Pomar's arrival in San Miguel coincided with the appearance of another expatriate, **Stirling Dickinson**. A native of Chicago and a graduate of Princeton University, Dickinson, as a writer and former art student, immediately showed a strong affinity for San Miguel's unique atmosphere and people. Not long after his arrival, Cossío appointed Dickinson the first art director at his school.

Dickinson helped Cossío to recruit American students for the school, and his efforts were bolstered by the passage of the GI Bill, which granted World War II veterans a free college education. San Miguel's art school was accredited in the United States, and by the mid-1940s, a few GIs had come to study. Then, in 1948, *Life Magazine* ran a photo spread showing Mexico's art students living cheaply in "paradise"; immediately thereafter, the school received more than 6,000 applications. While the school couldn't accommodate all its prospective students, many Americans came to San Miguel on their own.

Over the course of his lifetime, Stirling Dickinson would see many changes take place in San Miguel, as the city transformed from a sleepy outpost to an internationally recognized tourist and retirement destination. Today, expatriates make up an estimated 10 percent of the town's population, and foreigners have become an integral part of San Miguel's identity and culture. Dickinson himself would become an important figure in the city, both as the director of the Instituto Allende, an art school still in operation on the Ancha de San Antonio, and as a founder of numerous charity organizations. After Dickinson's death in an automobile accident, the city of San Miguel named a street in the San Antonio neighborhood after him. He is remembered as one of San Miguel's most influential citizens, as well as one of its greatest benefactors.

Housing will probably make up a rather large part of your total budget in San Miguel de Allende, though the costs vary widely depending on whether you rent or buy, where you choose to live, and what type of lifestyle you are looking for. Around the center of town, rental costs vary from as little as US$300 a month for an apartment to US$2,000 a month for a spacious multibedroom colonial home. In fact, big and centrally located colonial properties can demand even higher prices if they come equipped with a pool or are located on one of the most desirable streets. Fortunately, outlying neighborhoods and the surrounding countryside provide considerably cheaper alternatives for those on a budget.

FOOD AND MARKETS

Eat a bagel for breakfast; have a taco for dinner. For a town of its size, San Miguel has a remarkable variety of places to eat, drink, and shop. You'll never want for a nice loaf of bread or a freshly grown tomato, nor will you pine for barbecue sauce or provolone cheese. In the country's heartland, food is in abundance, and the town's many grocers offer specialty products not readily sold in the rest of Mexico.

Most Mexicans buy the majority of their fresh produce, dry goods, and tortillas at one of San Miguel's traditional markets. There are several covered markets in town, as well as the weekly Tuesday Market, a massive open-air marketplace that feels like a mix between a farmer's market and swap meet. Several organic farms have begun operating around the city; buyers can visit the farms to buy produce directly or pick up their leafy greens at one of the organic stores in town.

San Miguel's grocery stores cater to foreign residents by stocking more unusual or luxury items, like dried cranberries, prepared pesto, Brie, or tahini. Though these items may be inexpensive and easy to find at home, the prices can be much higher when imported south of the border. Thrifty shoppers can stick to items produced in Mexico, which are generally much more inexpensive than their equivalent in the United States or Canada.

Downtown, San Miguel still functions like an old-fashioned small town. There are butchers, dairies, bakeries, fruit markets, and specialty grocery stores, each carrying a distinct line of products. In some cases, shopping for tonight's dinner can mean stopping at three or four different places. For those who value convenience, large one-stop chain supermarkets have begun to crop up on the outskirts of town.

SHOPPING

Decorating a home can be great fun in San Miguel, and it's easy to do on a wide range of budgets. Some of the best craft traditions in Mexico are united here, and there are numerous well-curated shops throughout the city center, as well as contemporary galleries showing work from local artists. Iron and other metalwork has been a craft specialty in San Miguel since the colonial era, and you can order custom pieces from local artisans. There are several local designers who manufacture unique lines of modern furniture, though you can also find traditional Mexican furnishings throughout town.

When stocking your house, you can find everything you need in San Miguel, from dishwashers to ceramic casserole dishes. There are numerous smaller shops in the center of town, as well as several large grocery and department stores that have opened around the perimeter of town. They carry necessities like electronics, clothing, and kitchen supplies. However, most folks looking for household basics take the hour drive to Querétaro, where there are several malls, as well as big international chain stores like Costco and Home Depot.

HEALTH CARE

San Miguel is a small town, so it has more limited health care options than you'd find in a big city. There are several English-speaking general doctors, if you have the flu or stomach upset. For seniors, it is relatively easy and inexpensive to hire in-home nursing care.

For sudden illness and emergencies, there are several small hospitals in San Miguel de Allende, as well as emergency response services operated by the volunteer Cruz Roja Mexicana (Red Cross). For the best care, the neighboring city of Querétaro is home to several large hospitals, including well-regarded Hospital de los Angeles. If the situation isn't an emergency, it is worth the drive to get care in Querétaro.

In addition to hospitals and allopathic doctors, there are numerous options for alternative therapies and treatments throughout San Miguel, including healing massage, Reiki, acupuncture, and naturopathic medicine. For mental health, several expatriates have set up counseling and therapy practices in San Miguel.

EDUCATION
Primary and Secondary Education

For families relocating from the United States or Canada, there are a few private schools in San Miguel de Allende that offer curriculum in a combination of English and Spanish, from kindergarten through high school. These schools are usually attended by a mix of Mexican and expatriate children. Some of these programs can be accredited in the United States.

For college students, there are fewer options in San Miguel, though several local nonprofit organizations offer summer internship programs appropriate for college-age students. The language school Academia Hispano Americana also offers college credit for a year of Spanish-language study via the University of Guanajuato.

Language and Arts Schools

San Miguel seems to naturally inspire creative growth and personal reinvention. The oldest art academy in Mexico, the Instituto Allende, as well as popular cultural center and art academy Centro Cultural Ignacio Ramírez offer classes to the community. In addition to these institutions, many local artists and art studios offer individual or group instruction in drawing, painting, ceramics, printmaking, jewelry making, and watercolor. For those seek-

© ARTURO MEADE

courtyard of the Instituto Allende, one of the oldest art academies in Mexico

ing an advanced degree, the Instituto Allende operates an MFA program in the visual arts, principally aimed at foreign graduate students.

For Spanish-language programs, San Miguel offers a plethora of options, especially for students at the beginner levels. Whether you want to take an intensive summer course or simply attend a few hours of private lessons each week, the town's many schools will be happy to accommodate you. Many language schools offer cultural programs and cooking classes to complement their Spanish courses.

Where to Live

HOUSING

There are diverse housing options in San Miguel de Allende, from empty lots to full-service condominiums. Whether you are renting or buying, old or colonial-era houses are the most coveted properties in town. Colonial homes are often oversized and airy, with thick stone walls, high ceilings, and interior gardens. (By the way, when it comes to San Miguel's real estate, you can't judge a book by its cover: Some of the smallest and most unassuming facades open onto lavish colonial-era mansions.) Those looking for more modern accommodations will find them, too, especially in some of the growing neighborhoods surrounding the city center.

Although San Miguel has a long history as an expatriate destination, foreign immigration has surged during the past few decades. One by one, the houses in San Miguel's historic downtown district have been sold to foreign buyers who generally remodel them to meet modern standards. If you want to buy an old home, you will likely be purchasing it from another expatriate. While it may not have the same romantic appeal as remodeling your own property, the advantage is that the previous owners will likely have brought the house up to speed with regards to wiring, heating, and other modern utilities.

Those looking to buy will find plenty of eager help in the city's rapidly multiplying real estate agencies. Most of these agents are representing the same properties (few have exclusive listings), so the best bet is to find someone you trust and who can help you with the paperwork. Since the contracts for all real estate transactions are complicated and must be completed in Spanish, find a broker who will keep you informed throughout the process.

Since the worldwide economic crisis of 2008, San Miguel's markets have slowed a bit. However, buyers and renters can expect to pay big prices for a nice place in San Miguel, with some properties exceeding US$1 million. Real estate prices run the gamut, though. Thrifty buyers can find plenty of options under US$250,000, especially if they don't mind living outside the *centro histórico.*

SAN MIGUEL DE ALLENDE

San Miguel isn't a very big town, but it offers a nice array of neighborhoods and housing options for a varied populace.

The Centro

You'll find the highest density of expatriates living in and around the *centro histórico* of San Miguel. The lush and quiet streets around Parque Juárez and El Chorro, as well as the tangle of narrow streets climbing east from the *jardín,* classically demand the highest prices. In the 10 square blocks around the town square, homes are usually older constructions, and some have unique history. Spacious properties tend to cost US$500,000–1 million, but like everywhere in San Miguel, prices vary.

San Miguel covers a hillside overlooking a valley; neighborhoods along the eastern slope often afford beautiful views and more peace and quiet than you'd find downtown. In some cases, these luxuries come with a higher price tag. The surprisingly lush **Atascadero** neighborhood hovers over the *centro* *histórico* to the east, with shady trees fed by a brook running through the canyon. Largely residential yet centrally located, this neighborhood is one of San Miguel's most desirable. Along the edge of the canyon that leads to El Charco del Ingenio, San Miguel's botanical gardens, **Balcones** is another upscale neighborhood, dominated by newer constructions in the colonial style. Views of downtown from Balcones can be breathtaking.

To the south of the central square, both the **San Antonio** and **Guadiana** neighborhoods are popular with foreigners, offering more inexpensive prices than the blocks immediately surrounding the central square. Guadiana has a very pleas-

© ARTURO MEADE

San Miguel de Allende's downtown district is ribboned by picturesque, cobblestone alleys.

ant suburban atmosphere, while San Antonio is a larger neighborhood with more Mexican residents. In the San Antonio, most expatriates buy places in the blocks closest to downtown. Those who don't mind a brisk walk to the *centro* can still get a good deal in the San Antonio, where many properties are listed at under US$300,000. To the north of the city, **Guadalupe** and **Aurora** are low-lying residential neighborhoods. Typically Mexican, these *colonias* have become more popular with foreign residents since the Fábrica La Aurora, an art and design center, opened nearby. They are typically far more inexpensive than the *centro histórico,* or even the San Antonio.

Outlying Neighborhoods

Just before you depart the city on the highway to Celaya, you'll come to **Los Frailes,** a suburban neighborhood with wide cobbled streets and leafy trees. During the week, Los Frailes can be rather quiet, as a large number of homes belong to part-time residents from Mexico City. Homes here tend to be oversized and colonial style, and some have views overlooking the municipal reservoir. Prices in Los Frailes are all across the board, from surprisingly inexpensive homes to million-dollar properties. You can rent a large family home for around US$1000.

Those looking to rent or buy in a more inexpensive neighborhood have plenty of good options. San Miguel de Allende is not a particularly large town, and even outlying neighborhoods are relatively close (even within walking distance) to the center of town. Since the turn of the 21st century, more foreign residents have been buying properties in the **Independencia,** a hilltop neighborhood just to the south of the *centro.* Other outlying neighborhoods, like **Santa Julia, San Rafael,** and **Cinco de Mayo,** are slowly beginning to attract foreign buyers, and prices are much lower in these communities. Although prices are steadily rising, you can rent a place here for under US$500 and buy one for less than US$100,000.

Surrounding Communities

The beautiful countryside around San Miguel de Allende can offer a quiet alternative to the city. For those who'd like to construct their own home, the country can also be a good choice, where there are many more vacant lots than in the city of San Miguel.

Among the most popular places with foreign buyers, the community of **Atotonilco** is located about 10 minutes north of San Miguel de Allende, on the road to Dolores Hidalgo. The Río Laja runs past Atotonilco, making the area particularly green and water thankfully abundant. Of particular note, there are natural hot springs under the ground in and around Atotonilco; lucky homeowners often find their water lines reach thermal water. This tiny rural community is dominated by Santuario de Jesús Nazareno, a massive church and religious retreat that has been an important pilgrimage site since its construction the 18th century. Most of the time, the community is incredibly quiet; however, the town attracts masses of people during an important religious event. Those living near the center of Atotonilco should be prepared for some noisy weekends and traffic.

The Santuario de Jesús Nazareno, a church and religious retreat in Atotonilco, is located just ten minutes from downtown San Miguel de Allende.

Just south of Atotonilco, the community of **La Cieneguita** is another popular spot for foreign buyers, especially those planning to construct their own home. The area has become a lot more attractive (or a lot less attractive, depending on your point of view) since the state government expanded the highway system to link La Cieneguita with Mexico 67, the highway between Celaya and Guanajuato. Many lots in La Cieneguita do not have links to water or power supplies. It is possible to dig a well; however, the depth of these wells (and their related costs) can vary widely. Do your research before committing to a property.

It is possible to get lucky and find a rental home in both Atotonilco and La Cieneguita; however, in most cases, those who want to live in these communities will have to consider buying. A few foreigners have also bought land in **San Miguel el Viejo,** a small and surprisingly marginalized community just past the train station.

MINERAL DE POZOS

Nestled along the hillsides of the high desert chaparral, the small town of Mineral de Pozos is a former mining settlement with a distinctly romantic atmosphere. Abandoned in the early 20th century, this hillside community was left in near ruin. The town has experienced a modest resurgence, with a small but elegant collection of boutiques, galleries, and cafés in the main square—most only open on weekends. Expatriates in search of lower prices and a quieter atmosphere (but who want to retain proximity to San Miguel) have begun to move here. With its old, crumbling properties and sleepy rural vibe, Pozos is often compared to a former San Miguel de Allende.

It takes about 45 minutes to drive to Pozos from San Miguel de Allende. Basic services are scarcer here. There are few phone lines in town, and even electricity will unexpectedly go out—sometimes for days. However, those who like peace, quiet, and home improvement projects may find true happiness in this remote and otherworldly city. Whereas San Miguel has already sold most of its old homes, Pozos is brimming with half-ruined adobe buildings with centuries of history.

Those looking to rent will have a greater challenge in Pozos; most available properties are for buyers, and even those aren't particularly abundant. There is one real estate agent in town, who can help you locate properties that are legally for sale. Prices aren't as cheap as you may expect them to be, but there are still plenty of opportunities in this small town. If you are willing to invest time and money, spacious and romantic (but literally crumbling) fixer-uppers can cost well below US$100,000, though the average cost for a functioning home in town is a bit under US$200,000. Note that homes that have already been remodeled by foreigners will often cost several times the local average.

Getting Around

AIR

Though it's a well-known tourist destination, San Miguel de Allende can sometimes feel a bit off the beaten track. It takes more than an hour to drive to the closest airports, León-Bajío (BJX) in Silao and Querétaro (QRO), just outside the city of Querétaro. From there, it is usually necessary to book a shuttle or taxi to San Miguel de Allende; several companies provide this service.

BUS

Every half hour, buses run between San Miguel de Allende and the city of Querétaro, until about 10 P.M. For trips to the capital, there is daytime bus service between Mexico City and San Miguel de Allende, operated by both Primera Plus and ETN first-class bus lines. Some buses stop in the larger city of Querétaro on their way north, adding travel time to the journey.

CAR

For shopping excursions to Querétaro, day trips near town, or big grocery runs, it can be convenient to have a car in San Miguel de Allende. Drivers are generally courteous and cautious. The biggest hassle is finding parking in the *centro histórico*'s narrow streets.

TAXI

To the delight of many foreigners, taxis are an inexpensive and popular way to get around town. Constantly circling through the streets of the *centro*, taxis charge about US$2 to take you anywhere in the central neighborhoods. A longer trip might cost another buck, but generally speaking, it's a cost-effective and hassle-free way to get your grocery bags home.

PRIME LIVING LOCATIONS

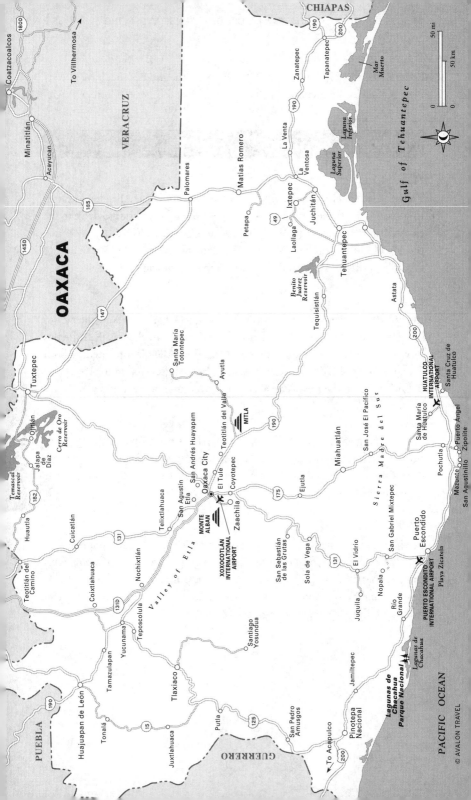

OAXACA

It takes almost six hours by highway to reach the city of Oaxaca, in the state of Oaxaca, from the capital in Mexico City. The landscape becomes more remote and more beautiful with every passing mile, dotted with tiny pueblos, grazing donkeys, and distant cornfields. In many ways, this very remoteness defines daily life in Oaxaca, a timeless region that seems far removed from the modern world even as it embraces contemporary ideas, art, and culture.

The state of Oaxaca covers a large, diverse, and beautiful swath of land along the Pacific Coast and the southern Sierra Madre. It is, end to end, a culturally vibrant region, home to some of the largest indigenous communities in Mexico, as well as some of the country's most impressive artisanal traditions. Living in Oaxaca is a true adventure for anyone born outside the state: Here, there are hundreds of tiny towns to explore, a varied natural landscape, and a different *mole* sauce in every home kitchen. Oaxaca produces what is arguably the country's finest mescal (a distilled spirit that is cousin to tequila), in addition to presiding over an incredibly distinctive and rich local cuisine, often

© ARTURO MEADE

imitated but rarely approximated outside the region. Adventurous eaters will be rewarded with bites like chili-fried *chapulines* (grasshoppers) and rich hot chocolates made with water rather than milk.

Despite the state's vibrant culture and popularity with tourists, Oaxaca remains one of the poorest and most disenfranchised regions in Mexico. A large percentage of the population lives below the poverty line, with many communities lacking basic services and health care. Oaxaca's industrious people have begun to organize on their own, developing communal farming systems, community-based ecotourist resorts, and autonomous village governments. Despite their efforts, corruption at the highest level continues unabated. Here, there are constant political demonstrations in the capital, and protests can bring the city of Oaxaca to a standstill.

True, Oaxaca's singular culture can make the transition here a bit more difficult for expatriates, who may always feel a bit "foreign" within the local community. But living here is also about moving outside your natural comfort zone to discover a place that is, quite literally, unlike anywhere else on Earth.

Oaxaca City

A splendid city of sandstone churches, pedestrian walkways, and flowering trees, Oaxaca de Juárez (usually just called Oaxaca) is one of Mexico's most famous cultural destinations. Stately and charming, Oaxaca has long been recognized as one of the country's great cultural and architectural jewels, with shady cobblestone streets lined with sandstone chapels, world-class museums, colorful craft shops, and bohemian cafés.

Despite the romance of Oaxaca's environment, the city's noisy urban buses, strident political groups, and surprisingly modern viewpoints temper the romance. It's a fascinating mix of culture and people, though the city isn't without its challenges. In Oaxaca, the expatriate community is smaller, foreigners are less readily accepted into local life, and the distinctive local culture can cause greater culture shock. Still, foreign residents do make a fulfilling life here. Even if you don't lay down permanent roots, Oaxaca is an excellent choice for people looking to spend a few months to a few years in Mexico, fully immersing themselves in the culture, language, and people.

THE LAY OF THE LAND

The city of Oaxaca is located in the Valles Centrales (central valleys) of Oaxaca state, at the juncture of three major plains between the Sierra Juárez and the

Sierra Madre del Sur. This region has been continuously inhabited for thousands of years, and there are numerous archaeological sites in the valley. Of these, the former Zapotec city of Monte Alban is the largest and most celebrated, located on a flattened hilltop just west of the modern city of Oaxaca.

At about 5,000 feet above sea level, Oaxaca is built atop high-altitude grassland, rather than the deciduous forest and tropical jungle that blanket the majority of the mountainous state. Farms and small towns surround the city on all sides, and as the capital of the state, Oaxaca represents a mix of people and cultures from across the region. The population rings in at fewer than half a million people, and the city retains a very low-key atmosphere, even in the downtown region. With a local economy largely dedicated to commerce, tourism, and agriculture, Oaxaca has no high-rise buildings or major business centers.

© ARTURO MEADE

Many large Catholic convents were constructed in Oaxaca during the colonial era.

The city is laid out around the *zócalo,* or central plaza, which is adjoined by the cathedral and ringed by sidewalk cafés. In the blocks surrounding the *zócalo,* you'll find the majority of the city's eateries, arts venues, shops, and markets. Heading north, the pedestrian street Alcalá runs past the beautiful Iglesia de Santo Domingo, a sandstone church and former convent now home to Oaxaca's interesting regional museum. Beyond the *centro histórico,* residential communities ring the center of town to the north, south, east, and west.

History

As early as 500 B.C., the Zapotec people built one of Mesoamerica's earliest city-states, Monte Alban, near the modern-day city of Oaxaca. A highly organized, religious society, Monte Alban dominated the surrounding valley, reaching its peak in the 6th century. As Monte Alban declined, smaller cities began to appear around the same valley, in places like Mitla and Yagul.

Around 1140, the entire region fell under the control of the Mixtec people,

Located on a hillside overlooking modern Oaxaca City, Monte Alban was once the capital of the great Zapotec empire.

who lived to the north and northwest of the valley. They overtook the Zapotec cities, including Monte Alban, and left their stamp on both the culture and aesthetics of early Oaxaca. Several hundred years later, the Mixtec fell to the Mexica; when the Spanish arrived in Mexico, the region was subject to the rulers of Tenochtitlan in present-day Mexico City.

The Spanish were the next to invade the valley. After Cortés successfully raised and conquered Tenochtitlan in 1521, he sent Francisco de Orozco and Pedro de Alvarado to Huaxyacac (today, Oaxaca), where they took control of the region. Now New Spain's most powerful general, Cortés claimed Oaxaca as his home, parsing out land to his children; eventually, the Spanish crown granted him an extensive land grant in the region, though it excluded the settlement that would eventually become the capital of the state.

During the early colonial era, Oaxaca was one of the most important settlements in New Spain. Religious missionaries were active in the region, building massive convents and churches, which are today some of the most striking buildings in the city. With the introduction of European diseases, the population in Oaxaca collapsed during the early colonial era, but over the centuries remote communities were able to grow their numbers; unlike many parts of Mexico, Oaxaca maintained a large native population.

Despite its prominence, the city remained rather quiet until the 20th century, when Oaxaca experienced the massive urban migration that affected much of Mexico. Today, it is home to close to half a million people.

© CARLOS MEADE

The ruins in Mitla, Oaxaca, are known for their finely carved stonework.

Climate

On a typical day in Oaxaca, the sun is shining, the sky is deep blue and dotted with puffy clouds, and a light humidity keeps the air pleasantly warm, even indoors or in the shade. Throughout the year, daytime temperatures hover in the 70s and 80s F (in the 20s in C), dropping 10–20 degrees in the evening. April and May are the warmest months, with temperatures in the high 80s (F) and a nice touch of humidity in the air.

By summer, the heat is tempered by daily thunderstorms, which flood the city in a matter of minutes and give way to an awe-inspiring abundance of flowering plants, fruit trees, and green grasses. December and January may bring a few chilly days, but even during the coldest months, the temperature rarely drops below 70°F (21°C) in the day and the mid-40s F (around 7°C) at night. Evenings are generally clear and cool, often with dazzlingly starry skies. During the winter, the verdant landscape slowly browns.

Language

Oaxaca is a predominantly Spanish-speaking city, and expatriates living there for any period of time will benefit from learning to speak the language, at least on a conversational level. Tourists can generally get by with a few words and phrases, but here, more than many places in Mexico, locals expect long-term residents to make an effort to speak their language. It is not just a matter of basic communication, but respect for your adopted home.

While Spanish predominates in daily life, there is a great deal of linguistic

PROTEST AND POLITICS IN OAXACA

Oaxacan people are outspoken, progressive, and proud. They are expert organizers, with active unions and citizens' groups both in the city and in the countryside. As you'll quickly notice, Oaxaca's streets are filled with creative, politically charged graffiti, including impressive stencils created by the artist collective **ASAR-O** (www.asar-oaxaca.blog-spot.com). Public demonstrations are remarkably common in Oaxaca – don't be surprised to see several thousand people marching through town with banners and flags, or a group of protesters occupying the *zócalo*. In fact, protests are such a common occurrence that Oaxaca's residents rarely bat an eyelash at them.

Despite the protests of the citizenry, Oaxaca city and state have a long history of corruption and are often overseen by politicians who seem out of step with the populace. After conflicts arise between the government and citizenry, there is often a failure to investigate claims of human rights abuse, and the state has drawn criticism from numerous international organizations, including Amnesty International. Unlike the majority of Mexico, the state has never shaken free of the **PRI (Institutional Revolutionary Party)**, and absenteeism is a major problem during elections.

Generally, political conflict is a loud but benign aspect of life in Oaxaca. However, Oaxaca's super-charged political climate can occasionally explode. In 2006, the city was locked in conflict for almost a year after a strike by the local teachers union clashed with local authorities. Their cause was taken up by the **Popular Assembly of the Peoples of Oaxaca (APPO)** political organization, which called for PRI governor Ulises Ruiz to step down. Ruiz resisted, a large-scale conflict ensued, and the city was all but shut down for close to year. At least 11 people were killed during this time, and others disappeared. During the conflict, the indigenous Triqui community of San Juan Copala declared itself autonomous of the Mexican government, and it has suffered both military occupation and violence in the years following.

diversity in Oaxaca. There are 16 recognized indigenous languages spoken in the state, with large Zapotec and Mixtec communities still living in and around the capital. Most of these indigenous languages are mutually unintelligible and are further complicated by the prevalence of dialects. Highly complicated, inflected, and, like Chinese, tonal, these languages are not easy for nonnative speakers to learn. You'll notice that informational texts at museums and archaeological sites are often printed in Spanish, English, and Zapotec or Mixtec.

Indigenous Communities

After the conquest, the vast majority of Mexico's indigenous groups went into sharp decline. Those who survived war, slavery, and famine eventually mixed with the ruling Spanish population, eventually forming Mexico's great mestizo (mixed race) population. In Oaxaca, native communities were similarly devastated by the Spanish invasion, but they slowly rebounded in the region's relative isolation. Today, Oaxaca has one of Mexico's largest and most active indigenous communities, with an estimated 40 percent of the population identifying with a native culture. The largest indigenous groups are the Zapotecos (Zapotecs) and the Mixtecos (Mixtecs), with populations of more than 400,000 and 350,000 respectively.

Although Mixtecs and Zapotecs dominate, there are 16 recognized indigenous groups in the state of Oaxaca, the most ethnically diverse state in the republic. Oaxacan people generally identify with their regional providence, rather than their language group or ethnicity. The majority of the state's indigenous population lives in small towns or in the countryside, but the influence of these communities is strongly felt in the capital as well. Not far from the city center are small towns where traditional markets have been held in the same place since the pre-Columbian era.

The Arts

The state of Oaxaca has one of the most robust craft traditions in Mexico. Here, many traditional artisans continue to work out of their home communities, and prices for beautiful handmade wares are surprisingly cheap. Weaving, embroidery, hand-dyed wool rugs, carved wooden animals, toys, baskets, fine silver jewelry, and glazed ceramics are some of the craft specialties for which Oaxacan artisans are renowned. The center of this bounty, the city of Oaxaca has numerous craft shops specializing in Oaxacan artistry; you can also visit one of the surrounding communities where artisans live and work. Usually, a village will be dedicated to a single craft tradition. For example, the community of San Bartolo Coyotepec produces burnished black pottery, whereas San Antonio Arrazola is the source of Oaxaca's famous *alebrijes,* carved and painted wood animals.

© ARTURO MEADE

Oaxacan families gather on the steps outside the Basilica de la Soledad for a concert.

In addition to craft traditions, Oaxaca is well-known for its active contemporary-art scene. One of the great modern masters, Rufino Tamayo, was born in Oaxaca, eventually reaching international fame during the mid-20th century for his expressive and colorful paintings. Following in his footsteps, a new generation of Oaxacan artists have helped to define a distinctly Oaxcan school of art. Among the most prominent is Francisco Toledo, a celebrated contemporary artist and one of the city's great benefactors.

Downtown, there are several important public galleries and museums, including the Museo de Arte Contemporaneo de Oaxaca (Contemporary Art Museum of Oaxaca), Centro Fotografico Manuel Alvarez Bravo (Manuel Alvarez Bravo Photography Center), and Instituto de Artes Gráficas de Oaxaca (Graphic Arts Institute of Oaxaca), a wonderful library and gallery space.

Cuisine

Oaxaca is well-known for its cuisine, which is quite distinct from what you'll generally find in Mexico. The fresh mozzarella-like cheese, known in Oaxaca as *quesillo,* is popular throughout the country (elsewhere it is called *queso oaxaca*), as is Oaxaca's most famous flavor, *mole negro,* a sauce made of chocolate and spices and served with turkey, chicken, or folded tortillas. On the street, you'll often find *tlayudas,* large corn tortillas stuffed with beans, cheese, cabbage, and salsa, and toasted on coals. Street vendors also sell *memelas,* thick corn flatbreads with meat or beans, and empanadas, giant handmade tortillas stuffed with cheese or *mole amarillo,* a spiced yellow sauce with chicken. Chocolate has been cultivated in this region for centuries, and it remains a staple of the diet (though traditional Oaxacan hot chocolate is prepared with water rather than milk). Seasoned and toasted grasshoppers are served alongside Oaxaca's famous mescal, the agave spirit that is a fiery cousin to tequila.

Oaxaca's cuisine is one of the country's most celebrated, but don't expect massive variety from the city. Here, most residents love their traditional dishes, and there is little demand for import. If you are craving flavors from afar, you'd do best to prepare them in your home kitchen. Even Mexican basics, like tacos, are less common in Oaxaca than elsewhere.

Holidays and Events

Oaxacans love a good fiesta. National and religious holidays are colorfully celebrated here, from Independence Day to Christmas, and the city's celebrations for Day of the Dead are among the most extravagant and colorful in the country. In addition, Oaxaca is known for its many unique festivals and traditions. During the summer, the city's largest cultural festival, La Guelaguetza, is celebrated in July. The Guelaguetza centers around traditional dance and music performed by various indigenous communities from the state. The dance performances take place on the first two Mondays following July 16, but the city is alive with arts, entertainment, and tourism throughout the two weeks of the festival (including many more dance performances on public stages in the city center). Another popular and uniquely Oaxacan tradition is the Radish Festival, wherein local artists and families celebrate the Christmas holidays by building elaborate holiday-themed dioramas using fresh radishes. It is held in the *zócalo* on December 23.

DAILY LIFE

Life in Oaxaca is a wonderful mix of contemporary and traditional. You can choose to do your shopping at a big-box supermarket or in a rambling traditional market. On Saturday night, you can see a Hollywood movie at a cinema or go out to dance salsa with a live band.

Oaxaca is, however, best for those people who enjoy a slower pace of life and who aren't expecting every modern luxury at their fingertips. You can eat incredibly well, enjoy cosmopolitan events and exhibitions, and meet people from across the world. You can't, however, expect to rent a modern penthouse apartment or have access to a well-stocked department store.

Cost of Living

Living in Oaxaca is comparatively inexpensive. Fresh food is abundant and inexpensive, with lots of produce grown right in the state. When shopping at a market, you can fill your grocery bag with a week's worth of beautiful produce for less than US$10. You may pay a bit more for imported items, like wine or cheese, if you are shopping in the grocery store, but never a higher price than what you'd find in the rest of Mexico. Utilities here are reasonable, too, running a touch lower than in other parts of the country.

Like most parts of Mexico, the cost of homes and property can really run the gamut in Oaxaca due to the absence of a multiple listing service (MLS) or any centralized real estate listings. There are plenty of bargains to be had, but you'll need to spend some time getting to know the city and the real estate market first. For renters, it is possible to find a simple apartment in the city center for as little as US$350 a month. However, a comparable apartment in a similar area may rent for $200 more for no apparent reason. Bigger homes also vary widely in price. A multibedroom home could run US$500–1,000 per month to rent, or even more, in the center of town. Beyond the basics, Oaxaca is a bargain. Meals at restaurants, movies in the cinema, drinks at bars, live

NORMA HAWTHORNE, A CULTURAL NAVIGATOR

An expert Oaxaca traveler and cultural enthusiast, Norma Hawthorne organizes cultural immersion programs in and around the city through her organization Oaxaca Cultural Navigator (oaxacaculture.com). Here, she shares her perspective on the city's unique culture.

Tell me a little about Oaxaca. What makes it special?

Oaxaca is a blend of past, present, and future. It represents all that Mexico has to offer: warm and welcoming people, extraordinary art, innovative food, lively music, colonial ambience, indigenous values, majestic scenery, ancient archaeological sites, a place to do and to be. The city is energizing and a cacophony of sound, aroma, and color. One could spend a lifetime in Oaxaca and never see it all. It is a place to expand one's imagination and creativity.

When did you first visit Oaxaca?

I first traveled to Mexico years ago but didn't discover Oaxaca until much later, in 2005. It was heaven – a complex layering of color, food, art, crafts, indigenous culture, history and archaeology, biodiversity and sustainable agriculture, mountains and beach. I fell in love with it immediately, and after three days there I began planning my next visit.

I know you are very interested in Oaxaca's artisanal traditions. What is some of the best or most emblematic craftwork from Oaxaca?

Artisanal traditions in Oaxaca take on many forms – all handcrafted: spicy cinnamon and pepper enhanced chocolate, *quesillo* cheese, mescal, wool rugs, hand-carved copal wood figures decorated with primary colors, and hand-stamped tinwork. Probably the most em-

musical performances, and other entertainment are much more inexpensive than in Mexico City, Guadalajara, or other medium-size cities.

It all sounds very appealing, but remember that salaries here are much lower, too. Foreigners who come to Oaxaca with some savings or who telecommute to jobs will be able to live comfortably. Those planning to work in Oaxaca will have to pinch pesos to make ends meet; fortunately, many of the city's greatest pleasures (strolling in the *centro,* browsing in markets) are free.

Food and Markets

Like in many culinary capitals, the quality of Oaxacan food isn't only reflected in its excellent restaurants and food stands, but in its abundant local food and produce. Every neighborhood has its own market selling fresh vegetables, fruits, grains, cheese, tortillas, bread, and meat, in addition to prepared foods like tamales and salsas. The city's largest market, the *central de abastos,* has an astonishing mix of products; you can buy hand-woven wicker baskets,

blematic for me is a traditional handwoven wool rug with the ancient Zapotec caracol design that symbolizes communication and continuity of life.

Can you tell me about any traditions that stand out in Oaxaca?

To be in Oaxaca is to experience all that is incredible about Mexico in one location. Yet what differentiates Oaxaca, in my opinion, is the range of extraordinary textiles created on back-strap looms by very creative and talented people who have been working this way for centuries. The work is intricate, and the materials include native cotton, silk, and wool with natural dyes. There is an attention to both tradition and innovation.

What are some of your favorite places to visit?

To me, getting to know an artist or artisan personally is what amplifies the value of the travel experience and makes it memorable. I have relationships with artists and artisans who I visit repeatedly to track the evolution of their work.

Cuisine is a big part of Oaxacan culture, too. What do you love to eat?

I love to eat *fiesta tamales con mole amarillo* (tamales with yellow *mole* sauce — a local tradition for special occasions) made by hand in the kitchen of Las Granadas Bed and Breakfast in Teotitlan del Valle by Magda and Josefina. They are made with masa (stone-ground corn dough) stuffed with tender chicken, hand rolled in corn husks from the local crop, and steamed to a creamy perfection — all organic, and delicious. This is heaven on earth!

PRIME LIVING LOCATIONS

tiny guitars, five types of mango, or even a live hen, if so inclined. Even the central market downtown (often derided for being touristy) sells a beautiful and inexpensive array of fruits, vegetables, meat, chocolate, and other local products. In addition to stationary markets, the city has numerous rotating markets that open in local neighborhoods each week.

Most Oaxaca residents will quickly learn that the markets are the best places to find fresh food, though there are several large supermarket chains outside the city center, for those who want to augment their purchases with a traditional grocery-store selection. (Oaxaca's city planners were smart in relegating the behemoth chains to the city's outskirts, reducing their visual impact on the city center.) Just southeast of the *centro*, you'll find Sam's Club and Walmart, in addition to Mexican-owned Soriana. Although Oaxaca has plenty of beautiful, handmade clothing for sale in its artisanal markets, it can be more difficult to purchase brand-name or department store clothing.

Health Care

Health care options in Oaxaca are more limited than those in big cities like Mexico City or Guadalajara, or even in other cities of a similar size. There are some hospitals and clinics here, but there are few English-speaking physicians. Resources in the city are much better than in the surrounding countryside (where the government is still trying to bring basic care to all communities), though they still lag behind other parts of Mexico. For private care, there are a few hospitals and clinics in the *centro,* as well as several large health care facilities in the residential Reforma neighborhood, north of the *centro.* For those with IMSS (public health care) coverage, there is also an IMSS clinic located on Calzada Niños Héroes De Chapultepec in the *centro.* You can check with the U.S. or Canadian consular agencies for a list of recommended physicians.

WHERE TO LIVE

Although the city of Oaxaca is large, most foreign residents live in one of a few places: the city center, the residential neighborhoods in the northern metropolitan area, or, to a lesser extent, the small towns in the Valley of Etla. In general, expatriates should expect to look in these areas. Not only are there slim pickings in other parts of Oaxaca, but not every community is open to foreign buyers or foreign residents; some small communities outside the city are openly hostile to the idea.

Buying and renting in Oaxaca isn't as easy as it is in other parts of Mexico. Here, you'll find a much smaller rental market and, relative to the low cost of living in the city, rather elevated real estate prices in the most desirable areas. Unlike many parts of Mexico, people in Oaxaca know what their land is worth, and they aren't willing to part with it for bargain-basement prices. The best advice for anyone planning to buy is to rent first, get a feeling for the local area, and then look into investing.

With its warm and sunny climate, Oaxaca City's residential neighborhoods are filled with flowering plants and trees.

Housing

Oaxaca's real estate market is fairly modest. Plainly put, there's not that much for sale, especially when compared with the incredible real estate offerings in San Miguel de Allende, Ajijic, or other popular expatriate destinations. If you are moving to Oaxaca and you'd like to buy a home or a piece of land, rent first and plan to spend some time getting to know the city. There are several real estate agents who can help you find a place, though some owners do their own selling, too.

Finding a place to rent can be a bit more challenging in Oaxaca than it is in, say, Guadalajara, but with a little time and patience, most people are able to find a place that suits their needs. There are few rental options available at any given time, but looking through the newspapers, driving around and spotting For Rent signs, and asking locals are all effective ways to find a place.

Because the city attracts many long-term visitors, language students, and tourists, there are many furnished rentals in the *centro,* which can be a good interim option. Some hotels and guesthouses have bungalows with small kitchens, which can serve as a good temporary solution while looking for something more permanent. If you can, take your time and look for something that suits your needs.

While there are few new constructions in Oaxaca, there are some housing developments cropping up in the north of the city, near San Felipe del Agua. You'll pay more for colonial-era or older colonial-style homes, but there are also a range of mid-20th-century constructions, which may be charmingly retro, pleasingly comfortable, or horribly ugly. Homes in Oaxaca rarely have heat or air-conditioning, and they can be airy, with rooms opening onto patios or rooftops.

Throughout the center of town, in the surrounding neighborhoods, and to the north of the *centro,* family homes generally fall into the US$150,000–250,000 range, though large and historic properties can cost significantly more. Rentals run the gamut, but average around US$600 for a good-sized two-bedroom apartment or modern home. In the very center of town, rental prices are elevated by the short-term tourist market.

Centro Histórico and Jalatlaco

The *centro histórico* is the heart of the city. Here, the atmosphere is charming and vibrant, with loads of beautiful architecture, wonderful restaurants, shops, galleries, and markets all within the 10 square blocks surrounding the *zócalo.* By and large, homes in the *centro histórico* will be older, some with quite a bit of history. Thick stone walls keep these homes cool throughout the year, and many have charming central patios or roof decks. Older homes may require more maintenance. The nicest central neighborhoods are north, northwest, and northeast of the *zócalo,* including the lovely areas around Parque Juárez.

To the northeast of the *centro,* the charming, cobblestone neighborhood of Jalatlaco is an ideal place to live—if only there were more properties available! If you are lucky enough to find a place to rent or buy here, it will likely be an older property with a Spanish colonial design. While this neighborhood is quiet and relaxing, it is just a short walk away from everything in the *centro histórico.*

For all its charm, there are some drawbacks to living in Oaxaca's central districts. Of particular note, there is not always sufficient water in the center of town, and underground cisterns occasionally run dry. Despite the copious summer rains, city infrastructure isn't sufficiently modern to capture and distribute water downtown. If your taps run dry, you can purchase water from a mobile truck, which will fill the tank on your roof for a fee. The *centro* can also be quite noisy, especially during holidays when fireworks continuously explode in the sky. Even the garbage collection truck (which roars to a halt while ringing a large cowbell) often seems unnecessarily noisy.

La Reforma and San Felipe del Agua

North of the *centro histórico,* there are several large and lovely residential communities, popular with foreigners and middle-class Oaxacans. La Reforma, just north of the avenue Niños Héroes de Chapultepec, is a beautiful, quiet, and green neighborhood filled with family homes. If you live here, you won't need to run your errands in the *centro;* there is a small but excellent traditional market, wine shops and bakeries, grocery stores, banks, pharmacies, and doctors. There are also restaurants and cafés.

From the northern edge of the Reforma to the city's northernmost edge, the beautiful neighborhood of San Felipe del Agua is one of Oaxaca's nicest areas. As the name implies, San Felipe has plenty of *agua* (water), so residents won't suffer from the same frustrating dry spells that plague the *centro.* Nestled in the foothills of the sierra, San Felipe is incredibly picturesque; it's not uncommon to see chickens wandering the sidewalk or a herd of goats being led down a side street. There are fewer markets and less commerce in San Felipe than in the Reforma, though there is a farmer's market in the main square twice a week.

Transportation to these neighborhoods runs along main arteries; it may be easier to have a car if you live on one of the quieter, residential streets. Street

San Felipe del Agua, a residential neighborhood on Oaxaca City's northern edge, is popular with expatriates.

parking is easier to find the farther north you go, though many houses will also include garages.

To the east of San Felipe del Agua, **Los Volcanes** is another large residential community. Though less peaceful, it is another good option for a lower-priced apartment, and it is closely linked to the city center through bus routes. Here, as in the Reforma, you'll find markets, dairies, bakeries, and so on.

Valley of Etla

One of the most appealing areas outside the city proper are the communities in the Valley of Etla, just northwest of Oaxaca de Juárez on the road toward Mexico City. This fertile region has been inhabited for centuries—no surprise considering its abundant water and significant natural beauty. The region is peaceful and largely traditional, yet most communities in Etla are more comfortable with foreigner residents than in other areas around Oaxaca. There is even an organic farm in the Etla valley that participates in the international WWOOF (World Wide Opportunities on Organic Farms) program.

There are natural springs in the Etla vicinity, so water runs freely in many communities here, even in the dry season. Of the many little towns in the Etla valley, **San Agustín Etla** is among the most picturesque and home to the Instituto de Artes Gráficas de Oaxaca (Graphic Arts Institute of Oaxaca), a multipurpose school and exhibition space launched by contemporary Oaxacan artist Francisco Toledo.

The Valley of Etla, especially San Agustín, is a very desirable place to live, and properties can really run the gamut. Family homes for sale will generally run in the neighborhood of US$200,000, though they can be higher near the art school in San Agustín or for a larger property.

San Andrés Huayapam

With its cobbled streets and tranquil country atmosphere, the suburban community of San Andrés Huayapam feels miles away from the bustle of downtown Oaxaca. In reality, it is only 20 minutes from Huayapam to the city center by car (and you probably want to own a car if you live in Huayapam, as public transportation is more limited here).

The benefits to living in Huayapam are readily apparent: fresh air, peace and quiet, and a charming small-town atmosphere where roosters wander freely in the streets and children play outside old adobe dwellings. While the donkey watching is good, you won't get much by way of nightlife, restaurants, or shopping in this little community, so be prepared to run errands, stock up on groceries, and go out to eat in the city proper. For those who value a quiet atmosphere at home, Huayapam is ideal.

When it comes to finding a place to rent or buy, there are fewer options here, though they do occasionally come up. If you have your heart set on Huayapam, try chatting with locals to see if any place is for rent in town. If you aren't able to find a place to rent in central Huayapam, you might also try looking just south, in the large residential neighborhoods north of Niños Heroes.

You can reach San Andrés Huayapam by following Niños Heroes west out of the city center (where it becomes the Panamerican Highway), then following the road to the cemetery (*panteón*) or Highway 175. From there, Huayapam is noted on various road signs.

Valles Centrales

The grassy valleys surrounding the city of Oaxaca, known as the Valles Centrales, are filled with picturesque small towns and ancient archaeological sites. Most of these towns have very little to offer in terms of real estate, and most are generally resistant to the idea of foreign residents. However, if you have your heart set on living in a small town here, you may be able to find places for rent or buy in pretty little towns like **El Tule** or **Teotitlan del Valle.**

GETTING AROUND

Oaxaca is well connected to the rest of the country by air and highway, though it is also more remote than it might appear on a map. This remoteness has served Oaxaca well, helping to preserve its cultural traditions into the modern era and limiting the influence of Mexico City on daily life. However, residents will find travel to and from the city—especially to international destinations—can be more arduous and expensive than in other major destinations.

Car

In a car, it takes 5–6 hours to drive to Oaxaca from Mexico City, provided there is no road construction (which, unfortunately, there often is). If you are new to Oaxaca, the scenic road is best traveled in the daytime; hairpin turns, high mountain passes, and uneven pavement can make the trip feel like a bit of an obstacle course. Within the city, Oaxacans are generally fast and aggressive drivers; here, accidents are not uncommon. Drive defensively and never under the influence of alcohol.

Bus

The road linking Oaxaca to the capital is scenic but can also be dangerous thanks to high-speed drivers, lumbering big rigs, and uneven pavement. If you prefer to let someone else do the driving, you can do like most locals and take a first-class bus to Mexico City for around US$25–30. There are dozens of daily departures to the capital, as well as frequent service to other southern destinations, like Puebla, San Cristóbal de las Casas, and the Oaxacan coast. If you want to head north of the capital, you'll likely need to connect through Mexico City.

With their own massive bus terminal on the northern edge of the *centro,* the bus company ADO (Autobuses del Oriente) is the king of the hill, offering hourly departures to Mexico City throughout the day and night, as well as dozens of other locations throughout Mexico. Their first-class buses are clean, safe, air-conditioned, and equipped with bathrooms; for an even cushier ride, you can pay extra for their GL (executive) or UNO (premium) service.

For most long trips, first-class buses are the best bet for safety and comfort; however, second-class buses can be easier and more inexpensive when traveling short distances within the state of Oaxaca. The second-class bus terminal is located just west of the city's largest market, the *central de abastos,* with buses frequently departing to neighboring towns. If you are heading east to destinations like Mitla, Teotitlan de Valle, or Tlacolula in the Valles Centrales, you can also catch a bus on Niños Heroes de Chapultepec, just a block before the baseball stadium; look for the destination written in the window.

Note that if you are heading to the coast of Oaxaca, first-class buses take a longer route to popular destinations via the highway to Salina Cruz on the Isthmus of Tehuantepec. They then travel north along the ocean (it can take around 12 hours to reach the hub city of Pochutla). For that reason, many travelers prefer to take second-class buses, which travel one of the incredibly curvy highways through the Sierra Madre and can reach Pochutla or Puerto Escondido in about half the time.

Air

Located just twenty minutes south of the city center, the small Oaxaca-Xoxocotlán International Airport (OAX) has a single landing strip, which currently receives several daily flights from Mexico City (about an hour's trip), as well as more infrequent service to Monterrey, Tijuana, Mérida, Tuxtla Guiterrez, and Huatulco and Puerto Escondido on the coast of Oaxaca. In addition, Continental Airlines offers direct flights between Houston and Oaxaca; for all other international destinations, you must connect through the capital. Once you are on the ground, you can take private or shared taxi service into the city. There are official taxi booths at the airport's exit where you can pre-pay for your trip.

Public Transportation

All major neighborhoods in Oaxaca are serviced by city buses. Bus routes and schedules aren't published, but you can learn the ropes without too much difficulty. Most buses travel along central avenues and have their destinations marked in the windows. Look for major east–west routes along Avenida Independencia and Avenida Hidalgo in the *centro,* or major north–south routes (including buses to and from the Reforma neighborhood and San Felipe del Agua) along Avenida Juárez and Pino Suárez, which run alongside Parque Juárez.

Taxi

Taxis are a ubiquitous and inexpensive form of transport in the city of Oaxaca. The easiest thing to do is simply hail a taxi in the street; they circle the central districts throughout the day and evening. You can also call a cab if you are in a more remote location (though they may not always be reliable in the wee hours). Taxis charge a flat rate depending on the distance you are traveling. Usually, a fare doesn't exceed a couple dollars, though it can be higher if you are covering a lot of ground. If you are concerned about the cost, ask in advance.

Coastal Towns

Due south from the city of Oaxaca, the coastal mountains rise as high as 10,000 feet before dropping to the balmy Pacific Coast. With its year-round tropical weather and sleepy atmosphere, the coast of Oaxaca is among Mexico's most rustic and low-key shorelines. North of the Isthmus of Tehuantepec (Mexico's slimmest point from east to west), there are numerous beach communities that hold the promise of endless surf, a carefree lifestyle, and all the coconut milk you can drink. Unlike Acapulco, Mazatlan, Puerto Vallarta, or other Pacific resorts, Oaxaca's coast primarily appeals to adventurous travelers seeking something cheaper, less polished, and more laid-back. For dollars a day, you can pitch a hammock, kick back some brews, and sunbathe before the roaring Pacific.

THE LAY OF THE LAND

Traveling south over the Sierra Madre, the Pacific Coast of Oaxaca is a lush, tropical, and largely undeveloped stretch of shoreline. The area has attracted backpackers and travelers for decades but has remained remarkably rustic nonetheless. West of the Isthmus of Tehuantepec and about 170 miles from the city of Oaxaca, Bahías de Huatulco is the largest resort area on the coast. A series of small bays and their associated communities, the Huatulco region receives a modest amount of tourism to its numerous hotels and resorts (all of which are relatively inexpensive when compared with other Pacific resort towns), though it has yet to become one of Mexico's major destinations. Powerful offshore currents render a good portion of this coastline unsafe for swimming, but the bays around Huatulco are generally sheltered and nice for swimming and snorkeling.

Huatulco has its share of attractions, but those looking to spend an extended time on the Oaxacan coast usually head farther northeast to some of the rustic, picturesque, and amazingly inexpensive communities along the coast. About 30 miles west of Huatulco, you'll reach the city of Pochutla, one of the coast's larger communities and a transportation hub (though by no means a large place). Just south of Pochutla on the Pacific Coast, Puerto Ángel, Zipolite, San Agustinillo, and Mazunte are rustic, hippie beach towns that, despite their longtime popularity with backpackers, feel far from "discovered." Head another 30 miles northwest to reach Puerto Escondido, a charming surf town with an ever-growing community of foreign part-time and full-time residents.

DAILY LIFE

Those looking for a laid-back, get-away-from-it-all lifestyle will have their wish fulfilled along Oaxaca's rugged coast. Here, simple pleasures are the spice of life: Swimming, sunbathing, walking along the beach, and tipping back a cold beer are the most popular pastimes.

Being so far off the beaten path means you won't find extensive offerings with regards to health care, education, and shopping, so you'll likely make periodic trips home, to Mexico City, or, at the very least, to the city of Oaxaca to get necessities, buy clothes, or stock up on more exotic groceries. Especially in the Puerto Ángel area, many plots of land may not have access to electricity or telephone lines, though service is slowly improving. At the same time, locals learn to get by with the basic services available, and living more simply is a big reason to choose this area in the first place.

WHERE TO LIVE

The Oaxacan coast is largely undeveloped, and those who settle down on this rustic stretch of shoreline are usually looking to get away from it all. Most foreigners who live part time or full time on the coast of Oaxaca like the surf town of Puerto Escondido, though even more hardy bohemians may settle down along the bucolic string of beaches north of Puerto Ángel. Some also purchase land along the coast, either in these areas or near Huatulco.

Housing

You can pitch a hammock for dollars a day and spend several happy months along the Oaxacan coast, though those looking for four walls and a roof will be able to find inexpensive, basic digs along the coast near Pochutla. The Puerto Escondido area offers a bit more variety, from simple bungalows to condos and villas. Those looking to invest in a bit more luxury might look at the newer developments around Puerto Escondido, where many homes are equipped with pools and gardens.

No matter where you choose to live, the climate on the coast is perpetually warm and balmy, so homes are often breezy, outdoorsy constructions, many with thatched palm roofs and mosquito-screen windows.

Puerto Ángel

Situated aside a tranquil bay, Puerto Ángel is a traditional fishing village with a small sandy beach and a decidedly sleepy atmosphere. To get here, you must first get yourself to Pochutla, a crossroads town with the only large bus terminal in the area. From there, cabs or *colectivos* will drive you down the winding path to the Pacific shore.

Puerto Ángel itself doesn't offer much more than a few beachside restaurants and a dusty little downtown, but a handful of foreigners have begun to purchase properties in the hills surrounding the bay. It's great place to go if you want to open a hippie café or practice meditation, and it offers a touch more services than the adjoining beach towns, including an ATM, a pharmacy, and a tourist office. At the same time, you have to head up the hill to Pochutla if you need to go to the bank or to the grocery store. Fishing is still the town's principal industry (tourism comes in second), and you can hire a boat from the bay if you'd like to tour the open seas.

If you are planning to buy land, especially in off-the-beaten-path locations around Puerto Ángel, make sure you have paid close attention to the *ejido* rules and work with a trusted notary.

Zipolite, San Agustinillo, and Mazunte

If you continue east along the coastal road from Puerto Ángel, you'll reach the laid-back beach community of Zipolite about a mile later. This long stretch of sand is a famed reunion point for intrepid backpackers and party-oriented tourists, and during the winter high season it can feel a bit like an international love-in. Though still fairly rustic (there are no banks or ATMs in town, no grocery stores, and no police force), Zipolite has grown over the years. Today, there is a pleasant selection of restaurants and cafés along the main drag, as well as a few bed-and-breakfasts (though you can still tap into Zipo's classic vibe by pitching a hammock and hanging out at the Playa del Amor, a popular spot for nude sunbathing).

From Zipolite, you can catch a *colectivo* north to a small bay called San Agustinillo. It's a little more laid-back than Zipo, and you won't get many late-night parties here, but you can still watch the stars from the sand. Mazunte, another few miles north along the same sandy coastal road, is another relaxed beach town, this one with a famous sea-turtle sanctuary. It remains entirely rustic, even as it draws backpackers and tourists to its fabled shores.

There is a small community of younger Europeans, Americans, and other foreigners, as well as hippie-minded *chilangos* (Mexico City natives), that lives in these little beach towns, trading urban atmosphere for the simple pleasures of the *playa*. Some come to spend a few months; others settle down for a longer stint, opening restaurants or selling handmade jewelry to tourists. In reality, few foreigners invest in property in Zipolite and vicinity, and you should definitely use care when conducting real estate deals here. The predominance of *ejido* land can make purchasing property a precarious decision.

The greater Mexican real estate boom hasn't reached this secluded stretch of beach, and many of the properties available are still *ejido* land. If you are interested in purchasing here, you will need to make contacts in the local community to explore your options, as there are very limited real estate offices that represent properties in this region. Rent a *palapa* and get to know the area before you settle down.

Puerto Escondido

The big waves at Playa Zicatela have made Puerto Escondido a popular destination for high-adrenaline surfers, while its off-the-beaten-track charms herald backpackers and bohemians from around the world. Most foreigners make their way to this laid-back beach town for a week or two of rest and relaxation, though some find the area so appealing, they decide to stay.

There was little in Puerto Escondido before the early 20th century, when it was first established as a Pacific shipping port. In the 1960s, the coastal highway was extended between Guerrero and Oaxaca, making Puerto Escondido more accessible to tourists from Acapulco and other Pacific beaches. Since then, tourism has played a major role in the town's culture and economy. However, Puerto Escondido remains decidedly more down-to-earth than other popular resort destinations, with no high-rise hotels or all-inclusive resorts.

The beaches are the town's main attraction, and, in addition to the big-wave surf at Playa Zicatela, there are numerous quieter shores safe for swimming and sunbathing. Pérez Gazga Avenue, known as El Adoquin locally (which refers to the street's paved stones), is filled with surf and swim shops, cafés, bars, and restaurants, including many tasty pizza and pasta joints thanks to a preponderance of Italian expatriates in town. You'll also find most of the practical stuff along this corridor: banks, Internet cafés, pharmacies, hardware stores, and liquor stores. Along the main highway, Puerto Escondido's traditional market is the best place to shop for inexpensive fruits, vegetables, eggs, meat, fish, tortillas, flowers, and prepared foods.

While you'll get all the basics, Puerto Escondido is not as connected, developed, or contemporary as beach towns like Puerto Vallarta or Cabo San Lucas. Living here is about enjoying life's simple pleasures and living within the region's limitations. You won't be able to get your hands on many imported foods. You'll probably do most of your clothes shopping when visiting a bigger city, and, though there are some doctors, you will likely have to get your health-care needs met elsewhere. Plus, travel to and from other parts of the country can be long or expensive.

Puerto Escondido literally means Hidden Port, and that moniker once suited this laid-back beach town well. Today, things have changed. There is an ever-increasing community of foreign homeowners in the area, and prices have been steadily increasing. Nonetheless, home prices run the gamut from luxurious villas with million-dollar price tags to multibedroom homes for less than US$150,000. Some places have pools, and most sport *palapas* (open-air dwellings with a thatched-palm roof). Coastal land is also available in a number of new developments, but remember to work with a trusted notary and set up the correct trusts at the bank if you are going to buy beachfront property. Avoid buying converted *ejido* land, as these are often embroiled in legal battles even after the land has been sold. There is a big market for vacation rentals in Puerto Escondido, which tend to be pricier (around US$600 to US$1000 per week for a place with a pool and multiple bedrooms) than long-term rentals, which average less than US$1000 per month.

GETTING AROUND

It is neither quick, nor easy, nor inexpensive to get to and from the coast of Oaxaca, yet locals will tell you that the region's relative inaccessibility is precisely what has given it such a low-key, off-the-beaten-track atmosphere.

Air

For the quickest (and also, unfortunately, most expensive) journey to the coast, there is the Puerto Escondido International Airport (PXM), where national carriers VivaAerobus and Aeromar operate daily flights to and from Mexico City. If you are traveling to the Puerto Ángel vicinity, you can fly into Bahías de Huatulco International Airport (HUX), which receives flights from Mexico City and Oaxaca. To get to Puerto Ángel and beyond, you will need to arrange ground transportation from the Huatulco airport to Pochutla, and from there to the coast.

Bus

Some people drive to the beach, but another common way to get to the Oaxaca coast is via bus. From Mexico City, there are first-class buses to Puerto Escondido, Pochutla, and Bahías de Huatulco; the ride is about 12 hours, and most departures leave in the evening and travel overnight. From the city of Oaxaca, you have two options. You can take a first-class bus to the coast, which will travel the more modern highway out to the Isthmus of Tehuantepec, then follow the coastline north. Since traveling to the isthmus takes you considerably farther south, the ride is about 10 hours to Puerto Ángel in a first-class bus, and another hour to Puerto Escondido. The second option is to take a second-class bus from the city of Oaxaca directly over the Sierra Madre to Pochutla or Puerto Escondido; the ride, though considerably bumpier and more winding, only takes about six hours. In addition to second-class buses, there are private shuttle companies that make the trek over the Sierra Madre.

PRIME LIVING LOCATIONS

BAJA CALIFORNIA SUR

The long, slender Baja California peninsula extends more than 750 miles from the U.S. border to its southernmost point at Cabo San Lucas. Flanked to the east by the Sea of Cortez and to the west by the powerful Pacific Ocean, Baja is rimmed by more than 3,000 miles of coastline and home to some of the richest marine ecosystems in the world.

Though today it is a well-known playground for outdoor activities, adventure sports, and good old-fashioned sunbathing, Baja California's sparsely populated deserts were relatively undeveloped until the 1970s. Since the introduction of large hotels and tourist resorts, there has been a steady growth in population around the southernmost point in Los Cabos, as well as in the capital of La Paz. Places that were once off the beaten track now feel thoroughly discovered as expatriates, tourists, and new national residents arrive on the peninsula to partake of its natural beauty and promising economic growth.

Despite ongoing development, Baja California has maintained its mystique

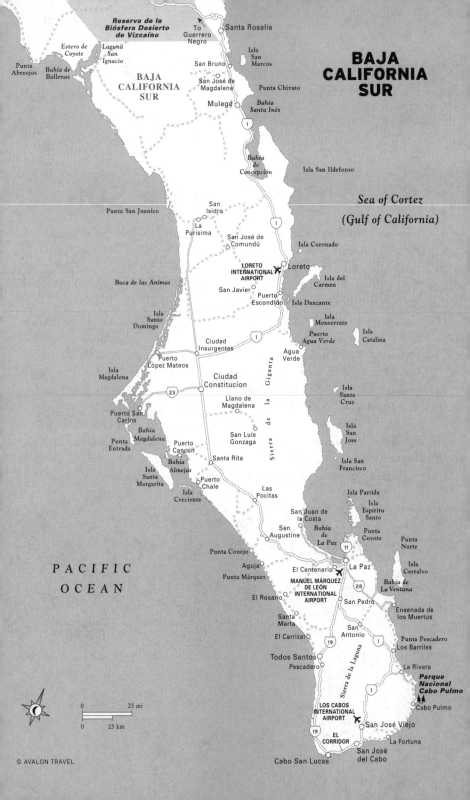

as an undiscovered paradise with empty deserts punctuated by tiny oases, hidden surf towns, and remote highways patrolled by bandits. The spirit of Baja California is still alive (without the bandits, of course!), just as the natural scenery remains some of the most striking in Mexico.

While it is still a romantic place, today's Baja is both safe and modern, especially around the large resort towns of Cabo San Lucas and San José del Cabo on the southern cape. The area is close to the United States both physically and culturally, so you may not feel as much culture shock here as you would in, say, Mexico City. Still, the region has received a substantial influx of residents from Northern Mexico, so there's still a distinctly Mexican feeling from the moment you cross the border.

Los Cabos

At the southernmost cape of the Baja California peninsula, the twin towns of Cabo San Lucas and San José del Cabo (often referred to jointly as "Los Cabos") occupy a particularly dramatic stretch of coastline. Here, the Sea of Cortez and the powerful Pacific Ocean converge at Land's End, an outcropping of giant granite boulders that extends from the sierra above Cabo San Lucas into the sea. On a sheltered bay just behind this dramatic scene, the city of Cabo San Lucas has a earned a place as one of Mexico's most famous resort destinations, with a pleasant downtown, beautiful scenery, and amenable climate.

Follow the cape east from Cabo, and you'll arrive in the mellower city of San José del Cabo, overlooking the Sea of Cortez. Low-key and charming, San José has a nice Mexican atmosphere, with low stucco buildings throughout the downtown and a pleasant central square. Here, you'll find boutiques, restaurants, galleries, and some old-fashioned hotels (in addition to some newer, swankier accommodations). While still fairly relaxed, San José has become more popular in recent years; there are several luxury developments near town, and prices have been steadily rising.

A short flight from Los Angeles, Cabo San Lucas and environs is popular with Californians and Southwesterners, though the region's unique desert atmosphere, beautiful beaches, and numerous exclusive high-end resorts attract visitors from all over the world. For those who choose to settle down here, spectacular sunsets, noisy nightclubs, and Baja's famous fish tacos are all a part of daily life.

PRIME LIVING LOCATIONS

THE LAY OF THE LAND

The Baja California peninsula is divided into two states: Baja California Norte (North Baja) and Baja California Sur (South Baja). Mexican Federal Highway 1, also known as the Transpeninsular Highway, runs over 1,000 miles from Tijuana to the cape, passing through tiny towns, unexpected oases, and miles of untouched desert before arriving at its southernmost point in Cabo San Lucas. From there, the highway travels 18 miles down a stretch of coast called the Corridor, arriving in the town of San José del Cabo. A single municipal government oversees both Cabo and San José, as well as the adjoining Corridor.

Though San José is a bit larger in terms of population, Cabo San Lucas is the more famous of the two cities, having blossomed into a major resort destination. Downtown Cabo spreads from behind the city's pretty marina and sandy beach, and is definitely the most glitzy and upbeat place in all of Baja California, with a slew of nightclubs, famous restaurants, souvenir shops, and boutiques.

While there are residential neighborhoods around town, the eastern Corridor has absorbed a lot of the spillover from Cabo. Today, it has been built up with condominiums, gated communities, luxury hotels, and shopping centers, and many expatriates end up living in one of the communities along this strip of coast. The development thins out a bit before arriving in San José del Cabo, where a low-key Mexican atmosphere still defines the downtown area, even as the town's outskirts are being developed.

Climate

The Tropic of Cancer slices through tip of the Baja California peninsula, placing both Cabo and San José in the northernmost tropics. The unusual combination of tropical and arid climates translates into year-round sunshine and warm weather in Cabo San Lucas and San José del Cabo. In the winter and spring, average temperatures hover in the low to mid-70s F (around 21–24°C). The weather warms up in the late summer and early autumn, often getting a bit too hot for comfort. Expect 80°F- (27°C) and 90°F-plus (32°C) weather throughout July, August, and September, as well as a bit more humidity than you'll see during the winter, spring, and fall. Generally, however, the dry air helps keep excessive heat at bay, and after each glorious Pacific sunset, the temperature drops a good 10 degrees in the evening.

The Baja California peninsula is affected by the Pacific hurricane season, which runs from May to November. Although Los Cabos is rarely hit directly with a storm, there will often be massive rainfall as a result of Pacific hurricanes.

History

Though humans have lived on the Baja California peninsula for thousands of years, societies here never advanced to the point of organized civilization and city building, as on the Mexican mainland. During the 18th century, Spanish missionaries ventured onto the peninsula as they colonized Northern Mexico and the Californias. They built a mission in San José del Cabo in 1730, though the settlement never had much success and was eventually abandoned.

With its deep and abundant seas, the Cabo area was popular with wealthy sportfishermen as early as the 1940s, but tourism was largely restricted to the few who could afford to get down there. By 1974, the Mexican government completed work on the Transpeninsular Highway, clearing the way for more development in the region. At that point, fewer than a thousand people lived in Cabo San Lucas. Over the following decades, the cape transformed from a sleepy fishing community to one of Mexico's most desirable and expensive resort towns. The cities of Baja California Sur continue to grow at a rapid rate, with thousands of new residents arriving every year.

Natural Environment

While Baja California is largely covered in desert, there are more varied terrestrial ecosystems along the cape. Here, the southerly stretch of the Baja sierra receives a bit more rainfall than the rest of the range, creating greener vegetation than you'd find along most of the peninsula. Just outside the center of

Cactus and scrub fill the empty desert in Baja California.

San José del Cabo, the San José Estuary is one of the largest freshwater lagoons in southern Baja, and its marshy, green, palm-filled environment is a popular place for walks and bird-watching.

The land is beautiful, but the sea is where Baja offers its most incredible abundance. Cabo San Lucas is located on the southernmost tip of Baja California, flanked on one side by the tranquil Sea of Cortez and on the other by the Pacific Ocean. The convergence of these two seas has made Cabo San Lucas and the surrounding area one of the most interesting marine habitats in the world. People come here to watch the annual whale migration from the Pacific to the Sea of Cortez, and it is not unusual for snorkelers and scuba divers to see manta rays, nurse sharks, dolphins, and elephant seals. More than 900 bird species live around the Sea of Cortez, and close to 40 percent of the world's marine mammal species visit its waters.

Culture

Physically isolated from the rest of the country, the Baja California peninsula is very different from mainland Mexico, mixing a heavy dose of gringo culture with a more typically northern Mexican atmosphere. For many expatriates, living in Los Cabos isn't all that different than living in San Diego, though you shouldn't come to Los Cabos expecting an extension of the United States. You'll still find a generally friendly, Mexican attitude among the people, plenty of tacos and tortillas to feast on, and, despite the prevalence of the English language, plenty of opportunities to practice your Spanish. On the whole, Los Cabos is a friendly, mellow, laid-back place where it is easy for foreigners to feel welcome and at home.

Culturally, Los Cabos doesn't have much of a legacy. The entire Baja California peninsula was sparsely populated throughout its history, only seeing a considerable population increase during the past few decades. Cabo and San José have been principally developed as tourist resorts, and they do have a bit of the typical spring break mayhem downtown, in addition to more elegant and upscale dining and nightlife options. As these cities grow, they have also become more culturally rich. Some of the best restaurants in Mexico have opened in the area, artists have begun to open gallery spaces, and, in towns like Todos Santos, there are funky boutiques and cool cafés somewhat akin to what you'd find in Santa Fe, New Mexico.

Tourism

Cabo San Lucas, like Cancún in Quintana Roo, was developed as a tourist resort. Tourism plays a major role in the region's character and sustains the local economy; indeed, the city would barely exist if it weren't for the people who spend their money on hotels, restaurants, beachwear, souvenirs, and tour boats. There are high-rise hotels all along the coast, but the influence of tourism is particularly prominent near the marina and beachfront in Cabo San Lucas, where you'll find strings of loud nightclubs, bathing-suit-sporting tourists, time-share hawkers, jewelry shops, and massive restaurants catering to carefree vacationers. If you are on vacation yourself, it's a great place to go out and have fun; some residents also partake of the action, while others avoid the downtown district entirely.

That said, most residents are comfortable living among (or entirely ignoring) the ongoing throng of tourists, though Los Cabos won't appeal to everyone. Living in such a popular tourist resort can be great for retired or semiretired people, though those who need to work may find a bit of a culture clash between themselves and the windsurfers, partygoers, and sportfishermen who have come to spend a week living it up in paradise.

DAILY LIFE

While Cabo San Lucas is one of Mexico's premier resort towns, it is actually a rather small city. Clearly, the ongoing influx of tourists plumps up the population at any given time, but residents will find that a friendly, small-town attitude reigns among locals. You'll often bump into familiar faces in Cabo or San José, and many expatriates get together or participate in social groups. Both Cabo and San José are fairly compact cities geographically, so driving distances between one point and another are rarely far. And, even as these cities grow, they have managed to avoid typical urban problems like pollution, traffic, and crime. For most happy residents, the warm weather, sunny skies, laid-back atmosphere, and incredible natural beauty define daily life in Los Cabos. Most people who live here spend their free time swimming, sailing, hiking, or otherwise enjoying an active, outdoorsy lifestyle.

Cost of Living

The cost of living in the Baja California peninsula—and the cape region in particular—is more elevated than almost all of mainland Mexico. Prices here are roughly on par with Mexico City for a middle-class lifestyle, though there isn't the same variety of housing, shopping options, and restaurants you'd find in the capital. In many cases, expatriates in Los Cabos aren't necessarily looking for a reduced cost of living, but a much better lifestyle for their money.

While the Los Cabos area is generally upscale, not everyone who lives here is wealthy. The region offers plenty of laid-back charms, and there is a crowd of expatriates who choose Cabo for the mellow surf-and-sand lifestyle rather than its glitzy side. As everywhere, finding a good deal on housing is the most important piece of the puzzle. Though they aren't the majority, there are homes for sale that are less than US$200,000. And though most end up paying more than US$1,000 a month (or far more) to rent an apartment or condo in the area, there are some deals for US$500 a month, for those who cast a wide net.

Other basic expenses can be costlier in Los Cabos than on the mainland. Groceries tend to be pricey, as the limited agricultural capabilities of a desert environment mean almost everything but seafood must be imported from the Mexican mainland or the United States. Many foreigners also find it is both more inexpensive and more satisfying to shop for clothes or electronics back home, rather than purchase basics in Los Cabos's tourist-price environment.

Food and Shopping

There is a variety of delicious, inexpensive, and incredibly fresh fish and sea-food sold throughout the Baja California peninsula. Seafood is featured on the menu at almost every Cabo restaurant, and it takes center stage at most dinner tables at home. With its distinct northern Mexican influence, Los Cabos is also a great place to sample traditional *norteno* staples: delicious flour torti-llas (as opposed to the ubiquitous corn tortilla in south and central Mexico), grilled meats, and burritos (stuffed tortillas).

Unfortunately, Cabo's arid natural environment doesn't support much agri-culture, so most fresh fruits and vegetables must be imported from elsewhere. Though Mexico has a robust agricultural sector, there are some restrictions on fresh food imported from the Mexican mainland. Believe it or not, you may find a pineapple in Cabo comes from Hawaii rather than Veracruz. This situation, once far more pronounced, has been improving. Today, there are far more vegetable and fruit options in the supermarket, as well as a weekly organic farmer's market in San José del Cabo. You can buy dry goods, cereal, pastas, dairy, deli items, and other staples at the Mexican supermarket chains Soriana and CCC, both in Cabo, or at international giants Costco and Walmart.

Anything else you might want or need can probably be purchased some-where in Cabo. The large Puerto Paraiso shopping mall has clothes and shoe stores, beach shops, boutiques, and even galleries; however, most residents do the majority of their shopping back home. Prices are usually lower outside the resort area.

BAJA'S CUISINE

Baja California's unique environment has produced a rather distinctive culinary palate. Here, agriculture is highly limited by the arid climate, yet seafood is fresh and abundant. With many mainlanders making the jump over the Sea of Cortez, you'll also get a strong influence from Northern Mexico in the culinary offerings. Throughout the peninsula, you can buy soft and delicious flour tortillas, grilled meats, and burritos (large stuffed flour tortillas, typical to the north). The following is what to eat when you're in Baja.

- *tacos de pescado:* Fish tacos are Baja California's quintessential snack. Invariably delicious, battered and deep fried white fish (halibut is among the most common) is dropped into a warm tortilla, then topped with shredded cabbage, sour cream, and salsa.

- ceviche: Popular in coastal areas throughout Latin America, ceviche is lime-cured fish, often mixed with cilantro and vegetables, and served on tostadas. The fresher the fish, the tastier the ceviche, and Baja's fish can't get any fresher.

- *machaca:* An influence from Baja's northern neighborhoods, *machaca* is shredded beef that has been salted and dried before it is cooked with vegetables and spices. A popular alternative preparation of *machaca* is made with marlin rather than beef.

- *almejas brujas:* Stuffed clams are traditionally prepared with vegetables and spices. Clams are particularly popular in Loreto and other cities along the Sea of Cortez.

- dates: Date palms were introduced to the Baja California peninsula and now grow liberally in the region's oases, including the town of San Ignacio in the northern state, as well as Mulegé and Loreto.

- wine: Though you won't see any vineyards in southern Baja, the northern regions of the peninsula have begun to grow grapes and produce some very good wines. Many of Baja California Sur's fine restaurants feature Baja wines, though they aren't from the local area.

- *cerveza* Pacífico: This light pilsner-style beer is practically the symbol of the Baja. Originally founded on the Pacific coastal town of Mazatlan, it is the most popular brand of brew on the peninsula.

- *agua de cebada:* Similar to *horchata,* this refreshing beverage is made by soaking barley grains in water, sweetening the brew, and serving over ice.

PRIME LIVING LOCATIONS

Health Care

With its large tourist economy, Los Cabos has swiftly ramped up its health care services and hospitals, offering a generally good range of medical services, especially for basic needs. Most medical care is considerably less expensive than in the United States. There are many private walk-in clinics and full-service hospitals in both Cabo San Lucas and San José del Cabo, as well as a public IMSS clinic in San José (you must be enrolled in the IMSS insurance program to use this facility). Many clinics are staffed by English-speaking doctors, and there are even a few American physicians in private practice around town. You can get low-cost dental work done in Cabo, too, and there is a growing medical tourism market, with plastic surgery, rehab clinics, and elective surgery options offered at lower prices than in the United States. A rarity in most of Mexico, there are also some English-speaking counseling and psychotherapy services in the Cabo region.

While health care is generally sufficient in Los Cabos, some expatriates prefer to return to the United States or Canada for their medical needs; thanks to the area's proximity to its northern neighbors, it may be not be out of the question to get most of your medical services at home. Some expatriates maintain special international insurance plans that will airlift you back home in the case of a serious emergency. When contracting one of these plans, ask around for recommendations; many companies that offer these services have folded.

In addition to allopathic medicine, there are plenty of alternative health-care options in Cabo, including spas, therapeutic massage, and chiropractic treatments. Perhaps the most important point, though, when thinking about your health and well-being is the active and outdoorsy lifestyle enjoyed by most Baja California residents. Here, swimming, golf, and other outdoor activities are abundant, and it's easy to stay in shape. Generally speaking, sanitation standards are very high in the Cabo area.

Recreation and Entertainment

Los Cabos isn't the type of place to tie a hammock between two palm trees and sleep away the afternoon. For those who love the great outdoors, Baja is a paradise. The list of outdoor activities is virtually inexhaustible: swimming, hiking, snorkeling, scuba diving, whale watching, sailing, fishing, canoeing, wave running, surfing, parasailing, horseback riding, sunbathing, golfing, tennis, motocross, and yachting. There are a number of activities (like dinner cruises or water taxis) aimed principally at tourists, but living here is all about getting outside and taking advantage of the recreational opportunities in the region.

Entertainment in Los Cabos skews toward vacation-friendly nightspots, though of course you'll find some more low-key, locals-only watering holes and restaurants, especially in the town of San José. During the high season, there are frequent art walks in the San José del Cabo galleries.

At the tip of the Baja California peninsula, the coastline is particularly dramatic and picturesque.

Expatriate Community

There is a growing community of foreign residents in Los Cabos. Most find plenty of ways to fill up their free time, including an active social life among the expatriate community. Sandra Landsman, a writer, copy editor, and former real estate broker from Texas who lives in Cabo San Lucas, shares her perception of other expatriates in Los Cabos:

> *A typical day for those of us who are retired are busier than when we worked full time! Most are involved in some type of charity, networking, or social organization. Most are interested in their health, so some type of exercise is part of the day, with Pilates, a health club, water aerobics, or walking the marina or the mountain. More and more families with children are moving to Cabo, therefore there is a work environment, usually time-share selling, if no other field is available.*

Sandra notes that, thanks to the cost of living in Los Cabos, expatriates often come from a stable financial background, investing in a luxury home or second property. But she adds, "Los Cabos also attracts those who just wanted to get out of the rat race and move to a slower-paced, less-expensive area. The expats are from all backgrounds and run the gamut from ex-schoolteachers, nurses, and former airline pilots to retired lawyers, businesspeople, and doctors. Many have bought businesses or opened their own hair salon or health clinic. It is a good mixture of cultures."

PRIME LIVING LOCATIONS

WHERE TO LIVE

There has been extensive development all along the cape: in the tourist town of Cabo San Lucas, along the eastern corridor, in and around the town of San José del Cabo, and in the nearby surf community of Todos Santos. The entire region shares sunny skies, great beaches, and ocean views, though you may find that some areas fit your lifestyle and budget a bit better than others.

Housing

The Cabo San Lucas area was conceived as an upscale resort, so the vast majority of housing for rent or sale is in planned neighborhoods or condominiums. While many of these come at a premium, the local real estate market has bottomed out since the worldwide financial crisis of 2008. Big homes still cost top-dollar, though there are options for less than US$250,000 in many gated neighborhoods, especially for properties farther from the water.

Planned developments and high-end condominiums crowd the market for attention, but they aren't the only options along the cape. For those looking for something more low-key, there are some options in both Cabo San Lucas and San José. With a little luck, there are even places for as low as US$500 per month (try the online classifieds service Craigslist for some more-inexpensive options). If you want to buy or rent long-term outside of a planned community, plan to invest some time looking for a place.

© BRUCINE DOHERTY

Many of the homes in Cabo San Lucas are located in planned and gated communities just outside of town, many with private access to the ocean.

© BRUCINE DOHERTY

view of Cabo San Lucas from the water

Cabo San Lucas

If you want your finger on the pulse, Cabo San Lucas is the undeniable locus of the cape's action, with all of the area's most famous restaurants, cantinas, nightclubs, shops, and so on. Many Cabo residents actually live on the Corridor to the east of the city, but there are also several residential neighborhoods and condominiums in Cabo proper, such as Cabo Viejo, which are within walking distance of the marina, the beaches, and some of the area's great restaurants. Some places are available for long-term rental as well as for purchase.

Just west of the *centro,* in the hills above the bay, there are also several up-scale communities, such as **El Pedregal.** Here, you'll enjoy a quieter side of Cabo, with excellent views of the ocean and easy access to downtown. If you are willing to live farther from the sea, you may also be able to find a place in one of the traditionally Mexican neighborhoods, though the quality of services is variable in these communities.

El Corridor

A string of rocky shores and sandy beaches runs along the cape from Cabo San Lucas to San José del Cabo. At the turn of the 21st century, this picturesque strip of coastline was virtually uninhabited. Today, much of the coastline is covered in gated communities with gorgeous views, multimillion-dollar properties, recreational facilities, and, often, golf clubs. Here, you'll enjoy a much quieter atmosphere than in Cabo proper, though you'll still likely use Cabo San Lucas as your base for shopping, eating, and other recreational activities.

When it comes to housing, there are major planned and gated communities along the Corridor, some of the most famous of which include **Cabo Real, Cabo del Sol, Oasis Palmilla, Querencia,** and **Punta Ballena.** Many of these have a golf course, recreational facilities, and private beaches, with prices ranging from as low as US$200,000 for a golf-course condo to more than US$1 million for multibedroom properties. Though prices vary widely, anyone interested in buying in these exclusive communities should be prepared to make an investment. In the Espiritu del Mar development, for example, starting prices for homes are well over US$1 million. Many people buy these properties as second homes or investment properties, while others make them a permanent home base. Most rentals in this area are aimed at vacationers, but long-term renters can find homes and condos averaging around US$2,000 per month. Luxury homes in gated communities can run much higher.

San José del Cabo

Though it is just 18 miles down the coast, San José del Cabo feels more like a quaint small town than a major resort destination, with narrow streets, stucco homes, and a mix of boutiques and galleries. There are some residential neighborhoods near the center of town, as well as a growing number of luxury town houses, condos, and new developments in the area. Housing prices here are

© BRUCINE DOHERTY

San José del Cabo retains the feeling of an old Mexican town, with this historic church near the main square and charming cobbled streets.

generally a touch lower than Cabo San Lucas, though San José has become increasingly popular over the past decade, nudging up the cost of living.

Downtown San José is charming, though it isn't easy to find a place to rent or buy here, unfortunately. Luck may be on your side, but if not, there are plenty of condominiums to rent or buy within the city limits. If you are renting, most two- or three-bedroom condos will run somewhere around US$1,000 per month for a basic place, though there are cheaper options for those willing to shop around. For buyers, real estate prices here are similar to El Corridor and Cabo San Lucas, with many properties located in gated communities or condominiums.

San José del Cabo has several large master-planned neighborhoods with recreational activities and golf courses, such as the golf-club community of Cabo del Sol along the Sea of Cortez. These types of planned communities were once unusual in San José but have become increasingly common as developers seek out new regions to exploit along the cape.

Todos Santos

About an hour north of Cabo San Lucas on the Pacific Coast, Todos Santos has transformed from a sleepy surf spot to a lively artists' enclave, with historic homes, pretty bed-and-breakfasts, romantic restaurants, assorted galleries, and cute boutiques. Nestled in a natural palm grove at the foothills of the Sierra de la Laguna, Todos Santos is home to an interesting multicultural community, attracting writers, musicians, artists, and surfers drawn to its laid-back pace and magical atmosphere. On that note, Todos Santos was the first place in Baja to be inducted into the Mexican government's Pueblos Magicos (magic towns) program, which allocates funds to restore and promote culturally, historically, and architecturally significant cities throughout the republic.

Life is laid-back here yet offers just the right amount of stimulation and culture. There are some great restaurants, art and music festivals, and lively local parties, yet the vibe is far more relaxed than Cabo San Lucas, with no major high-rise all-inclusive resorts or noisy nightclubs. At the same time, it doesn't offer the many conveniences you'd find in a larger city. Surrounded by a natural oasis, Todos Santos produces fruits and vegetables locally, though you are likely to travel to Cabo (one hour south) or La Paz (one hour north) to stock up on groceries or other modern necessities. You'll likely fly in and out of the airport in Los Cabos, too.

Like most of southern Baja's towns, Todos Santos was originally founded as a mission settlement, garnering an important place in the local sugarcane industry during the 19th century, after the town's natural aquifer was discovered.

One of the more historic cities in the region, the downtown area feels like a quaint pueblo. Even so, development is rapidly picking up in and around the town; there are major communities planned along the Pacific Coast, real estate prices have spiked, and it's not as easy to find a deal in town as it once was. There are stand-alone properties for less than US$250,000 in the region, though most homes run higher (with multibedroom ocean-view villas peaking at more than US$1 million). Note that you'll likely work with a real estate broker in Cabo San Lucas if you are looking to buy in Todos Santos. Most rentals here are aimed at seasonal tenants and vacationers.

GETTING AROUND

Los Cabos International Airport (SJC) is located just outside the city of San José del Cabo. It receives international flights daily, with many coming from nearby California. From the airport, there are shuttle services that will take you to both San José and Cabo San Lucas.

Once on the ground, you will likely need a set of wheels to get around the region—much as you do in Southern California. Most expatriates from the United States choose to drive their cars down to Cabo, as there is a much more limited variety of automobiles for sale in Baja.

La Paz

La Paz is a bustling seaside town and the commercial and governmental capital of the state of Baja California Sur. Whereas San José and Cabo San Lucas have a distinctly vacation-oriented atmosphere, La Paz has the pleasant bustle of a low-key yet functioning city, despite the fact that tourism is also a big part of the local economy. With its bare desert landscape and sparkling blue waters, La Paz and its surrounding region offer some of the most distinctive and beautiful natural scenery in all of Baja. Along the coast, both north and south of the city, there are numerous sandy bays and quiet beaches with calm, clear waters and abundant marine life.

Like most of the Baja California peninsula, the settlement at La Paz got off to a slow start. The famous conquistador Hernán Cortés came ashore here during the 16th century, and other Spanish explorers followed in his wake, though the forbidding environment impeded them from founding a settlement. In the 18th century, Jesuits arrived and built a mission in La Paz, though it was unsuccessful and abandoned after just a few decades in operation.

FRAGILE BEAUTY: THE SEA OF CORTEZ

A narrow gulf between Baja California and the Mexican mainland, the Sea of Cortez is one of the ocean's most distinctive environments. The sea is estimated to be 5.3 million years old, produced by the movement between the Pacific plate and the North American plate (which ripped the Baja California peninsula away from the Mexican mainland). Geographically unusual, the sea is both narrow and deep: While the gulf has an average width of just 150 miles east to west, the sea floor is dramatically ridged, plunging to depths of more than two miles.

Sustaining major plant and animal populations, as well as one of the northern Pacific's largest coral reefs, the Sea of Cortez is the most diverse sea on the planet. It is home to more than 900 vertebrate species and more than 2,000 invertebrates. Large fish and marine mammals are astonishingly abundant, from whale sharks, hammerhead sharks, moray eels, and marlin to elephant seals, California sea lions, Guadalupe fur seals, and bottlenose dolphins. Every year, gray, humpback, and killer whales migrate thousands of miles to the sea (along with a flurry of whale-watching tourists), and both sea turtles and manta rays also visit the waters to breed. Of particular note, there are several creatures endemic to the region, including the *vaquita marina,* the world's smallest marine mammal. Near land, the gulf also supports tidal zones and estuaries where hundreds of species of birds and crustaceans thrive.

Unfortunately, this marvelous ecosystem is also very fragile. As humans rapidly develop the Baja California peninsula, the Sea of Cortez has come under great environmental threat. Fishing sustains local economies throughout Baja, but overfishing, as well as the massive amount of bycatch pulled from the waters, has drastically reduced fish communities. (Anecdotally, many sportfishermen note that their prize catches generally measure far smaller today than a decade ago.) Coastal developments have affected mangrove estuaries, and many worry that continued development will lead to pollution and improper sewage treatment (the peninsula's lack of freshwater makes it a particularly difficult place to develop responsibly). In the north, the sea is fed by the Colorado River, which has produced some interesting tidal communities and wetlands at its mouth. The river's famous damming, however, has drastically reduced the amount of freshwater flowing into the sea and dried up the former estuaries.

There are many active environmental organizations in Baja California, some with a specific interest in protecting the Sea of Cortez. As responsible citizens of such a special place, residents should consider getting involved. Just as importantly, before buying into a planned community or neighborhood, make sure the developers have already fully considered the environmental impact.

La Paz was again settled in the 19th century, and it eventually became the capital of the Baja California province after a hurricane destroyed the former capital of Loreto. Pearls and oysters were the region's major exports, and, after the bivalve colonies were wiped out by disease, fishing formed the base of the economy. In the 1940s, wealthy Americans, including many celebrities like Bing

Crosby, bought homes in the region. But La Paz only began to grow substantially after the completion of the Transpeninsular highway in the early 1970s.

Today, La Paz is a warm, laid-back, medium-size city with a distinctly coastal atmosphere and a strong cultural influence from Northern Mexico. Nestled against the glassy waters of the Sea of Cortez, La Paz's downtown district is a mix of pastel-colored buildings overlooking a paved boardwalk lined with palms. Despite its beautiful location and proximity to Los Cabos, La Paz has managed to stay off the tourist circuit to a large extent. It hasn't entirely escaped notice of the foreign community, however. More than 4,000 expatriates spend their winters here, with many staying on year-round.

THE LAY OF THE LAND

La Paz is located on the Sea of Cortez, just off the Transpeninsular Highway, about an hour and a half north of Cabo San Lucas and 900 miles south of San Diego by highway. With a population of around 250,000, La Paz is the capital of Baja California Sur and seat of both the municipal and state government. The city is also home to the state university, Universidad Autónoma de Baja California Sur, in addition to several local colleges and marine biology schools.

To the south of the city, there are numerous secluded sandy beaches, and off the coast, the islands near La Paz are popular for bird-watching, whale watching, snorkeling, and scuba diving. Of particular note, the Isla Espíritu Santo, a large island just 25 miles from the city, is renowned for its dramatic scenery and abundant community of marine mammals, birds, and fish. Because of its remarkable diversity, the island has been protected by the United Nations' World Heritage program.

Climate

La Paz has a similar climate to the Baja California cape: It is arid, warm, and slightly humid throughout the year. July through September are the hottest months, when the air is perpetually warm and muggy, and temperatures rise to the high 90s F (high 30s C). On most days, heat is lightly tempered by a constant westerly breeze that blows over La Paz from the Sea of Cortez. Winters are lovely, with daytime temperatures ranging between the high 60s and mid-70s F (approximately 20–24°C).

DAILY LIFE

Life in La Paz is different from other southern Baja cities, with a bit more bustle and industry than you'd find in the more vacation-oriented spots along the cape. There is certainly tourism in La Paz, as well as a community of international expatriates; however, it remains a predominantly Mexican city with a culture strongly influenced by the many northern Mexican families who have relocated here over the past few decades.

For most foreign residents, life in La Paz is not about restaurants and adventure sports, but tipping back an *agua fresca* on the street, dining on some fish tacos, or watching the sunset over the Sea of Cortez. Downtown, there is some modest spring-break-style spillover from Los Cabos, with tourist-friendly restaurants like Carlos and Charlie's and Applebees. But on the whole, the city has yet to reach the level of tourist-ready development that you'd find in Cabo San Lucas and San José.

Cost of Living

La Paz is more inexpensive than Cabo San Lucas or San José del Cabo, with prices more on par with much of mainland Mexico. Following a budget, you can likely reduce your cost of living significantly. At the same time, La Paz, like the rest of Baja, is rapidly being developed. There are fewer bargains here than you'd have found at the turn of the new millennium, though you can still rent or buy for a lower cost than in most coastal towns in the United States or Canada.

Food in La Paz is similar to the rest of Baja California: Fruits and vegetables are imported and are generally pricey. To get the best deals, check out the traditional municipal market, where more local produce is for sale (grocery stores import all their food from the mainland or California). Only seafood is the real bargain in these parts, where fresh sea bass, tuna, halibut, shrimp, and other pricey catch are sold at the lowest imaginable prices.

Health Care

Health care in La Paz is good quality and far more inexpensive than in the United States. There are five major hospitals in the city, including a public IMSS clinic (available only to IMSS-covered patients) and a public military hospital (which may be available to expatriates on a space-available basis).

WHERE TO LIVE
Housing

There are plenty of housing options in and around La Paz, especially for those who plan to buy property. Here, a lot or a home in planned gated community will cost far less than in Cabo San Lucas, though there are plenty of independent properties for sale as well. Depending on how much time and energy you want to invest in the property, you can find everything from large ocean-view lots along the coast, to simple homes in Mexican neighborhoods, to luxury furnished condominiums.

Downtown and Vicinity

Many foreigners love the relaxed atmosphere and quirky coastal charm of central La Paz. Near the *malecón* (promenade), you'll find a mix of simple beach bungalows and more upscale condos throughout the tree-lined, pastel-colored neighborhoods. You rent a simple, two-bedroom home within walking distance to the sea from US$600 and up per month. If you want a bit more luxury or ocean views, plan to spend double that, even in the downtown district. Also near the *centro,* the **Lomas de Palmira** area is popular with Mexicans, as well as some expatriates, and has homes for rent or sale; you can find a multibedroom home rental for anywhere between US$1,500 and US$3,000 monthly, often with a nice view of the ocean. Housing prices in this area cost on average around $US350,000.

El Pedregal and Other Planned Communities

Master planned communities, like El Pedregal (by the same group that developed El Pedregal in Cabo San Lucas), are cropping up all around La Paz. Though growth has slowed since the economic crisis, you can still buy into a master planned community near La Paz, though it will cost you less than it would along the cape. In many communities, houses start at less than US$200,000.

The **Mogote peninsula** extends into the bay opposite La Paz, and until recently it was most easily accessible by kayak. Today it has been slated for development, with many large lots for sale. As with all planned communities, do your homework before investing; the development has come under fire from ecological groups for disturbing the unique habitat on the peninsula.

El Centenario

In the greater La Paz municipality, there are some smaller communities that can make a quiet and inexpensive alternative to living near the city center. About 10 miles west of La Paz, El Centenario is a small, traditionally Mexican pueblo, which has become a popular place for American and Canadian expatriates to buy land and own houses. You may be able to find a more inexpensive option in this area. Across the bay from La Paz, **El Comitan** is another smaller community with both lots and houses for sale. It is still rather easy to commute from these communities to La Paz for shopping, food, entertainment, or a job, if you work in the city.

GETTING AROUND

The Manuel Márquez de León International Airport (LAP) is located just outside the city and runs flights to the mainland, as well as some limited service to Los Angeles. There are two ferry lines that run between La Paz and mainland Mexico from the port at Pichilingue outside the *centro*. There are daily departures to Mazatlán and Topolobampo, Sinaloa, on the Pacific Coast, with the trip lasting 15–17 hours. Cars and pets can ride the ferry along with ticketed passengers, but you must book ahead.

On the ground, there are city buses running though La Paz's central districts, but the automobile is a vastly more popular option for getting around town. There is also a bike lane alongside the *malecón*.

Loreto and Vicinity

Mexican Federal Highway 1 heads north from La Paz, cutting across the peninsula toward the Pacific Ocean before swinging back to the Sea of Cortez. Arriving on the eastern shore, this fabled roadway runs past remote and beautiful beaches, small towns, and RV parks where road-trippers and intrepid expatriates have found a little piece of paradise far off the beaten track.

The coast along the Sea of Cortez is an unusual, otherworldly mix of glassy turquoise waters and brittle brown desert. The region's amazing abundance is largely beneath water in the diverse marine ecosystem of the Sea of Cortez. Water sports and natural scenery are the big attractions here, since this remote shore is far removed from the modern world.

THE LAY OF THE LAND

Heading north from La Paz, the Transpeninsular Highway meanders across the peninsula 200 miles before hitting the coast just south of Loreto, a town of fewer than 15,000 inhabitants. While certainly not a massive metropolis, Loreto is the largest community along this stretch of coast, and it's the former capital of Baja California. Head a bit farther north, and you'll find many secluded beaches and a few more small communities, including the oasis of Mulege, a popular stopover for RVers and road-trippers.

Climate

The coast along the Sea of Cortez enjoys a warm and sunny climate year-round, with average temperatures in the mid-70s F (around 24°C). The weather heats up from June to September, with temperatures rising into the 90s F (32°C and up). It can be uncomfortably hot and humid during the summer, when there is little breeze to break the heat; many foreign travelers and residents avoid the area in July, August, and September.

DAILY LIFE

The quiet beach towns along the coast of the Sea of Cortez are best for those who love water sports, silence, and free time. There are few modern amenities—forget seeing the latest Hollywood movie or going out for a gourmet meal. Yet those types of distractions are hardly missed in such a laid-back and beautiful area. The cost of living is generally low here, and you can still get some great deals on real estate, even on the water. Work with a trusted broker if you plan to buy beachfront property, and be especially careful about investing in *ejido* land. In terms of services and shopping, you'll likely make the trek to La Paz for most of your basics, if not to the United States or Canada.

WHERE TO LIVE

Living on this remote coastline isn't for everyone, though it has become much easier now that Loreto has a functioning international airport. When weighing where to live, consider access and convenience in addition to costs and lifestyle.

Housing

There is very little development along the Sea of Cortez coast, and the area has never been known as a luxury destination. In the areas around Loreto, most homes are simple and modern, some with large surrounding properties. There are also many popular RV parks in the region, where foreigners spend extended seasons by the sea. Those looking for more posh amenities should look in the city of Loreto, where there are some newer developments and condominiums in addition to traditional residential neighborhoods. Of particular note, there are many empty lots for sale in this area, both for homes and commercial development, and many have views of the sea or beach access.

Loreto

The small city of Loreto was, until the mid-2000s, a sleepy fishing village. Founded in the 18th century, Loreto was the site of the first mission in Baja

California; it was the capital of the province for years thereafter. La Paz later surpassed Loreto as the most important Sea of Cortez port, and Loreto languished for decades. As tourism to the Baja California peninsula has become more popular, Loreto has also begun to grow. Loreto's municipality was officially established in the 1990s, with its first mayoral election held in 1993.

Loreto has always drawn some modest tourism from sportfishermen who come to partake of the famous abundance of mahimahi in surrounding waters. However, for many foreigners, Loreto was put on the map with the opening of its first resort community, Loreto Bay, which was designed to be ecologically friendly, as well as aesthetically tied into the region's particular environment. Because of mismanagement, as well as the bottoming out of the worldwide real estate market, the resort community folded, and much of the development expected for Loreto has been put on hold. Word has it that the Mexican government plans to develop Loreto for tourism. But today, there are still plenty of lots and some homes for sale around central Loreto, as well as the adjoining coasts. Simple homes in town often cost about US$200,000, though beachfront properties are three times that amount.

The city itself is arranged around its most historic landmark, the Mission of Our Lady of Loreto, which is also accompanied by a regional museum. The center of town has a low-key, beachy feeling, and there are a few casual places to eat or tip back a beer.

Mulegé

Driving along the Transpeninsular Highway, it is a surprise to come across the green, palm-fringed valley of Mulegé. Fed by the Río Santa Rosalía, this tiny oasis supports a local community of fewer than 4,000 permanent residents, many working in the fishing industry. Though the town is fairly rustic, it receives a fairly consistent stream of tourists and road-trippers, and there are a few nice places to eat and sleep, as well as a bank and ATM. The town's mission is one of the nicer landmarks in Baja California, with a view of the palm-filled valley below. However, the area's true attraction is the endless array of quiet, sandy beaches and coves that dot the coastline of the Sea of Cortez.

Despite its incredibly off-the-beaten-track feeling, Mulegé draws some foreign residents and travelers who love getting away from it all. Here, you can find some inexpensive properties (some less than US$100,000), and the region is also very popular with RV enthusiasts.

Santa Rosalía

The small community of Santa Rosalía, north of Mulegé, has about 10,000

THE YUCATÁN PENINSULA

The Yucatán Peninsula extends east from the Mexican mainland into the Atlantic Ocean, separating the Gulf of Mexico from the Caribbean Sea. Once the locus of the great Late Classic Mayan civilization, the region remains a place of tremendous culture and tradition, as well as some of the most spectacular scenery in all of Mexico.

The Yucatán Peninsula has always been culturally, geographically, and politically distinct from the mainland. It was with some reluctance that the region became part of the Mexican republic, and, in the 19th century, ethnic Maya and Yucatecos launched a long and large-scale offensive against the largely white rulers of the region, in what is known as the Caste War of Yucatán. Over the course of its turbulent history, the peninsula has been shaped by myriad cultures, including native Maya, Spanish settlers, the greater Caribbean, mainland Mexico, and immigrant populations.

While the peninsula is often regarded as a single social and geographical region, it is actually diverse, both culturally and physically. In the southeastern

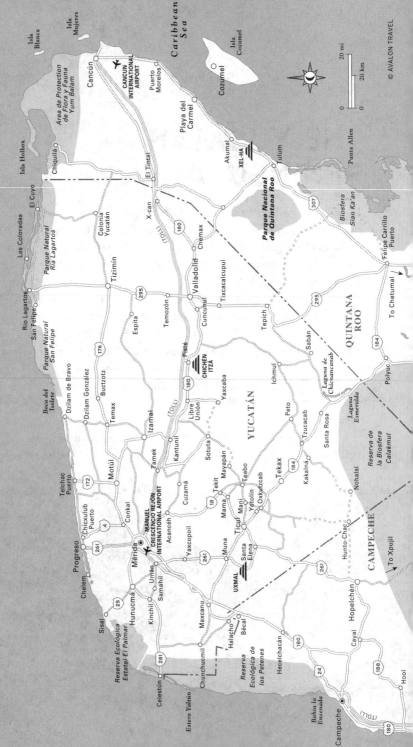
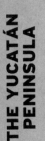

THE YUCATÁN PENINSULA

state of Quintana Roo, the Caribbean coastline defines daily life for most residents. With its stunning beaches, lush jungles, and warm turquoise waters, it is a naturally breathtaking place, as well as the home of Mexico's largest and most famous resort town, Cancún.

To the northwest, the state of Yucatán adjoins the Gulf of Mexico. Here, the attraction isn't the pristine beaches (though there is some nice coastline along the Gulf), but vibrant culture, historic cities, and a low-key environment. Mérida, the capital of the state of Yucatán, is a handsome and colorful colonial city with wonderful food and a friendly atmosphere. Though not undiscovered by tourists and expatriates, Mérida remains a traditional, old-fashioned, and inexpensive place to live.

a beach on the Caribbean coastline

© INDI ERICKSEN

PRIME LIVING LOCATIONS

The Caribbean Coast

On the eastern edge of the Yucatán Peninsula, the state of Quintana Roo is a postcard-worthy paradise. Stretching from the city of Cancún to the border with Belize, the coastline is blanketed with miles of palm-fringed white-sand beaches, sinking into glassy, gentle, impossibly turquoise sea. With its abundant marine life, large barrier reef, and naturally transparent water, the Caribbean coast is popular for scuba diving and snorkeling, as well as good old-fashioned rest and relaxation. It has also become increasingly popular with foreign residents looking to get away from it all—either for a few years or for a lifetime.

Though there were Mayan communities living along the Caribbean coast for centuries, the population declined drastically in the years following the conquest. Throughout the colonial era and into the 20th century, the Caribbean coast was remote, largely uninhabited, and viewed as wild and forbidding. Though today it is a major resort destination, the city of Cancún was just a small fishing community until the 1970s, when the Mexican government launched a plan to develop the region for tourism. In a matter of a few decades, this once-empty beach was filled with high-rise hotels. Today, luxury tourism and rapid urban development define the region almost as much as its natural beauty.

After Cancún's success as a resort, other Caribbean beach towns began to develop their tourist industry. Now the previously quiet stretch of coast at Playa del Carmen is another popular vacation destination, with smaller cities like Tulum and Akumal also on the rise. Despite the rapid growth in tourism and the region's international flavor, Quintana Roo is still a largely Mexican place, with a friendly and easygoing character.

THE LAY OF THE LAND

The Caribbean coast of Mexico is located in the state of Quintana Roo, which spans the eastern side of the Yucatán Peninsula and is bordered by the states of Campeche and Yucatán, to the west and northwest respectively. Though Chetumal is the capital of Quintana Roo, Cancún is the region's biggest and most famous city. It was the first major tourist resort to be developed along the Caribbean coast, and in the four decades since the city was founded, it has become one of the largest and most important tourist towns in Mexico. It continues to draw millions of visitors each year, and, as the location of the international airport, it is the jumping-off point for any destination in the region.

Heading south along Highway 307 from Cancún, the stretch of shoreline between Playa del Carmen and Punto Allen is known as the Riviera Maya. For many years, this string of coastal communities remained quiet and relatively unvisited, even as the resort at Cancún blossomed throughout the 1980s and '90s. With time, tourists inevitably found their way down to these quieter, more inexpensive, and more laid-back Caribbean hideaways, and development followed. Today, the largest of these "small" resorts is Playa del Carmen, with around 150,000 permanent residents. Just south of Playa, Tulum is the site of a large, seaside archaeological site, which overlooks the town's beautiful white-sand beaches.

In addition to mainland communities, there are several islands off the Caribbean coast with resident populations. Just across from Cancún, you can take a ferry to Isla Mujeres, a small six-mile-long island with white-sand beaches and a very easygoing attitude. Cozumel, a popular destination with scuba divers, is the largest island off the Quintana Roo coast, located right across from Playa del Carmen.

© INDI ERICKSEN

Hammocks and *palapas* dot a beach on Isla Mujeres.

Climate

The eastern coast of Quintana Roo has a tropical climate, with warm and balmy weather year-round. It is slightly cooler during the winter months, with temperatures ranging from the low 70s to high 80s F (around 21–32°C), and warmest from mid-May through August, when the temperature can peak at more than 100°F (38°C). There is a short rainy season, which typically runs from August to November; during this time, afternoon thundershowers are common. As has been unfortunately witnessed on several occasions, the Caribbean coast is often affected by tropical storms during the Atlantic hurricane season, which runs from June to November annually.

Natural Environment

The state of Quintana Roo, like all the Yucatán Peninsula, is located atop a flat limestone bedrock covered with thick jungle. There is little surface water in the region, though the porous limestone sediment has given rise to long subterranean rivers and natural sinkholes called cenotes. (Once a source of drinking water for the Maya, they are popular for swimming today.) Along the coasts, white-sand beaches are punctuated with swampy mangrove estuaries and wide lagoons, which shelter fragile aquatic ecosystems and bird communities.

A whole other world exists beneath the surface of the Caribbean's warm and turquoise waters. Running all along the eastern coast of the Yucatán Peninsula to the Bay Islands in Honduras, the great Mesoamerican Reef is the largest barrier reef in the Atlantic, home to hundreds of fish species, dolphins,

PRIME LIVING LOCATIONS

ATLANTIC HURRICANE SEASON

On September 14, 1988, a category five storm named Hurricane Gilbert hit the Caribbean coast of Mexico, making landfall at the island of Cozumel. This massive, slow-moving storm pummeled the shoreline with 180 mile per hour winds and waves of up to 23 feet. The largest Atlantic storm on record at the time, Gilbert caused damage, landslides, and flooding in countries as far away as Venezuela and Honduras. In a matter of hours, it had beached ships, ripped trees from the ground, destroyed thousands of homes, and left more than 200 people dead along the coast of Quintana Roo.

At this moment in its history, Cancún was at the top of its game: a sparkling beach paradise in full development, with high-rise hotels and luxury condominiums spanning its white beaches. Mexico's Caribbean coast hadn't been directly hit by a major storm in decades, and a storm the size of Gilbert had never been recorded. As a result, the region wasn't fully prepared for the strength of the storm and the resulting damage.

Fortunately, Mexico's Caribbean coast has become far better equipped to deal with tropical storms. In 2005, Hurricane Wilma hit the Quintana Roo coast at Felipe Carrillo Puerto. Although this category five storm was the largest ever recorded (beating Gilbert for that dubious title), the local governments took early action. Classes were suspended at public schools, and residents of low-lying areas were evacuated. As Wilma hit the coast, three-story waves hit the shore, 64 inches of rain fell, and many of the area's beaches were permanently altered in size and shape; however, the impact on human life was much lower, with only eight people reported dead as result of the storm. The resulting damage, without calculating the loss of tourist dollars, was estimated at around US$7.5 billion.

Hurricanes don't strike every year, but for anyone living along the Caribbean coast, they are a threat from June to November (with August and September usually seeing the worst storms). Before a hurricane, secure your home, stock up on essential supplies, and develop an emergency plan for both your family and your pets. The National Hurricane Center (www.nhc.noaa.gov/prepare) offers tips for preparing for a tropical cyclone and creating an emergency kit.

sharks, manatees, a slew of crustaceans, and loggerhead, hawksbill and green sea turtles. There are also sea turtle nesting beaches along the coast, particularly in and around the community of Akumal.

While the coastline has been developed for tourism and fishing, most of the interior in the Yucatán Peninsula is still rather remote, inaccessible, and forbidding, covered in thick tropical jungle. Here, fruit trees and hardwoods like ceiba, mahogany, and cedar provide an emerald canopy to the jungle floor, where orchids grow wild. Deep in this verdant ecosystem, a variety of unusual creatures thrive, including toucans, macaws, anteaters, tapirs, howler monkeys, and the elusive puma.

© INDI ERICKSEN

Tropical jungle surrounds the pyramids in Cobá, northwest of Tulum.

Culture

The Yucatán Peninsula was an important center of the Classic and Late Classic Mayan culture; though many of the region's most famous sites are located in the state of Yucatán, powerful city-states and smaller communities also cropped up along the Caribbean coast. East of Tulum, the city of Cobá flourished around A.D. 200–600, controlling a vast swath of peninsula until the rise of Chichén Iztá. Right on the coast, the Late Classic city of Tulum reached prominence in the 13th century.

Visiting the ruins of these great city-states is one of the undeniable highlights of a trip to the region, and many ethnic Maya continue to live in the state, particularly in the southwestern regions, far from tourist centers like Cancún. Along the coast, the area has attracted Mexicans from across the republic, creating a distinctly amiable and Mexican atmosphere, despite the constant stream of international tourism. Although most of the region's large cities are international places, smaller towns in Quintana Roo are still home to more traditional communities. Throughout the Yucatán Peninsula, food and markets, traditional crafts, and local customs reflect the Mayan people who have lived on this land for centuries, in addition to the traditions from greater Mexico.

Language

Like all of Mexico, Spanish is the official language along the Caribbean coast, though English is also widely spoken in the tourist areas. Residents may not need to learn Spanish in order to go about their daily lives, but they will have a richer and more fulfilling experience if they do. In addition, a large population still speaks Yucatec Maya (generally just referred to as Maya) throughout the peninsula. You are most likely to hear Maya spoken in smaller communities rather than tourist areas.

DAILY LIFE

The impossibly perfect combination of powdery white sand and crystalline sea has won the heart of many a weary traveler, though visitors are often surprised to find that the Caribbean coast of Mexico is also a friendly, livable, and culturally interesting place. Most people who relocate to the Caribbean coast choose this area because they are avid divers or are looking to get away from the grind of daily life. Websites and books about the region are peppered with phrases about the easy pace of life in "paradise."

Maybe it's the warm weather or the calming effect of the sea, but life generally is a lot more slow paced for most people in the Caribbean—though not necessarily for everyone. The rapid development of the Yucatán Peninsula has created quite a bit of local industry; while some people come to chill out or retire, others come to work or raise families. There are foreigners employed as English teachers, in time-share sales, and in real estate, as well as those who open their own businesses, like bed-and-breakfasts or restaurants, or telecommute to their jobs back home.

Your lifestyle, however, depends in large part on where you plan to live.

IF I HAD A HAMMOCK

A swinging hammock, or *hamaca*, is the perfect accessory for a backyard garden or an ocean-view balcony. Durable, attractive, and surprisingly inexpensive, handmade hammocks are sold throughout Yucatán. Once you've learned how to position yourself in a hammock (try lying diagonally to find a balance), they can be extremely comfortable and supportive. In fact, many Yucatecos prefer sleeping in a hammock to sleeping on a mattress.

The best Yucatec hammocks are made of brightly colored, finely woven cotton. When buying your first hammock, try a specialty shop, like Hamacas El Aguacate (www.hamacaselaguacate.com.mx) in Mérida, where you can also give the hammock a test swing before you buy. Later, when you have a good idea of what makes a hammock comfortable, you can browse the artisanal market or buy from beach vendors. A great one-person hammock often doesn't cost more than US$30; larger two-person hammocks are also common and cost just a touch more.

Once you've got your hammock home, you can hang it between two metal hooks about 13 feet apart (you can adjust for comfort). Climb in, recline, and swing along with the spirit of Yucatán.

a small plaza with restaurants in Playa del Carmen

Cancún will definitely keep you plugged into the modern world—there are plenty of dining, shopping, and nightlife options to keep you entertained for years, while the Riviera Maya remains more low-key and "away from it all," despite its growth and relatively modern atmosphere. Along the coast, Playa del Carmen is the chicest choice; there are great restaurants, bars, and entertainment options in this hip beach town, without the high-rise hotels in Cancún. If you want to really depart from the modern world, quieter cities along the coast or, even more drastically, slightly to the north in the jungle will bring you an entirely off-the-grid panorama.

Cost of Living

Like most parts of Mexico, the cost of living is extremely variable along the Caribbean coast. As it's an internationally popular tourist destination, luxury can come with a significant price tag here, especially in well-known places like Cancún or Playa del Carmen. Like many beach communities, including Puerto Vallarta or Cabo San Lucas, costs here tend to run higher than in the interior of the country. However, if you are willing to forgo the vacation lifestyle and live like a local, the area can be surprisingly reasonable. If you want to keep your cost of living down, look for cheaper rents a few blocks from the beach or in a residential neighborhood, shop in traditional markets, and eat at the more understated local joints. Note that air-conditioning can be a significant cost, especially during the summer.

Health Care

For health care and dental work, Cancún has the most options in the region, though there are also several hospitals and clinics in Playa del Carmen, which have English-speaking doctors on staff. If you live in a smaller town like Tulum, you will likely have to travel to see the doctor. Generally, both medical and dental services are far more inexpensive on the Caribbean coast than in the United States. The area does not have a robust medical tourism industry, like other states.

Food and Shopping

Eating well—and inexpensively—is one of the best parts of life in this abundant region, where tropical fruits grow naturally and the ocean provides a bounty of fresh fish and seafood. There are big chain grocery stores all along the Caribbean coast, but savvy shoppers will take advantage of the inexpensive, traditional markets in the area. In Cancún, you can get excellent fresh produce, meats, cheese, tortillas, and prepared foods at the Mercado 23, in addition to clothes and shoes, kitchenware, crafts, and other necessities. Along the Riviera Maya, you will find smaller traditional markets for grocery shopping, where you can buy mangoes, tomatoes, gourds, herbs, peppers, banana leaves, and a slew of other tropical produce.

For clothing, there are beach shops and clothing boutiques in Cancún and Playa del Carmen, though most foreigners find they still buy many of their staples at home (prices can be elevated here). In addition to smaller shops, you can pick up some necessities, like socks or beach towels, at chain stores like Soriana or Costco, which are also located in Cancún and Playa. If you live in a smaller community, you'll likely travel to a larger city for occasional shopping trips.

Recreation and Entertainment

Living along the Caribbean coast is all about a slower pace of life, but taking advantage of outdoor activities is also a must. Kayaking, snorkeling, swimming, and scuba diving are all popular activities with locals, as are day trips to more remote beaches like Xcalacoco. You will find tour operators equipped for adventure sports, like zip lining and parasailing, though most of these activities are geared toward tourists rather than locals. In addition to beach-related activities, many expatriates participate in social groups, volunteer, take yoga or language classes, or otherwise get involved in their local communities.

In addition to public beaches, there are several ecoparks along the Quintana

Roo coast, where visitors pay an admission ticket to access beautiful wilderness and beach areas. The most popular is Xel-Ha, a massive water park located in a beautiful coastal inlet, which the resort calls a "natural aquarium." Admission includes access to the grounds for swimming and snorkeling, as well as unlimited drinks and snacks; it can be a great day for families. Just south of Playa del Carmen, Xcaret is another ecopark in the region. For a more low-key (and equally gorgeous) wilderness experience, you can visit Sian Ka'an, a huge biosphere reserve and UNESCO World Heritage Site, which includes a portion of the barrier reef.

Living on the coast, nightlife is never hard to come by. For a slushy drink with an umbrella, a wild night out, or an upscale meal, Cancún is the locus for nightlife in the region, a place known as much for its spring-break-style parties as its beautiful beaches. For the young and hip, Playa del Carmen has largely replaced Cancún as the region's nightlife hub; trendy clubs in Playa may even fly in popular DJs from Mexico City during the high season.

WHERE TO LIVE

There are a lot of options along the Caribbean coast, and the area seems to grow with every season. Most beachfront condos or luxury homes are rented to tourists, who are happy to pay several hundred dollars (or more!) a night for their piece of paradise. If you are moving to the area permanently, you'll have more options. Those who don't need an ocean view or private beach access can find great deals, either in the city of Cancún, in Playa del Carmen, or in smaller communities along the coast. Even living five or six blocks from the beach can save you several hundred dollars a month. Along the Riviera Maya, if you look on the northwestern (nonbeach) side of Highway 307, you can find particularly good deals on lots and rentals. If you are investing in a property, take a good look at the area around you and consider how it may change in the next 5–10 years.

Housing

Mexico's Caribbean coast is in rapid development, so there are a wide range of options and lifestyles available. You can find folks living in rustic homes with palm-thatched roofs, just as luxury condominiums and beachfront villas are being rushed into development all along the coastline. More upscale towns like Akumal have many multibedroom, ocean-view vacation homes with private pools and gardens, while bigger cities like Cancún have high-end developments, as well as more low-key residential neighborhoods where simple concrete houses are surprisingly cheap and luxury-free. Since the region was developed only recently, most housing is modern (no colonial properties here), and paint jobs tend toward pastel, Caribbean-inspired hues.

Cancún and Isla Mujeres

The great glittering city of Cancún is divided into two distinct sections: the tourist area, where high-rise hotels march across a gorgeous white-sand beach, and the *centro,* the residential city center. Most tourists head straight to the hotel zone, while most residents live in the main town. Note that time-shares and vacation rentals are generally located in the hotel district, as is the beautiful area around the lagoon and golf course, which is one of the Caribbean's most upscale residential communities.

For those who have visited Cancún on vacation, it may be hard to imagine living there long-term. But beyond the all-inclusive resorts and nightclubs, there is a mellow, tree-filled, tropical city, which can make a nice home base on the Caribbean Sea. In town, there is an excellent traditional market and plenty of locals-only restaurants, as well as a range of housing options. Just outside the hotel zone, there are modern homes and luxury condos, and, if you are on a serious budget, you can rent a very simple place for less than US$500 a month in a traditionally Mexican neighborhood (with costs rising from there, if you want something furnished, closer to the beach, or with more comforts). Homes and condos for sale run the gamut in Cancún, from under US$200,000 to over US$1,000,000. An average family home in the residential areas of the city generally costs around US$300,000, though luxury condos and beachfront villas near the tourist areas are much pricier. Though it is slightly more expensive than other parts of Mexico, Cancún remains a surprisingly well-priced option for those willing to live simply. Do keep in mind, though, that with so many vacationers living it up around you, living simply may take greater willpower than in other destinations! On that note, some residents find the constant stream of tourism and party atmosphere grating; spend some time in Cancún before you settle down there.

From Cancún, you can take a ferry to the teensy island of Isla Mujeres, about 15 minutes by boat. Most real estate here is designed as a vacation rental or time-share, and prices can be high, as the tiny bit of available land on this paradise island is in short supply. Still, a few expatriates have settled or retired in Isla Mujeres, or they spend winters on the island and summers at home. Others simply come to Isla Mujeres from Cancún to swim at Playa Norte, a turquoise beach with gentle waves and a sandy floor. There isn't a lot of ground to cover, so most people use golf carts and mopeds to get around this teensy isle.

Playa del Carmen

Playa del Carmen was once a small fishing town on the Quintana Roo coast, accessible via the bumpy, tree-covered Highway 307. After a port was built to run a ferry to the island of Cozumel (which lies directly east of Playa del Carmen), the city began to grow. As the roads improved and the jungle was cut back, Playa became a popular alternative to Cancún. Its long white-sand beach and gentle surf are nice for swimming and sunbathing, and the city has an appealingly laid-back atmosphere, with small hotels, lots of mellow hangout spots, great shopping, yoga classes, and a range of dining options, from gourmet to street grub.

One of the fastest-growing cities in Mexico, Playa del Carmen has all the bases covered. Here, you'll find a range of grocery stores, health care facilities, boutiques and clothing shops, language schools, banks, real estate agencies, and other services. For fun and nightlife, the focus of the town is the Quinta Avenida (5th Avenue), a paved pedestrian walkway just behind the beach. It's the perfect place for people-watching with a *cappuccino frio* or wandering around in flip-flops while window shopping. For restaurantgoers, food here is among the best along the coast, with a range of internationally inspired options as well as great Mexican joints.

The residential district in Playa runs north from the Quinta Avenida, becoming increasingly rustic and ramshackle with every block farther from the beach. For nice properties, prices in Playa del Carmen are higher than most of the region (even Cancún can be a better place to look for deals, depending

© INDI ERICKSEN

an overgrown property for sale in Playa del Carmen

PRIME LIVING LOCATIONS

on what you are looking for). You can still find deals, though; the farther from the shore, the more inexpensive the property will likely be.

Playa del Carmen has a big real estate market, which even includes properties under US$100,000, though average costs for a home or condo are closer to US$250,000 in residential parts of town. Like everywhere along the coast, prices are much higher for waterfront lots and luxury developments. Many real estate agents principally represent higher end developments in the US$300,000 to US$600,000 range and up.

Cozumel

The largest island off the coast of the Yucatán Peninsula, Cozumel has a longer history with foreigners than most of the Riviera Maya. In fact, it has been popular with divers since Jacques Cousteau first visited the island in 1961, touting it as one of the world's most beautiful reefs and coastlines. Even today, Cozumel is a renowned spot for scuba diving and snorkeling, with incredible marine life swimming around in its transparent, turquoise waters. Expatriates who settle down here are generally escaping the daily grind, and some work in the dive industry as dive masters.

San Miguel de Cozumel is the island's only city, and it's the landing dock for cruise ships. There's the inevitable bustle of commerce and people where the cruisers land, but residents will generally enjoy a low-key atmosphere on the island. When it comes to the nuts and bolts of island life, you can find all the basics in Cozumel: banks, restaurants, pharmacies, Laundromats, and a medical clinic. In terms of entertainment, shops stay open into the evening, and there are some nice restaurants where you can have dinner. Because it has a cruise ship dock, Cozumel does have a more raucous zone, though residents will find it's entirely avoidable.

Like Isla Mujeres, there are very defined limits to how much Cozumel can expand; in other words, land comes at a premium here, with prices for lots, houses, and rentals running over the average for similar properties in Cancún. That said, there are fixer-uppers for less than US$100,000, though you'll likely spend double or triple that, even for something simple.

Akumal

Just south of Playa del Carmen, the small community of Akumal is growing, but it still feels a bit more subdued than its neighbors. Here, upscale residential communities are built along several pretty bays with gentle, sparkling blue water. There are a few places to eat, but don't come here for nightlife and parties; Akumal is a quiet, lazy, traffic-free town where even a golf cart is sufficient transportation.

When it comes to daily life, Akumal has most of the bases covered: There are several good supermarkets and a fishmonger in town, ATMs, pharmacies, a few doctors, and some cute beachfront restaurants for a plate of fish tacos. Plus, it's wired for Internet, cable television, and all other communication services, so you'll never feel cut off. However, you'll have to travel to other towns for some basic services, like banks, veterinarians, hospitals, or clothing shops.

Because tourism is more limited in Akumal, it can be a great place to live peacefully; however, it isn't necessarily the best spot for people on a budget. Akumal's residential neighborhoods are generally upscale, and many private homes have pools, patios, multiple bedrooms, and views of the water. You can find more-inexpensive options in the jungle or in more undeveloped areas around town. Both Akumal and Tulum have much smaller real estate markets than Playa del Carmen and Cancún, but the housing prices are generally on par with the rest of the Caribbean Coast, in terms of ranges and averages.

Tulum

One of the most distinctive communities on the coast, Tulum was once the site of an important Postclassic Mayan city, today a beautiful archaeological site overlooking the turquoise sea. Despite this unique scenery, Tulum was not always a tourist magnet. For many years, even as Playa del Carmen blossomed into a full resort, Tulum remained famous for its inexpensive

PRIME LIVING LOCATIONS

© INDI ERICKSEN

Tourists flock to the ruins of the Mayan port of Tulum.

beach *palapas,* where you could pitch a hammock along the sugary white-sand beaches for a couple dollars a day. Though prices have risen, the halcyon days aren't over. Even as the tourist sector grows by leaps and bounds, Tulum has maintained a somewhat alternative, laid-back atmosphere. It is a popular place for spas and yoga retreats, as well as gourmet locavore restaurants and ecohotels.

Tulum itself is somewhat spread out: The ruins are located aside the beach area (Tulum Playa), while the town itself straddles Highway 307 to the northwest of the coast. Downtown, you'll find some residential streets, as well as restaurants and shops, language schools, banks, and other necessities. Most hotels and some of the best restaurants are located right on the beach. If you are looking to live in Tulum, cast a wide net; you may find something in town or along the highway. There are also a few condominium complexes planned for the area.

GETTING AROUND
Air
The largest airport in the region is Cancún International Airport (CUN), which runs daily flights to locations across Mexico, the United States, Canada, and Europe, as well as more limited service to South America and the Caribbean (notably Havana, Cuba). Transporting more than 12 million passengers annually, it is the country's second-busiest airport, after Mexico City. If you live in Cancún or anywhere along the Riviera Maya, you will likely use CUN as your primary connection to the rest of the world. From the airport, you can arrange taxi or shuttle service to any of the towns along the coast.

Car
Owning a car can be useful for residents of the Caribbean coast, especially if they live in a more remote area or are going to be lugging groceries or kids around. Even if you only use your car for day trips, many

an intersection along the coastal highway

of the best sights, hidden beaches, and interesting ruins are harder to get to using public transportation.

Public Transportation

First-class and second-class buses run between all the cities on the Riviera Maya and Cancún, as well as the major archaeological sites. There are also *combis,* collective transport vans, that run between Cancún and Playa del Carmen 24 hours a day, and more *combis* connecting Playa with the communities farther south. Ferries depart for Cozumel from Playa del Carmen every couple hours 7 A.M.–10 P.M.

Taxi

There are taxis available in every town, and most offer very low rates for intercity travel. In towns like Playa del Carmen, Tulum, or Akumal, you may also be able to get to most places you need to go by simply walking.

Mérida

The capital of the state of Yucatán, Mérida is a big old-fashioned city known for its stately colonial downtown, tropical climate, and vibrant local culture. With almost a million people, this handsome metropolis may be one of the biggest cities in Mexico, but it is still a warm and easygoing place with colorful cultural traditions. Here, celebration, music, and dance are a big part of daily life, and you'll frequently hear live bands playing in the streets downtown. Every Sunday night, the blocks around the main square are closed to traffic for a festive local music and dance party. At the same time, the city offers a fairly large dose of sophistication, with some fine museums and wonderful restaurants.

Visually, Mérida is splendid, its streets lined with colonial-era mansions and some of the most historic buildings in Mexico. The Catedral de San Ildefonso, which overlooks Mérida's pleasant tree-filled central square, was built in the early years of New Spain in the 16th century, as were many of the stone churches and public plazas that dot the city center. There are also many archways, public squares, and other neoclassical or French-inspired architecture from the Porfiriato era of the late 19th century.

Mérida is less trafficked than the Caribbean coast, or even cultural havens like Oaxaca. However, it does receive quite a bit of tourism during the winter months, principally from north-of-the-border travelers and snowbirds, as well as from national vacationers. As an expatriate destination, it is also on the rise, as its many charms, low cost of living, and friendly community make it a particularly appealing place to settle down.

THE LAY OF THE LAND

The city of Mérida is the capital of the state of Yucatán, located about 20 miles inland from the Gulf of Mexico. Mérida's population is close to a million, making it the largest city on the Yucatán Peninsula, as well as one of the biggest cities in Mexico. Even so, Mérida maintains a rather charming and provincial atmosphere, especially downtown, where there is a growing art scene, frequent live music in the streets, and a pleasant hum of diners and tourists day and night.

Mérida's central square is the Plaza Mayor, also called the *zócalo*. This 16th-century plaza remains the physical and cultural heart of the city, and it is in the *centro histórico* that you'll find the majority of Mérida's colonial architecture, interesting regional museums, restaurants, and markets. Traditionally affluent residential neighborhoods extend north from the city center toward the Yucatán Country Club. To the south of the city center, there are large poor and working-class neighborhoods, typically a bit grittier and less popular with foreigners. Throughout the city center, even-numbered streets run north to south, while odd-numbered streets run east to west. Addresses here generally note the house number and street number, as well as the cross streets.

Around Mérida and in the greater state of Yucatán, there are many culturally interesting and beautiful small towns, archaeological sites, and ecological attractions. From the flamingo colony at Celustún to the massive Mayan ruins of Uxmal, Yucatán is one of the most vibrant states in Mexico. And, though it isn't a coastal city, Mérida is very close to the Gulf Coast. On weekends, many city residents head to the wide sandy beach in Progreso, which is also home to a small community of foreign residents.

History

What is today the state of Yucatán was once the center of the powerful Mayan civilization, which flourished throughout the peninsula during the Terminal Classic and early Postclassic eras of Mesoamerican history. Major Mayan cities flourished and collapsed as smaller city-states also cropped up around the region. Just 75 miles from Mérida, the city of Chichén Itzá reached its peak around A.D. 600, following the fall of Tikal in Guatemala. Mayapan, just over 25 miles from Mérida, grew in the wake of Chichén Iztá's decline, while south of Mérida, the city of Uxmal dominated the western peninsula from roughly A.D. 850 to 950, peaking as the Mayan civilization went into decline.

The cause of the collapse of Classic Mayan civilization is unknown, and it is the subject of great debate among anthropologists. However, long after their largest cities were abandoned, the Maya continued to live in great numbers on the Yucatán Peninsula. In 1542, Spanish conquistadors took control of the Mayan city of T'ho, which was still thriving when the Spanish arrived in the Americas. They renamed the city Mérida, after the Spanish city of the same name, dismantling T'ho's pyramids and using the stones to build a new Spanish city. One of the fruits of their efforts, the Catedral de San Ildefonso, stands on the site of the former Mayan temple in central Mérida.

Mérida and the surrounding region never fully integrated into greater Mexican society, and throughout the colonial era, it was governed more directly by Spain than Mexico City. During the War of Independence, Yucatecos fought for their own sovereignty, not on behalf of the Mexican army, though they eventually joined the Mexican empire and, later, the Mexican republic.

Nonetheless, frustrations came to a head during the War of the Castes. From 1847 to 1901, the native people of the Yucatán Peninsula rose up against the white, European leaders of the region in a violent conflict known as the Caste War of Yucatán. Though the conflict eventually ended with the peninsula returning to the Mexican republic, resentment lingered into the 20th century in all three Yucatec states. Today, Yucatán and its people remain culturally independent of the larger country, with traditions in food, culture, craft, and religion entirely their own.

Climate

Mérida has a hot and humid climate, with temperatures hovering in the 80s and 90s F (around 27–37°C) throughout the year. Since it is not located on the coast, it is warmer in Mérida than in Yucatán's coastal cities, where there are stronger breezes offshore; Mérida does receive the benefit of some light trade winds, though. The northeastern corner of the Yucatán Peninsula, including Mérida, is actually rather dry, receiving a third of the rainfall of the southerly parts of the peninsula adjoining Guatemala and Belize, where as much as 118 inches of rain can fall per year. As a result, the ecosystems around Mérida are generally broadleaf forest, rather than the more verdant rainforest along the Caribbean coastline.

Culture

Continuously inhabited for centuries, the city of Mérida is a vibrant mix of people and traditions. Throughout the colonial era, the Spanish made numerous attempts to colonize the region, and though they left a lasting imprint on local religion, architecture, and customs, they were never fully successful in eradicating native culture. Today, the world's largest group of ethnic Maya lives on the Yucatán Peninsula, and much of Mérida's culture borrows from the Maya's age-old traditions. The Mayan language is still spoken around the state, and the region's unique cuisine leans heavily on native flavors.

At the same time, modern Mérida's myriad influences are not limited to the Spanish and Maya. The greater Caribbean region introduced many traditions in music and dance, and the popular *guayabera* (a lightweight men's blouse) is traditionally worn at weddings and special events in Mérida, as it is in Cuba. At the end of the 19th century, Lebanese immigrants arrived in Mexico to escape Ottoman rule, many settling in the state of Yucatán (a second wave arrived in the 1920s and '30s). Though they largely assimilated into the greater culture, Mexico's Middle Eastern population is largely visible through their influence on the regional cuisine, where dishes like *jocoque* (a fresh, spreadable cow's milk cheese), *pan arabe* (pita bread), and kibbe (seasoned meatballs) are common fare.

In and around the downtown area, Mérida has many cultural attractions, including the Museo Regional de Antropología (Regional Anthropology Museum), Museo de Arte Contemporáneo (Contemporary Art Museum), and the Museo de la Ciudad (City Museum), in addition to its wonderful mix of colonial-era and 19th-century architecture. There is a growing local art scene, and—not surprising considering the excellent traditional cuisine—some wonderful restaurants.

Language

Mérida has become increasingly popular with tourists and expatriates, which has made English more prevalent in the city, especially in service industries. However, Mérida and environs are predominantly Spanish-speaking areas; as an expatriate, your experience will be far better if you learn to communicate in Spanish. Fortunately, there are many inexpensive and high-quality language schools in Mérida—if you don't speak Spanish already, consider enrolling in courses when you arrive. In smaller communities near Mérida, as well as in the city itself, ethnic Maya still speak their native tongue in addition to Spanish (and a very small percentage do not speak Spanish at all).

Cuisine

Yucatec food is among the most distinct and delicious cuisines in Mexico. Yucatecos make great use of pork, turkey, *lima* (a sour lemonlike fruit), and the condiment achiote, which is derived from the fruit of a shrub called *achiotl.*

© JULIE DOHERTY MEADE

Sopa de lima is a traditional dish from the state of Yucatán, made with chicken broth and lemon.

The blisteringly spicy habanero chili is also ubiquitous in the region, often served in fiery salsas with pickled onion. Some signature Yucatec dishes include *sopa de lima* (lemon soup), *cochinita pibil* (pulled pork marinated in spices), *papadzules* (egg-stuffed tortillas covered in a pumpkin-seed sauce and topped with more egg), and *queso relleno* (a hollowed-out Gouda cheese wheel filled with spiced ground beef).

DAILY LIFE

Mérida is a big and modern city with a charming colonial downtown district and an easygoing tropical atmosphere. While the city has attracted more expatriates—in addition to Mexicans relocating from other cities—it is not a place that offers the same contemporary lifestyle you might get in other big Mexican cities. For most residents, that's a good thing! Life in Mérida is about the simple pleasures, friends and family, and a sense of community.

Cost of Living

Mérida and its surrounding communities are fairly inexpensive relative to the rest of Mexico. You can always ratchet up your monthly budget with extras like eating out, going to the movies, buying imported wines, or other luxuries, but, on the whole, basics are very inexpensive. As Mérida becomes more popular with expatriates and Mexicans from other states, the cost of living is quickly inching up. Even so, it remains one of the most reasonably priced places to live in Mexico.

EXPAT PROFILE: ELLEN FIELDS

Ellen Fields knows a thing or two about expatriate life in Mérida. With her husband, Jim, she runs the popular website Yucatán Living, a massive archive of articles and information about visiting and moving to the Yucatán Peninsula. Here, Ellen shares her own take on her job, other expatriates, and life in Mérida:

How did you first visit the Yucatán Peninsula, and why did you move there?

We first visited looking for a place to move to. We were looking for something outside the USA, somewhere we could learn a second language, be in a European-style city with cathedrals and a central square, somewhere we could start a business, somewhere close to scuba diving (one of our passions), and a place from which we could get back to California easily.

What do you love about the area?

The variety of experiences, the people, the culture, the weather, the colors, the skies, the food...there is a lot to love, and we discover more all the time.

Tell me a little about your website, Yucatan Living. How did it get started?

We had been doing websites for other people (still do), many of whom were in the tourist business. We realized, however, that there were a lot of people both looking to get out of the United States and Canada, and a lot of English speakers moving to the Yucatán. They needed to know things. We were photographers and knew how to write, and we had a lot of information to share. So YucatanLiving.com was born. After many years in operation, it continues to fill a growing niche.

What is something anyone should know about the state of Yucatán before deciding to move there?

It gets hot here. If you don't like the heat, stay out of the kitchen. On the other hand, I never thought I liked the heat. But I have grown fond of it and the culture that has built up around it.

I also think it is important that people move to another country with the understanding that they are guests, and not try to change the country they are coming to in a big way.

Are there many expatriates in the area, and if so, what type of people does Mérida or other Yucatán locales seem to attract?

There are expatriates here, but if you never want to see one, you don't have to. It isn't an expatriate community in that sense. Mérida is a city of over a million people, and the expats are spread out. The biggest concentrations are along the beach and in the historic *centro*, of course. This area seems to attract people who want to explore Mexico and get to know the country and the culture. There are mostly retired people, or people starting new businesses. And there are a growing number of young professionals with families.

Do you see the expatriate population growing in the future?

Yes, everything points to it. The demographics, the high cost of living in the two northern countries, and the increasing availability of goods and services globally.

Of particular note, housing is cheaper in Mérida than in most other parts of the country, especially for those who'd like to rent or buy a historic or colonial-era home. In the downtown area, a large home might rent between US$500 and US$1,000 per month (less for something basic), and you can still find simple fixer-uppers for sale for less than US$100,000. One thing to keep in mind is that Mérida is hot and humid, so many people use air-conditioning almost year-round. When planning your budget, remember to factor in a higher energy bill.

Shopping

Mérida's inexpensive and well-stocked municipal market, Mercado Lucas de Gálvez, is located southeast of the Plaza Mayor. The entire district surrounding the market is a busy commerce zone bustling with shops and shoppers. Head here for the best prices on fruits, vegetables, flowers, fresh fish, and sundry housewares and clothing. In addition to the main market area, there are small local markets all over town, which can also be great spots to eat or pick up food for the house. Like all big cities in Mexico, Mérida has plenty of national and international chain stores for grocery shopping, including Superama, Chedraui, and many others. Most of these carry some imported items in addition to basics like milk, bread, pasta, cheese, and other items.

Mérida is also famous for some regional crafts, including handmade hammocks, panama hats, and *guayaberas* (traditional lightweight men's shirts). You can find these in the market area or in shops around the *centro.* For home decoration, Mérida's colorful concrete and ceramic tiles, called *mosiaco,* are produced and sold in the city.

Health Care

There are both public and private hospitals in Mérida, as well as a good medical school at the state university, Universidad Autónoma de Yucatán. Most expatriates use private facilities, as health care costs are generally very inexpensive here.

WHERE TO LIVE

Whether you choose to live in central Mérida, in a suburban neighborhood, or on the nearby coast, there are lots of housing options in the area. Many foreigners are immediately attracted to central Mérida, and with good reason. The downtown district gets the most action, and there are many beautiful, historic, and colonial properties both for rent and sale. However, for those who'd prefer a little less action and a little more quiet, there are outlying neighborhoods that may also fit the bill.

Housing

There are beautiful historic homes throughout Mérida's central neighborhoods. These centuries-old buildings are often worn and full of character, built with thick stucco-covered stone walls, incredibly high ceilings, and wrought-iron details. A wonderfully commonplace feature in homes of this region, floors are often made of *mosiaco,* ceramic tiles in bold colors and patterns. Because these tiles have been produced in the region for centuries, many old homes have lovely floors already installed; if they don't, it is inexpensive to pour concrete and lay the tiles yourself.

You can still find a historic fixer-upper in Mérida at low prices, a rarity in many parts of Mexico today. However, for those who would prefer to move into a fully functional home, there are also renovated colonial houses with modern kitchens and bathrooms, as well as air-conditioning systems, for sale. Though its traditional appeal is the colonial areas, Mérida also has some modern communities in the northern neighborhoods, which some expatriates prefer to the older places in the center of town.

Central Mérida

The neighborhoods of central Mérida are the oldest, busiest, and most bustling parts of town, filled with blocks and blocks of historic homes, old pastel-painted chapels, and lovely tree-filled urban parks and plazas. There are a few options to rent or buy in the blocks directly surrounding the **zócalo,** but you can spread your housing search out much farther, as lovely residential neighborhoods extend around the center of town in all directions, especially to the north and to the west. Though the entire city has a fairly relaxed atmosphere, there is a pleasant bustle of people and traffic downtown. Those who don't mind a bit of noise and energy will be happiest here.

Traditionally one of the more popular areas with Mérida's expatriates, the **Santiago** neighborhood is located about four blocks from the main square and surrounds a lovely urban park called the Parque Santiago. There are shops and restaurants around the park, as well as a traditional market for food shopping. A little farther west, the area around the Centenario Zoo and Parque Centenario has a mix of architecture, from simple concrete homes to belle epoque mansions built during the late 19th century. Among the residential neighborhoods in the northern *centro histórico,* the **Santa Ana** is another historic district with a growing arts and gallery scene.

Most expatriates tend toward the neighborhoods north and northwest of the main plaza, but there is a nice central square with an 18th-century church at the center of the **San Juan** neighborhood, south of the Plaza Mayor. Here, you'll find a bit of commerce and bustle, as well as some good deals on older homes. The twin neighborhoods of **San Sebastian** and **Ermita** have also begun to attract more attention, lower prices making them a good alternative in the central district.

North Mérida

Many nice and newer neighborhoods spread north from the city center. Although most of these areas don't have the same energy you'd find downtown, they are well connected to the *centro* by car or by city bus, and they offer a slightly quieter and more peaceful setting.

Heading north from the Santa Ana and passing the Centro Médico de las Americas, the lovely **Itzimna** neighborhood was also once its own township, built by wealthy Mérida families as a country resort. There is a mix of old colonial-era buildings, turn-of-the-20th-century architecture, and newer constructions along Itzimna's tree-filled streets; it feels more relaxed than the downtown district, even though it only takes about five minutes to drive to the *zócalo*.

Farther north, there are newer residential neighborhoods, like **Chuburná,** where you can find inexpensive modern homes in small, gated communities. These areas may be well priced, and many offer a more relaxed and suburban setting than in the center of town. There are also luxury apartments and condominiums in a development around the Yucatán Country Club.

Just a few miles northeast of the city, **Cholul** is a residential community that was once an independent township. Today it has become a part of the larger Mérida metropolitan area, yet it still feels far removed from the city, with a quiet country atmosphere. (A car is a necessity if you live out here.) Most homes available to foreigners in this area are modern constructions.

Progreso

Progreso is a port city on the Gulf of Mexico, popular with Mérida families and long the home of a small but happy expatriate community. Progreso has a wide, sandy beach located on a generally gentle and shallow stretch of surf. Here the winds off the Gulf make the weather slightly cooler than in the city of Mérida, and there are a few beachfront bars and restaurants to tip back a beer or a plate of seafood. Progreso receives cruise ships during the winter months, and there is a bustle of cruise-related tourism around the pier.

PRIME LIVING LOCATIONS

While Progreso isn't as famous as Cancún (and lacks that city's spectacular turquoise sea), many foreigners enjoy the low-key and low-cost options in Progreso. The town is particularly popular with snowbirds, who spend the winter at the beach and, as the temperature rises, head home for the summer months.

GETTING AROUND
Air

Southwest of the city center, Mérida's Manuel Crescencio Rejón International Airport (MID) has service to numerous national destinations, including Mexico City, Cancún, Guadalajara, and Monterrey. There are also more limited international routes with flights to Houston, Miami, and Havana. (Depending on your final destination, it may be easier to catch a connecting flight in Mexico City.)

Car and Taxi

Taxis are an inexpensive alternative if you're in a hurry. Many residents also own a car to facilitate grocery shopping or day trips around the region.

Bus

There are first- and second-class buses from Mérida to all other cities on the Yucatán Peninsula, as well as the capital in Mexico City. Within the city, major neighborhoods are linked by public bus routes.

RESOURCES

Consulates and Embassies

UNITED STATES
EMBASSY OF THE UNITED STATES IN MEXICO CITY
Paseo de la Reforma 305
Colonia Cuauhtemoc, México D.F. 06500
tel. 55/5080-2000
acsmexicocity@state.gov
http://mexico.usembassy.gov

CONSULATE GENERAL OF THE UNITED STATES IN GUADALAJARA
Progreso 175, Colonia Americana
Guadalajara, Jalisco, Mexico C.P. 44160
tel. 33/3268-2100
fax 33/3826-6549
guadalajara.usconsulate.gov

CONSULAR AGENT IN PUERTO VALLARTA
Paseo de los Cocoteros 85
Sur Paradise Plaza, Interior L-7
Nuevo Vallarta, Nayarit 63732
tel. 322/222-0069

CONSULAR AGENT IN SAN MIGUEL DE ALLENDE
Plaza La Luciernaga
Libramiento Jose Manuel Zavala No. 165,
Locales 4 y 5
San Miguel Allende, Guanajuato 37745
tel. 415/152-2357
fax 415/152-1588

CONSULAR AGENT IN OAXACA
Macedonio Alcala No. 407, Office 20
Oaxaca, Oaxaca 68000
tel. 951/514-3054 or 951/516-2853
fax 951/516-2701

CONSULAR AGENT IN CABO SAN LUCAS
Blvd. Marina Local C-4, Plaza Nautica
Cabo San Lucas, B.C.S. 23410
tel. 624/143-3566
fax 624/143-6750

U.S. CONSULAR AGENCY CANCÚN
Blvd. Kukulcan Km 13 ZH
Torre La Europea, Despacho 301
Cancún, Quintana Roo, Mexico C.P. 77500
tel. 998/883-0272
fax 998/883-1373

CONSULAR AGENT IN PLAYA DEL CARMEN
Calle 1 Sur, entre Av. 15 y Av. 20
Playa del Carmen, Quintana Roo 77710
tel. 984/873-0303
fax 984/873-0481

CANADA
EMBASSY OF CANADA IN MEXICO CITY
Schiller 529
Col. Bosque de Chapultepec, Del. Miguel Hidalgo
Mexico City D.F. 11580
tel. 55/5724-7900
www.canadainternational.gc.ca/mexico-mexique

CONSULATE OF CANADA IN GUADALAJARA
World Trade Center
Av. Mariano Otero 1249, Piso 8, Torre Pacífico
Col. Rinconada del Bosque 44530
tel. 33/3671-4740
fax 33/3671-4750
gjara@international.gc.ca

CONSULAR AGENCY OF CANADA IN CABO SAN LUCAS
Plaza San Lucas, Carretera Transpeninsular Km 0.5, Local 82
Col. El Tezal 23454, Cabo San Lucas, Baja California Sur–Mexico
tel. 624/142-4333
fax 624/142-4262
lcabo@international.gc.ca

CONSULAR AGENCY OF CANADA IN CANCÚN
Centro Empresarial Oficina E7
Blvd. Kukulcan Km 12
Zona Hotelera
Cancún, Quintana Roo-Mexico 77599
tel. 998/883-3360 or 998/883-3361
fax 998/883-3232
cncun@international.gc.ca

CONSULAR AGENCY OF CANADA IN OAXACA
Multiplaza Brena, Pino Suárez 700, Local 11B
Col. Centro, Oaxaca, Oaxaca 68000
tel. 951/513-3777

fax 951/515-2147
oaxaca@canada.org.mx

CONSULAR AGENCY OF CANADA IN PLAYA DEL CARMEN

Plaza Paraíso Caribe, Oficina C21-24
Av. 10 Sur, Colonia Centro
Playa del Carmen, Quintana Roo 77710
tel. 984/803-2411
fax 984/803-2665

CONSULAR AGENCY OF CANADA IN PUERTO VALLARTA

Plaza Peninsula, Local Sub F
Blvd. Francisco Medina Ascencio 2485
Puerto Vallarta, Jalisco 48300
tel. 322/293-0098 or 332/293-0099
fax 322/293-2894
pvrta@international.gc.ca

EUROPE
BRITISH EMBASSY
Río Lerma 71
Col. Cuauhtémoc, México D.F. 06500
tel. 55/1670-3200
fax 55/1670-3224
http://ukinmexico.fco.gov.uk

EMBASSY OF GERMANY IN MEXICO CITY
Lord Byron No. 737
Col. Polanco Chapultepec, México D.F. 11560
tel. 55/5283-2200 or 55/5281-2588
info@embajada-alemana.org.mx
www.mexiko.diplo.de

EMBASSY OF IRELAND IN MEXICO
Cda. Blvd. Avila Camacho 76-3
Col. Lomas de Chapultepec, México D.F. 11000
tel. 55/5520-5803
fax 55/5520-5892
mexicoembassy@dfa.ie
www.irishembassy.com.mx

PACIFIC AND ASIA
AUSTRALIAN EMBASSY
Ruben Dario 55
Col. Bosque de Chapultepec, México D.F. 11580
tel. 55/1101-2200
fax 55/1101-2201
www.mexico.embassy.gov.au

NEW ZEALAND EMBASSY MEXICO
Jaime Balmes 8, Piso 4-404A
Col. Los Morales Polanco, México D.F. 11510
tel. 55/5283-9460
fax 55/5283-9480
www.nzembassy.com/mexico

MEXICAN EMBASSIES OVERSEAS
MEXICAN EMBASSY IN THE UNITED STATES
1911 Pennsylvania Ave.
Washington DC 20006
U.S. tel. 202/728-1600
http://embamex.sre.gob.mx/eua

MEXICAN EMBASSY IN CANADA
Plaza Juárez No. 20, Piso 19
Col. Centro, C.P. 06010, México D.F.
tel. 55/9159-5100 (within Mexico City)
http://embamex.sre.gob.mx/canada_eng

Planning Your Fact-Finding Trip

MEXICO TOURISM OFFICIAL WEBSITE
www.visitmexico.com
The Mexican government maintains this website for foreign visitors, with information about history, culture, and travel to popular tourist destinations.

CONSEJO NACIONAL PARA LA CULTURA Y LOS ARTES
(CONCULTA)
Av. Paseo de la Reforma 175, Piso 14
Col. Cuauhtémoc, Del. Cuauhtémoc 06500, México D.F.
tel. 55/4155-0200
www.conaculta.gob.mx
The National Council for Culture and Arts is the government body that oversees museums, arts and cultural organizations, and sponsorship for artistic projects.

RESOURCES

MEXCONNECT
www.mexconnect.com
Mexconnect features hundreds of feature articles on Mexican travel, food, history, and culture from independent contributors across the country. They also have advice about relocation and visas.

PEOPLE'S GUIDE TO MEXICO
www.peoplesguide.com
This website, by the authors of the book *People's Guide to Mexico,* offers practical advice, a travel blog, articles, and links that complement their popular guidebook about Mexican travel.

MÉXICO DESCONOCIDO
www.mexicodesconocido.com.mx
A Spanish-language travel magazine focusing on off-the-beaten-track destinations, interesting cultural traditions, and the natural environment throughout Mexico.

MOON
www.moon.com
Read excerpts from various Moon titles and tips from Moon authors, including many of the destinations featured in this book.

Making the Move

VISAS AND OFFICIALDOM

U.S. DEPARTMENT OF STATE
www.state.gov
The United States Department of State provides information on passports and visas, as well as travel advisories.

INSTITUTO NACIONAL DE MIGRACION
Homero 1832, Col. Los Morales Polanco
Delegación Miguel Hidalgo, México D.F. 11510
tel. 800/004-6264
www.inm.gob.mx
The National Institute of Migration is the branch of the federal government that oversees migration to Mexico, including the administration of resident visas.

Local Immigration Offices

MEXICO CITY
Av. Ejército Nacional 862
Col. Los Morales Sección Palmas
Delegación Miguel Hidalgo, México D.F. 11570
tel. 01/800-46264
informesdrdf@inami.gob.mx

GUADALAJARA
Alcalde No. 500 4 Palacio Federal
Col. Centro, C.P. Guadalajara, Jalisco 44280
tel. 333/942-0290
fespinosap@inami.gob.mx

SAN MIGUEL DE ALLENDE
Calzada de la Estación de FFCC s/n
San Miguel de Allende, Guanajuato 37769
tel. 415/152-8985 or 415/152-2542
cvillalpando@inami.gob.mx

OAXACA
Av. Independencia 709
Col. Centro, Oaxaca de Juárez, Oaxaca 68000
tel. 951/502-0004
aarredondog@inami.gob.mx

BAJA CALIFORNIA SUR
Lázaro Cardenas 1625
Col. Centro, Cabo San Lucas, B.C.S. 23410
tel. 624/105-1638
radame@inami.gob.mx

CANCÚN
Av. Carlos J. Nader, Supermanzana 5 Lote 1
Cancún, Quintana Roo 77500
tel. 998/881-3560
jarmas@inami.gob.mx

MÉRIDA
Av. Colón Núm 507
Col. García Ginerés, Mérida, Yucatán 97070
tel. 999/925-5009 or 999/925-7034
brosel@inami.gob.mx

IMMIGRATION AND RELOCATION ASSISTANCE

THE RELOCATION CONNECTION
Guadalajara, Jalisco
tel. 33/3686-0067
info@relomexico.com
www.relomexico.com

AJIJIC LAW
Carretera Oriente 58-D
Ajijic, Jalisco C.P. 45920, Mexico
info@ajijiclaw.com
www.ajijiclaw.com

PATTY GARCIA, IMMIGRATION ASSISTANCE
San Miguel de Allende
cell tel. 415/115-1078
patgar5@yahoo.com

SECRETARÍA DE RELACIONES EXTERIORES (SRE)
Av. Juárez 20, Col. Centro
México D.F.
tel. 55/3686-5100
www.sre.gob.mx
Office of the Mexican foreign ministry.

YUCATÁN EXPATRIATE SERVICES
Calle 25 157, Colonia García Ginerés, Mérida, Yucatán
tel. 999/927-2437
info@yucatanyes.com
www.yucatanexpatriateservices.com

U.S. EMBASSY
List of Attorneys in Mexico City
http://mexico.usembassy.gov/eng/eacs_attorneys.html

MOVING COMPANIES

MEXICO FORWARDING
2404 Wilson Rd.
Harlingen TX 78552
U.S. tel. 800/684-3894
www.mexico-forwarding.com

STEVENS INTERNATIONAL
P.O. Box 1323
Tucson AZ 85702
U.S. tel. 520/331-9995 or 877/644-7102
http://stevensmx.com

ALAN KENT TRANSPORTES SAN MIGUEL
20 de Enero 70 San Antonio
San Miguel de Allende, Gto. 37750
tel. 415/152-3924

MOVING TO MEXICO GUY
tel. 66/9176-0893
U.S. tel. 213/928-6214
movingtomexicoguy@yahoo.com
http://movingtomexicoguy.com

EXPATRIATE GROUPS

AMERICAN LEGION CHAPALA
Calle Morelos 114
Chapala, Jalisco
tel. 376/765-2259

AMERICAN LEGION GUADALAJARA
San Antonio 143, Colonia Las Fuentes
Guadalajara, Jalisco
tel. 33/3631-1208

AMERICAN LEGION MEXICO
Celaya 25, Col. Hipódromo
México, D.F. 06100
tel. 55/5564-3386
www.amlegion-mexico.org
American service organization for men and women who served in the U.S. Armed Forces during wartime.

AMERICAN LEGION SAN MIGUEL DE ALLENDE
Bar Casino, Calle Canal #14
San Miguel de Allende, Guanajuato
U.S. tel. 714/525-8434

AMERICAN SOCIETY OF JALISCO
Av. San Francisco 3332
Guadalajara, Jalisco
tel. 33/3121-2395
amsoc@megared.net.mx
www.amsocguadalajara.org

CANADIAN CLUB OF LAKE CHAPALA
Ajijic, Jalisco
tel. 376/766-0201
info@canadianclubmx.com
www.canadianclubmx.com

EXPATS IN VALLARTA
Mike and Sara Wise, Puerto Vallarta, Jalisco
tel. 322/209-1381
U.S. tel. 612/605-3790
www.expatsinvallarta.com

INTERNATIONAL WOMEN'S CLUB OF CANCÚN
Cancún, Quintana Roo
www.iwccancun.com
www.facebook.com/IWCCANCUN

THE INTERNATIONAL WOMEN'S CLUB OF MERIDA
Mérida, Yucatán, Mexico
www.iwcmerida.org

INTERNATIONS
Schwanthaler Strasse 39
Munich, 80336, Germany
info@internations.org
www.internations.org/guadalajara-expats

LAKE CHAPALA SOCIETY
16 de Septiembre 16-A
Ajijic, Jalisco
tel. 376/766-1140 or 376/766-4685
www.lakechapalasociety.org

MEXICO CITY HASH HOUSE HARRIERS
www.mchhh.com
The Mexico City division of the international running club meets for group runs and social events.

NEWCOMERS CLUB OF CUERNAVACA
info@newcomerscuerna.org
www.newcomerscuerna.org

NEWCOMER'S CLUB OF MEXICO CITY
Paseo de la Reforma 1870, Col. Lomas de Chapultepec
México D.F., C.P. 11000
tel. 55/5520-6912
www.newcomers.org.mx

RED ROYAL ROOSTER CLUB (MEN'S BREAKFAST CLUB)
Cabo San Lucas, Baja California Sur
tel. 624/125-6056
jc@royalredrossterclub.org
www.royalredroosterclub.org

LOS CABOS TOMATOES
Cabo San Lucas, Baja California Sur
tel. 624/125-6056
loscabostomatoes@yahoo.com

Housing Considerations

MEXICO MORTGAGE LENDERS
MORTGAGES IN MEXICO
18936 S. 4185 Rd.
Claremore, OK 74017
tel. 55/5350-6331
U.S. and Canada tel. 918/398-9588
info@mortgagesinmexico.com
www.mortgagesinmexico.com

GE MONEY MEXICO
Avenida Santa Fe 495, Col. Cruz Manca
México D.F. 05349
tel. 800/284-4020
www.gemoney.com.mx/mortgage

MEXLEND
Insurgentes 441

Puerto Vallarta, 48380
tel. 322/222-7377
U.S. tel. 917/779-9061 or 800/364-2272
www.mexlend.com.mx

BANCOMER
Liverpool 18, Col. Juárez
México, D.F., 06600
tel. 800/122-6630
www.nacionalhipotecaria.com.mx

REAL ESTATE AND RENTAL AGENTS

Mexico City
LOMELIN BIENES RAICES
Mariano Escobedo 752
Col. Anzures, México D.F.

tel. 55/2581-0300 or 55/2581.0350
www.lomelin.com.mx

CENTURY 21 CEDROS
Etla No. 26
Colonia Condesa, México D.F.
tel. 55/5277-1888
fax 55/5277-1888
century21cedros@yahoo.com.mx
www.century21cedros.com

Guadalajara and Ajijic
GRUPO LLOYD
Av. Mariano Otero 1915 D
Residencial Victoria
Guadalajara, Jalisco
tel. 33/3647-5047
www.grupolloyd.com.mx

COLLINS REAL ESTATE
Carretera Chapala–Jocotepec 160-A
San Antonio Tlayacapan, Jalisco, Mexico
tel. 376/766-4197
www.livinglakechapala.com

Puerto Vallarta
COLDWELL BANKER LA COSTA
Calle Ancla Local 24
Marina Vallarta, Puerto Vallarta
tel. 322/223-0055 or 322/221-1122
U.S. tel. 877/309-2686
Canada tel. 877/303-2376
www.cblacosta.com

TROPICASA REALTY
Púlpito 145-A at Olas Altas
Col. Emiliano Zapata, Puerto Vallarta
tel. 322/222-6505
cell tel. 322/227-6064
U.S. tel. 866/978-5539
http://tropicasa.com

San Miguel de Allende
ALMA REALTY SAN MIGUEL
Zacateros 21, Centro
San Miguel de Allende, Gto.
tel. 415/154-8164
cell tel. 415/103-4141
international tel. 877/878-4141
greg@almarealtysanmiguel.com,
ben@almarealtysanmiguel.com
www.almarealtysanmiguel.com

ATENEA REALTY
Jesús 2
San Miguel de Allende, Guanajuato
tel. 415/152-1337 or 415/152-0785
U.S. and Canada tel. 210/587-7755
info@atenearealty.com
http://atenearealty.com

Oaxaca
CENTURY 21
Av. Hidalgo 1106
Colonia Centro, Oaxaca de Juárez
tel. 951/516-0367
www.century21mexico.com

Baja California Sur
BAJA PROPERTIES
Plaza Coral Baja No. 5 y 6
San José del Cabo, Baja California Sur
San Jose Del Cabo tel. 624/142-0988
Cabo San Lucas tel. 624/143-2560
Toll-free tel. 877/464-2252
www.bajaproperties.com

REMAX CABO SAN LUCAS
Plaza Aramburo
Cabo San Lucas, Baja California Sur
tel. 624/144-4169
U.S. and Canada tel. 619/955-7082
info@remaxcaboSanlucas.com
www.remaxcabosanlucas.com

The Yucatán Peninsula
MEXICO INTERNATIONAL REAL ESTATE
Calle 29 #80 x 12 y 10, Colonia México
Mérida, Yucatán
tel. 999/920-6856
info@mexintl.com
www.mexintl.com

REMAX PLAYA
Av. Aviación Fracc. II Mzna. 29
Plaza Paseo Cobá Local 201
Playa del Carmen, Quintana Roo
tel. 984/803-2539 or 984/803-2540
www.remax-playa.com

Language and Education

LANGUAGE SCHOOLS

Mexico City

CENTRO DE ENSEÑANZA PARA EXTRANJEROS (FOREIGN STUDENT TEACHING CENTER)
Universidad Nacional Autónoma de México
Av. Universidad 3002
Ciudad Universitaria, México D.F.
tel. 55/5622-2470
fax 55/5616-2672
cepe@servidor.unam.mx
www.cepe.unam.mx

FRIDA SPANISH SCHOOL
Insurgentes Sur #307
Colonia Hipodromo, México D.F.
tel. 55/5264-7018
www.fridaspanish.com

INSTITUTO CHAC-MOOL
Privada de la Pradera #108, Colonia Pradera
Cuernavaca, Morelos
U.S. tel. 530/622-4262 or 866/439-9634
spanish@chac-mool.com
www.chac-mool.com

Guadalajara and Lake Chapala

CENTRO DE ESTUDIOS PARA EXTRANJEROS (FOREIGN STUDENT STUDY CENTER)
Universidad de Guadalajara
Tomás V. Gómez 125, Colonia Ladrón de Guevara
Guadalajara, Jalisco 44600
tel. 33/3616-4399
infopv@cepe.udg.mx
www.cepe.udg.mx

IMAC SPANISH LANGUAGE PROGRAMS
Donato Guerra 180
Guadalajara, Jalisco
tel. 33/3613-1080
U.S. and Canada tel. 866/306 5040

Puerto Vallarta

CENTRO DE ESTUDIOS PARA

EXTRANJEROS (FOREIGN STUDENT STUDY CENTER)
Universidad de Guadalajara, Puerto Vallarta
tel. 322/223-2082
infopv@cepe.udg.mx
www.cepe.udg.mx

SOLEXICO LANGUAGE AND CULTURAL CENTER
Juárez 793, Colonia Centro
Puerto Vallarta, Jalisco
tel. 322/223-9778
www.solexico.com

San Miguel de Allende

ACADEMIA HISPANO AMERICANA
Mesones 4
San Miguel de Allende, Guanajuato
tel. 415/152-0349
fax 415/152-2333
info@ahaspeakspanish.com
www.ahaspeakspanish.com

CENTRO BILINGÜE DE SAN MIGUEL
San Francisco 1
San Miguel de Allende, Guanajuato
centrobilingue@gmail.com
www.centrobilingue.com

WARREN HARDY SPANISH
San Rafael 6
San Miguel de Allende, Guanajuato
tel. 415/154-4017 or 415/152-4728
info@warrenhardy.com
http://warrenhardy.com

Oaxaca

INSTITUTO AMIGOS DEL SOL
Pino Suárez 802
Calzada San Felipe del Agua 322
Oaxaca de Juárez, Oaxaca
tel. 951/133-6052
www.oaxacanews.com

INSTITUTO CULTURAL OAXACA
Av. Juárez 909
Oaxaca de Juárez, Oaxaca
tel. 951/515-3404 or 951/515-1323
fax 951/515-3728
info@icomexico.com
www.icomexico.com

Los Cabos
SPANISH IN CABO
Paseo de los Marinos esq. Retorno del
Rompehielos
Colonia El Chamizal
San José del Cabo BCS, Mexico
tel. 624/146-9975
malena@spanishincabo.com
eduardo@spanishincabo.com
www.spanishincabo.com

The Yucatán Peninsula
**PLAYA DEL CARMEN
LANGUAGE INSTITUTE**
Condominio Hacienda del Cármen Depto. A2,
Calle 14 bis
Playa del Carmen, Quintana Roo
contacts@cancunspanish.com
www.cancunspanish.com

INSTITUTE OF MODERN SPANISH
Instituto de Espanol Moderno
Calle 15 #500B X 16A y 18
Col. Maya, Mérida, Yucatán
tel. 999/911-0790
U.S. tel. 877/463-7432

HABLA
Calle 26 #99 B
Col. México, Mérida, Yucatán
tel. 999/948-1872
U.S. tel. 401/374-3237
www.habla.org

PRIVATE SCHOOLS (PRIMARY, SECONDARY, HIGH SCHOOL)

Mexico City
**THE AMERICAN SCHOOL
FOUNDATION (PRE-K-12)**
Bondojito 215, Col. Las Américas
Tacubaya, México D.F. 01120
tel. 55/5227-4900
fax 55/5227-4928
asf@asf.edu.mx
www.asf.edu.mx

GREENGATES SCHOOL (K-12)
Av. Circunvalación Pte. 102
Balcones de San Mateo, Edo. de México 53200
tel. 55/5373-0088

fax 55/5373-0765
www.greengates.edu.mx

ETON SCHOOL (K-12)
Domingo García Ramos s/n
Santa Fe, México D.F. C.P. 11000
tel. 55/5261-5800
fax 55/5292-1950
www.eton.edu.mx

COLEGIO PETERSON
Colegio Peterson, Cuajimalpa
Huizachito 80, Lomas de Vista Hermosa
Cuajimalpa, México D.F. 05720
tel. 555/813-0114
fax 555/813-1385
www.peterson.edu.mx

LYCEE FRANCO-MEXICAIN
Homero 1521
Polanco, México D.F. 11560
tel. 55/9138-8080
Cerro Xico 24
Coyoacan, México D.F. 04310
tel. 55/5339-0370
www.lfm.edu.mx

WESTHILL INSTITUTE, S.C.
Domingo García Ramos 56
Prados de la Montaña, Santa Fe
Cuajimalpa, México D.F. 05610
tel. 555/292-6627 or 555/292-6628
fax 555/292-6627
www.westhill.edu.mx

Guadalajara and Lake Chapala
**AMERICAN SCHOOL FOUNDATION
OF GUADALAJARA**
Colomos 2100, Col. Providencia
Guadalajara, Jalisco 44640
tel. 333/648-0299 or 333/817-3377
fax 333/817-3356
www.asomex.org

Puerto Vallarta
**COLEGIO AMERICANO DE PUERTO
VALLARTA, A.C. (PRE-K-12)**
Albatros 129, Col. Marina Vallarta
Puerto Vallarta, Jalisco 48354
tel. 322/221-2604 or 322/221-1525
fax 322/221-2373
www.aspv.edu.mx

BRITISH AMERICAN SCHOOL
Primary School
171 Pavo Real, Colonia Aralias
tel. 322/224-5614, 322/224-9354, or
322/224-1011
Secondary and High School
552 Marlyn
Colonia Jardines de Vallarta
Puerto Vallarta Mexico, Jalisco
tel. 322/225-0562 or 322/293-3099

San Miguel de Allende
COLEGIO LOS CHARCOS (WALDORF SCHOOL, PRESCHOOL-6)
Carretera a Dolores Hidalgo Km 6.5
tel. 415/155-9603
fax 415/110-2040
info@waldorfsanmiguel.org
www.waldorfsanmiguel.org

COLEGIO ATABAL (MONTESSORI)
Guardaujas No. 12, 37765 San Miguel de
Allende, Mexico
tel. 415/155-8248
educacionconcorazon@gmail.com
http://carrusel-atabal.com

JOSÉ VACONCELOS ESCUELA BILINGUE
Col. El Obraje s/n
tel. 415/152-1869 or 415/152-8050
jose-vasconcelos.edu.mx

Oaxaca
INSTITUTO CARLOS GRACIDA A.C. DE OAXACA (K-12, SPANISH)
Carretera Cristóbal Colón Km 542 s/n
tel./fax 951/516-2888

INSTITUTO SAN FELIPE
Calzada San Felipe del Agua 323
Oaxaca de Juárez, Oaxaca 68020
tel. 951/520-0232 or 951/520-0752
www.isf.edu.mx

Baja California Sur
COLEGIO AMARANTO (K-6)
Km 6.7 Carretera Transpeninsular s/n
Col. El Tezal C.P. 23454
Cabo San Lucas, B.C.S. México
Tel. 624/145-8700
www.amaranto.edu.mx

INSTITUTO PENINSULAR
Carretera Transpeninsular Km 6.5
Colonia El Tezal
Cabo San Lucas, B.C.S. 23454
tel. 624/1043-455
contacto@institutopeninsular.edu.mx

The Yucatán Peninsula
INTERNATIONAL AMERICAN SCHOOL OF CANCÚN (7-12)
Calle de Aceso SM309 Lote 36
Av. De los Colegios
Cancún, Quintana Roo 77560
tel. 998/882-2269 or 998/882-2273
www.iasces.com

UNIVERSIDAD LA SALLE CANCÚN
Carretera Cancún-Playa del Carmen, Km 11.5
Mza. 1 Lote 1 SM. 299
Cancún, Quintana Roo 77565
tel. 998/886-2201
www.lasallecancun.edu.mx

PUBLIC SCHOOLS
COLEGIO DE CIENCIAS Y HUMANIDADES
Insurgentes Sur y Circuito Escolar
Ciudad Universitaria de la UNAM,
Mexico D.F. 04510
www.cch.unam.mx
This prestigious public high school is
overseen by the National Autonomous
University of Mexico (UNAM).

ESCUELA NACIONAL PREPARATORIA
Adolfo Prieto 722
Colonia Del Valle
Mexico D.F. 03100
dgenp.unam.mx
Mexico's oldest and arguably most presti-
gious high school is overseen by the Na-
tional Autonomous University of Mexico
(UNAM).

COLLEGES AND UNIVERSITIES
UNIVERSIDAD AUTÓNOMA DE BAJA CALIFORNIA SUR
Carretera al Sur KM 5.5
La Paz, Baja California Sur
tel. 612/123-8800
www.uabcs.mx

UNIVERSIDAD NACIONAL AUTÓNOMA DE MÉXICO (NATIONAL AUTONOMOUS UNIVERSITY)

Avenida Insurgentes Sur 3000
Ciudad Universitaria, Coyoacán
México, D.F. 04510
www.unam.mx

UNIVERSIDAD AUTÓNOMA DE YUCATÁN

Central Campus
Calle 60 No. 491-A por 57
Centro Histórico
Mérida, Yucatán, México
tel. 999/930-0900
www.uady.mx

INSTITUTO POLITÉCNICO NACIONAL (NATIONAL POLYTECHNIC INSTITUTE)

Unidad Profesional "Adolfo López Mateos"
Zacatenco, Del. Gustavo A. Madero
México D.F. 07738
tel. 55/5729-6000, 55/5729-6300, or
55/5624-2000
www.ipn.mx

TECNOLÓGICO DE MONTERREY (MONTERREY INSTITUTE OF TECHNOLOGY)

Santa Fe Campus, Mexico City
Calle del Puente No. 222. Col. Ejidos de
Huipulco
Tlalpan, México D.F. 14360
tel. 55/5483-2020

UNIVERSIDAD AUTÓNOMA DE GUADALAJARA

Av. Patria 1201, Lomas del Valle, 3a Sección
Zapopan, Jalisco C.P. 45129
tel. 33/3648-8463
www.uag.mx

UAG SCHOOL OF MEDICINE

Av. Patria 1201, Lomas del Valle, 3a. Sección
Guadalajara, Jalisco C.P. 45129
tel. 800/531-5494
www.uag.edu/medicine

UNIVERSIDAD DE GUANAJUATO

Lascuráin de Retana No. 5 Centro C.P. 36000
tel. 473/732-0006
www.ugto.mx

INSTITUTO ALLENDE (ART SCHOOL)

Ancha de San Antonio 22, San Miguel de
Allende
tel. 415/152-0190
www.instituto-allende.edu.mx

UNIVERSIDAD VERACRUZANA

Av. Luis Castelazo Ayala s/n, Col. Industrial
ánimas
Xalapa, Veracruz
tel. 228/841-8900
www.uv.mx

UNIVERSIDAD DE LAS AMERICAS

Sta. Catarina Mártir
Cholula, Puebla
tel. 222/229-2000 or 800/227-7400
www.udlap.mx

Exchange Programs

SCHOOL FOR INTERNATIONAL TRAINING (CERTIFICATE PROGRAM)

1 Kipling Road, P.O. Box 676
Brattleboro, VT 05302
United States
U.S. tel. 800/257-7751
www.worldlearning.org

RESOURCES

Health

GENERAL RESOURCES

COMISIÓN NACIONAL DE PROTECCIÓN EN SALUDO (SEGURO POPULAR)
Gustavo E. Campa 54, Col. Guadalupe Inn
México D.F. 01020
tel. 55/5090 - 3600
www.seguro-popular.gob.mx
Find information on Mexico's public health coverage for citizens that is not associated with social security or other health systems.

INSTITUTO MEXICANO DEL SEGURO SOCIAL (MEXICAN SOCIAL SECURITY INSTITUTE, IMSS)
www.imss.gob.mx
Mexico's national health-care program for employed workers is also open to foreign nationals.

HEALTHCARE RESOURCE VALLARTA
tel. 322/222-9638
cell tel. 322/107-7007
www.healthcareresourcespv.com
Puerto Vallarta-based health-care consultant provides medical referrals, home health care, insurance, and other services.

HOSPITALS AND CLINICS

Mexico City

AMERICAN BRITISH COWDRAY (ABC) HOSPITAL
Sur 136 No. 116
Col. Las Américas, C.P. 01120
tel. 55/5230-8000
Emergencies Observatorio 55/5230-8161

AMERICAN BRITISH COWDRAY (ABC) HOSPITAL
Av. Carlos Graef Fernández No. 154
Col. Tlaxala, Del. Cuajimalpa, C.P. 05300
tel. 55/1103-1600
Emergencies 55/1103-1666

CENTRO MÉDICO DALINDE
Tuxpan 25 Colonia Roma
C.P. 06760 México D.F.
tel. 55/5265-2800, ext. 1601
Emergency tel. 55/5265-2805
contacto@dalinde.com
www.dalinde.com

CLINICA LONDRES (HOSPITAL ANGELES)
Durango 50, Col. Roma, C.P. 06700
tel. 55/5229-8400
Emergency tel. 55/5229-8445
www.hospitalangelesclinicalondres.com

HOSPITAL ANGELES PEDREGAL
Camino a Santa Teresa 1055
Col. Héroes de Padierna
C.P. 10700 México D.F.
tel. 55/5449 5500
Emergency tel. 55/5652-6987 or 55/5568-1540
www.hospitalangelespedregal.com.mx

HOSPITAL ESPAÑOL
Ejercito Nacional 613
Granada, Ciudad Mexico
tel. 55/5255-9660 or 55/5255-9645 (emergencies)
www.hespanol.com

HOSPITAL NACIONAL HOMEOPÁTICA
Obrero Mundial No. 358, Col. Piedad Narvarte
Mexico D.F. 03000
tel. 55/5761-177 or 55/5005-4053
www.hnh.salud.gob.mx

MÉDICA SUR (VARIOUS LOCATIONS)
Puente de Piedra 150, Toriello Guerra
C.P. 14050 México D.F.
tel. 55/5424-7200
www.medicasur.com.mx

MÉDICA SUR LOMAS
Acueducto Rio Hondo 20 Lomas Virreyes, C.P. 11000
tel. 55/5520-9200 or 800/501-0101
www.medicasur.com.mx

Guadalajara
AMERICAS HOSPITAL
Av. Americas 932
Guadalajara, Jalisco
tel. 33/3817-0478 or 33/3817-3141
www.americashospital.com

CLINICA AJIJIC
Carr. Oriente No.33
Ajijic, Jalisco
tel. 376/766-0662 or 376/766-0500

HOSPITAL BERNADETTE
Hidalgo 930, Col. Centro
Guadalajara, Jalisco
tel. 33/3825-4365
www.hospitalbernardette.com.mx

HOSPITAL MÉXICANO-AMERICANO
Colomos 2110
Col. Ladrón de Guevara, C.P. 44620
tel. 33/648-3333 or 800/462-2238

HOSPITAL ÁNGELES DEL CARMEN
Tarascos 3435
Col. Fracc. Monraz, C.P. 44670
tel. 33/3813-0042
Emergency tel. 33/3813-1224 or
33/3813 2546

HOSPITAL SAN JAVIER, GUADALAJARA
Av. Pablo Casals 640, Col. Prados Providencia
Guadalajara, Jalisco
tel. 33/3669-0222
www.sanjavier.com.mx

Puerto Vallarta
AMERIMED PUERTO VALLARTA
Blvd. Francisco Medina Ascencio No. 3970
Col. Villa las Flores
Puerto Vallarta, Jal.
tel. 322/226-2080
www.amerimed.com.mx

HOSPITAL CMQ
Av. Francisco Villa 1749
Col. Vallarta Villas, C.P. 48300
tel./fax 322/226-6500
info@hospitalcmq.com
www.hospitalcmq.com

San Miguel de Allende
HOSPITAL DE LA FÉ
Libramiento José Manuel Zavala Zavala PPK-BZON No. 12
San Miguel de Allende, Gto.
tel. 415/152-2233 or 415/152-2320
hospitaldelafe@prodigy.net.mx
www.hospitaldelafe.com

HOSPITAL ÁNGELES QUERÉTARO
Bernardino del Razo 21, Ensueño
Santiago de Querétaro, Querétaro 76178
tel. 442/192-3000
Emergency tel. 442/215-5901
www.hospitalangelesqueretaro.com

Oaxaca
CLINICA HOSPITAL CARMEN
Abasolo 215
Colonia Centro, Oaxaca 68000
tel. 951/516-2612 or 951/514-7545
fax 951/516-0027

CLINICA 2002
Emiliano Zapata 316
Colonia Reforma, Oaxaca 68050
tel. 951/515-7200 or 951/513-1169

HOSPITAL REFORMA
Reforma 613
Colonia Centro, Oaxaca 68000
tel. 951/516-0989 or 951/516-6090
fax 951/514-6277

Baja California Sur
AMERIMED
Blvd. Lazar Cárdenas s/n
Col. El Médano, C.P. 23410
tel. 624/881-3400
www.amerimed.com.mx

BAJA MEDICAL RESOURCE
Lopez Mateos Esq. Leona Vicario
Cabo San Lucas, Baja California Sur
tel. 624/143-7777
Emergency tel. 624/144-3434
www.bajamedicalresourcecenter.com

CENTRAL DE ESPECIALIDADES MÉDICAS
Transpeninsular, Campestre
La Paz, Baja California Sur
tel. 612/124-0400

RESOURCES

The Yucatán Peninsula

HOSPITEN
Av. Bonampak, Lote 7
MZ 2, SM 10, Cancún, Quintana Roo 77500
tel. 998/881-3700
fax 998/881-3737
Cancún@hospiten.com
www.hospiten.es

AMERIMED
Av. Tulum Sur Mza. 4, 5 y 9, No. 260
Municipio Benito Juárez
Cancún, Quintana Roo 77503
tel. 998/881-3400
www.amerimed.com.mx

**CENTRO MEDICO DE
LAS AMERICAS**
Calle 54 No. 365. 33-A y Perez Ponce
Col. Centro, Mérida, Yucatán 97000
tel. 999/926-2111
Emergency tel. 999/927-3199
cma@centromedicodelasamericas.com.mx
www.centromedicodelasamericas.com.mx

STAR MEDICA
Calle 26 No. 199
Col. Altabrisa, Mérida 97133
tel. 999/930-2880
Emergency tel. 999/930-2880, ext. 5
http://starmedica.com

INTERNATIONAL INSURANCE

**HCC MEDICAL INSURANCE
SERVICES**
251 North Illinois Street, Suite 600
Indianapolis, IN 46204
U.S.317/262-2132, 800/605-2282
www.hccmis.com
U.S. company offering national, international, and travel health insurance packages.

ALLIANZ
18B Beckett Way
Park West Business Campus
Nangor Road, Dublin 12, Ireland
tel. 353/1-630-1301
client.services@allianzworldwidecare.com
www.allianzworldwidecare.com
Alianz is a European company specializing in worldwide health insurance plans.

BUPA GROUP
Victory House
Trafalgar Place
Brighton
BN1 4FY, U.K.
tel. 44/0/127/332-3563
www.bupa-intl.com
The BUPA Group has international and Mexican local health insurance plans.

IHI DANMARK
8, Palaegade, 1261
Copenhagen K, Denmark
tel. health insurance 45/3315-3099
tel. travel insurance 45/7020-7048
tel. sales (Spain) 34/902-15-00-09
globalsales@ihi.com
www.ihi.com
IHI Danmark is a European company offering travel insurance and international health insurance packages.

MEDICAL EVACUATION

SKYMED
13840 N. Northsight Blvd
Suite 109
Scottsdale, AZ 85260
Mexico tel. 800/203-7779
U.S./Canada tel. 800/475-9633
www.skymed.com
SkyMed offers air ambulance services for Americans and Canadians living more than 100 miles from the border.

POLICE AND EMERGENCIES

CRUZ ROJA MEXICANA
Juan Luis Vives No. 200, Col. Los Morales Polanco
México, D.F. 11510
tel. 55/1084-9000
www.cruzrojamexicana.org.mx

**SECRETARÍA DE
SEGURIDAD PÚBLICA**
Av. Constituyentes 947,
Col. Belén de las Flores
México D.F.
tel. 55/1103-6000
www.ssp.gob.mx

RESOURCES FOR THE DISABLED

ACCESSIBLE MEXICO

Océano Indico 399
Palmar de Aramara
Puerto Vallarta, Jalisco
tel. 322/225-0989 or 322/224-1868
info@accesiblemexico.com
www.accesiblemexico.com

This Puerto Vallarta-based company runs accessible tours to Mexico, and can also assist with home care and medical service for residents.

CONSEJO NACIONAL PARA EL DESAROLLO Y LA INCLUSIÓN DE LAS PERSONAS CON DISCAPACIDAD (CONADIS)

Paseo de la Reforma 450, Col. Juárez
México, D.F.
tel. 55/5514-5321 or 55/5514-5983
www.conadis.salud.gob.mx

The National Council for People with Disabilities was established in 2005 to help promote greater disabled access and services.

Employment

GENERAL SERVICES

AMERICAN CHAMBER OF COMMERCE MEXICO, MEXICO CITY

Blas Pascal 205, 3rd Floor
Col. Los Morales, México D.F. 11510
tel. 55/5141-3800
fax 55/5141-3835 or 55/5141-/3836
amchammx@amcham.org.mx
www.amcham.com.mx

The American Chamber of Commerce Mexico is an independent and nonprofit organization promoting trade and joint business ventures between the United States and Mexico.

AMERICAN CHAMBER OF COMMERCE MEXICO, GUADALAJARA

Av. Moctezuma 442, Col. Jardines del Sol
Zapopan, Jalisco 45050
tel. 33/3634-6606
fax 33/3634-7374
socios_gdl@amcham.org.mx
www.amcham.com.mx

The Guadalajara branch of the American Chamber of Commerce Mexico.

CÁMARA DE COMERCIO DE CANADÁ (CANADIAN CHAMBER OF COMMERCE)

Blvd. M. Ávila Camacho 1 Piso 8 Desp. 806
Col. Polanco, México D.F. 11560
tel. 55/5580-3690
fax 55/5580-4143
www.canchammx.com

Canadian Chamber of Commerce in Mexico.

PRO MÉXICO (BUSINESS AND INVESTING)

Camino a Santa Teresa No.1679
Col. Jardines del Pedregal
México D.F. 10900
tel. 55/5447-7000 or 800/397-6783
http://negocios.promexico.gob.mx

Pro México is the government office dedicated to promoting Mexico's participation in the global economy, as well as direct foreign investment in the country.

SECRETARÍA DE LA ECONOMIA (SECRETARY OF ECONOMY)

Alfonso Reyes No.30
Col. Hipódromo Condesa
México D.F. 06140
tel. 800/083-2666
www.economia.gob.mx

The Secretary of Economy is Mexico's government department overseeing economic affairs.

TEACHING ENGLISH

General Resources

INTERNATIONAL TEACHER TRAINING ORGANIZATION

Madero No. 469
Guadalajara, Jalisco C.P. 44100
tel. 33/3658-3224 or 33/3614-3800
fax 33/3614-2462

info@teflcertificatecourses.com
www.teflcertificatecourses.com

LANGUAGECORPS
53 Whispering Way
Stow MA 01775
U.S. and Canada tel. 877/216-3267
info@languagecorps.com
www.languagecorps.com
Teacher placement worldwide.

DAVE'S ESL CAFÉ
www.eslcafe.com
Job board.

EXECUTIVE SEARCH SERVICES
SHORE CONSULTING GROUP
Av. Constituyentes No. 117-5
San Miguel Chapultepec, Del. Miguel Hidalgo
México, D.F. 11850
tel. 55/5089-8800
info@shore.com.mx
www.shore.com.mx

SPENCER STUART S DE RL DE CV
Paseo de la Reforma 2620
Piso 10, Colonia Lomas Altas
México D.F. C.P. 11950
tel. 55/5002-4950
fax 55/5281-4184
contact@spencerstuart.com
www.spencerstuart.com

VOLUNTEERING AND NONPROFIT ORGANIZATIONS

General Resources
IDEALIST
www.idealist.org
Nonprofit job and volunteer board.

WWOOF MEXICO (WORLDWIDE OPPORTUNITIES ON ORGANIC FARMS)
www.wwoofmexico.org

GLOBAL ROUTES
1 Short Street
Northampton, MA 01060
U.S. tel. 413/585-8895

www.globalroutes.org
High school and college student volunteer organization.

HEALTH VOLUNTEERS OVERSEAS
1900 L Street NW, No. 310
Washington DC 20036
U.S. tel. 202/296-0928
fax 202/296-8018
info@hvousa.org
www.hvousa.org

Nonprofit and Nongovernment Organizations
HABITAT FOR HUMANITY MEXICO
Colonia Álamos
Delegación Benito Juárez
Av. Xola No. 162 C.P. 03400
tel. 55/5519-0113
info@habitatmexico.org

AMIGOS DE LAS AMÉRICAS
5618 Star Lane
Houston TX 77057
U.S. tel. 713/782-5290 or 800/231-7796
info@amigoslink.org
www.amigoslink.org

CASA (CENTRO PARA LOS ADOLESCENTES DE SAN MIGUEL DE ALLENDE)
Santa Julia 15, Colonia Santa Julia
San Miguel de Allende, Guanajuato
tel. 415/154-6060 or 415/154-6090
U.S. tel. 212/234-7940
www.casa.org.mx

CENTRO ECOLÓGICO AKUMAL
Apartado Postal 2
Akumal, Quintana Roo 77730
tel. 984/875-9095
www.ceakumal.org

GLOBAL EXCHANGE
2017 Mission Street, 2nd Floor
San Francisco, CA 94110
tel. 415/255-7296
web@globalexchange.org
www.globalexchange.org

PATRONATO PRO NIÑOS
Av. Reforma 75C, Fracc. Ignacio Ramírez
tel. 415/152-7290 or 415/152-7796

info@patronatoproninos.org
www.patronatoproninos.org

PLAYA LAS TORTUGAS
Las Palmeras No. 13

Colonia Las Fuentes
Otates, Nayarit
tel. 322/294-1477
www.playalastortugas.com

Finance

GENERAL FINANCIAL RESOURCES
BANCO DE MEXICO
Avenida 5 de Mayo 2
Colonia Centro
México D.F. 06059
www.banxico.org.mx
Mexico's central bank provides domestic currency and works to ensure the stability of the peso.

BOLSA MEXICANA DE VALORES
Av. Paseo de la Reforma 255
Col. Cuauhtémoc, México, D.F. 06500
tel. 55/5342-9000
www.bmv.com.mx
The Bolsa Mexicana de Valores is Mexico's only stock exchange, and it lists some of the country's biggest companies.

EXPORT-IMPORT BANK OF THE UNITED STATES
811 Vermont Avenue NW
Washington DC 20571
U.S. tel. 202/565-3946 or 800/565-3946
www.exim.gov

EXCHANGE RATES
www.exchangerate.com

BANKS
SCOTIABANK INVERLAT
tel. 800/472-6842
www.scotiabank.com

BANAMEX/CITIBANK
tel. 55/1226-2639 or 800/021-2345
www.banamex.com

BANCOMER
tel. 800/1122-999
www.bancomer.com

HSBC
tel. 55/ 5721-3390 or 800/7124-825
www.hsbc.com.mx

BANCO INBURSA
tel. 55/5447-8000 or 800/909-0000
www.bancoinbursa.com

BANCO SANTANDER MEXICANO
tel. 55/5169-4300 or 800/501-0000
www.santander.com.mx

IXE
tel. 55/5174-2000 or 800/493-2001
www.ixe.com.mx

BANCO AFIRME
tel. 800/223-4763
www.afirme.com.mx

BANSÍ
tel. 800/226-7400
www.bansi.com.mx

BANORTE
tel. 55/5140-5600 (Mexico City), 33/3669-9000 (Guadalajara), or 800/226-6783
www.banorte.com

BANCO DEL BAJIO
tel. 800/471-0400
www.bb.com.mx

WIRE TRANSFER SERVICES
MONEY GRAM
2828 N. Harwood St, Floor 15
Dallas, TX 75201
U.S. tel. 800/328-5678
www.moneygram.com

WESTERN UNION
Corporate Offices
12500 E. Belford Ave
Englewood, CO 80112

tel. 800/800-8930
U.S. tel. 800/325-6000
www.westernunion.com
www.westernunion.com.mx

Communications and Media

INTERNET SERVICE PROVIDERS
PRODIGY BY TELEFONOS DE MEXICO (TELMEX)
Parque Vía No. 190
Col. Cuauhtémoc
México D.F. 06599
tel. 800/123-1114
www.telmex.com
Mexico's largest telecommunications company offers home or business dial-up and DSL service, in addition to telephone service.

ACESO UNIVERSAL BY AXTEL
Blvd. Díaz Ordaz Km. 3.33 1er Piso
Colonia Unidad San Pedro, C.P.
San Pedro Garza García, Nuevo León 66215
tel. 55/1515-0050 (Mexico City), 81/1515-0050 (Monterrey), or area code + 505-0050
www.axtel.mx
Home or business dial-up and DSL service.

ALESTRA
Av. Lázaro Cárdenas 2321
Col. Residencial San Agustín
San Pedro, Garza García, Nuevo León 66260
tel. 800/112-6222
www.alestra.com.mx
Alestra is an Internet service provider principally focused on large business clients.

CABLE COMPANIES
CABLEVISION
Antonio M Anza 20
Cuauhtémoc, Mexico D.F. 06760
tel. 55/5574-5705
This national cable company offers cable television and high-speed Internet service.

MEGACABLE
Guadalajara, Jalisco 44900
tel. 33/3750-0020 (throughout Mexico area code + 690-0000)
www.megacable.com.mx

SKY MEXICO
tel. 809/560-9842
www2.sky.com.mx

TELECABLE
Av. Naciones Unidas 5526
Col. Vallarta Universidad
Zapopan, Jalisco
tel. 33/3770-0000
www.telecable.net.mx
Telecable offers cable television and Internet service for small towns and Puerto Vallarta. Check website for local service numbers and offices.

PHONE COMPANIES
TELEFONOS DE MEXICO (TELMEX)
Parque Vía No. 190
Col. Cuauhtémoc
tel. 800/123-1114
Service problems (from a landline) tel. 050
www.telmex.com

AXTEL
Blvd. Díaz Ordaz Km. 3.33 1er Piso
Colonia Unidad San Pedro
San Pedro Garza García, Nuevo León 66215
Mexico City tel. 55/1515-0050
Monterrey tel. 55/1515-0050
Rest of the country tel. area code + 505-0050
www.axtel.mx

CELL PHONE COMPANIES
TELCEL
Mexico D.F.
tel. 800/710-5687
www.telcel.com

RESOURCES

Telcel, owned by Carlos Slim's América Móvil, is Mexico's largest cellular phone company. Consult the website for service areas and phone numbers.

MOVISTAR
tel. 800/888-8366
www.movistar.com.mx
Movistar, owned by Spanish company Telefónica Móviles, is the second-largest cell phone provider in Mexico.

IUSACELL
tel. 800/333-0611
www.iusacell.com.mx
The Iusacell website provides a full list of shops and regional contact numbers for this mobile phone company.

NEXTEL
tel. 800/200-9300
Mexico City tel. 55/1018-3300
www.nextel.com.mx
The Mexican branch of an American-owned mobile communications company provides mobile phone service and Internet.

MAIL AND SHIPPING

Mail Forwarding
MAIL BOXES ETC.
Ejercito Nacional No. 253-A Piso 4
Colonia Anáhuac
México D.F. 11320
tel. 55/5004-1919
fax 55/5004-1900
www.mx.mbelatam.com
The mail forwarding service offers U.S. postal service to offices in Guadalajara, Puerto Vallarta, Mexico City, San José del Cabo, and other locations.

BORDER CROSSINGS
Mesones 57, San Miguel de Allende, GTO
tel. 415/152-2497
www.bordercrossingsma.com

LA CONEXION
Aldama 3, San Miguel de Allende, Guanajuato
tel. 415/152-1599
www.laconexion.com.mx

SOL Y LUNA LOGISTICS
Carretera Chapala-Jocotepec 424-4
tel. 376/106-1207
U.S. and Canada tel. 719/302-5459

HANDY MAIL
Carretera Chapala-Jocotepec 159C
Ajijic, Jalisco
tel. 376/766-3813
handmailtomx@gmail.com
www.handymailtomx.com

USA2ME
10685-B Hazelhurst Drive
Houston, TX 77043
U.S. tel. 281/361-7200
www.usa2me.com
USA2Me is an international mail forwarding service.

Shipping
CORREOS DE MÉXICO/MEXPOST
Tacuba No. 1
Col. Centro, Delegación Cuauhtémoc
México D.F. 06000
tel. 55/5340-3300
www.sepomex.gob.mx
Correos de México is the national postal service. MexPost is its faster and more reliable subsidiary.

ESTAFETA
Hamburgo 213 piso 14
Col. Juárez
México D.F. 06600
tel. 800/3782-3382
www.estafeta.com
Mexican-owned national and international packaging and shipping service.

DHL
tel. 55/5345-7000 (DHL Express) or
55/5133-1700 (global forwarding)
www.dhl.com.mx
The international shipping and expedited mail services company has offices throughout Mexico.

FEDEX
tel. 800/900-1100
www.fedex.com/mx_english
The U.S. shipping and freight company has offices throughout Mexico.

UPS
Eugenia No. 189, Col. Narvarte Oriente
México, D.F. 03020
tel. 55/5228-7900 or 800/902-9200
UPS offers expedited overseas shipping
and freight services.

NATIONAL NEWSPAPERS

EL UNIVERSAL
Bucareli 12, Col. Centro
México D.F. 06600
tel. 55/5709-1313
www.eluniversal.com.mx

LA JORNADA
Av. Cuauhtémoc 1236, Col. Santa Cruz Atoyac
México D.F. 03310
tel. 55/9183-0300
www.jornada.unam.mx

REFORMA
Av. México Coyoacán 40,
Col. Santa Cruz Atoyac
Del. Benito Juárez
México D.F. 03310
tel. 55/5628-7100
www.reforma.com

EL ECONOMISTA
Coyoacán 515, Col. Benito Juarez
México D.F. 03100
tel. 55/5237-0766 or 800/018-8000
http://eleconomista.com.mx

MILENIO
Morelos 16, Col. Centro
México D.F. 06040
www.milenio.com

REGIONAL NEWSPAPERS

CORREO
Carr. Guanajuato Juventino Rosas Km. 9.5
Guanajuato, Guanajuato
tel. 473/733-12-53, 473/733-12-66
correo@correo-gto.com.mx
vimarsa@prodigy.net.mx
www.periodicocorreo.com.mx

EL INFORMADOR
Independencia 300, Col. Centro
Guadalajara, Jalisco 44100

tel. 01/33-3678-7750
www.informador.com.mx

EL TRUEQUE
San Miguel de Allende
www.clasificadoseltrueque.com

EXCELSIOR
Bucareli 1, Col. Centro
México, D.F. 06600
tel. 55/5128-3000
www.excelsior.com.mx

GRINGO GAZETTE
P.O. Box 13168
Palm Desert, CA 92211
tel.624/143-0865
U.S. tel. 562/714-6735
www.gringogazette.com

MANO A MANO
Francisco Medina Ascencio 2849 Local 1
Puerto Vallarta, Jalisco
tel. 322/222-3888
www.manoamano.com.mx

MAGAZINES

ARTES DE MEXICO
Córdoba 69, Col. Roma
Mexico D.F. 06700
tel. 55/5525-5905 or 55/5525-4036
www.artesdemexico.com

ARQUEOLOGIA MEXICANA
Rodolfo Gaona 86, Col. Lomas de Sotelo
Mexico D.F. 11200
tel. 55/5557-5004 or 800-4724237
www.arqueomex.com

PRÓCESO
Fresas 13, Col. Del Valle
Mexico D.F. 03100
tel. 55/563-62080
www.proceso.com.mx

RADIO

RADIO UNAM
Adolfo Prieto 133, Col. del Valle
México D.F. 03100
www.radiounam.unam.mx

RADIO UNIVERSIDAD DE GUADALAJARA
Av. Juárez 976, Piso 12

Guadalajara, Jalisco
tel. 33/3134-2222 ext. 12823 or
800/5700-330
www.radio.udg.mx

RADIO UNIVERSITDAD GUANAJUATO

Palacio Federal
Sopeña 1, Casa de Moneda 2do Piso
Guanajuato, Gto. 36000
tel. 473/732-1684
www.radiouniversidad.ugto.mx

RADIO UNIVERSIDAD QUERETARO

Universidad Autónoma de Querétaro
Av. Hidalgo s/n
Santiago de Queretaro, Queretaro 76010
tel. 442/192-1293
http://radio.uaq.mx

XEW (96.9 FM)

Tlalpan 3000, Col. Espartaco
México D.F. 04870
tel. 55/5327-2000
www.wradio.com.mx

Travel and Transportation

AIRLINES

AERO CALAFIA

Calle Adolfo Lopez Mateos, Manzana 02,
Lote 11
Cabo San Lucas, Baja California Sur 23469
tel. 624/143-4302, 624/143-4255, or
800/5603949
www.aereocalafia.com.mx

AEROMÉXICO

tel. 55/5133-4000 or 800/021-4000
U.S. and Canada tel. 800/237 6639
www.aeromexico.com
The largest national and international
Mexican-owned airline.

AEROMAR

Aeropuerto de Acapulco
Blvd. de Las Naciones S/N
Plan De Los Amates, Acapulco, Gro. 39931
tel. 855/237-6627
calidad.servicio@aeromar.com.mx
www.aeromar.us
Aeromar is a national airline with service
to the Pacific Coast, the Gulf Coast, and
northern destinations.

AVIASCA

Eje 6 Sur (Av. de Las Torres)
México D.F.
tel. 55/559-3988
www.aviacsa.com

INTERJET

Mexico City tel. 55/1102-5555
tel. 800/011-2345
U.S. tel. 866/285-9525
atencionaclientes@interjet.com.mx
www.interjet.com.mx
Interjet is a low-cost Mexican airline with
service to national destinations, as well as
San Antonio, Texas, and Havana, Cuba.
Check the website for ticket offices.

VOLARIS

Prolongación Paseo de la Reforma 490 piso 1,
Col. Santa Fe
México D.F.
tel. 866/988-3527 or 800/122-8000
www.volaris.mx
Volaris is a low-cost Mexican airline with
destinations in the United States and
Mexico.

VIVAAEROBUS

Aeropuerto de Monterrey, Terminal C
Carretera Miguel Alemán Km. 24
Apodaca, Nuevo León
Mexico City tel. 55/4777-5050
Guadalajara tel. 33/4777-0770
Monterrey tel. 81/8215-0150
U.S. and Canada tel. 888/935-9848
www.vivaaerobus.com
Associated with several major bus com-
panies, this low-cost airline connects na-
tional and U.S. cities.

BUS COMPANIES

North and North-Central Mexico

GRUPO ESTRELLA BLANCA
tel. 800/507-5500
www.estrellablanca.com.mx

GRUPO SENDA
tel. 818/375-7577, 800/017-3632, or
800/890-9090
www.gruposenda.com

Central Mexico

ETN
tel. 800/800-0386
www.etn.com.mx

OMNIBUSES DE MEXICO
tel. 800/765-6636
www.odm.com.mx

ESTRELLA DE ORO
tel. 800/900-0105
www.autobus.com.mx

PRIMERA PLUS/FLECHA AMARILLA
tel. 800/375-7587
www.primeraplus.com.mx

TRANSPORTES DEL PACIFICO
tel. 33/3668-5920 or 800/00-1827
www.tap.com.mx

Southern Mexico

AUTOBUSES ADO
tel. 52/5133-2424, 800/702-8000, or
800/822-2369
www.ado.com.mx

CAR TRAVEL

Maps and Highway Information

GUIA ROJI
www.guiaroji.com.mx

CAMINOS Y PUENTES FEDERALES (FEDERAL ROADS AND BRIDGES)
tel. 074, 55/5200-2000, or 777/329-2100
www.capufe.gob.mx

Car Insurance

SANBORN'S INSURANCE
U.S. tel. 800/222-0158
info@sanbornsinsurance.com
www.sanbornsinsurance.com

MEXICO INSURANCE SERVICES
510 Camino de la Reina #336
San Diego, California 92108
U.S. tel. 858/663-6453
www.drivemexico.net

QUALITAS
tel. 800/800-2880 or 800/288-6770
www.qualitas.com.mx

SEGUROS ATLAS
Conjunto Arcos Bosques
Paseo de los Tamarindos 60
Edificio Norte B
Col. Bosques de las Lomas
Cuajimalpa, México D.F.
tel. 55/9177-5000
www.segurosatlas.com.mx

GNP
tel. 800/400-9000
Mexico City tel. 55/5227-9000
www.gnp.com.mx

FERRY INFORMATION AND TICKETING

BAJA FERRIES
tel. 800/337-7437
www.bajaferries.com

BUS TERMINALS IN MEXICO CITY

TERMINAL CENTRAL PONIENTE
Av. Sur 122
Del. Álvaro Obregón
México D.F.
tel. 55/5271-4518
www.centralponiente.com.mx

TERMINAL CENTRAL SUR "TASQUEÑA"
Avenida Tasqueña No. 1320, Col. Campestre
Churubusco
México D.F.
tel. 55/5689-9745

RESOURCES

TERMINAL DE ORIENTE "TAPO"
Calzada Ignacio Zaragoza y Av. Eduardo
Molina, Col. 10 de Mayo
México D.F.
tel. 55/5762-5977

**TERMINAL CENTRAL DE
AUTOBUSES DEL NORTE**
Eje Central Lázaro Cárdenas No. 4907, Col.
Magdalena de las Salinas

México D.F.
tel. 55/5587-1552
www.centraldelnorte.com.mx

BOATING AND FISHING
MEXICAN FISHERIES OFFICE
2550 5th Avenue
San Diego, CA
tel. 619/233-4324

Prime Living Locations

MEXICO CITY
THE NEWS
Montes Urales No. 425, Piso 1, Col. Lomas de
Chapultepec
México D.F. 11000
tel. 55/3099-3000
www.thenews.com.mx
The News is an English-language newspaper covering local, national, and international news, as well as Mexico City
culture and events.

QUEREMOS COMER
www.queremoscomer.com
This is a searchable online database
of Mexico City's restaurants and taco
stands.

GUADALAJARA
GUADALAJARA REPORTER
Duque de Rivas 254, Col. Arcos Sur
Guadalajara, Jalisco
tel. 33/3615-2177 or 800/024-9432
www.guadalajarareporter.com
The *Guadalajara Reporter* is a Guadala-
jara-based English-language newspaper
covering local news, events, and culture,
expatriate activities, and national and international news.

PUERTO VALLARTA
BANDERAS NEWS
info@banderasnews.com
www.banderasnews.com
Banderas News provides online

information and articles about life, culture, real estate, and health in Puerto Vallarta, including classifieds.

SAN MIGUEL DE ALLENDE
SAN MIGUEL DE ALLENDE–OFFICIAL WEBSITE
www.sanmigueldeallende.gob.mx

ATENCIÓN SAN MIGUEL
Biblioteca Pública
Insurgentes 25, Piso 2
San Miguel de Allende, Gto.
tel. 415/152-3770
www.atencionsanmiguel.org
Atención San Miguel is a weekly Spanish-
English newspaper covering local cul-
ture and news, including a weekly events
calendar.

FALLING IN LOVE WITH SAN MIGUEL
http://fallinginlovewithsanmiguel.com
On this site you'll find message boards
and information about life in San Miguel
de Allende, maintained by the authors of
the memoir, *Falling in Love With San
Miguel.*

BEST OF SAN MIGUEL
www.best-of-san-miguel.com
Find San Miguel de Allende travel tips
from a local on this site.

OAXACA

OAXACA DE JUÁREZ–OFFICIAL WEBSITE
www.municipiodeoaxaca.gob.mx

OAXACA MIO
www.oaxaca-mio.com

This is an online travel guide to the state of Oaxaca, including links to hotels, restaurants, and shops, and descriptions of attractions.

NOTICIAS
Libres No. 411, Centro
Oaxaca, Oax.
tel. 951/502-1016
www.noticiasnet.mx

Noticias is the city of Oaxaca's most popular Spanish newspaper, with a good classifieds section.

BAJA CALIFORNIA SUR

LOS CABOS MAGAZINE
Mexico Office: Apartado Postal No. 342
Flor de Pitaya, Lote 30, Mza. 7
Fracc. Jacarandas,
Cabo San Lucas, Baja California Sur
tel. 624/143-1346
U.S. Office: 7770 Regents Road 113-387
San Diego, CA 92122
U.S. tel. 800/208-3924
www.loscabosmagazine.com
www.loscabosguide.com

Los Cabos Magazine is a print and digital lifestyle magazine for residents and visitors to the Los Cabos area.

LOS CABOS NEWS
Avenida Cabo San Lucas, esquina con Emiliano Zapata
Cabo San Lucas, Baja California Sur
tel. 624/143-4644
www.loscabosnews.com.mx

Los Cabos News is a bilingual newspaper covering Cabo San Lucas, San José del Cabo, La Paz, and vicinity.

LOS CABOS GUIDE
www.loscabosguide.com

BAJA INSIDER
www.bajainsider.com

Baja Insider is an online magazine about living and traveling in Baja California.

THE YUCATÁN PENINSULA

YUCATAN LIVING
Calle 81 #522, Colonia Centro
Merida, Yuc.
tel. 999/176-6176
www.yucatanliving.com

This extensive online database has articles and information about life on the Yucatán peninsula, including events, art, lifestyle, real estate, shopping, health care, daily life, and more.

YUCATAN TIMES
tel. 999/316-3179
www.theyucatantimes.com

This online newspaper covers Mexico and the Yucatán peninsula, including state news, politics, and finance.

Glossary

abarrotes grocery store
abogado attorney
abuelo/a grandpa, grandma
achiote a seed used in traditional Yucatec cooking
acupunctura acupuncture
adobado a seasoned rub for meat
aduana customs
aeropuerto airport
agave large Mexican succulent plant
agave azul blue agave, used in tequila production
agente agent
agua water
aguas frescas or aguas de fruta cold fruit drink
aguinaldo annual bonus
ahuehuete cypress
alebrije hand-painted copal wood animals and figurines from Oaxaca
almuerzo meal eaten around midday
alquiler rent
amueblado/a furnished
andador pedestrian walkway
antigüedades antiques
antojitos snacks or appetizers
arquitecto architect
arrachera Mexican skirt steak
arredamiento lease
arte art
artesanía traditional handcraft
asiento lard
atole a sweet and hot beverage made with corn flour
autobus bus
autónomo autonomous
autopista highway
avalúo appraisal
ayuntamiento town council
azulejo tile
bachillerato high school (internationally accredited)
bajo sexto acoustic bass
banco bank
baño bathroom
barbacoa pit-cooked lamb
biblioteca library
bienes raíces real estate
birria slow-roasted goat

bolillo white roll
bomberos firemen
botana appetizer
buen provecho an expression used to say enjoy your meal
burro donkey
caballo horse
café coffee
café con leche coffee with milk
cajero cashier; automatic teller
caldo broth
caldo de pollo chicken broth
calle street
callejón alley
camion bus
cantina traditional bar or drinking establishment
capilla chapel
capitaleño capital resident (Mexico City resident)
carne meat
carne asada grilled meat
carnitas braised pork
carretera highway
casa house
casa de cambio exchange house
casita small house
cempasuchil marigold
cena dinner
cenote sinkhole
centavo cent
centro histórico historic district
certificación cetification
certificado de libertad de gravamen lien certificate
cerveza beer
ceviche lime-cured fish
chapulin grasshopper
charreada traditional Mexican show of horsemanship and ranch skills, similar to rodeo in the United States
charro traditional Mexican cowboy
chayote a green gourd native to Mexico
chilango Mexico City resident
chilaquiles fried tortilla strips bathed in salsa, cream, and cheese
chile relleno stuffed chili pepper
chiles en nogada poblano pepper stuffed with meat, dried fruit, and nuts;

covered in creamed walnut sauce; and sprinkled with pomegranate seeds

chipotle a smoky dried chili pepper, derived from fresh jalapeño pepper

chorro spring

churro a tube-shaped sweet bread, deep fried and dusted in sugar

clínica clinic

coatimundi coati, an animal in the raccoon family

cochinita pibil Yucatec-style pulled pork

cocina kitchen

cocina integral installed kitchen

colectivo shared taxi service

colegio school (private)

colonia neighborhood

comadre godmother

combi shared van

comida the large midday meal in Mexico, typically eaten around 2 P.M.

comida corrida an economical, set-price lunch served in restaurants

compadre godfather

comprador buyer

comunitario community council

consulado consulate

convento convent

correo postal service

corrida de toros bullfight

corrido popular ballad

costo cost

cotija a variety of aged Mexican cheese

criollo a term used in New Spain to describe a Mexican-born person of Spanish descent

Cruz Roja Red Cross

cuaresma Lent

cuatrimoto ATV

cultura culture

cumbia a traditional musical style from Colombia

darse de alta register, legalize status

delegacion borough

depósito deposit

depósito de confianza escrow

desayuno breakfast

Día de la Raza Day of the Race (Columbus Day)

Día del Amor y la Amistad Valentine's Day

Día de los Muertos Day of the Dead

distrito federal federal district, Mexico City

divino divine

doctor, doctora doctor

dulces sweets

dulces típicos traditional Mexican sweets

ejes vial traffic axis, thoroughfare (Mexico City)

ejido communally owned land

elote corn

embajada embassy

enchiladas mineras cheese-stuffed tortillas in guajillo sauce with sautéed potatoes and carrots

enchiladas verdes stuffed tortillas bathed in green salsa

enmoladas tortillas in mole sauce

entrada appetizer

epazote a fragrant herb used in cooking

equipal traditional wood and pigskin furniture from Jalisco

escritura deed

escritura de compraventa notarial purchase contract

escuela school

español Spanish

farmacía pharmacy

fería fair

festival festival

fiador cosigner (for a rental contract)

fideicomiso bank trust

fiesta party

fiestas patrias patriotic holidays

flan egg custard dessert

flauta deep fried and stuffed tortilla, topped with cream and salsa

flor de calabaza squash flower

FMM Forma Migratoria Multiple (tourist card)

FM3 nonimmigrant resident visa

FM2 immigrant visa

fonda casual restaurant

gachupín Spanish person

galería gallery

garrafón jug for drinking water

gas estacionario stationary gas tank

gordita stuffed corn cake

gringa a flour tortilla filled with melted cheese and meat

gringo American

guajolote turkey (Nahuatl)

guanabana soursop, a tropical fruit
guayaba guava
guayabera a men's dress shirt from the Caribbean region
güero/a light-colored; a fair-haired or fair-skinned person
guisado stew or side dish
habitación room
hacienda estate
hamaca hammock
hipoteca mortgage
hojalatería tinwork
homeopatía homeopathy
horchata traditional drink made with ground rice, sugar, and water
huapango a style of music typical to the Huasteca region
huarache torpedo-shaped corn flatbread
Huasteca Mexican region comprising northern Veracruz, southern Tamaulipas, a portion of San Luis Potosí, and the Sierra Gorda in Querétaro
huevo egg
huevos a la mexicana eggs scrambled with tomato, onion, and chili pepper
huevos rancheros fried eggs in tomato-chili sauce
huipil traditional women's tunic from Southern Mexico
huitlacoche corn fungus
iglesia church
impuesto tax
indigena indigenous person (n.) or indigenous (adj.)
ingeniero engineer
instituto institute
Instituto Federal Electoral Federal Electoral Institute
interés interest
jarana larger five-string guitar
jardín garden
jardín de niños preschool
jocoque fresh Middle Eastern–style cow's milk cheese
joyería jewelry
juego de pelota Mesomerican ball game
Las Mañanitas Mexico's birthday song
lavandería laundry
La Via Dolorosa Stations of the Cross
ley seca dry law
libertad liberty

libramiento freeway
librería bookstore
licenciado college graduate
licuado milk shake or fruit shake
lima lemon
limonada limeade
longaniza a type of sausage
macho traditionally masculine
maciza in *carnitas*, pork shoulder or leg
madre mother
maestro master; teacher
maguey large succulent plant common in Mexico
majolica tin-glazed pottery, originally from Italy
malecón promenade, boardwalk
mañana tomorrow; morning
manta lightweight cotton fabric frequently used in traditional Mexican clothing
manteca lard
mapache (Nahuatl) racoon
maquiladora manufacturing plant
maracuya passion fruit
mariachi a traditional Mexican music ensemble
masa dough
mercado market
mescal distilled spirit made from the maguey plant
mescal de gusano mescal distilled with the maguey worm
mesquite mesquite tree
mestizo a person of mixed ethnic heritage
michelada beer served with lime juice, salt, hot sauce, and Worcestershire sauce
migracion immigration
milagritos small tin ornaments
mixiote lamb steamed in agave leaf
mole flavorful sauce made of ground nuts and spices
mole negro ground sauce made of chocolate, nuts, and spices; from the state of Oaxaca
mollete a *bolillo* topped with beans, cheese, and salsa
mordida literally, bite; slang for bribe
mudanza movers
muebles furniture
municipio municipality

museo museum

narcotraficante drug dealer

navidad Christmas

nevería ice cream parlor

nieve ice cream

nopal prickly pear cactus

norteño north

notario publico notary public (a government-appointed attorney in Mexico)

novena nine days of prayer or worship

opción de compra purchase option

órgano organ

padre father

palapa structure with a thatched palm roof

pan bread

pan árabe pita

pan de dulce sweet bread

papadzules Yucatec tacos stuffed with hard-boiled egg

papelería stationery store

parque park

parroquía parish

partido political party

Partido Acción Nacional National Action Party

Partido de la Revolución Democrática Party of the Democratic Revolution

Partido Revolucionario Institucional Institutional Revolutionary Party

pascua Easter

pasilla a mild but flavorful dried chili pepper

pastor taco preparation using chili pepper and spices

PEMEX *Petroleos Mexicanos* (Mexican Petroleum)

peña rock

peninsular colonial-era term for a person born in Spain

pequeños contribuyente small contributor

permiso de salida y regreso permission to leave and return

pesero city bus (Mexico City)

peso Mexico's currency

petate woven rush mat

picadillo spiced ground beef

pico de gallo salsa made of chopped tomatoes, onion, cilantro, and chili peppers

pipián a sauce made of ground pumpkin seeds and spices

piso floor

planes de renta flat-rate contract (for cell phone service)

plata silver

playa beach

plaza plaza or public square

plaza de toros bullring

plazo term

plazuela small plaza

poblano from the state or the city of Puebla

Porfiriato Historical period during the presidency of Porfirio Díaz

posada inn

pozo well

pozole hominy soup

predial property taxes

preparatoria high school

presa reservoir

presidente municipal municipal president

préstamo loan

priista member of the PRI political party

primaria primary school

Protección Civil Civil Protection, or police

pueblo small town

pulque alcoholic drink made from fermented maguey sap

puntas de filete beef tips

querétense something or someone from Querétaro

quesadilla a warmed tortilla stuffed with cheese

queso cheese

queso de tuna prickly pear cheese, a regional sweet

queso fundido melted cheese

rajas strips of roasted chili pepper (usually poblano)

ranchera musical style from Northern Mexico

rebozo shawl

receta prescription

rentistas FM3 visa designation for foreigners who live but do not earn money in Mexico

restaurante restaurant

retablo devotional painting or altarpiece

río river

rosca de reyes a traditional fruitcake served on Three Kings' Day

salsa sauce

salsa roja condiment made with red tomatoes and chili peppers, or red chili peppers

salsa verde condiment made with green tomatoes, chili peppers, and spices

sangrita a tomato-based chaser for tequila

santa escuela a Jesuit school in the colonial era

sección amarilla yellow pages

Secretaría de Medio Ambiente y Recursos Naturals Secretary of Environment and Natural Resources

segundaria secondary school

Semana Santa Holy Week

señor Mr. or mister; sir; man

señora Mrs., madam; woman

señorita Miss; young woman

serape traditional Mexican wool shawl or cloak

se renta for rent

serrano variety of green chili pepper

se vende for sale

siesta nap

sobrino/a nephew, niece

sombrero hat

son traditional musical style

sopa soup

sope thick, round corn-based flatbread

subarrendar sublet

suegro/a father-in-law, mother-in-law

surtido mixed

taco seasoned meat or vegetables enclosed in a warm tortilla

tacos de guisado tacos prepared with a variety of fillings

tacos dorados deep-fried tacos

Talavera hand-painted majolica-style pottery from Puebla, Mexico

tamal tamale, or steamed corn cake (plural: tamales)

tapatíos resident of Guadalajara

teatro theater

techo roof

telenovela soap opera

templo temple

Tenochtitlan capital city of Mesoamerica at the time of the Spanish conquest

tequila a Mexican distilled spirit made from blue agave

tianguis open-air market

tierra land

tintorería dry cleaning

tío/a uncle, aunt

título title

tlayuda a large Oaxacan tortilla stuffed with beans and cheese

topografo surveyor

torta hot sandwich served on a white roll

transito transit

transpaso transfer

tranvía trolley

tú you, informal

tuna prickly pear fruit

turismo tourism

turista tourist or traveler's diarrhea

universidad university

usted you, formal

valor real value

vecindad neighborhood

vendedor seller

verano summer

verificación de crédito credit check

viceroy colonial governor

Viernes Santo Good Friday

vino wine

visa visa

zócalo central square adjoined by a cathedral

ABBREVIATIONS

Col. *colonia* (neighborhood)

IMN Instituto Nacional de Migración (National Institute of Immigration)

nte. *norte* (north)

ote. *oriente* (east)

PAN Partido Acción Nacional (National Action Party)

pp *por persona* (per person)

PRD Partido de la Revolución Democrática (Party of the Democratic Revolution)

PRI Partido Revolucionario Institucional (Institutional Revolutionary Party)

prol. *prolongación* (prolongation, usually of a city street)

pte. *poniente* (west)

s/n *sin número* (without number)

RESOURCES

Spanish Phrasebook

PRONUNCIATION

Once you learn them, Spanish pronunciation rules — in contrast to English — don't change. Spanish vowels generally sound softer than in English. (*Note:* The capitalized syllables receive stronger accents.)

Vowels

a like ah, as in "hah": *agua* AH-gooah (water), *pan* PAHN (bread), and *casa* CAH-sah (house)

e like ay, as in "may:" *mesa* MAY-sah (table), *tela* TAY-lah (cloth), and *de* DAY (of, from)

i like ee, as in "need": *diez* dee-AYZ (ten), *comida* ko-MEE-dah (meal), and *fin* FEEN (end)

o like oh, as in "go": *peso* PAY-soh (weight), *ocho* OH-choh (eight), and *poco* POH-koh (a bit)

u like oo, as in "cool": *uno* OO-noh (one), *cuarto* KOOAHR-toh (room), and *usted* oos-TAYD (you); when it follows a "q" the **u** is silent; when it follows an "h" or has an umlaut, it's pronounced like "w"

Consonants

b, d, f, k, l, m, n, p, q, s, t, v, w, x, y, z, and ch   pronounced almost as in English; **h** occurs, but is silent – not pronounced at all.

c like k as in "keep": *cuarto* KOOAR-toh (room), Tepic tay-PEEK (capital of Nayarit state); when it precedes "e" or "i," pronounce **c** like s, as in "sit": *cerveza* sayr-VAY-sah (beer), *encima* ayn-SEE-mah (atop).

g like g as in "gift" when it precedes "a," "o," "u," or a consonant: *gato* GAH-toh (cat), *hago* AH-goh (I do, make); otherwise, pronounce **g** like h as in "hat": *giro* HEE-roh (money order), *gente* HAYN-tay (people)

j like h, as in "has": *jueves* HOOAY-vays (Thursday), *mejor* may-HOR (better)

ll like y, as in "yes": *toalla* toh-AH-yah (towel), *ellos* AY-yohs (they, them)

ñ like ny, as in "canyon": *año* AH-nyo (year), *señor* SAY-nyor (Mr., sir)

r is lightly trilled, with tongue at the roof of your mouth like a very light English d, as in "ready": *pero* PAY-doh (but), *tres* TDAYS (three), *cuatro* KOOAH-tdoh (four).

rr like a Spanish r, but with much more emphasis and trill. Let your tongue flap. Practice with *burro* (donkey), *carretera* (highway), and Carrillo (proper name), then really let go with *ferrocarril* (railroad).

Note: The single small but common exception to all of the above is the pronunciation of Spanish **y** when it's being used as the Spanish word for "and," as in "Ron y Kathy." In such case, pronounce it like the English ee, as in "keep": Ron "ee" Kathy (Ron and Kathy).

Accent

The rule for accent, the relative stress given to syllables within a given word, is straightforward. If a word ends in a vowel, an n, or an s, accent the next-to-last syllable; if not, accent the last syllable.

Pronounce *gracias* GRAH-seeahs (thank you), *orden* OHR-dayn (order), and *carretera* kah-ray-TAY-rah (highway) with stress on the next-to-last syllable.

Otherwise, accent the last syllable: *venir* vay-NEER (to come), *ferrocarril* fay-roh-cah-REEL (railroad), and *edad* ay-DAHD (age).

Exceptions to the accent rule are always marked with an accent sign: (á, é, í, ó, or ú), such as *teléfono* tay-LAY-foh-noh (telephone), *jabón* hah-BON (soap), and *rápido* RAH-pee-doh (rapid).

BASIC AND COURTEOUS EXPRESSIONS

Most Spanish-speaking people consider formalities important. Whenever approaching anyone for information or some other reason, do not forget the appropriate salutation — good morning, good evening, etc. Standing alone, the greeting *hola* (hello) can sound brusque.

Hello. *Hola.*
Good morning. *Buenos días.*
Good afternoon. *Buenas tardes.*
Good evening. *Buenas noches.*
How are you? *¿Cómo está usted?*
Very well, thank you. *Muy bien, gracias.*
Okay; good. *Bien.*
Not okay; bad. *Mal or feo.*
So-so. *Más o menos.*
And you? *¿Y usted?*
Thank you. *Gracias.*
Thank you very much. *Muchas gracias.*
You're very kind. *Muy amable.*
You're welcome. *De nada.*
Goodbye. *Adios.*
See you later. *Hasta luego.*
please *por favor*
yes *sí*
no *no*
I don't know. *No sé.*
Just a moment, please. *Momentito, por favor.*
Excuse me, please (when you're trying to get attention). *Disculpe or Con permiso.*
Excuse me (when you've made a boo-boo). *Lo siento.*
Pleased to meet you. *Mucho gusto.*
What is your name? *¿Cómo se llama usted?*
My name is . . . *Me llamo . . .*
Do you speak English? *¿Habla usted inglés?*
Is English spoken here? (Does anyone here speak English?) *¿Se habla inglés?*
I don't speak Spanish well. *No hablo bien el español.*
I don't understand. *No entiendo.*
How do you say . . . in Spanish? *¿Cómo se dice . . . en español?*
Would you like . . . *¿Quisiera usted . . .*
Let's go to . . . *Vamos a . . .*

TERMS OF ADDRESS

When in doubt, use the formal *usted* (you) as a form of address.

I *yo*
you (formal) *usted*
you (familiar) *tú*
he/him *él*
she/her *ella*
we/us *nosotros*
you (plural) *ustedes*
they/them *ellos (all males or mixed gender); ellas (all females)*
Mr., sir *señor*
Mrs., madam *señora*
miss, young lady *señorita*
wife *esposa*
husband *esposo*
friend *amigo (male); amiga (female)*
sweetheart *novio (male); novia (female)*
son; daughter *hijo; hija*
brother; sister *hermano; hermana*
father; mother *padre; madre*
grandfather; grandmother *abuelo; abuela*

TRANSPORTATION

Where is . . . ? *¿Dónde está . . . ?*
How far is it to . . . ? *¿A cuánto está . . . ?*
from . . . to . . . *de . . . a . . .*
How many blocks? *¿Cuántas cuadras?*
Where (Which) is the way to . . . ? *¿Dónde está el camino a . . . ?*
the bus station *la terminal de autobuses*
the bus stop *la parada de autobuses*
Where is this bus going? *¿Adónde va este autobús?*
the taxi stand *la parada de taxis*
the train station *la estación de ferrocarril*
the boat *el barco*
the launch *lancha; tiburonera*
the dock *el muelle*
the airplane *avión*
the airport *el aeropuerto*

I'd like a ticket to . . . *Quisiera un boleto a . . .*

first (second) class *primera (segunda) clase*

round-trip *ida y vuelta; viaje redondo*

reservation *reservación*

baggage *equipaje*

Stop here, please. *Pare aquí, por favor.*

the entrance *la entrada*

the exit *la salida*

ticket *boleto*

the ticket office *taquilla*

(very) near; far *(muy) cerca; lejos*

to; toward *a*

by; through *por*

from *de*

the right *la derecha*

the left *la izquierda*

straight ahead *derecho; directo*

in front *en frente*

beside *al lado*

behind *atrás*

the corner *la esquina*

the stoplight *la semáforo*

a turn *una vuelta*

right here *aquí*

somewhere around here *por acá*

right there *allí*

somewhere around there *por allá*

road *el camino*

street; boulevard *calle; bulevar*

block *la cuadra*

highway *carretera*

kilometer *kilómetro*

bridge; toll *puente; cuota*

address *dirección*

north; south *norte; sur*

east; west *oriente (este); poniente (oeste)*

ACCOMMODATIONS

hotel *hotel*

Is there a room? *¿Hay cuarto?*

May I (may we) see it? *¿Puedo (podemos) verlo?*

What is the rate? *¿Cuál es el precio?*

Is that your best rate? *¿Es su mejor precio?*

Is there something cheaper? *¿Hay algo más económico?*

a single room *un cuarto sencillo*

a double room *un cuarto doble*

double bed *cama matrimonial*

twin beds *camas individuales*

with private bath *con baño*

hot water *agua caliente*

shower *ducha*

towels *toallas*

soap *jabón*

toilet paper *papel higiénico*

blanket *cobija*

sheets *sábanas*

air-conditioned *aire acondicionado*

fan *abanico; ventilador*

key *llave*

manager *gerente*

FOOD

I'm hungry *Tengo hambre.*

I'm thirsty. *Tengo sed.*

menu *carta; menú*

order *orden*

glass *vaso*

fork *tenedor*

knife *cuchillo*

spoon *cuchara*

napkin *servilleta*

soft drink *refresco*

coffee *café*

tea *té*

drinking water *agua pura; agua potable*

bottle of water *botella de agua*

bottled carbonated water *agua mineral*

bottled uncarbonated water *agua sin gas*

beer *cerveza*

wine *vino*

milk *leche*

juice *jugo*

cream *crema*

sugar *azúcar*

cheese *queso*

snack *antojito; botana*

breakfast *desayuno*

lunch *almuerzo*

daily lunch special *comida corrida (or el menú del día depending on region)*

dinner *comida (often eaten in late afternoon); cena (a late-night snack)*

wine list *lista de vinos*
the check *la cuenta*
tip *propina*
eggs *huevos*
bread *pan*
salad *ensalada*
fruit *fruta*
mango *mango*
watermelon *sandía*
papaya *papaya*
banana *plátano*
apple *manzana*
orange *naranja*
lime *limón*
fish *pescado*
shellfish *mariscos*
shrimp *camarones*
meat (without) *(sin) carne*
chicken *pollo*
pork *puerco*
beef; steak *res; bistec*
bacon; ham *tocino; jamón*
fried *frito*
roasted *asada*
barbecue; barbecued *barbacoa; al carbón*
spicy, hot *picante*

SHOPPING
money *dinero*
money-exchange bureau *casa de cambio*
I would like to exchange travelers checks. *Quisiera cambiar cheques de viajero.*
What is the exchange rate? *¿Cuál es el tipo de cambio?*
How much is the commission? *¿Cuánto cuesta la comisión?*
Do you accept credit cards? *¿Aceptan tarjetas de crédito?*
money order *giro*
How much does it cost? *¿Cuánto cuesta?*
What is your final price? *¿Cuál es su último precio?*
expensive *caro*
cheap *barato; económico*
more *más*

less *menos*
a little *un poco*
too much *demasiado*

HEALTH
Help me please. *Ayúdeme por favor.*
I am ill. *Estoy enfermo.*
Call a doctor. *Llame un doctor.*
Take me to ... *Lléveme a ...*
hospital *hospital; sanatorio*
drugstore *farmacia*
pain *dolor*
fever *fiebre*
headache *dolor de cabeza*
stomachache *dolor de estómago*
allergy *alergia*
burn *quemadura*
cramp *calambre*
nausea *náusea*
vomiting *vomitar*
medicine *medicina*
prescription *receta*
antibiotic *antibiótico*
pill; tablet *pastilla*
aspirin *aspirina*
ointment; cream *pomada; crema*
bandage *venda*
cotton *algodón*
sanitary napkins *toallas, or use brand name, e.g., Kotex*
birth control pills *pastillas anticonceptivas*
contraceptive foam *espuma anticonceptiva*
condoms *preservativos; condones*
toothbrush *cepilla dental*
dental floss *hilo dental*
toothpaste *crema dental*
dentist *dentista*
toothache *dolor de muelas*

POST OFFICE AND COMMUNICATIONS
long-distance telephone *teléfono larga distancia*
I would like to call ... *Quisiera llamar a ...*
collect *por cobrar*
station to station *a quien contesta*
person to person *persona a persona*

credit card *tarjeta de crédito*
post office *correo*
general delivery *lista de correo*
letter *carta*
stamp *estampilla, timbre*
postcard *tarjeta*
aerogram *aerograma*
air mail *correo aereo*
registered *registrado*
money order *giro*
package; box *paquete; caja*
string; tape *cuerda; cinta*

AT THE BORDER

border *frontera*
customs *aduana*
immigration *migración*
tourist card *tarjeta de turista*
inspection *inspección; revisión*
passport *pasaporte*
profession *profesión*
marital status *estado civil*
single *soltero*
married; divorced *casado; divorciado*
widowed *viudado*
insurance *seguros*
title *título*
driver's license *licencia de manejar*

AT THE GAS STATION

gas station *gasolinera*
gasoline *gasolina*
unleaded *sin plomo*
full, please *lleno, por favor*
tire *llanta*
tire repair shop *vulcanizadora*
air *aire*
water *agua*
oil (change) *aceite (cambio)*
grease *grasa*
My . . . doesn't work. *Mi . . . no sirve.*
battery *batería*
radiator *radiador*
alternator *alternador*
generator *generador*
tow truck *grúa*
repair shop *taller mecánico*
tune-up *afinación*
auto parts store *refaccionería*

VERBS

Verbs are the key to getting along in Spanish. They employ mostly predictable forms and come in three classes, which end in *ar*, *er*, and *ir*, respectively:
to buy *comprar*
I buy, you (he, she, it) buys *compro, compra*
we buy, you (they) buy *compramos, compran*
to eat *comer*
I eat, you (he, she, it) eats *como, come*
we eat, you (they) eat *comemos, comen*
to climb *subir*
I climb, you (he, she, it) climbs *subo, sube*
we climb, you (they) climb *subimos, suben*

Here are more (with irregularities indicated):
to do or make *hacer (regular except for hago, I do or make)*
to go *ir (very irregular: voy, va, vamos, van)*
to go (walk) *andar*
to love *amar*
to work *trabajar*
to want *desear, querer*
to need *necesitar*
to read *leer*
to write *escribir*
to repair *reparar*
to stop *parar*
to get off (the bus) *bajar*
to arrive *llegar*
to stay (remain) *quedar*
to stay (lodge) *hospedar*
to leave *salir (regular except for salgo, I leave)*
to look at *mirar*
to look for *buscar*
to give *dar (regular except for doy, I give)*
to carry *llevar*
to have *tener (irregular but important: tengo, tiene, tenemos, tienen)*

to come *venir (similarly irregular: vengo, viene, venimos, vienen)*

Spanish has two forms of "to be":

to be *estar (regular except for estoy, I am)*

to be *ser (very irregular: soy, es, somos, son)*

Use *estar* when speaking of location or a temporary state of being: "I am at home." *"Estoy en casa."* "I'm sick." *"Estoy enfermo."* Use *ser* for a permanent state of being: "I am a doctor." *"Soy doctora."*

NUMBERS

0 *cero*
1 *uno*
2 *dos*
3 *tres*
4 *cuatro*
5 *cinco*
6 *seis*
7 *siete*
8 *ocho*
9 *nueve*
10 *diez*
11 *once*
12 *doce*
13 *trece*
14 *catorce*
15 *quince*
16 *dieciseis*
17 *diecisiete*
18 *dieciocho*
19 *diecinueve*
20 *veinte*
21 *veinte y uno or veintiuno*
30 *treinta*
40 *cuarenta*
50 *cincuenta*
60 *sesenta*
70 *setenta*
80 *ochenta*
90 *noventa*
100 *ciento*
101 *ciento y uno or cientiuno*
200 *doscientos*
500 *quinientos*
1,000 *mil*
10,000 *diez mil*

100,000 *cien mil*
1,000,000 *millón*
one-half *medio*
one-third *un tercio*
one-fourth *un cuarto*

TIME

What time is it? *¿Qué hora es?*
It's one o'clock. *Es la una.*
It's three in the afternoon. *Son las tres de la tarde.*
It's 4 A.M. *Son las cuatro de la mañana.*
six-thirty *seis y media*
a quarter till eleven *un cuarto para las once*
a quarter past five *las cinco y cuarto*
an hour *una hora*

DAYS AND MONTHS

Monday *lunes*
Tuesday *martes*
Wednesday *miércoles*
Thursday *jueves*
Friday *viernes*
Saturday *sábado*
Sunday *domingo*
today *hoy*
tomorrow *mañana*
yesterday *ayer*
January *enero*
February *febrero*
March *marzo*
April *abril*
May *mayo*
June *junio*
July *julio*
August *agosto*
September *septiembre*
October *octubre*
November *noviembre*
December *diciembre*
a week *una semana*
a month *un mes*
after *después*
before *antes*

Courtesy of Bruce Whipperman, author of Moon Pacific Mexico.

RESOURCES

Suggested Reading

HISTORY, ANTHROPOLOGY, AND CULTURE

Brading, David. *Miners and Merchants in Bourbon Mexico.* Cambridge: Cambridge University Press, 2008. Widely recognized as one of the preeminent scholars of the early Spanish colonies, David Brading offers a look at life in colonial Mexico.

Coe, Michael D. *Breaking the Maya Code.* Rev. ed. London: Thames & Hudson, 1999. A fascinating story about the anthropologists who finally deciphered the ancient Mayan writing system.

Coe, Michael D. *From the Olmecs to the Aztecs.* London: Thames and Hudson, 2008. Yale anthropologist Michael D. Coe has written extensively about Mesoamerican civilizations. In this volume, he introduces the great cultures of pre-Columbian Mexico.

Collier, George. *Basta: Land and the Zapatista Rebellion in Chiapas.* Oakland, CA: Food First Books, 1994. An excellent introduction to indigenous communities and the 1994 Zapatista uprising in Chiapas.

De las Casas, Bartolome. *Short Account of the Destruction of the Indies.* London: Penguin Books, 1992. A Dominican friar and humanitarian, de las Casas recounts his firsthand observations about Spanish abuse of indigenous Americans during the colonial era.

Diaz Del Castillo, Bernal. *The Discovery and Conquest Of Mexico 1517–1521.* New York: Da Capo Press, 1954. A Spanish conquistador who accompanied Hernán Cortés to the Aztec capital of Tenochtitlan, Diaz Del Castillo wrote a firsthand chronicle of the conquest.

Hernandez, Daniel. *Down and Delirious in Mexico City: The Aztec Metropolis in the Twenty-First Century.* New York: Simon & Schuster, 2011. A series of essays about life and youth culture in modern Mexico City, written by a young journalist.

Herrera, Hayden. *Frida Kahlo.* New York: Harper Perennial, 2002. Art historian Herrera has written the definitive biography of famed Mexico City painter Frida Kahlo.

Krauze, Enrique. *Mexico: A Biography of Power.* New York: Harper Perennial, 1998. A history of Mexico written by one of the country's preeminent intellectuals.

Paz, Octavio. *The Labyrinth of Solitude.* New York: Grove Press, 1985. Mexico's first Nobel laureate in literature discusses the society and psychology of the nation in a series of pensive, elegantly written essays.

Poniatowska, Elena. *Massacre in Mexico.* Columbia: University of Missouri, 1991. Poniatowska recounts the events leading up to and following the Massacre of Tlatelolco in Mexico City in 1968.

Riding, Alan. *Distant Neighbors.* New York: Knopf, 1984. Though written in the 1980s, this book still offers a current perspective on the differences between U.S. and Mexican culture with incredible accuracy.

Womack, John. *Emiliano Zapata and the Mexican Revolution.* New York: Vintage, 1970. Written by Harvard Mexico expert John Womack, an exhaustive and well-researched history of the great hero Emiliano Zapata.

TRAVEL AND CUISINE

Franz, Carl, and Lorena Havens. *The People's Guide to Mexico*. Emeryville, CA: Avalon Travel Publishing, 2006. A cultural handbook to travel in Mexico, the *People's Guide* offers hard-won and well-placed advice for adventurous Mexico travelers.

Gilman, Nicholas. *Good Food in Mexico City: A Guide to Food Stalls, Fondas and Fine Dining*. Lincoln, NE: iUniverse, 2008. Finally, a massive and well-researched guide to the capital's restaurants by a resident foodie.

Kennedy, Diana. *My Mexico*. New York: Clarkson Potter/Publishers, 1998. As much an anthropological study as a cookbook, this guide offers detailed regional recipes from across Mexico, accompanied by personal observations and stories.

Wright, Ronald. *Time Among the Maya*. New York: Grove Press, 1989. A pensive travelogue about Mayan regions of Mexico, Belize, and Guatemala.

EXPATRIATE LIFE AND MEMOIR

Cohan, Tony. *On Mexican Time: A New Life in Mexico*. New York: Broadway Books, 2000. Cohan's best-selling memoir vividly recounts his first years of life as an expatriate in San Miguel de Allende.

Kras, Eva S. *Management in Two Cultures: Bridging the Gap between U.S. and Mexican Managers*. Yarmouth, ME: Intercultural Press, Inc., 1995. This book is a good introduction to the different social and cultural norms in Mexican and U.S. business culture.

Schmidt, Carol, and Norma Hair. *Falling...in Love with San Miguel: Retiring to Mexico on Social Security*. Laredo, TX: Salsa Verde Press, 2005. In this guide, which is more memoir than handbook, two women frankly and humorously recount their joyous adjustment to expatriate life in San Miguel de Allende.

POETRY AND FICTION

Bolaño, Roberto. *The Savage Detectives*. New York: Farrar, Straus and Giroux, 2007. Translation by Picador, 2008. Though Bolaño was Chilean, his novel about Mexican youth in the 1970s captures the spirit of the capital city.

Fuentes, Carlos. *The Old Gringo*. New York: Farrar, Straus and Giroux, 1985. Written by one of Mexico's most famous writers, this novel follows an American journalist during the Revolution of 1910.

Lawrence, D. H. *The Plumed Serpent*. Hertfordshire, UK: Wordsworth Editions Ltd., 1995. After Lawrence visited Mexico in the early 20th century, he penned this novel about an Irish woman visiting the country.

Lowry, Malcolm. *Under the Volcano*. New York: Harper Perennial Modern Classics, 2007. This English novel chronicles a day in the life of a British consul in a fictional Mexican city as he struggles with alcoholism and self-destruction.

Nezahualcóyotl. *Poemas de Nezahualcóyotl*. Barcelona: Linkgua S.L., 2008. An early-15th-century Acolhua prince, architect, and city planner, Nezahualcóyotl wrote beautiful poetry, which was passed down orally in the Nahuatl language.

Poniatowska, Elena. *Tinisima*. Albuquerque: University of New Mexico Press, 1995. Translation by Farrar, Straus and Giroux, LLC, 1995. One of Mexico's foremost intellectuals re-creates the life of Italian-born photographer Tina Modotti, who made her name as an artist and activist in Mexico.

RESOURCES

Rulfo, Juan. *Pedro Páramo*. New York: Grove Press, 1994. Written in 1955, this classic of Mexican fiction is a dark and magical novel about Juan Preciado's trip to his father's hometown.

Volpi, Jorge. *In Search of Klingsor*. New York: Scribner, 2007. This novel, about a U.S. military officer, brought contemporary Mexican writer Jorge Volpi international acclaim.

Suggested Films

Alamar. Directed by Pedro González-Rubio. 73 minutes. Mantarraya Producciones, 2009. A slow-moving, poignant, and beautifully shot quasi-documentary about a father and son living in a rural area along the Caribbean coast of Mexico.

Amores Perros. Directed by Alejandro González Iñárritu. 154 minutes. Lions Gate, 2000. A dark, gritty portrayal of life in modern Mexico City, told through four separate story lines.

A Toda Maquina. Directed by Ismael Rodríguez. 120 minutes. Producciones Rodríguez Hermanos, 1951. This movie follows the adventures of two friends who become members of Mexico City's motorcycle police squadron, played by the ever-enchanting Pedro Infante and Luis Aguilar.

Blossoms of Fire. Directed by Maureen Gosling. 74 minutes. New Yorker, 2001. This documentary explores gender roles and traditional life in the Isthmus of Tehuantepec, Oaxaca.

El Topo. Directed Alejandro Jodorowsky. 125 minutes. Starz/Anchor Bay, 1970. The Chilean filmmaker, thinker, cartoonist, and writer Alejandro Jodorowsky wrote and filmed this imaginative, violent, and surrealist film in Mexico, which depicts the quest of a spiritual cowboy through the desert.

Frida. Directed by Julie Taymor. 123 minutes. Miramax Films, 2002. Salma Hayek stars in the biopic about the life and work of famed Mexican painter Frida Kahlo and her romance with muralist Diego Rivera.

Los Olvidados. Directed by Luis Buñuel. 80 minutes. Films sans Frontieres, 1950. The great Spanish filmmaker Luis Buñuel made some of his most influential works in Mexico, including this movie about the poor in Mexico City.

Los Tres Garcia. Directed by Ismael Rodríguez. 118 minutes. Producciones Rodríguez Hermanos, 1947. This beloved and classic Mexican comedy features Jorge Negrete, Javier Solis, and Pedro Infante as *charro* cousins who fall in love with the same woman.

Pan's Labyrinth. Directed by Guillermo del Toro. 119 minutes. Picturehouse, 2006. An imaginative fairy tale set against the violent backdrop of the Spanish Civil War, directed by one of Mexico's most famous filmmakers.

Stellet licht. Directed by Carlos Reygadas. 136 minutes. Palisades Tartan, 2007. A quiet and artful award-winning movie about a family in one of Mexico's German-speaking Mennonite communities.

Vamonos Con Pancho Villa. 92 minutes. Directed by Fernando de Fuentes. Cinemateca, 1936. A group of young men hear of the Mexican Revolution and join Pancho Villa's forces in this classic Mexican film.

Y Tu Mamá También. Directed by Alfonso Cuarón. 106 minutes. MGM, 2001. A slangy, upbeat, and highly entertaining film about two Mexico City teenagers who take an older Spanish woman on a road trip to the coast.

Index

A

B

C

DE

Acknowledgments

From my first Spanish tutor in San Cristóbal de las Casas, Chiapas, to the airline representative who helped me board my dog on an international flight in Mexico City, there are literally hundreds of people who have contributed their insight to this book. I feel very lucky to have lived many happy years in Mexico, and I am truly grateful to everyone who lent a hand along the way. More specifically, I could not have written this book without the constant kindness and assistance from my life partner, Arturo Meade. *Muchas gracias, mi amor.* My gratitude to Brucine Doherty for the beautiful photos and the endless patience, and to Carson Brown, who began this journey with me. Thanks to Gabriela Peña Garavito for her beautiful photo contributions and friendship, and to Carlos Meade for snapping the last shots I needed. A very special thanks to the ever-helpful and lovely Alicia Wilson Rivero, Gary Thompson, Carmen Meade, Jeff Levy, Gabriela Gonazalez, Ana Meade, Melanie Harris, Brian Care, Terrence Jon Dyck, Carlos Rodal, Ghies van der Zwaal, Ben Calderoni, Scott Gagner, Lynn Rawden, Marie Moebius, Francis Doherty, Amy Doherty, and the many others who shared their experience and expertise during the research and writing process. Finally, many thanks to Erin Raber, Lucie Ericksen, Kat Bennett, Grace Fujimoto, and everyone at Avalon Travel, who always impress me with their knowledge and professionalism.

www.moon.com

DESTINATIONS | ACTIVITIES | BLOGS | MAPS | BOOKS

MOON.COM is ready to help plan your next trip! Filled with fresh trip ideas and strategies, author interviews, informative travel blogs, a detailed map library, and descriptions of all the Moon guidebooks, Moon.com is all you need to get out and explore the world—or even places in your own backyard. While at Moon.com, sign up for our monthly e-newsletter for updates on new releases, travel tips, and expert advice from our on-the-go Moon authors. As always, when you travel with Moon, expect an experience that is uncommon and truly unique.

KEEP UP WITH MOON ON FACEBOOK AND TWITTER
JOIN THE MOON PHOTO GROUP ON FLICKR

MAP SYMBOLS

▭	Expressway	○	City/Town	✗	Airfield	⬛	Archaeological Site
▭	Primary Road	◉	State Capital	✈	Airport	♦	Church
▭	Secondary Road					⬛	Gas Station
⋯	Unpaved Road	⊛	National Capital	▲	Mountain		Mangrove
⋯	Ferry	★	Point of Interest	♣♣	Park		Reef
⋯	Railroad	▪	Other Location	✗	Skiing Area		Swamp

CONVERSION TABLES

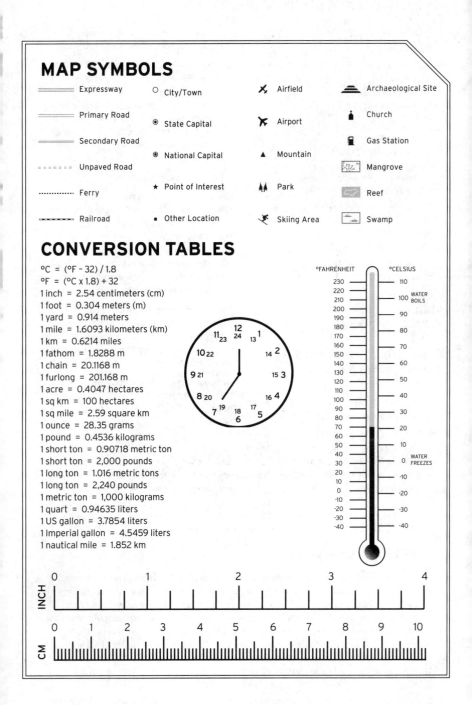

°C = (°F - 32) / 1.8
°F = (°C x 1.8) + 32
1 inch = 2.54 centimeters (cm)
1 foot = 0.304 meters (m)
1 yard = 0.914 meters
1 mile = 1.6093 kilometers (km)
1 km = 0.6214 miles
1 fathom = 1.8288 m
1 chain = 20.1168 m
1 furlong = 201.168 m
1 acre = 0.4047 hectares
1 sq km = 100 hectares
1 sq mile = 2.59 square km
1 ounce = 28.35 grams
1 pound = 0.4536 kilograms
1 short ton = 0.90718 metric ton
1 short ton = 2,000 pounds
1 long ton = 1.016 metric tons
1 long ton = 2,240 pounds
1 metric ton = 1,000 kilograms
1 quart = 0.94635 liters
1 US gallon = 3.7854 liters
1 Imperial gallon = 4.5459 liters
1 nautical mile = 1.852 km

MOON LIVING ABROAD
IN MEXICO

Avalon Travel
a member of the Perseus Books Group
1700 Fourth Street
Berkeley, CA 94710, USA
www.moon.com

Editor: Erin Raber
Series Manager: Elizabeth Hansen
Copy Editor: Justine Rathbun
Graphics and Production Coordinator:
   Lucie Ericksen
Cover Designer: Lucie Ericksen
Map Editor: Kat Bennett
Cartographer: Kaitlin Jaffe
Indexer: Greg Jewett

ISBN-13: 978-1-61238-179-4
ISSN: 1556-1321

Printing History
1st Edition – 2005
2nd Edition – May 2012
5 4 3 2 1

KEEPING CURRENT

Although we strive to produce the most up-to-date guidebook that we possibly can, change is unavoidable. Between the time this book goes to print and the time you read it, the cost of goods and services may have increased, and a handful of the businesses noted in these pages will undoubtedly move, alter their prices, or close their doors forever. Exchange rates fluctuate – sometimes dramatically – on a daily basis. Federal and local legal requirements and restrictions are also subject to change, so be sure to check with the appropriate authorities before making the move. If you see anything in this book that needs updating, clarification, or correction, please drop us a line. Send your comments via email to feedback@moon.com, or use the address above.